ARISA

5

Natsumi Ando

Translated and adapted by
Andria Cheng

Lettered by
Scott O. Brown

KC
KODANSHA
COMICS

A Kodansha Comics Trade Paperback Original

Arisa volume 5 copyright © 2010 Natsumi Ando
English translation copyright © 2011 Natsumi Ando

Published in the United States by Kodansha Comics, an imprint of Kodansha USA Publishing, LLC, New York.

Publication rights for this English edition arranged through Kodansha Ltd., Tokyo.

First published in Japan in 2010 by Kodansha Ltd., Tokyo.

ISBN 978-1-935-42919-7

Printed in the United States of America.

www.kodanshacomics.com

9 8 7 6 5 4 3 2 1

Translator/Adapter: Andria Cheng
Lettering: Scott O. Brown

CONTENTS

Words from the Author

I really like the white school uniform on the cover. The others were all black, so this was refreshing! I was happy that it continued onto the back cover so you can see the whole thing!

—Natsumi Ando

HONORIFICS EXPLAINED

Throughout the Kodansha Comics books, you will find Japanese honorifics left intact in the translations. For those not familiar with how the Japanese use honorifics and, more important, how they differ from American honorifics, we present this brief overview.

Politeness has always been a critical facet of Japanese culture. Ever since the feudal era, when Japan was a highly stratified society, use of honorifics—which can be defined as polite speech that indicates relationship or status—has played an essential role in the Japanese language. When addressing someone in Japanese, an honorific usually takes the form of a suffix attached to one's name (example: "Asuna-san"), is used as a title at the end of one's name, or appears in place of the name itself (example: "Negi-sensei," or simply "Sensei!").

Honorifics can be expressions of respect or endearment. In the context of manga and anime, honorifics give insight into the nature of the relationship between characters. Many English translations leave out these important honorifics and therefore distort the feel of the original Japanese. Because Japanese honorifics contain nuances that English honorifics lack, it is our policy at Kodansha Comics not to translate them. Here, instead, is a guide to some of the honorifics you may encounter in Kodansha Comics books.

-san: This is the most common honorific and is equivalent to Mr., Miss, Ms., or Mrs. It is the all-purpose honorific and can be used in any situation where politeness is required.

-sama: This is one level higher than "-san" and is used to confer great respect.

-dono: This comes from the word "tono," which means "lord." It is an even higher level than "-sama" and confers utmost respect.

-kun: This suffix is used at the end of boys' names to express familiarity or endearment. It is also sometimes used by men among friends, or when addressing someone younger or of a lower station.

-chan: This is used to express endearment, mostly toward girls. It is also used for little boys, pets, and even among lovers. It gives a sense of childish cuteness.

Bozu: This is an informal way to refer to a boy, similar to the English terms "kid" and "squirt."

Sempai/Senpai: This title suggests that the addressee is one's senior in a group or organization. It is most often used in a school setting, where underclassmen refer to their upperclassmen as "sempai." It can also be used in the workplace, such as when a newer employee addresses an employee who has seniority in the company.

Kohai: This is the opposite of "sempai" and is used toward under-classmen in school or newcomers in the workplace. It connotes that the addressee is of a lower station.

Sensei: Literally meaning "one who has come before," this title is used for teachers, doctors, or masters of any profession or art.

-[blank]: This is usually forgotten in these lists, but it is perhaps the most significant difference between Japanese and English. The lack of hon-orific means that the speaker has permission to address the person in a very intimate way. Usually, only family, spouses, or very close friends have this kind of permission. Known as yobisute, it can be gratifying when someone who has earned the intimacy starts to call one by one's name without an honorific. But when that intimacy hasn't been earned, it can be very insulting.

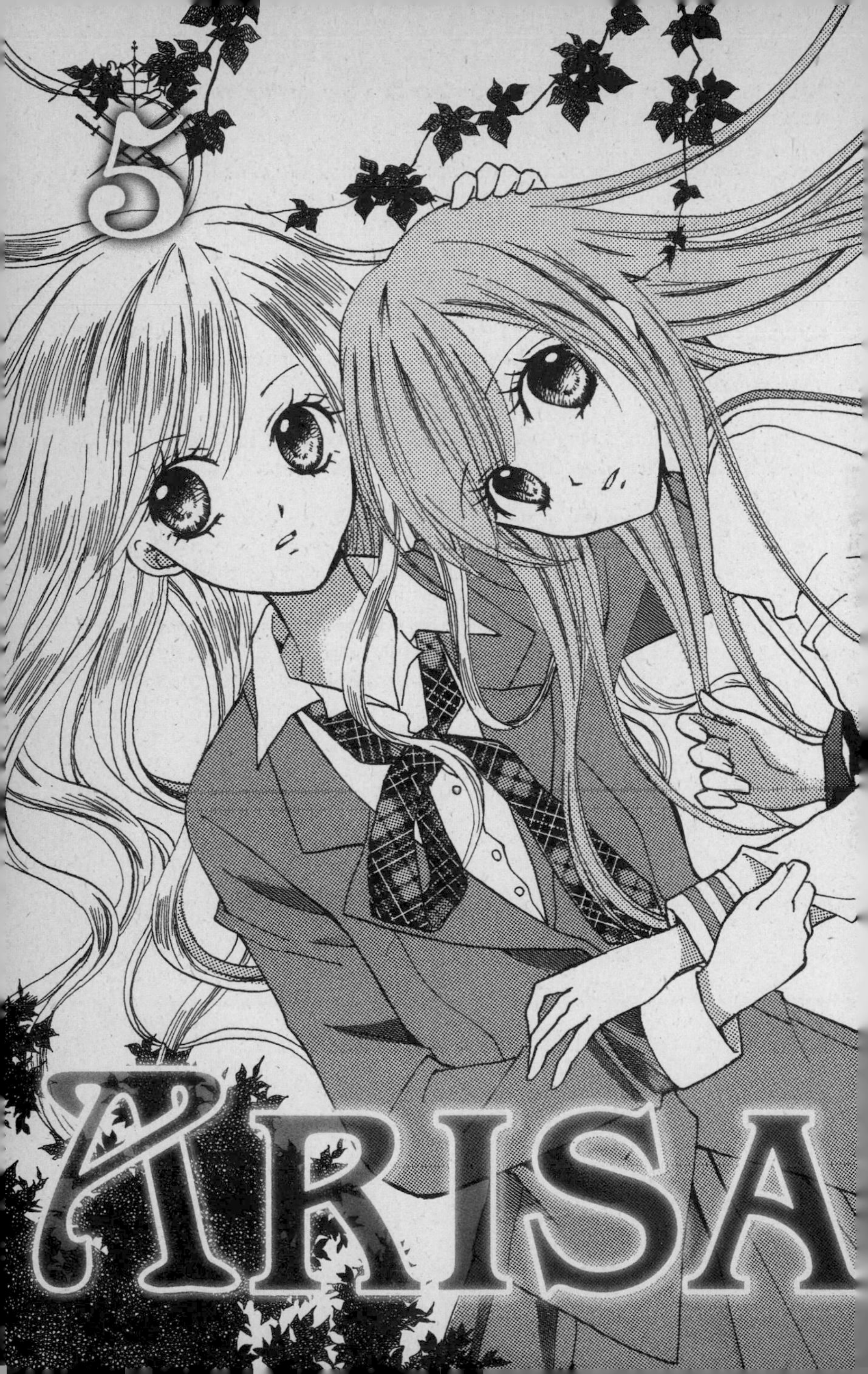
5
ARISA

Contents

ARISA

Secret King's Room

The story so far

Tsubasa and Arisa are twin sisters separated by their parents' divorce. They finally reunited after three years of being apart, but their happy time together came to an abrupt end when Arisa jumped out her bedroom window right in front of Tsubasa, leaving behind a mysterious card...

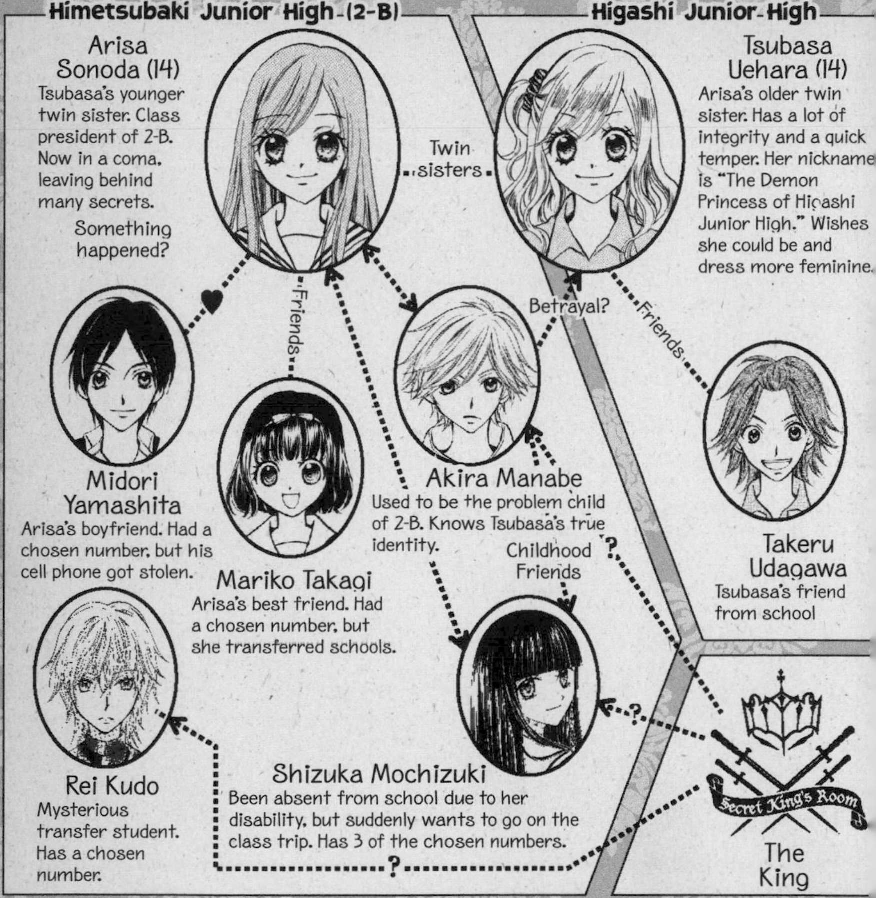
Himetsubaki Junior High (2-B)
Higashi Junior High
Arisa Sonoda (14)
Tsubasa's younger twin sister. Class president of 2-B. Now in a coma, leaving behind many secrets.
Twin sisters
Tsubasa Uehara (14)
Arisa's older twin sister. Has a lot of integrity and a quick temper. Her nickname is "The Demon Princess of Higashi Junior High." Wishes she could be and dress more feminine.
Something happened?
Friends
Betrayal?
Friends
Midori Yamashita
Arisa's boyfriend. Had a chosen number, but his cell phone got stolen.
Mariko Takagi
Arisa's best friend. Had a chosen number, but she transferred schools.
Akira Manabe
Used to be the problem child of 2-B. Knows Tsubasa's true identity.
Childhood Friends
?
Takeru Udagawa
Tsubasa's friend from school
Rei Kudo
Mysterious transfer student. Has a chosen number.
Shizuka Mochizuki
Been absent from school due to her disability, but suddenly wants to go on the class trip. Has 3 of the chosen numbers.
?
?
Secret King's Room
The King

In order to discover the secrets Arisa was hiding, Tsubasa pretended to be her and attended Himetsubaki Junior High. In Class 2-B, a mysterious internet presence called "The King" led strange incidents and bullying. It turns out that Arisa was the original "King," but someone else took over in order to control her classmates. The key to the King's identity are the five cell phones with the chosen numbers, but Manabe betrayed Tsubasa and took three of them from her. But on the day of the class trip, Tsubasa discovers that Manabe's childhood friend Shizuka has the cell phones now...

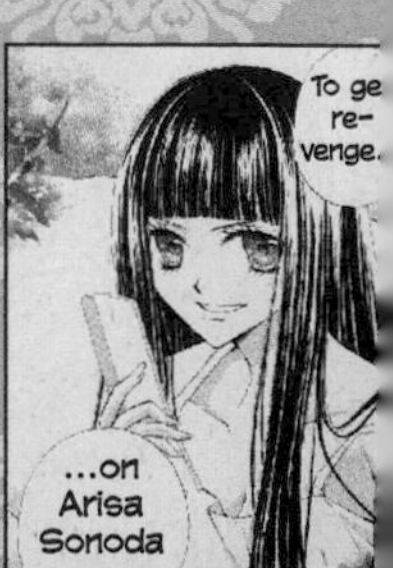
To get re-venge.
...on Arisa Sonoda

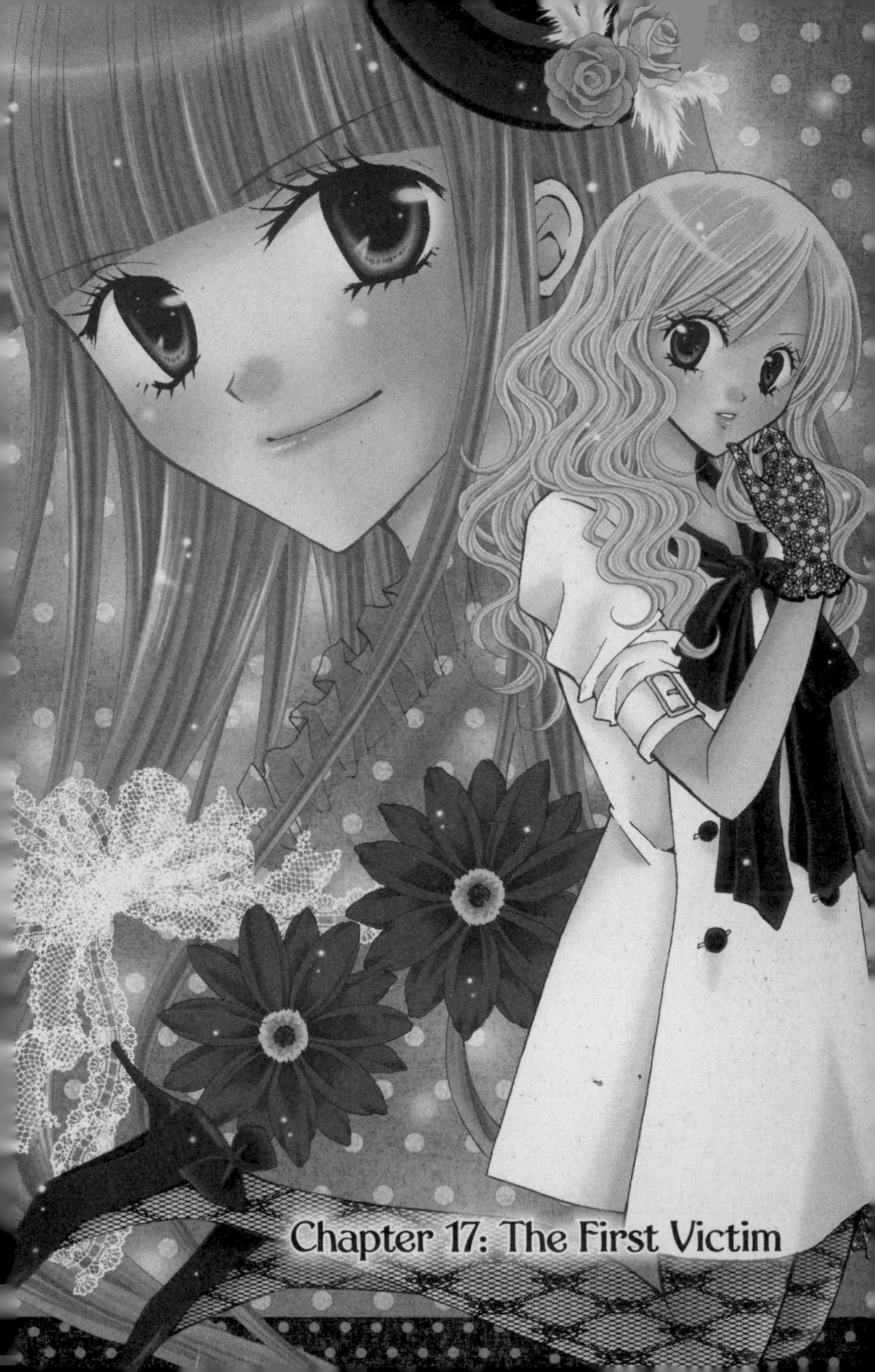
Chapter 17: The First Victim

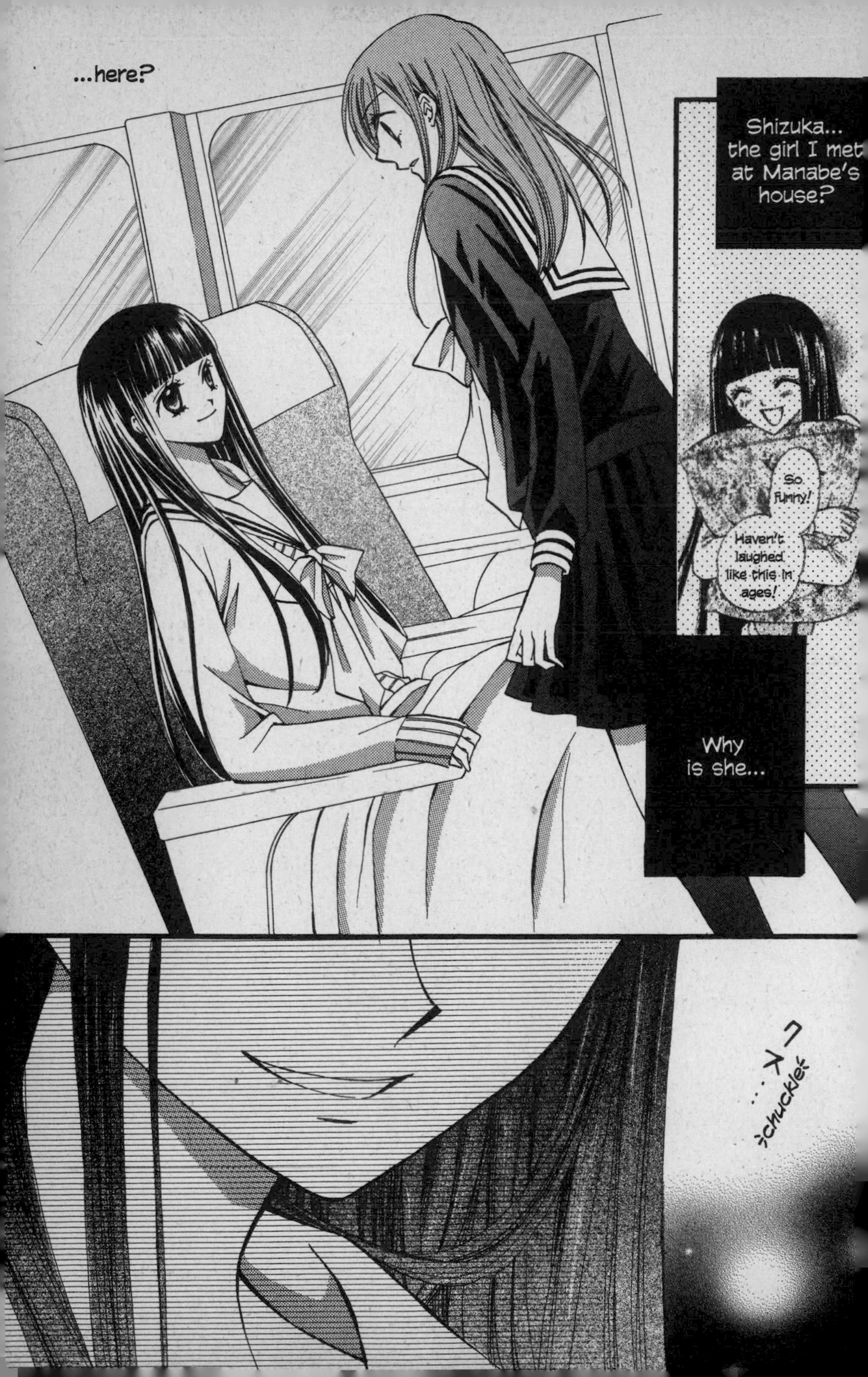
Shizuka... the girl I met at Manabe's house?
So funny!
Haven't laughed like this in ages!
Why is she...
...here?
chuckle

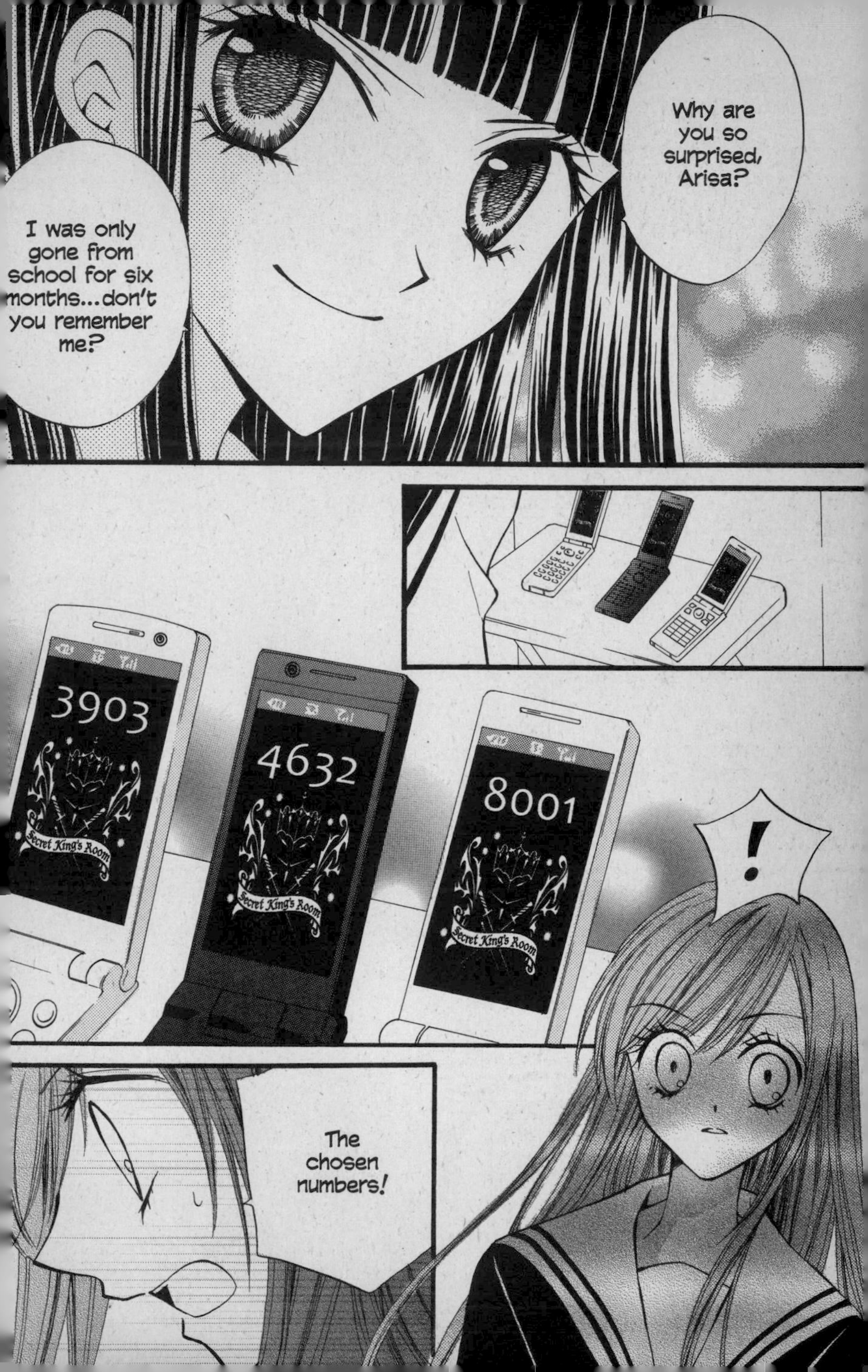
Why are you so surprised, Arisa?
I was only gone from school for six months...don't you remember me?
3903
Secret King's Room
4632
Secret King's Room
8001
Secret King's Room
!
The chosen numbers!

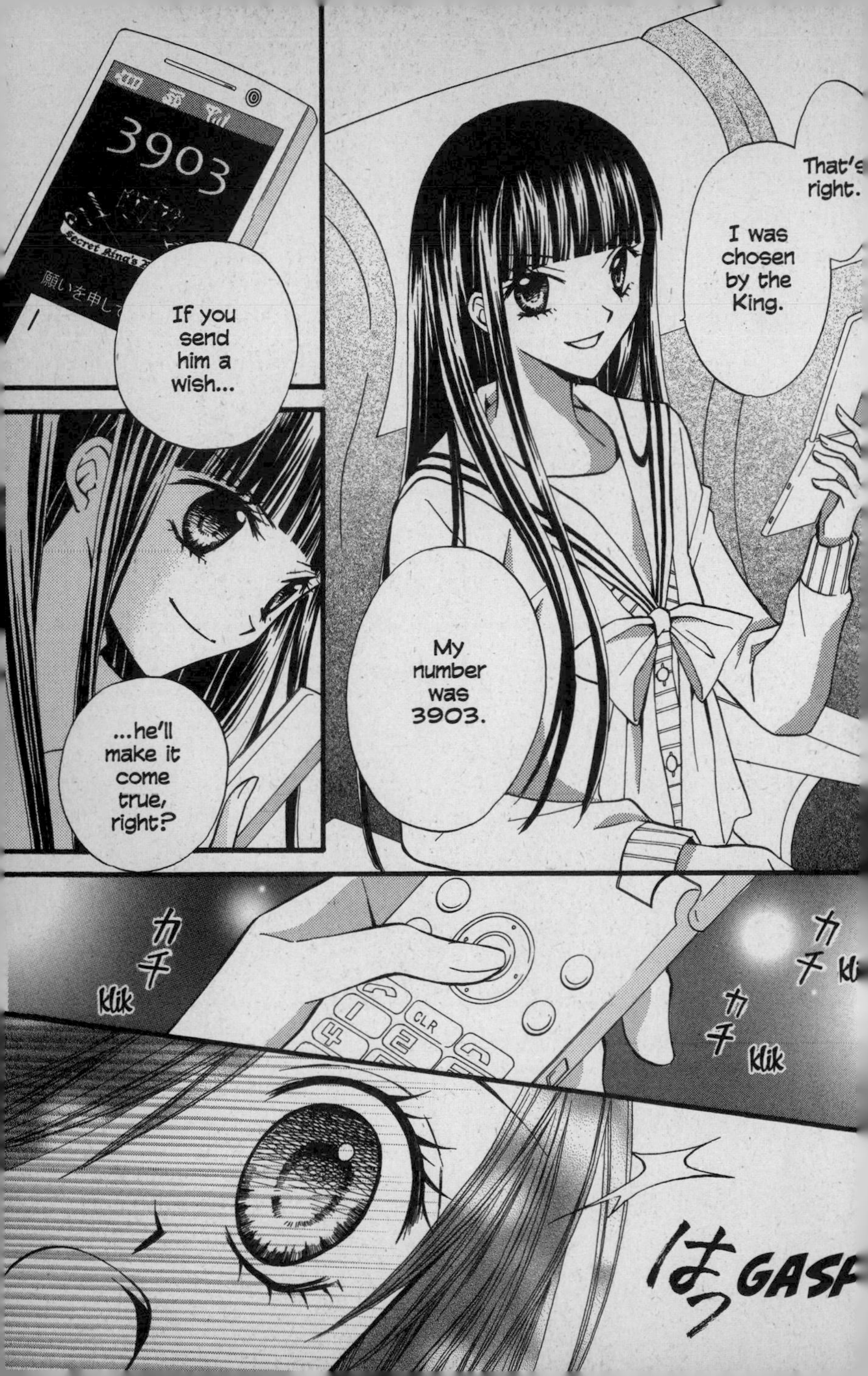
That's right.
I was chosen by the King.
My number was 3903.
3903
If you send him a wish...
...he'll make it come true, right?
カチ klik
カチ klik
カチ klik
CLR
はっ GASP

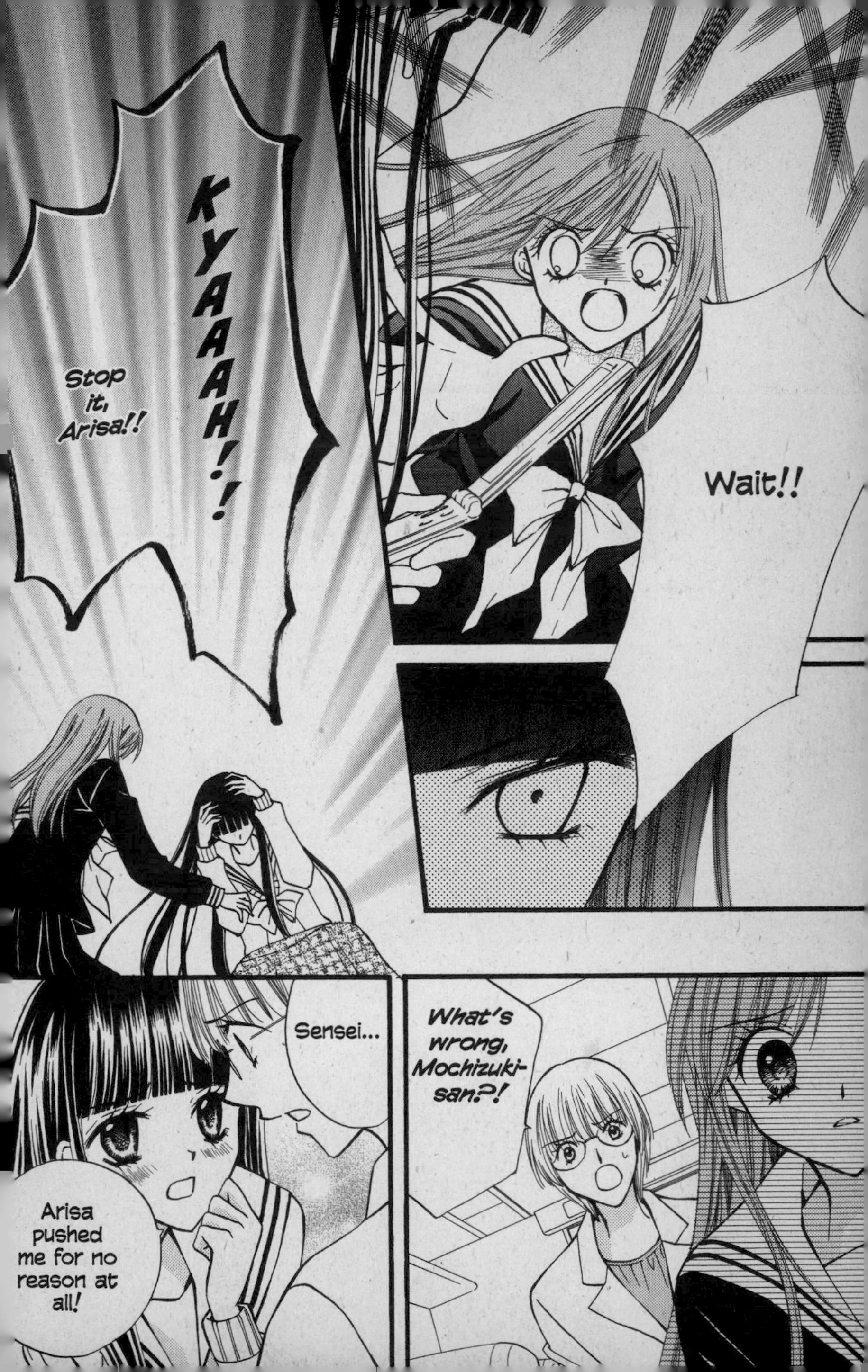
Wait!!
KYAAAAH!!
Stop it, Arisa!!
What's wrong, Mochizuki-san?!
Sensei...
Arisa pushed me for no reason at all!

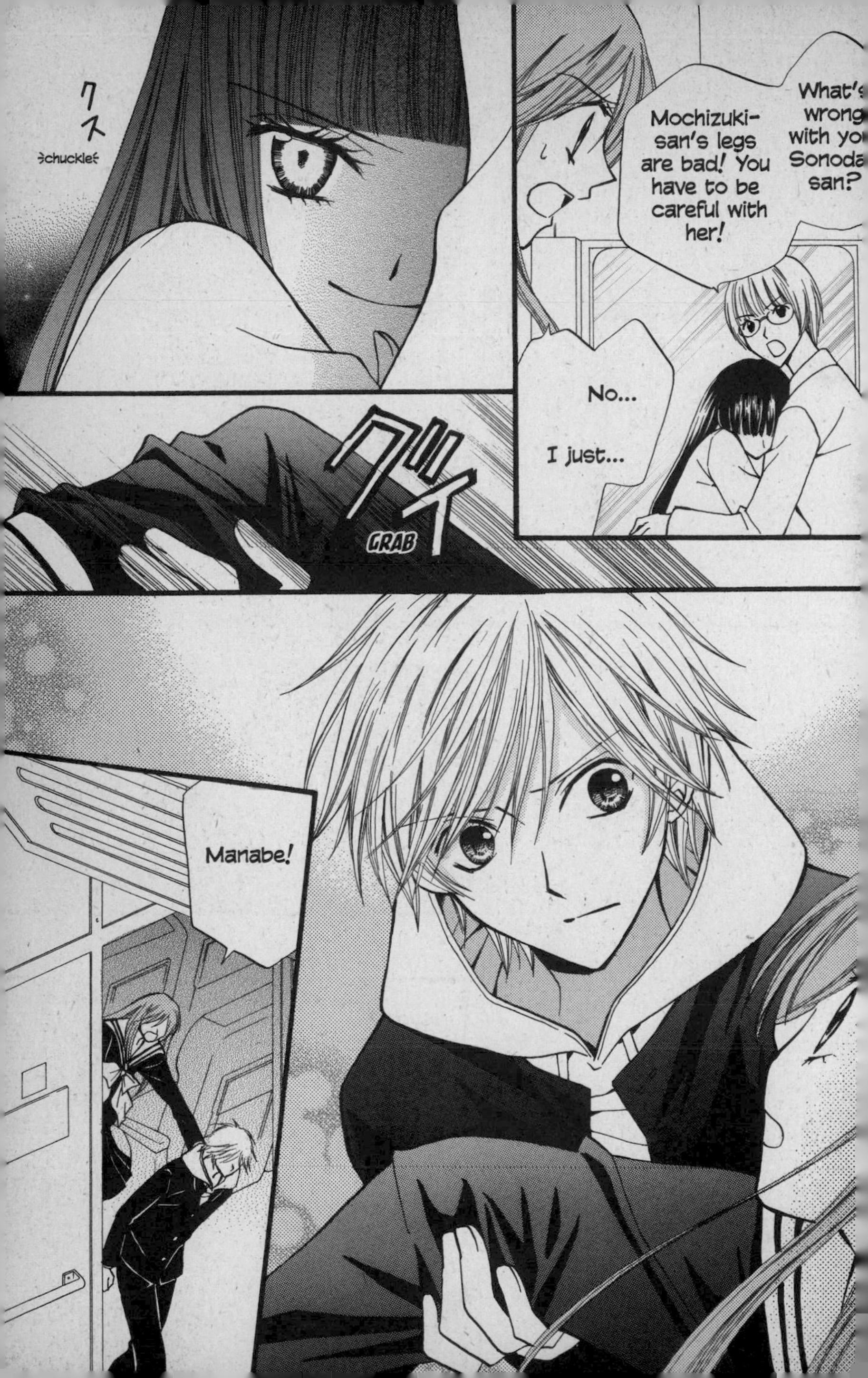
What's wrong with yo Sonoda san?
Mochizuki-san's legs are bad! You have to be careful with her!
No...
I just...
クス
chuckle
グイ
GRAB
Manabe!

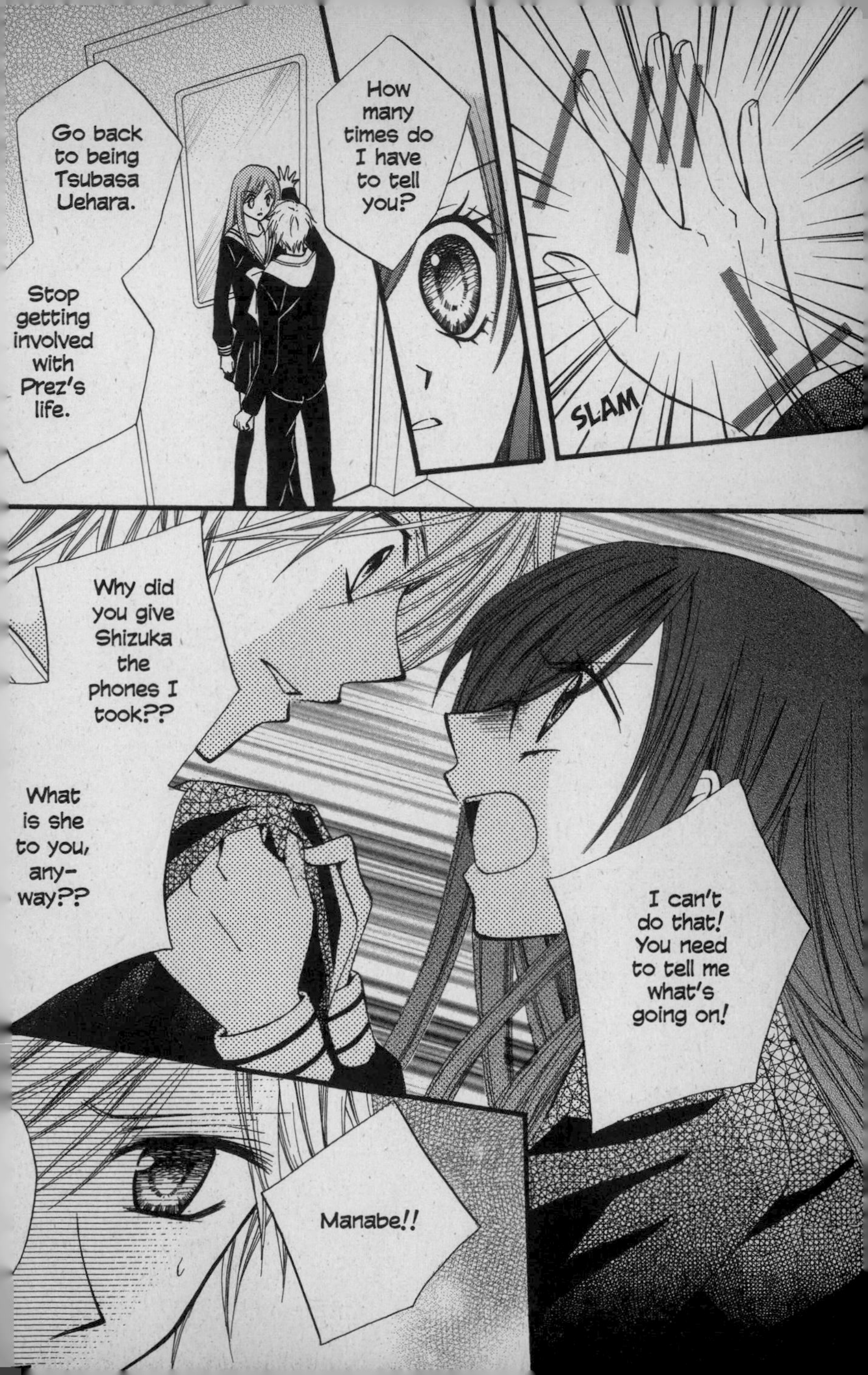
SLAM
How many times do I have to tell you?
Go back to being Tsubasa Uehara.
Stop getting involved with Prez's life.
Why did you give Shizuka the phones I took??
What is she to you, anyway??
I can't do that! You need to tell me what's going on!
Manabe!!

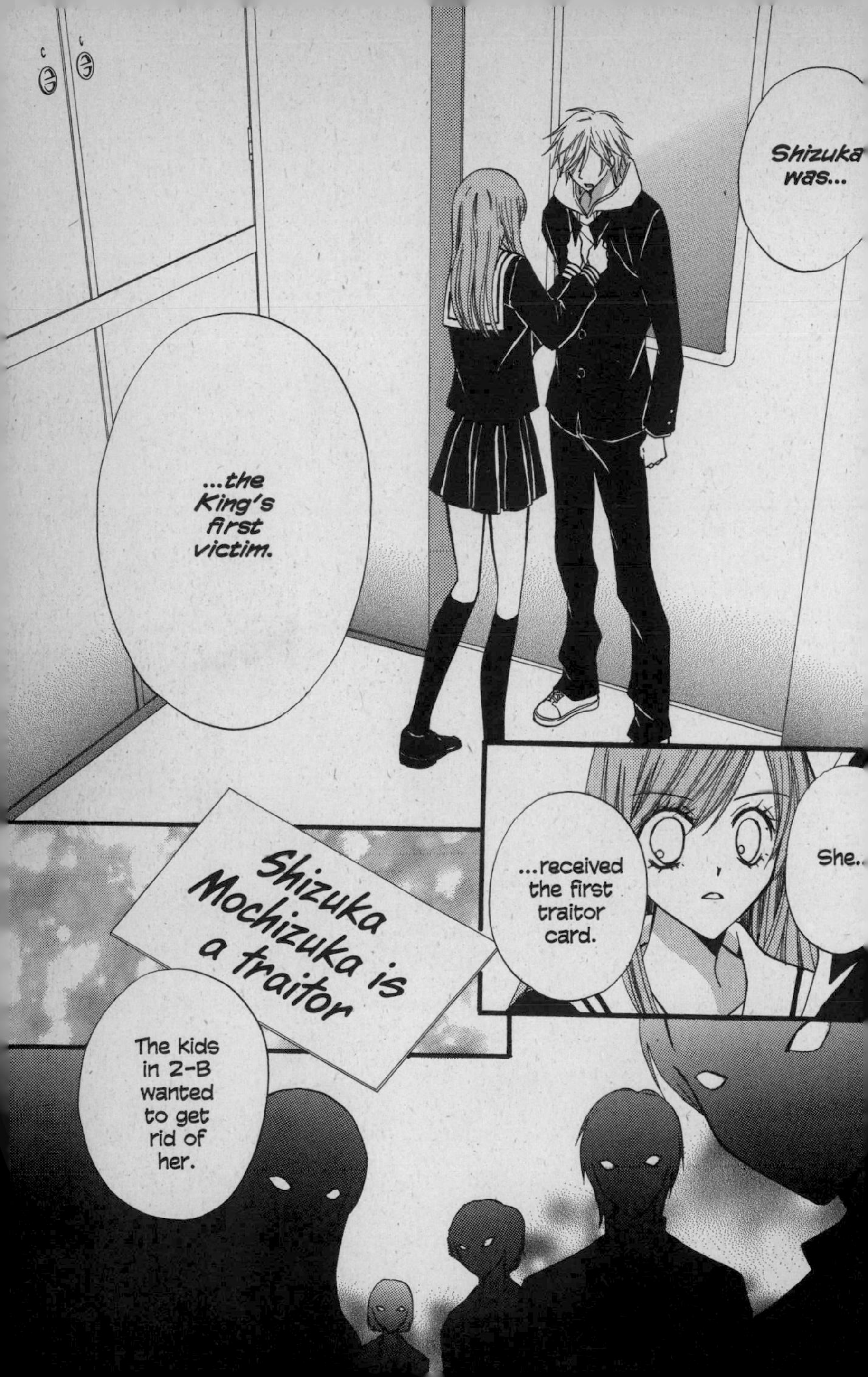
Shizuka was...
...the King's first victim.
She..
...received the first traitor card.
Shizuka Mochizuka is a traitor
The kids in 2-B wanted to get rid of her.

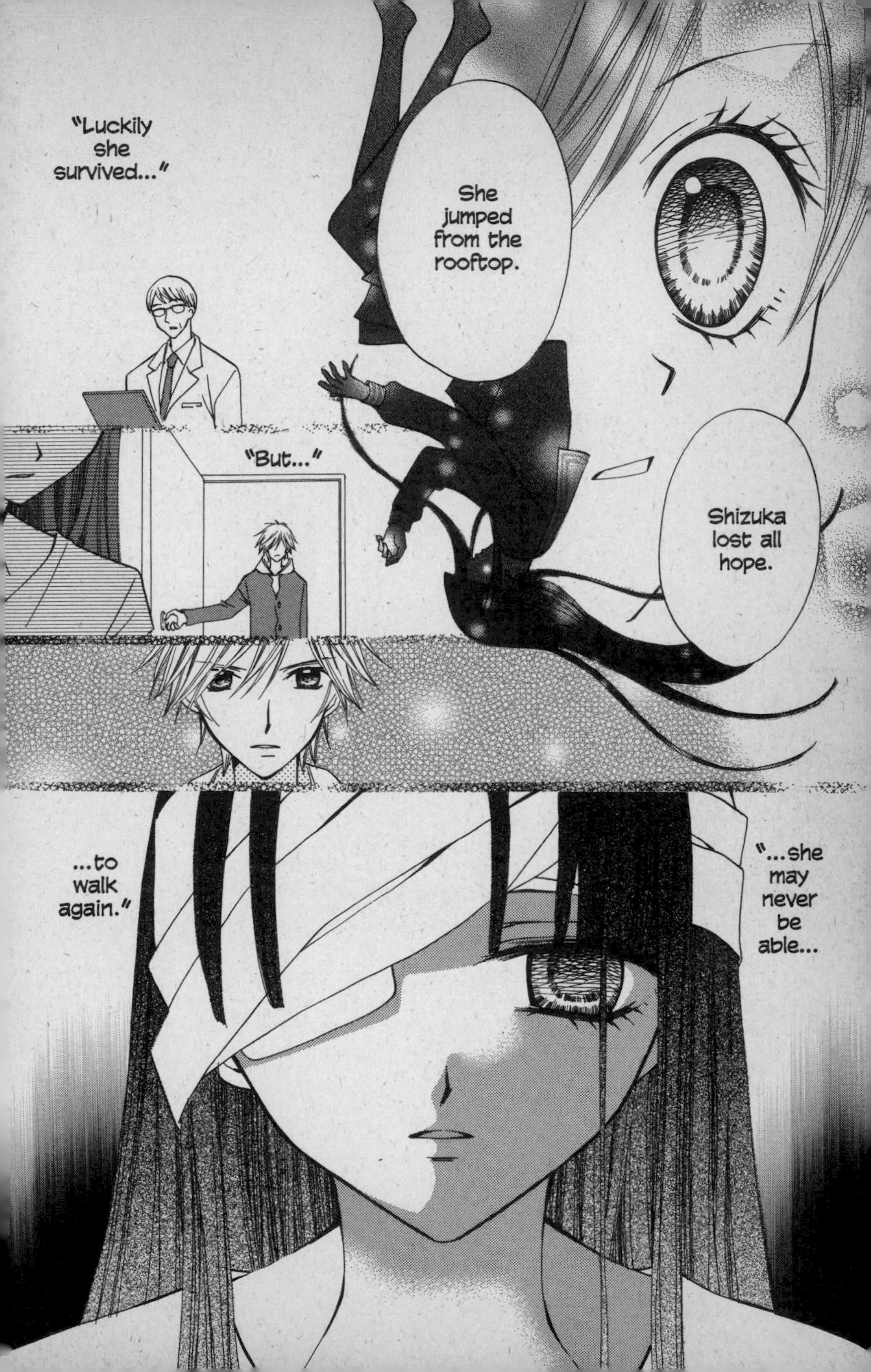
She jumped from the rooftop.
Shizuka lost all hope.
"Luckily she survived..."
"But..."
"...she may never be able...
...to walk again."

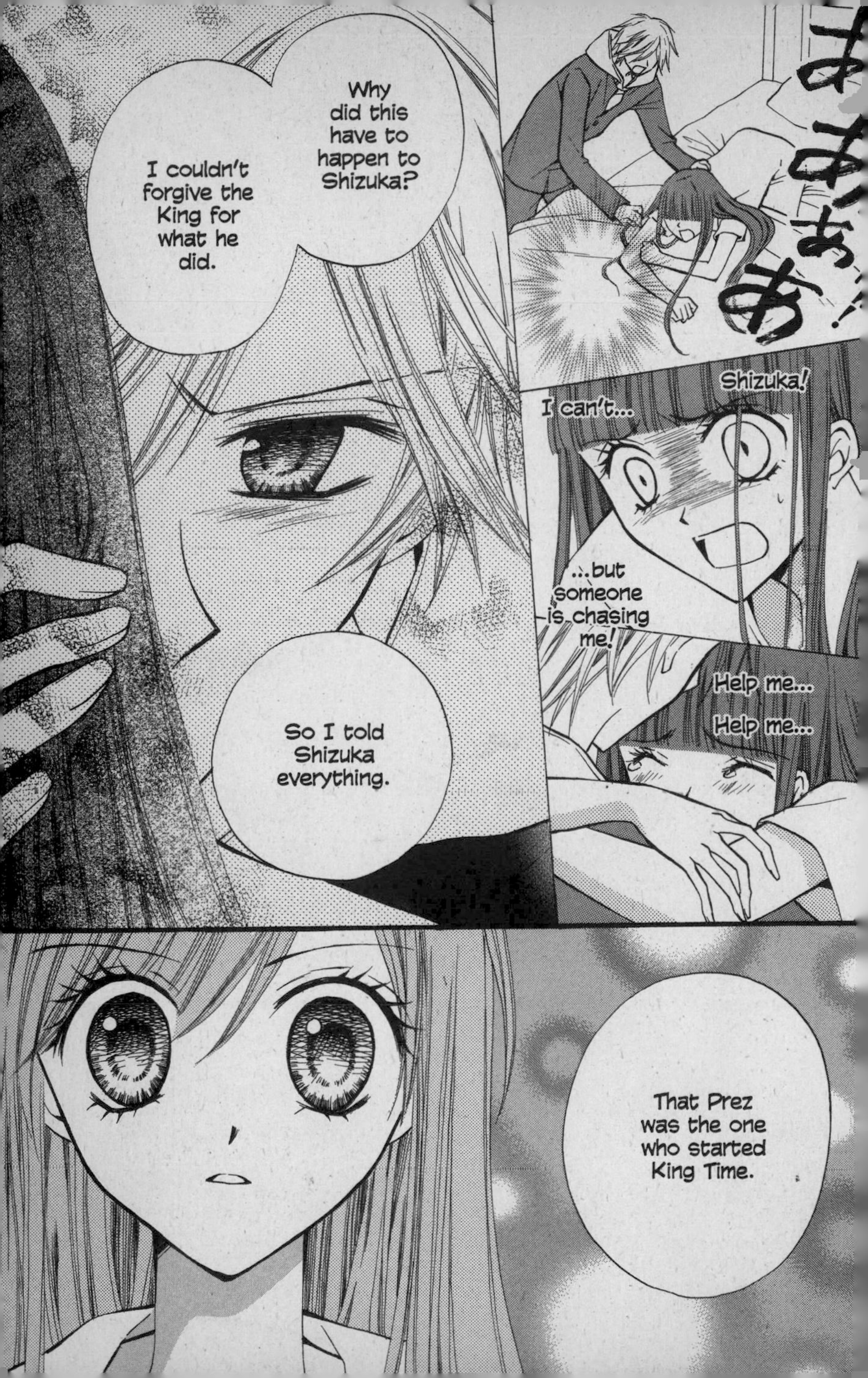
ああぁぁあ!!
Shizuka!
I can't...
...but someone is chasing me!
Help me...
Help me...
Why did this have to happen to Shizuka?
I couldn't forgive the King for what he did.
So I told Shizuka everything.
That Prez was the one who started King Time.

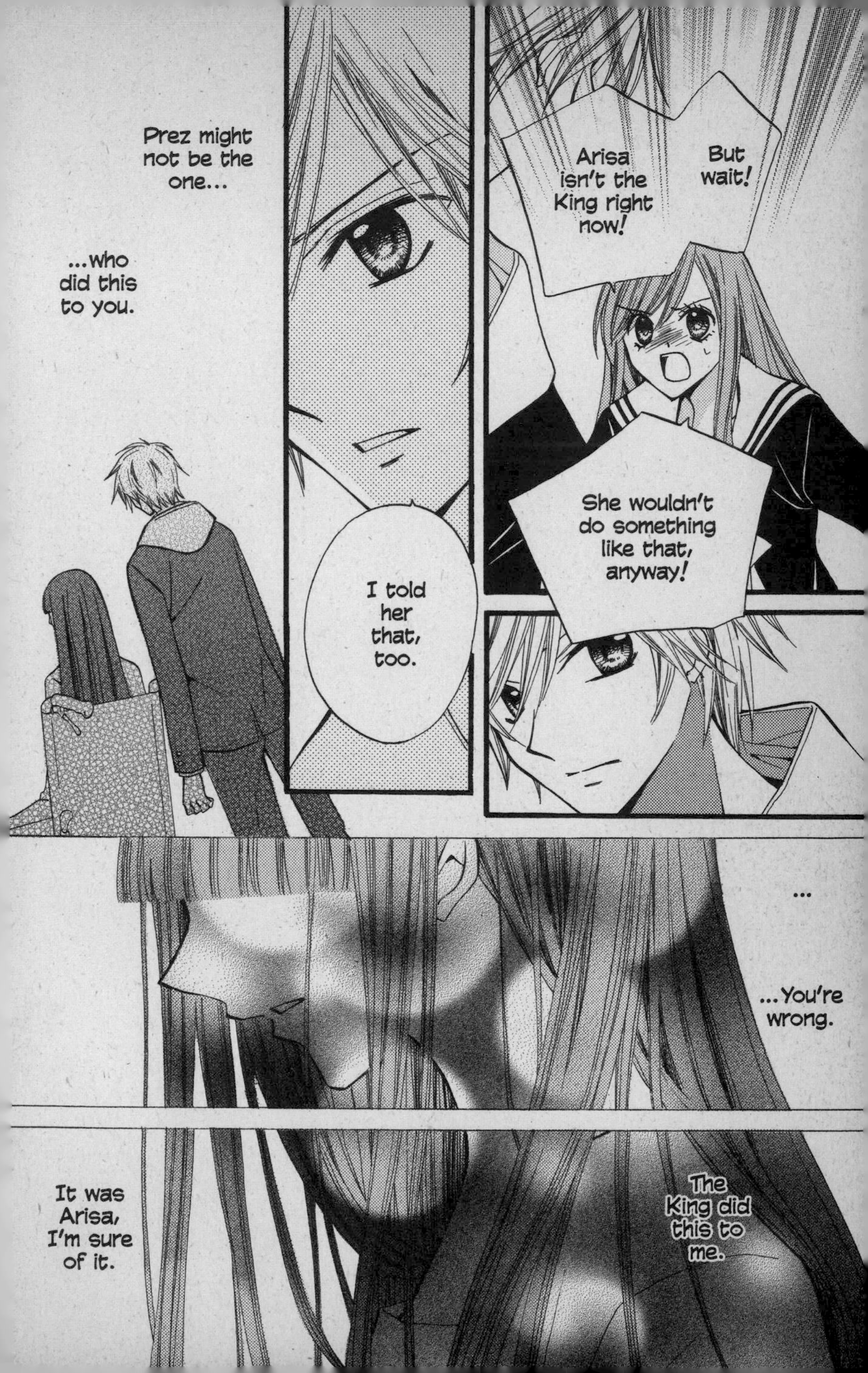
But wait!
Arisa isn't the King right now!
She wouldn't do something like that, anyway!
I told her that, too.
Prez might not be the one...
...who did this to you.
...
...You're wrong.
The King did this to me.
It was Arisa, I'm sure of it.

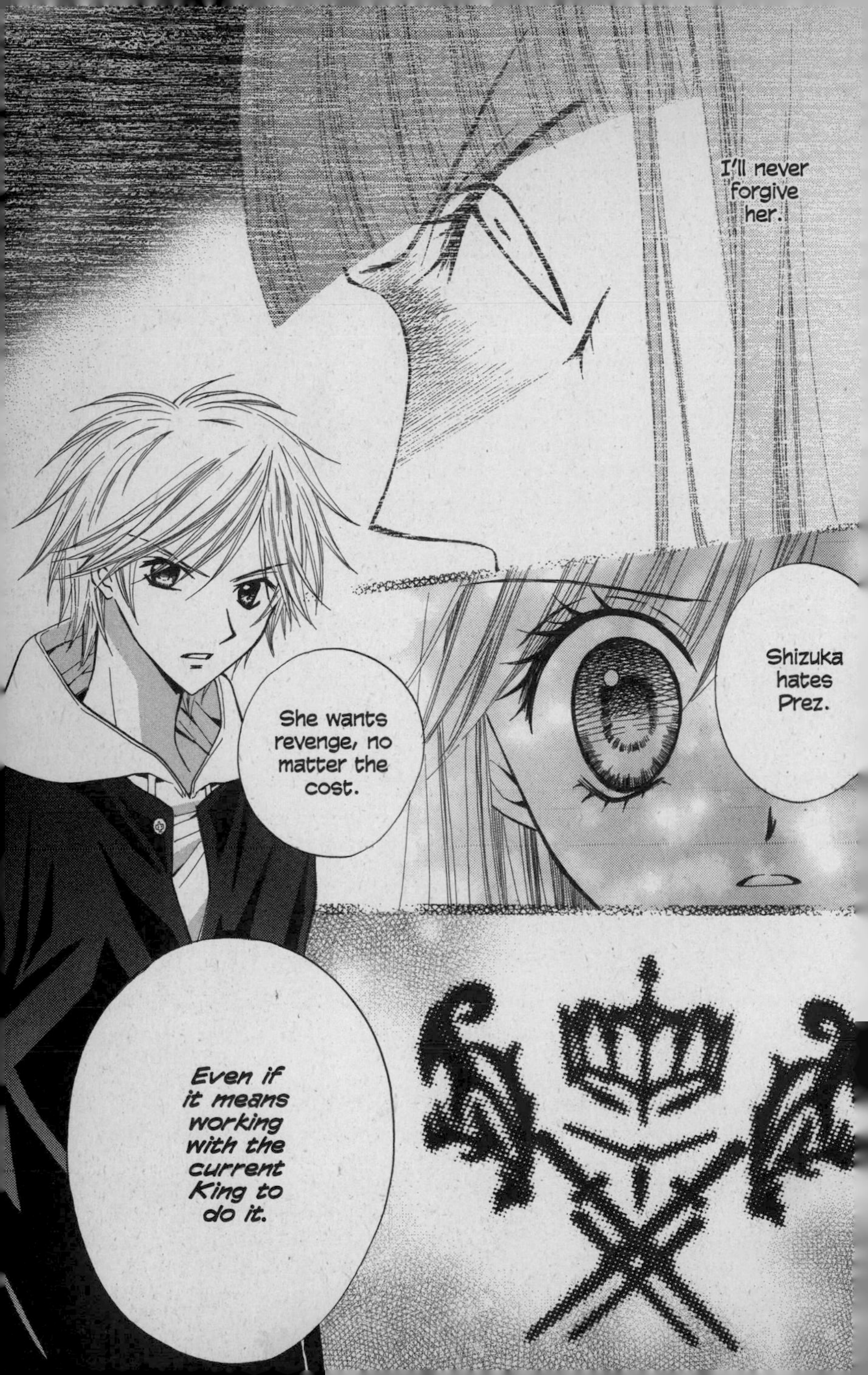
I'll never forgive her.
Shizuka hates Prez.
She wants revenge, no matter the cost.
Even if it means working with the current King to do it.

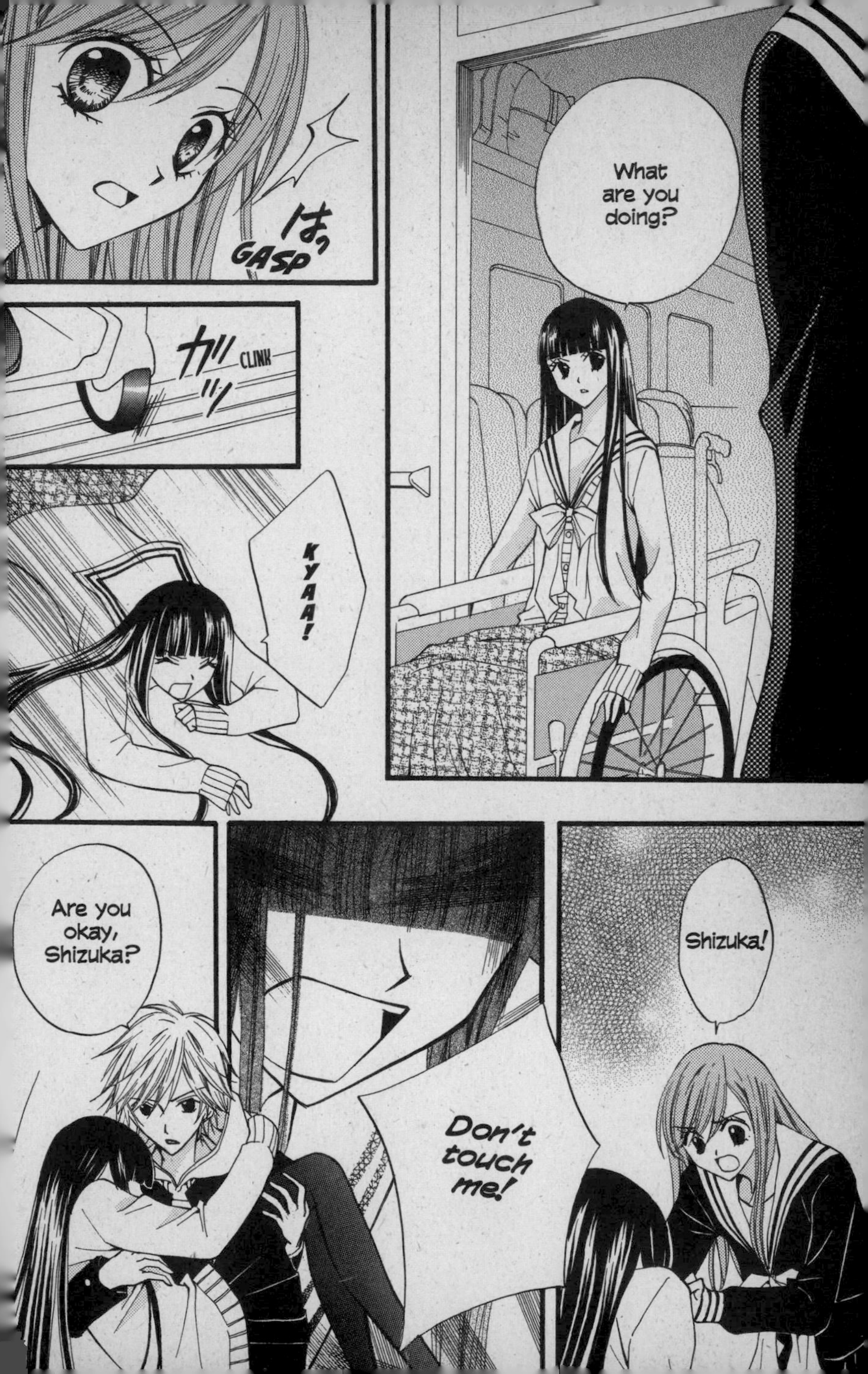
What are you doing?
はっ
GASP
ガッ
CLINK
KYAAA!
Shizuka!
Don't touch me!
Are you okay, Shizuka?

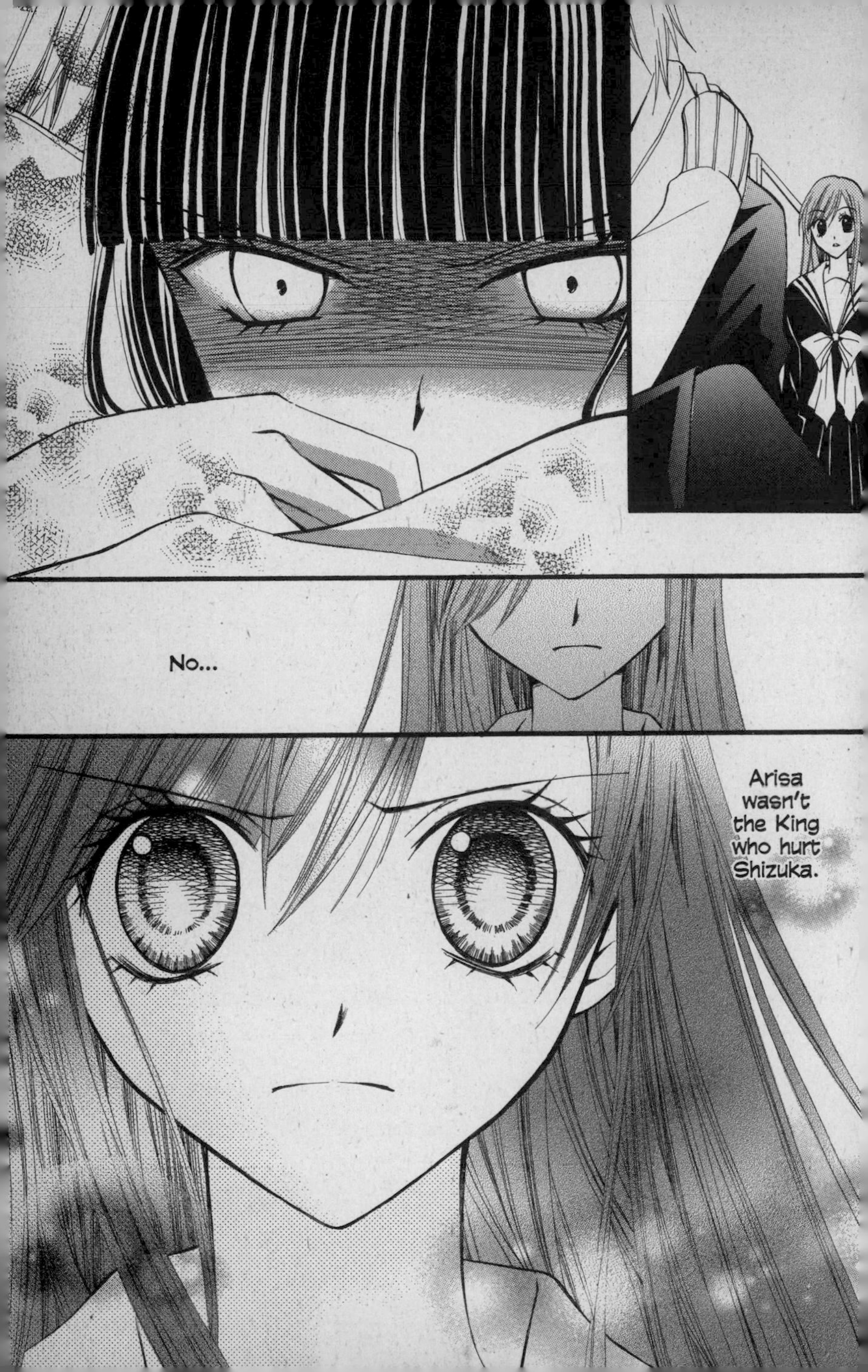
No...
Arisa wasn't the King who hurt Shizuka.

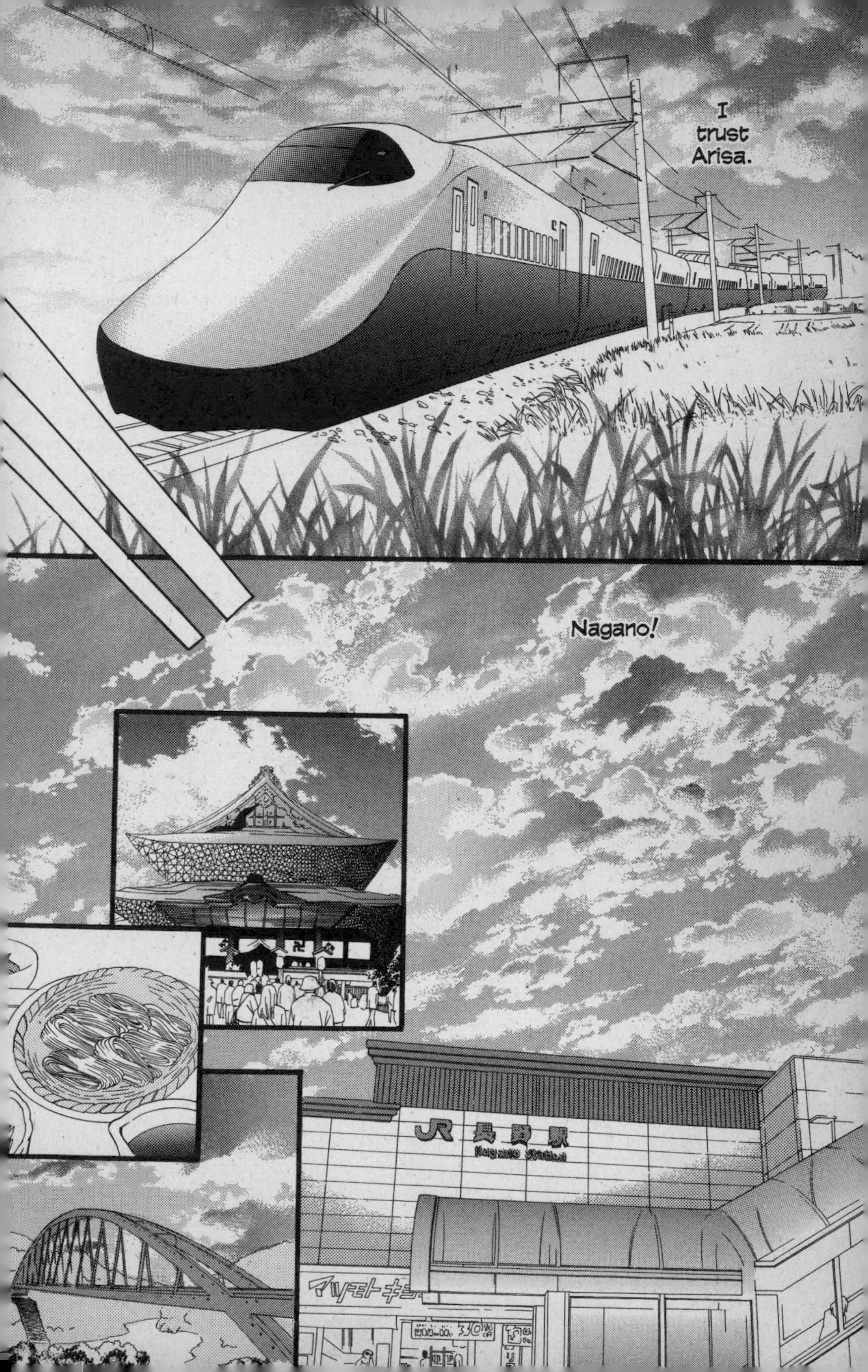
I trust Arisa.
Nagano!
JR 長野駅

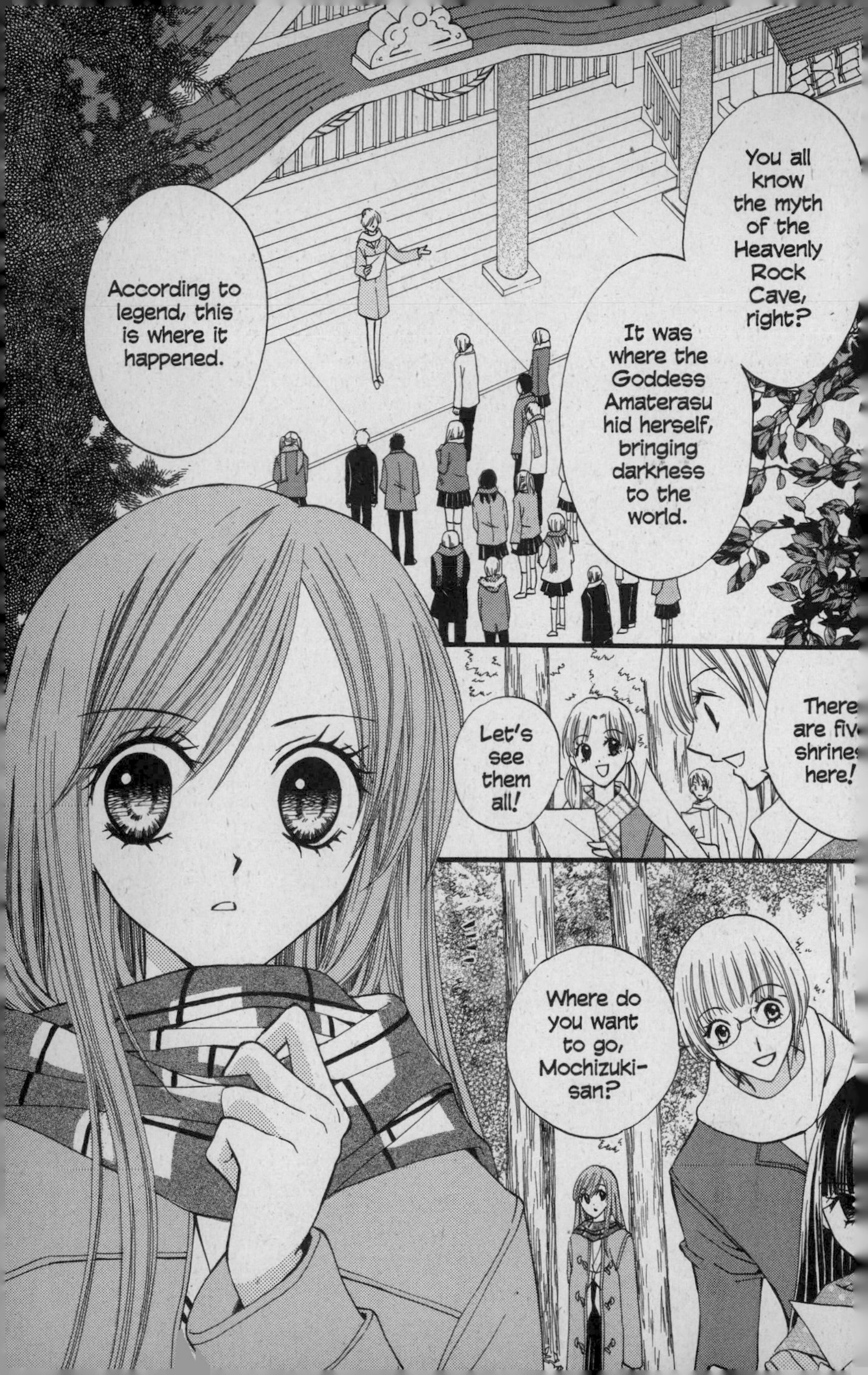
You all know the myth of the Heavenly Rock Cave, right?
It was where the Goddess Amaterasu hid herself, bringing darkness to the world.
According to legend, this is where it happened.
There are fiv shrine here!
Let's see them all!
Where do you want to go, Mochizuki-san?

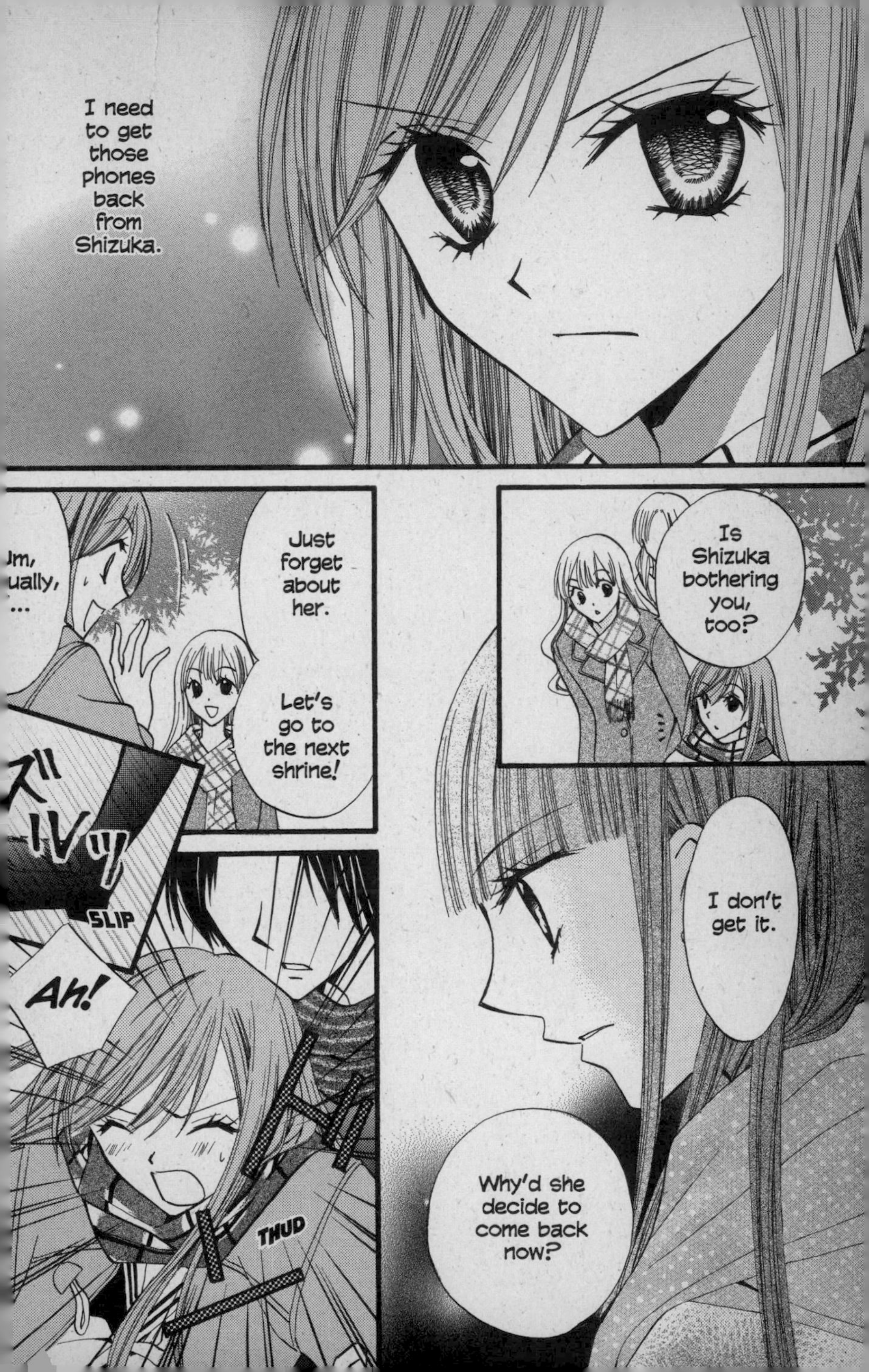
I need to get those phones back from Shizuka.
Is Shizuka bothering you, too?
Just forget about her.
Let's go to the next shrine!
Jm, ually, ...
I don't get it.
Why'd she decide to come back now?
ズルッ
SLIP
Ah!
THUD

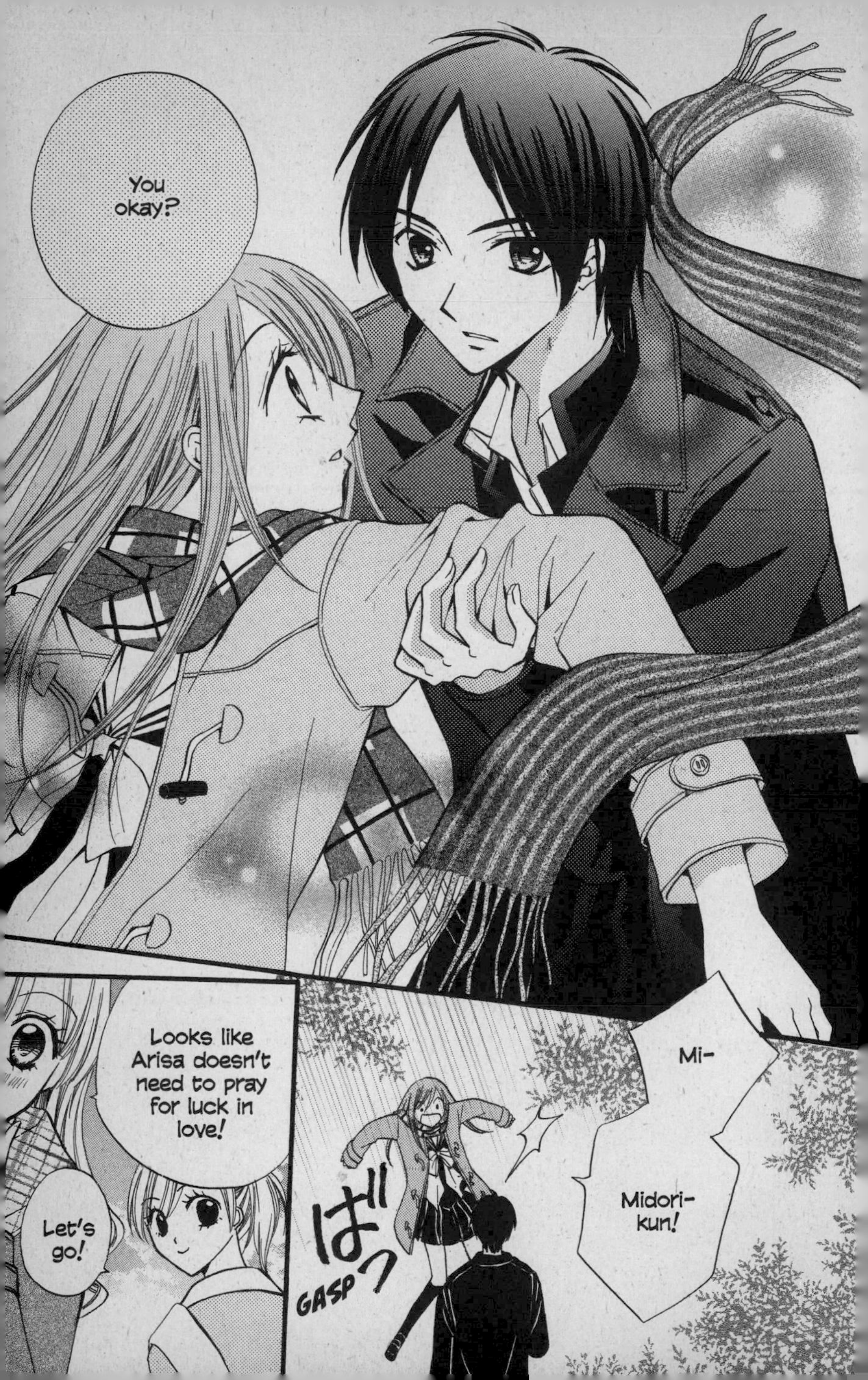

You okay?
Mi-
Midori-kun!
ばっ
GASP
Looks like Arisa doesn't need to pray for luck in love!
Let's go!

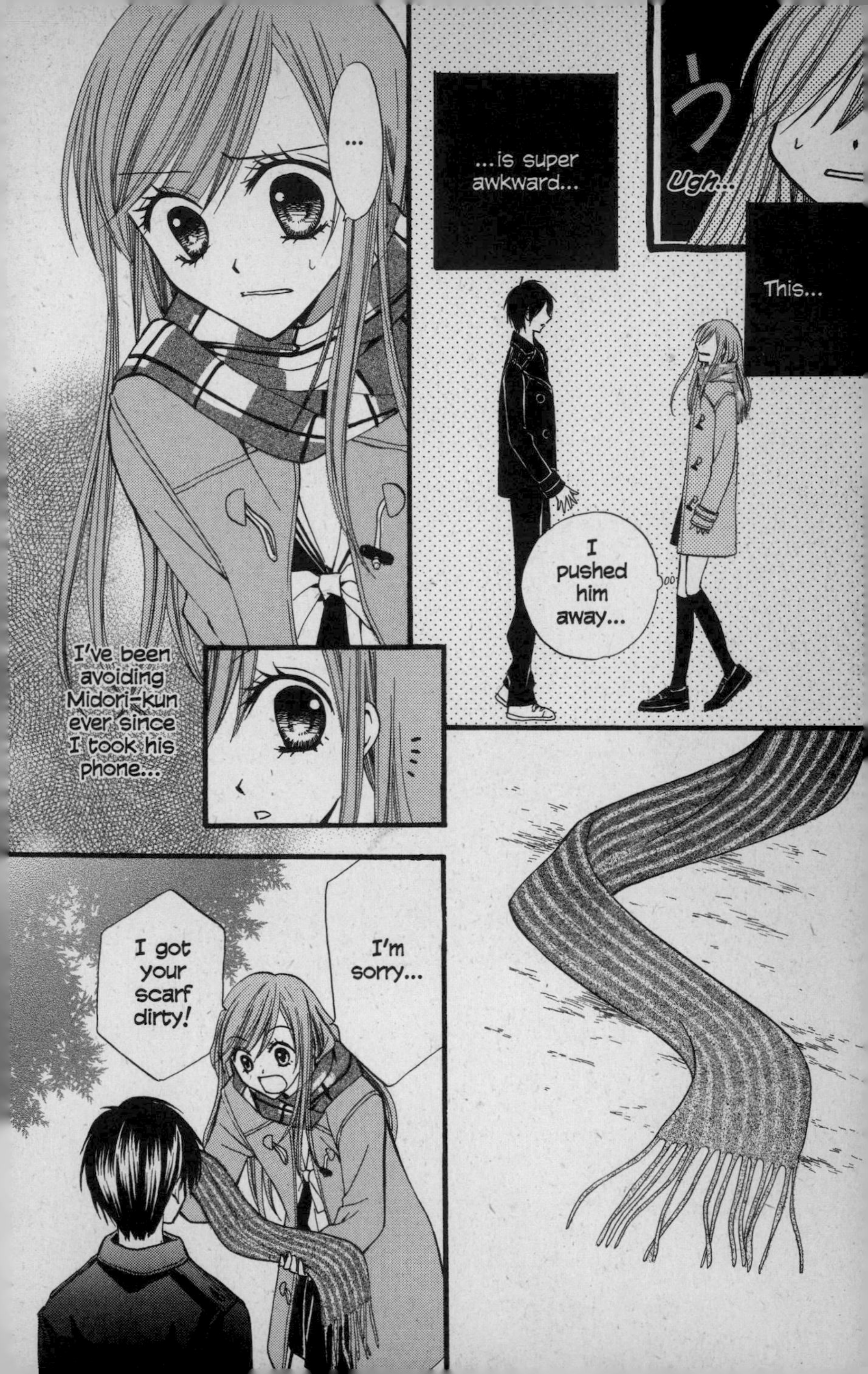
う
Ugh...
This...
...is super awkward...
I pushed him away...
...
I've been avoiding Midori-kun ever since I took his phone...
I'm sorry...
I got your scarf dirty!

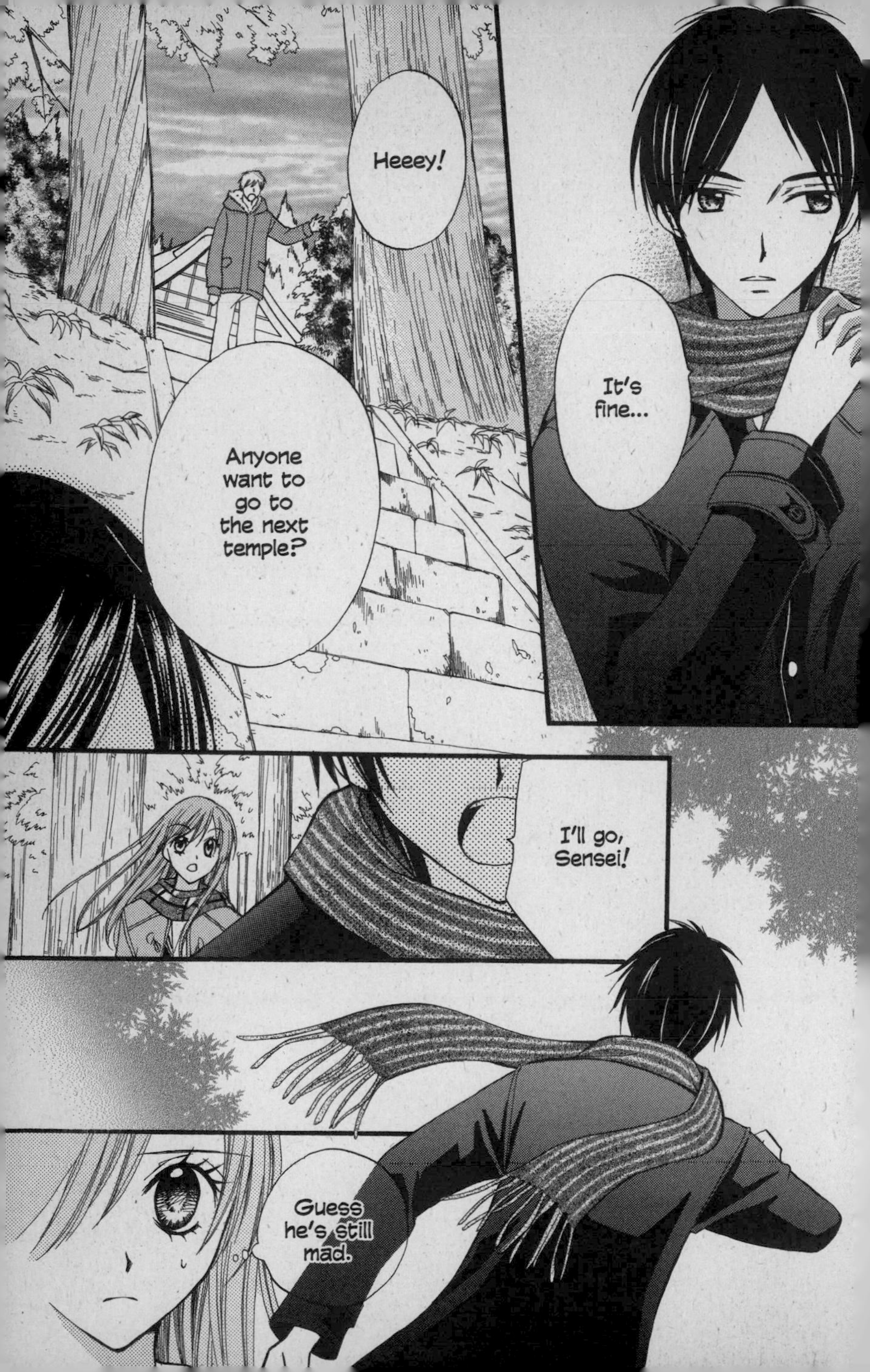
It's fine...
Heeey!
Anyone want to go to the next temple?
I'll go, Sensei!
Guess he's still mad.

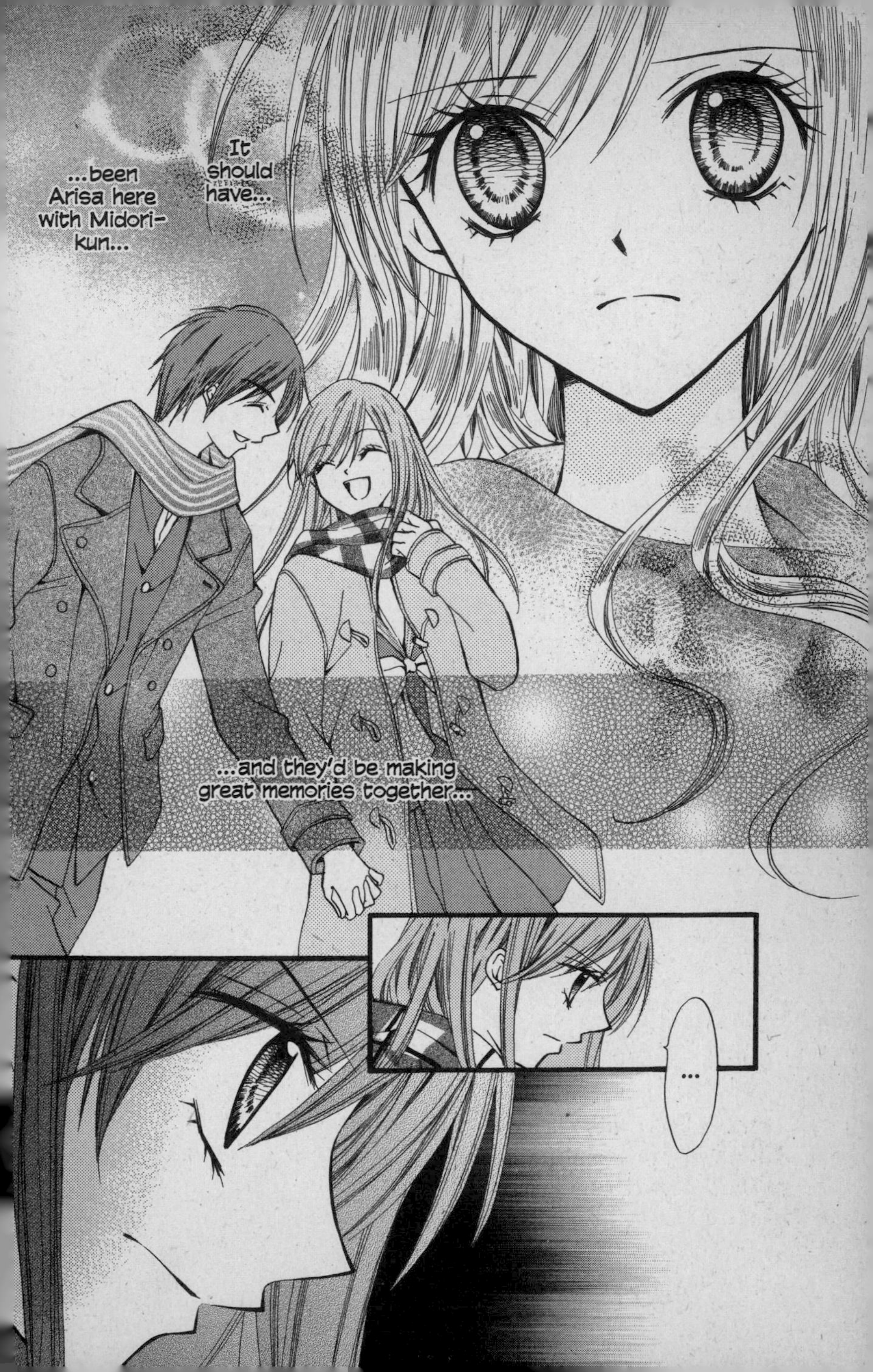
It should have...
...been Arisa here with Midori-kun...
...and they'd be making great memories together...
...

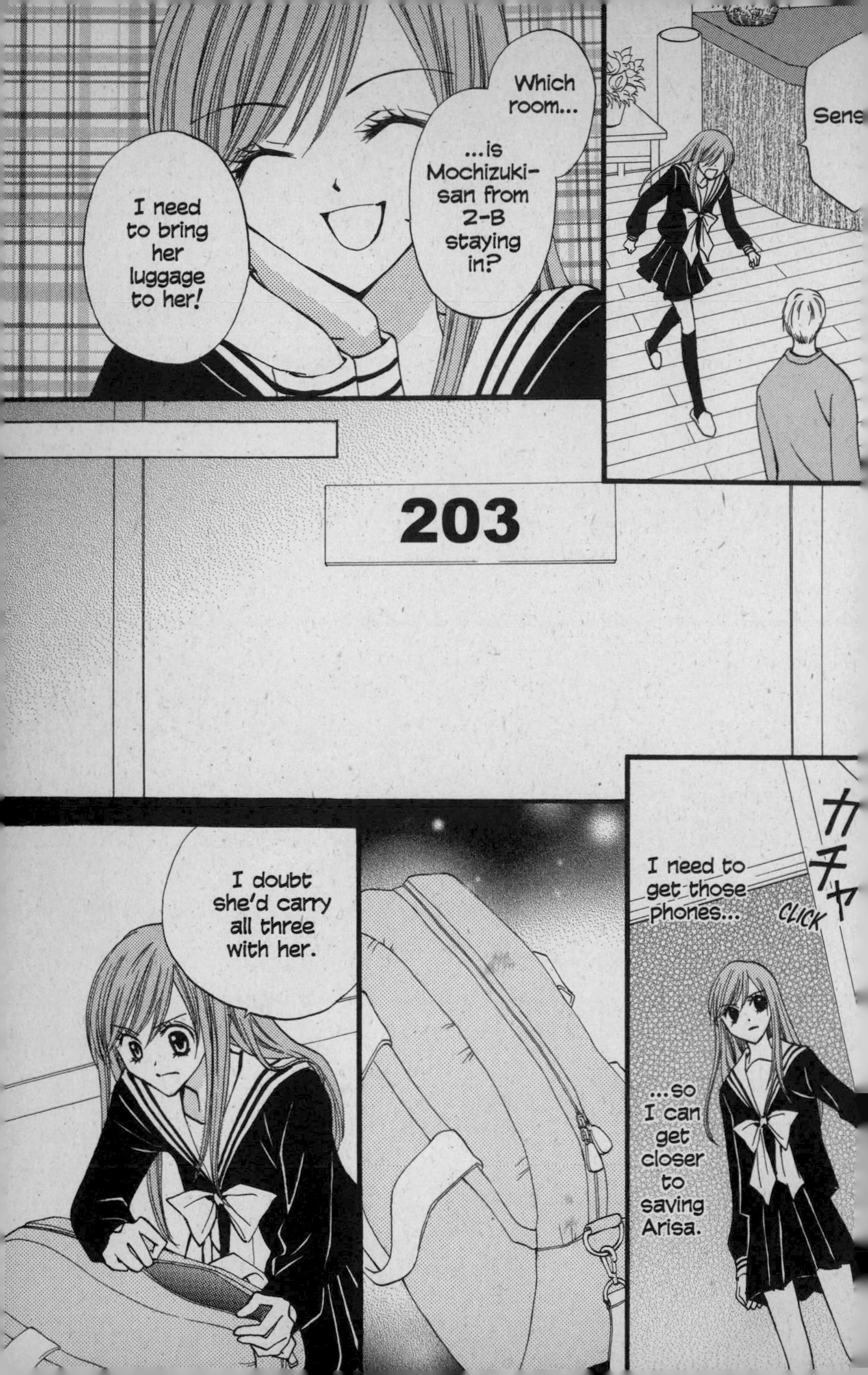

Sens
Which room...
...is Mochizuki-san from 2-B staying in?
I need to bring her luggage to her!
203
カチャ
CLICK
I need to get those phones...
...so I can get closer to saving Arisa.
I doubt she'd carry all three with her.

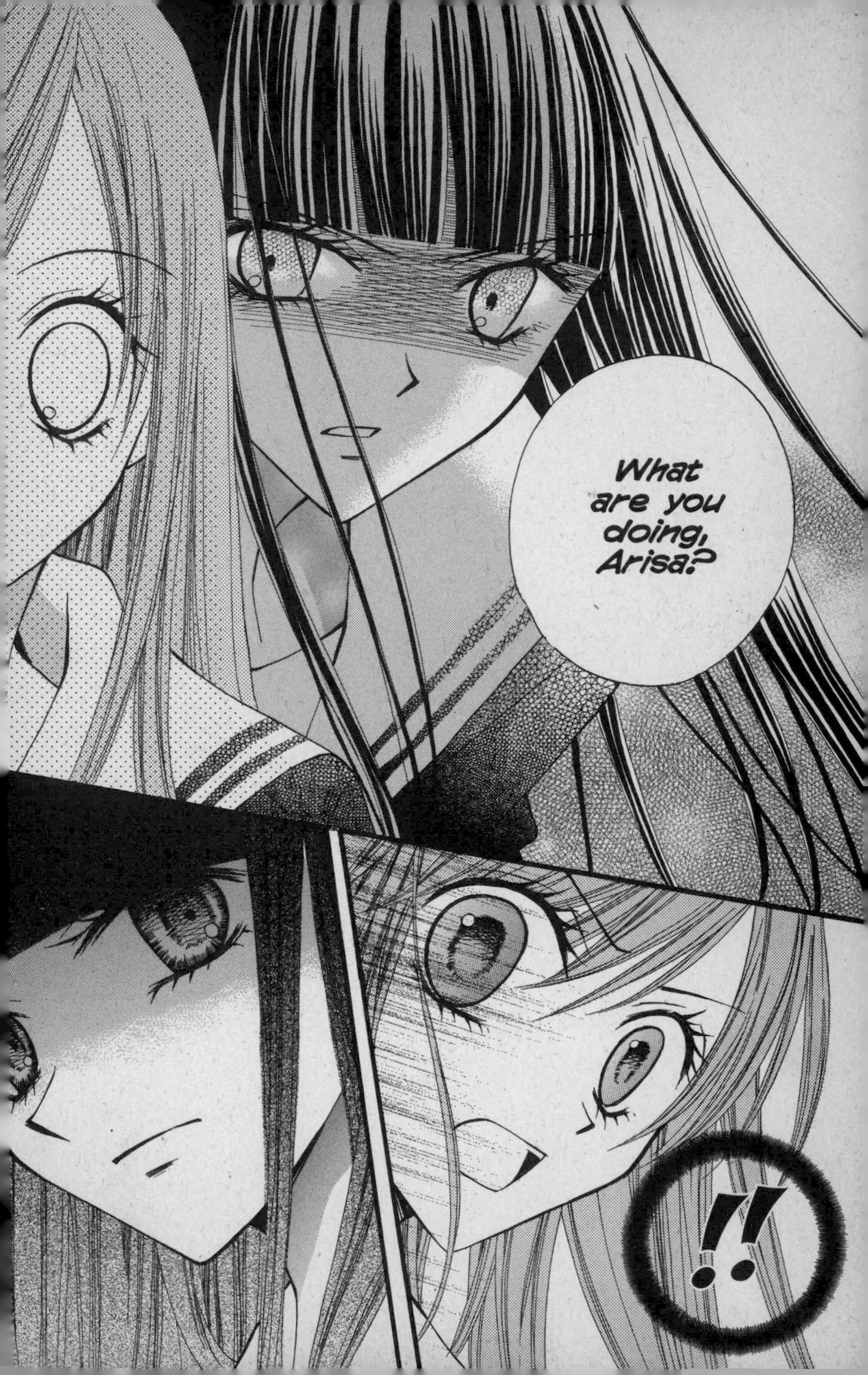
What are you doing, Arisa?
!!

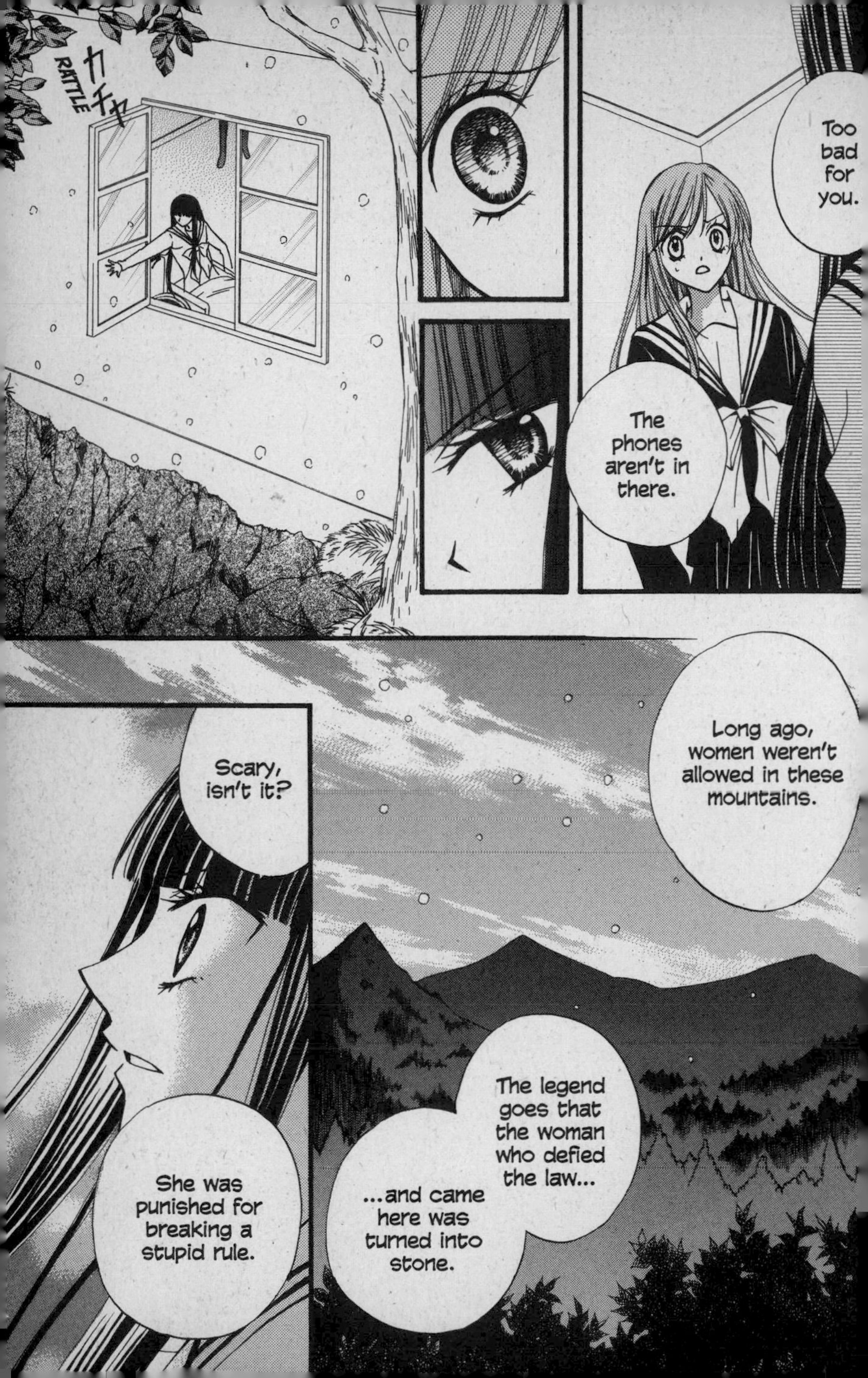
Too bad for you.
The phones aren't in there.
カチャ
RATTLE
Long ago, women weren't allowed in these mountains.
The legend goes that the woman who defied the law...
...and came here was turned into stone.
Scary, isn't it?
She was punished for breaking a stupid rule.

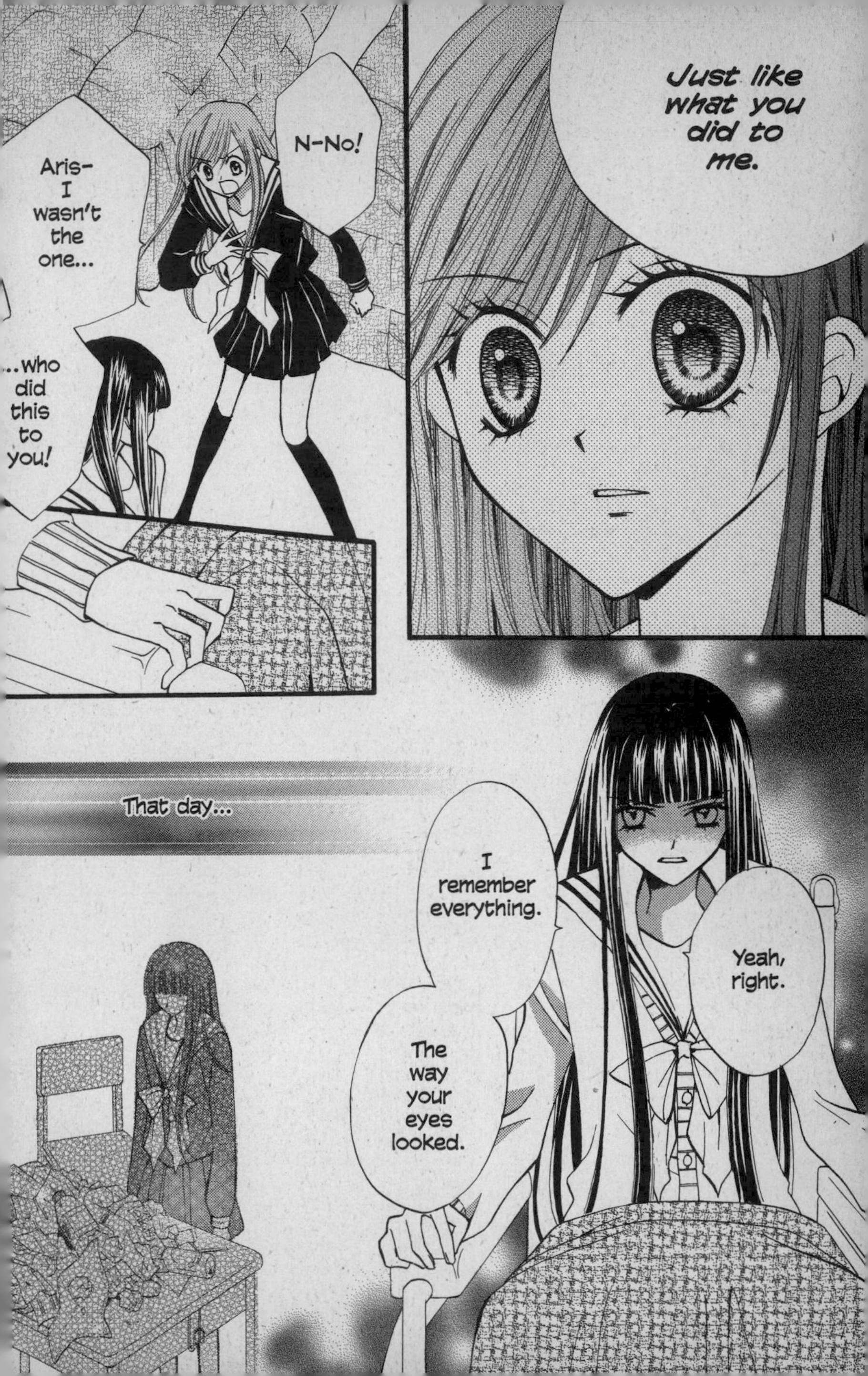
Just like what you did to me.
N-No!
Aris- I wasn't the one...
...who did this to you!
Yeah, right.
I remember everything.
The way your eyes looked.
That day...

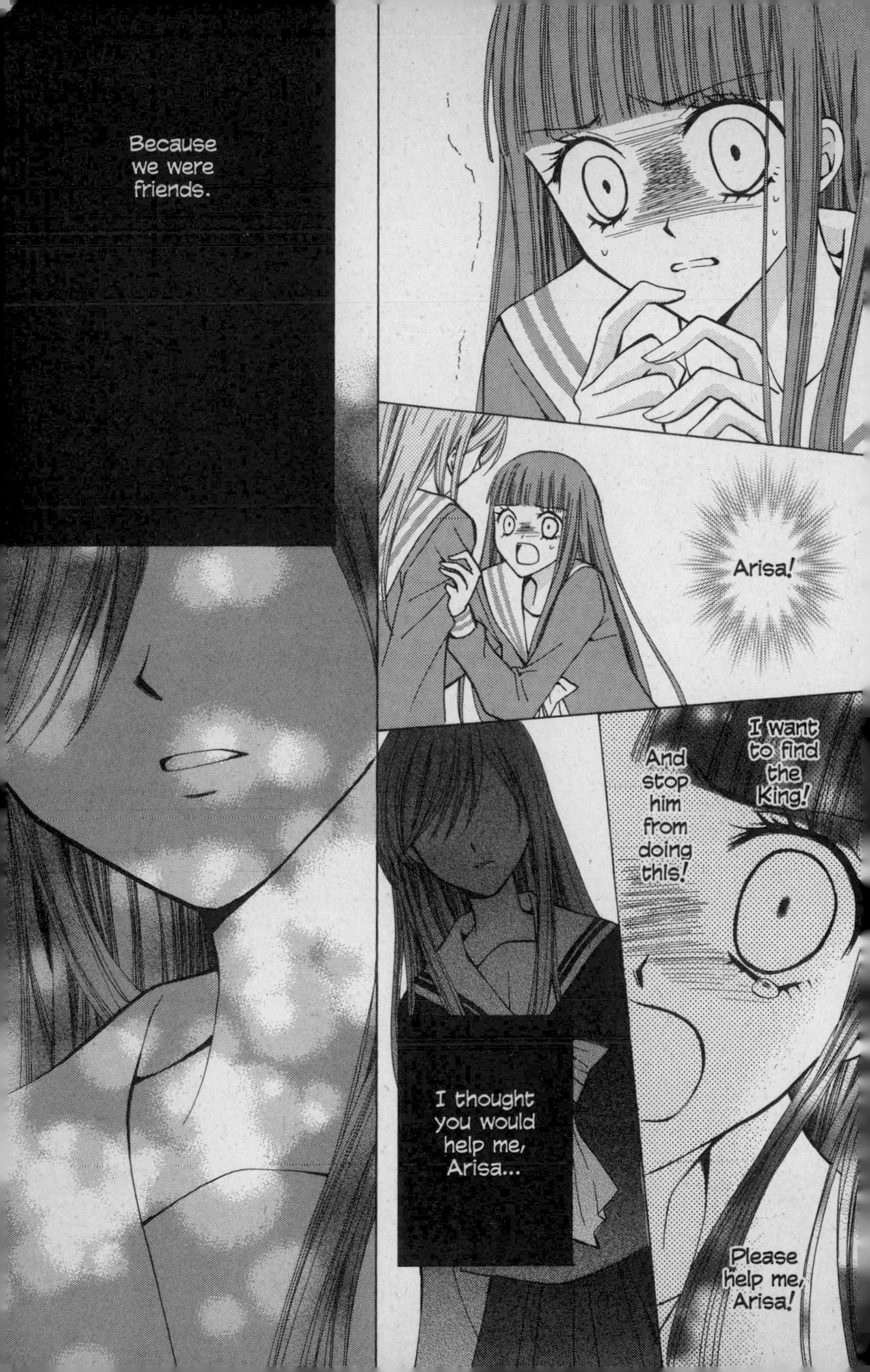
Arisa!
I want to find the King!
And stop him from doing this!
Please help me, Arisa!
I thought you would help me, Arisa...
Because we were friends.

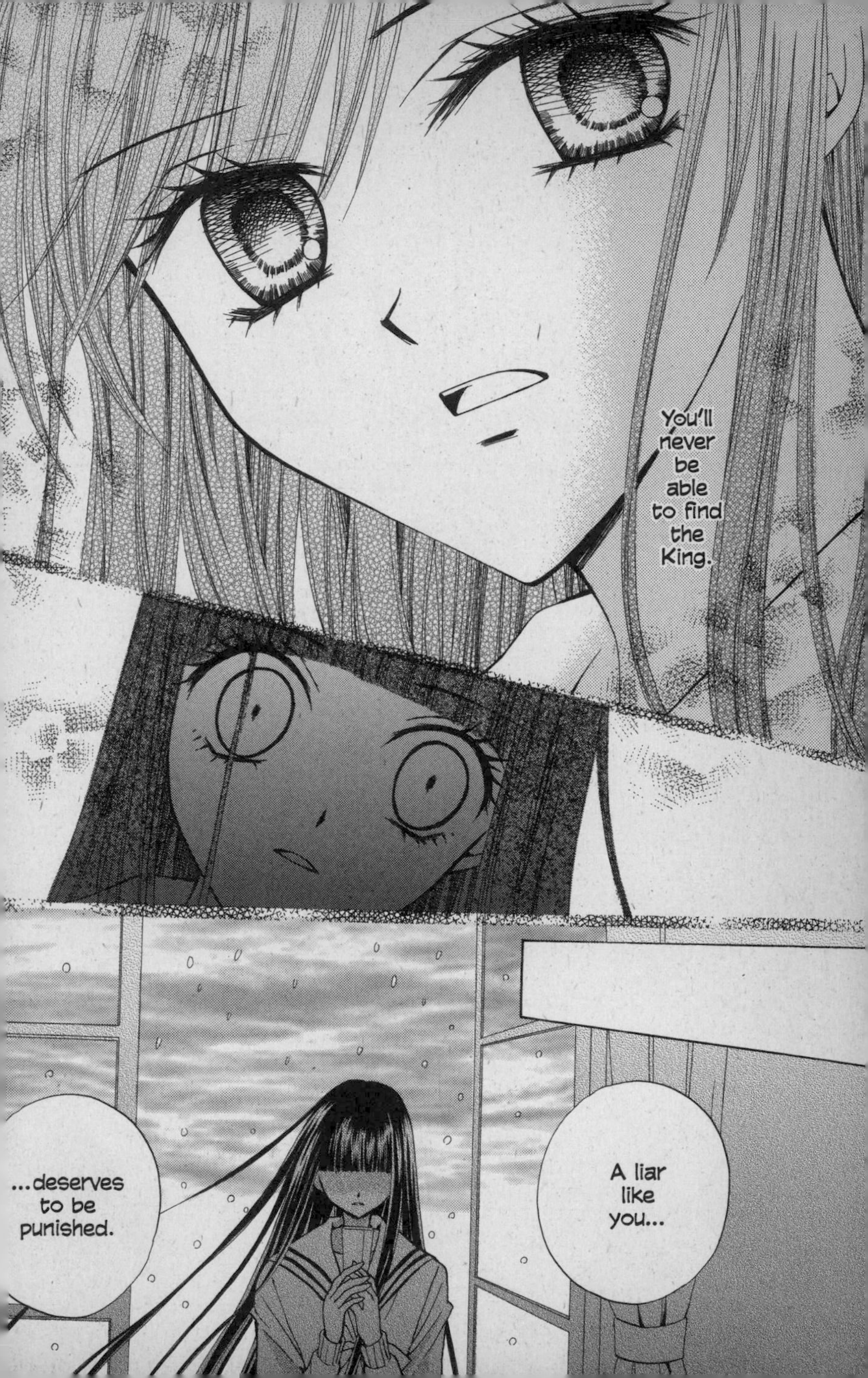
You'll never be able to find the King.
A liar like you...
...deserves to be punished.

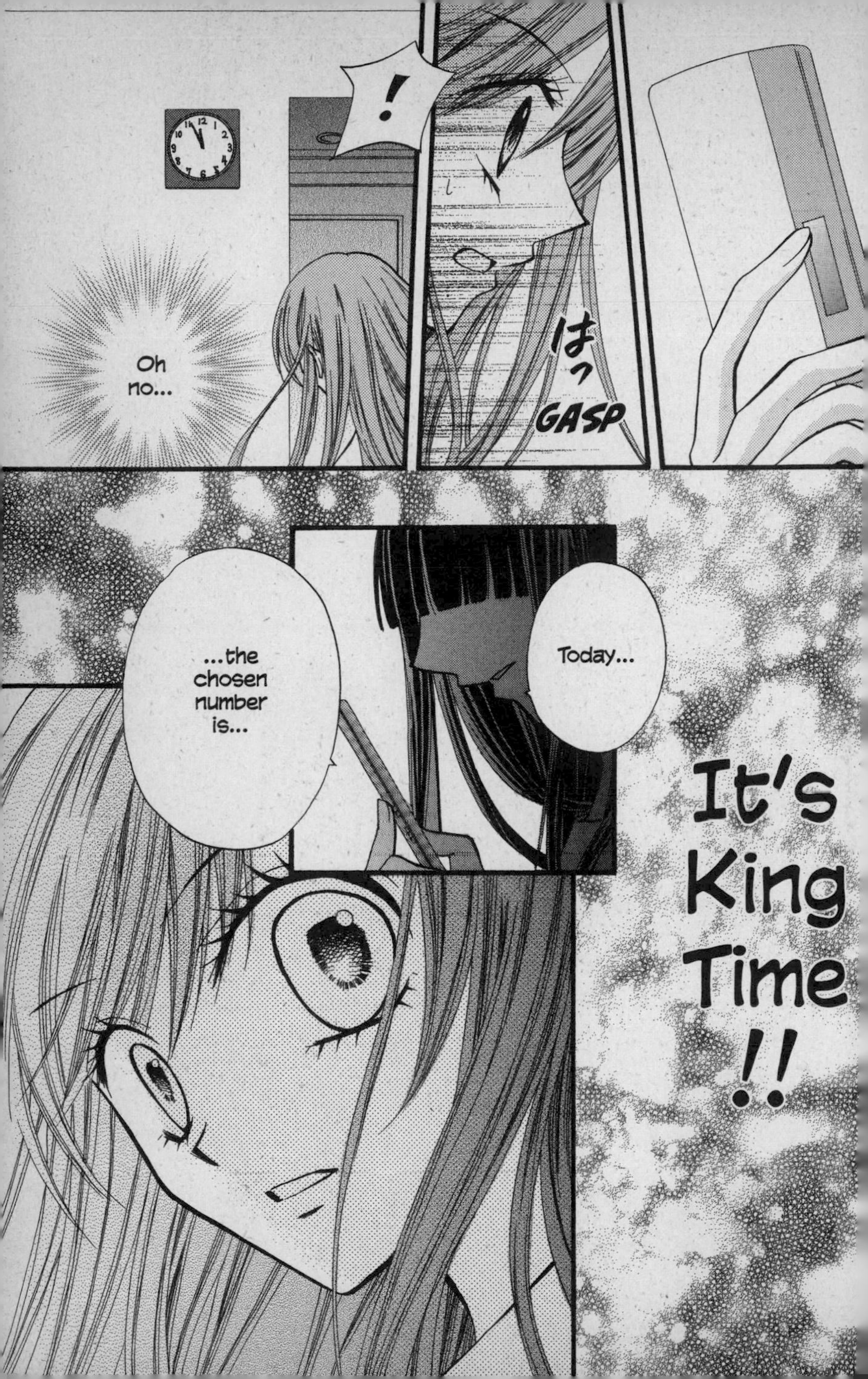
!
はっ
GASP
Oh no...
Today...
...the chosen number is...
It's King Time!!

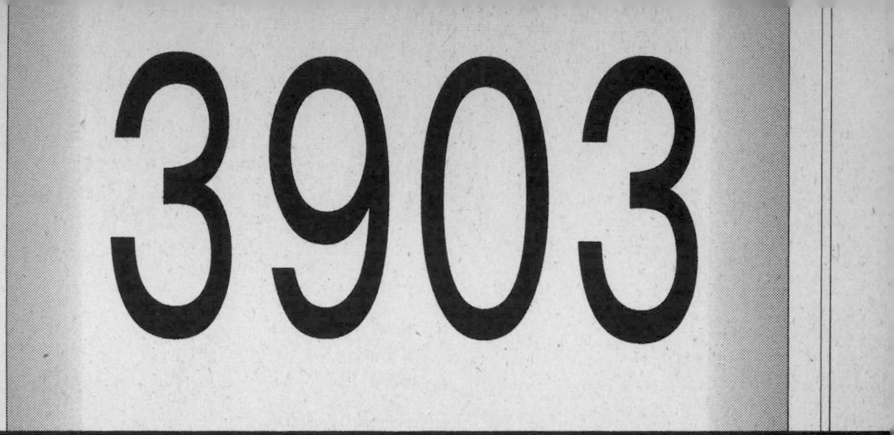
3903

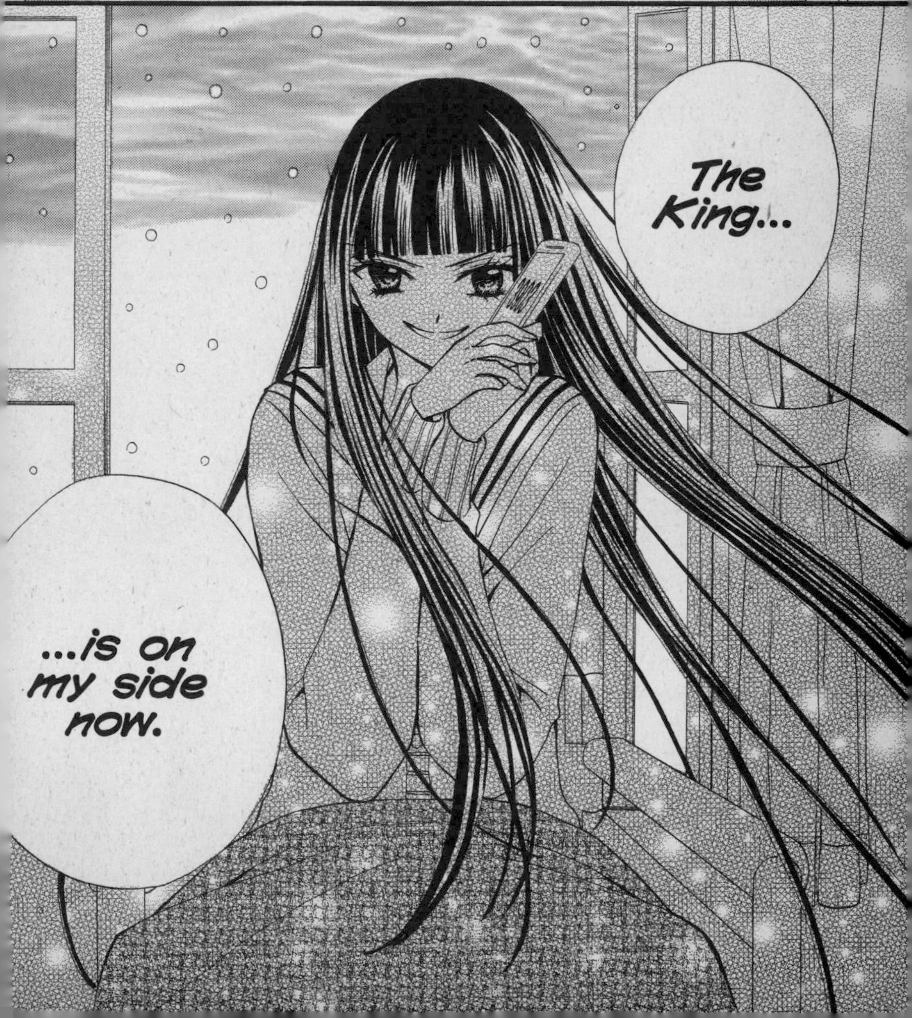
The King...
...is on my side now.

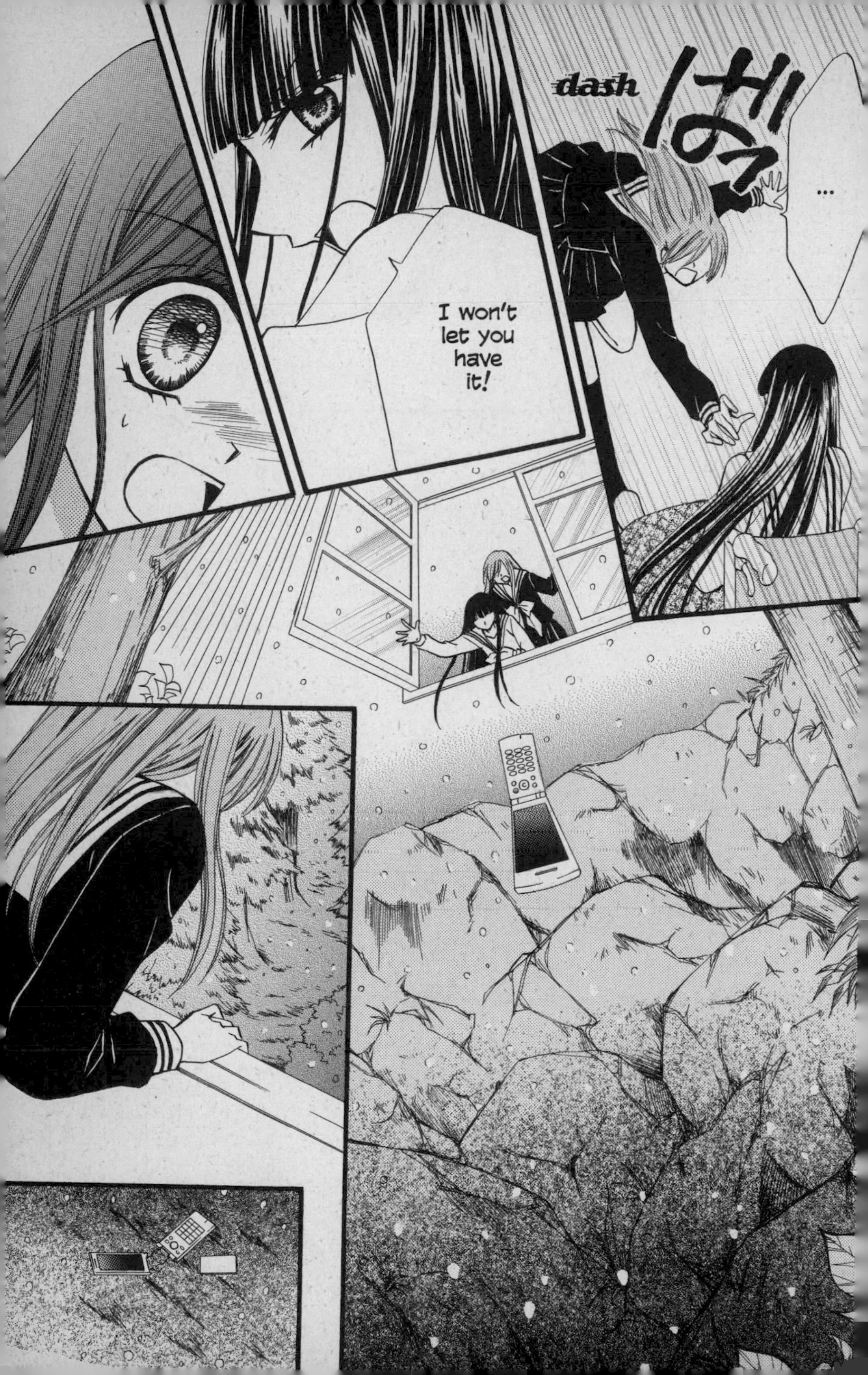
...
dash
I won't let you have it!

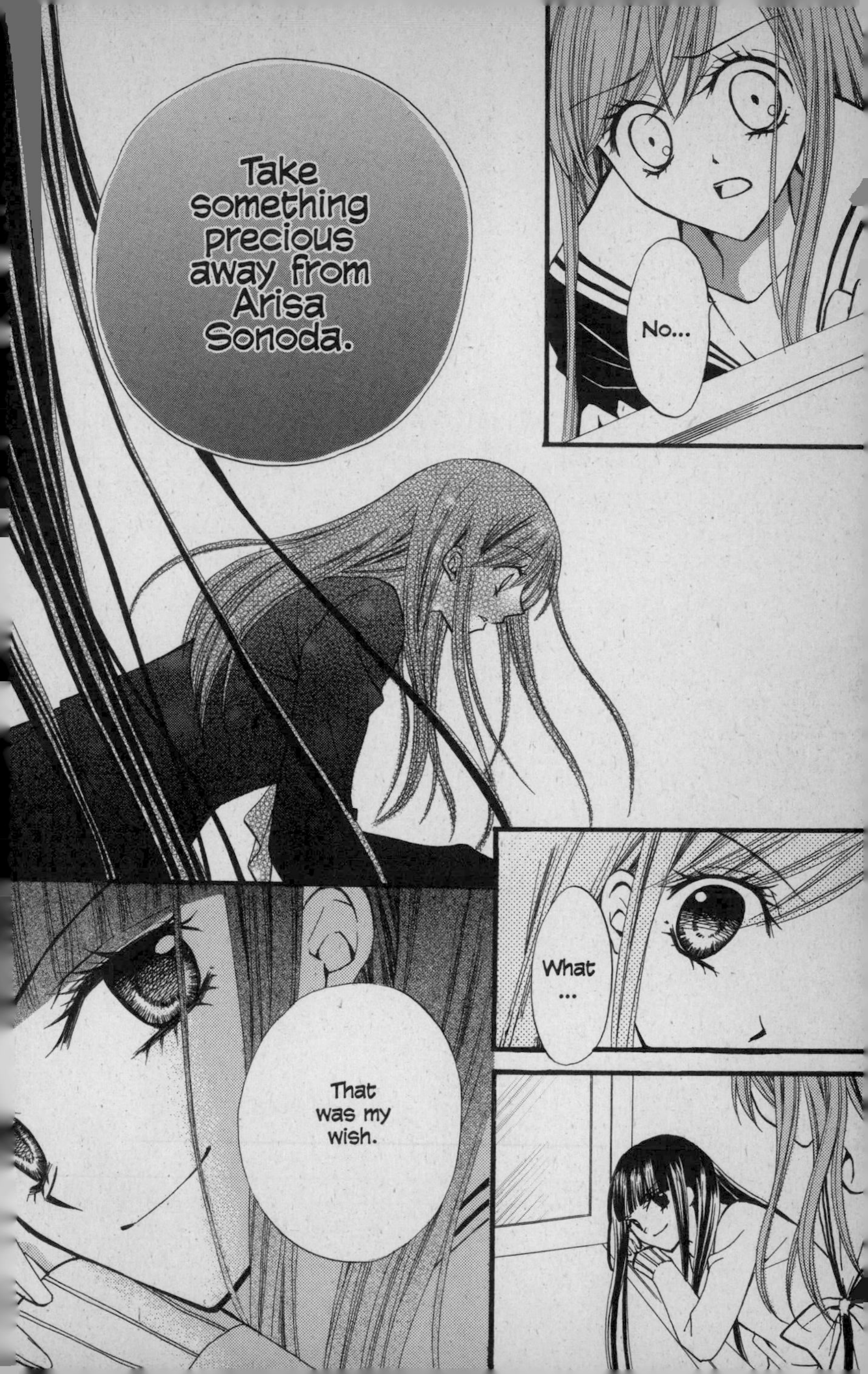
No...
Take something precious away from Arisa Sonoda.
What ...
That was my wish.

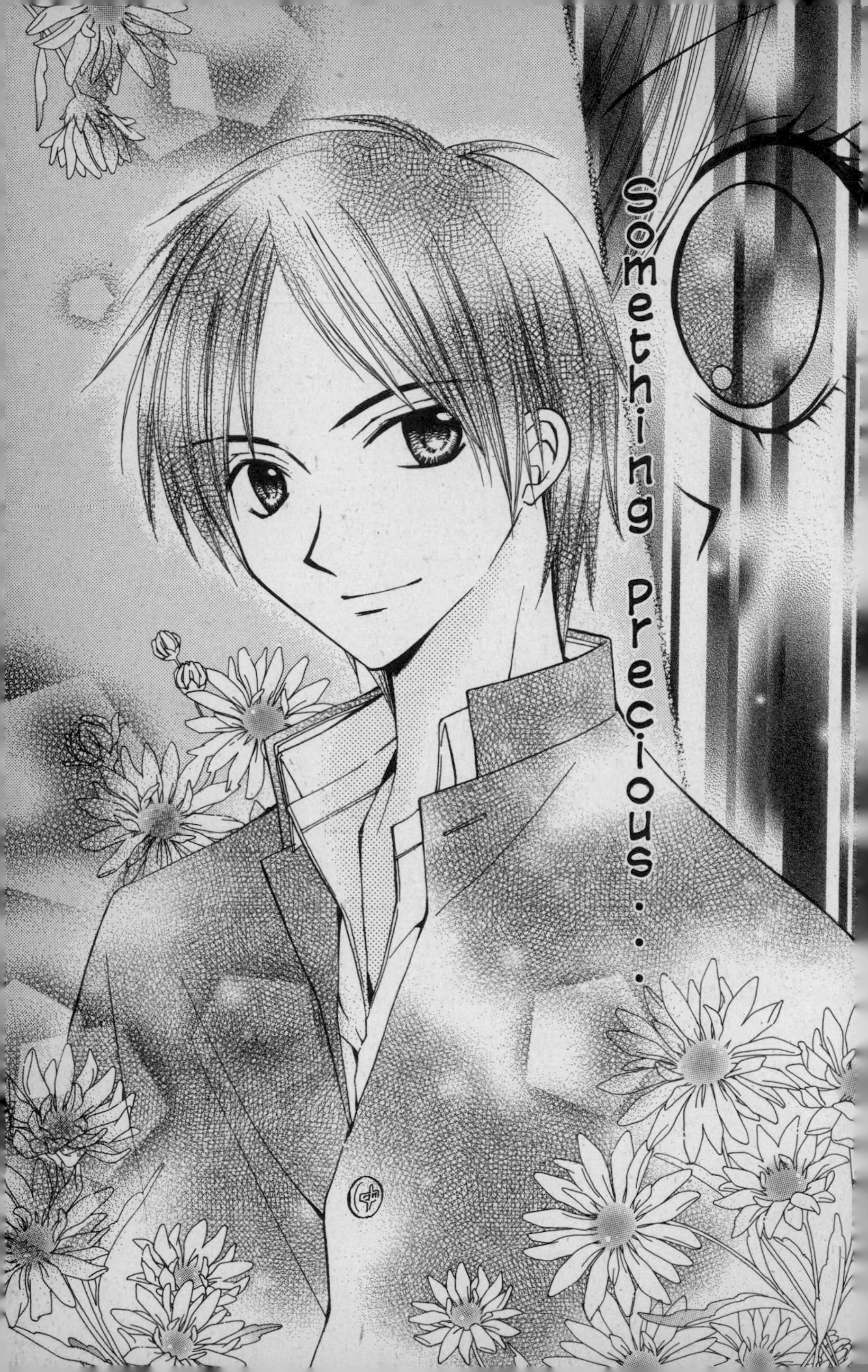
Something Precious...

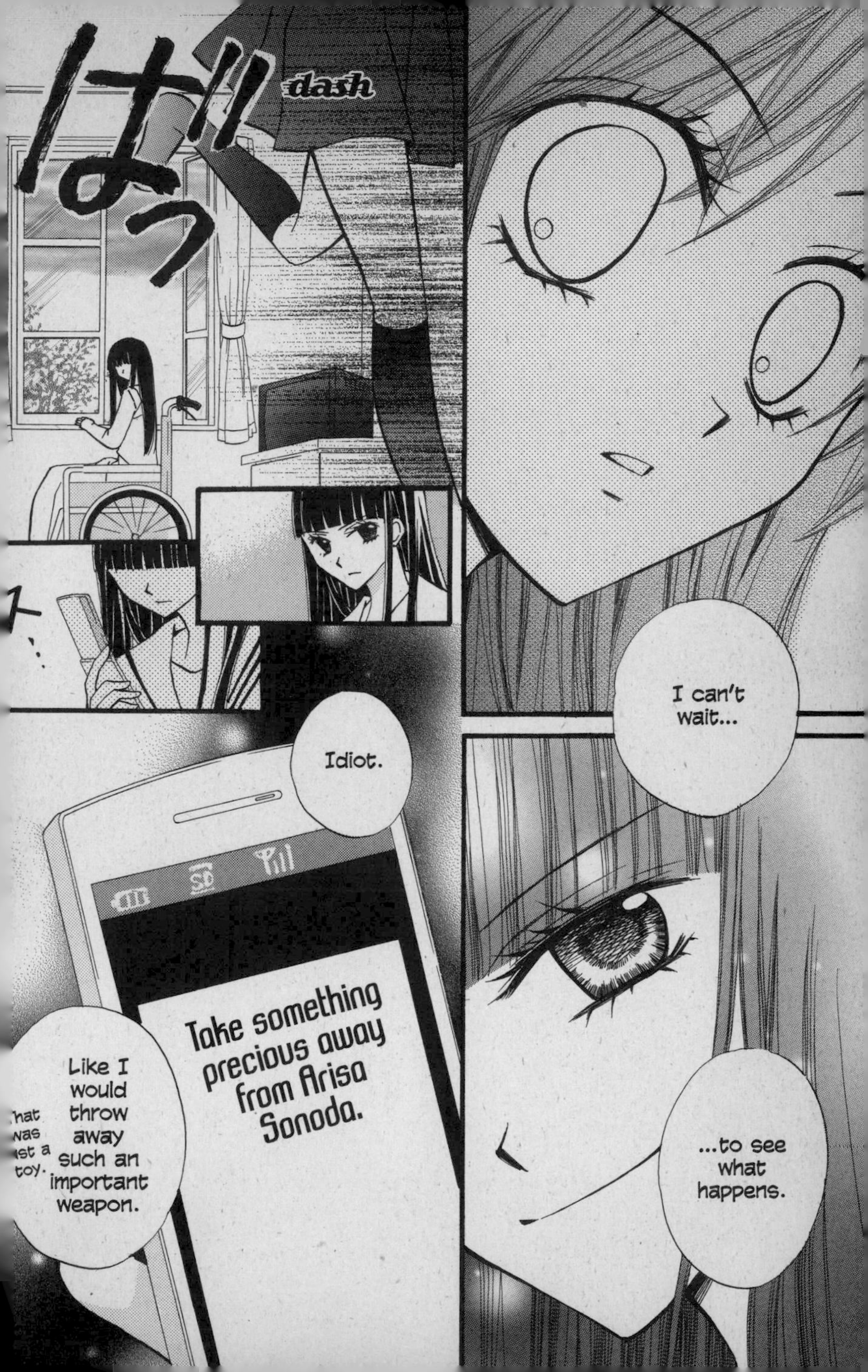
I can't wait...
はっ
dash
ス
...to see what happens.
Idiot.
Take something precious away from Arisa Sonoda.
Like I would throw away such an important weapon.
hat was ıst a toy.

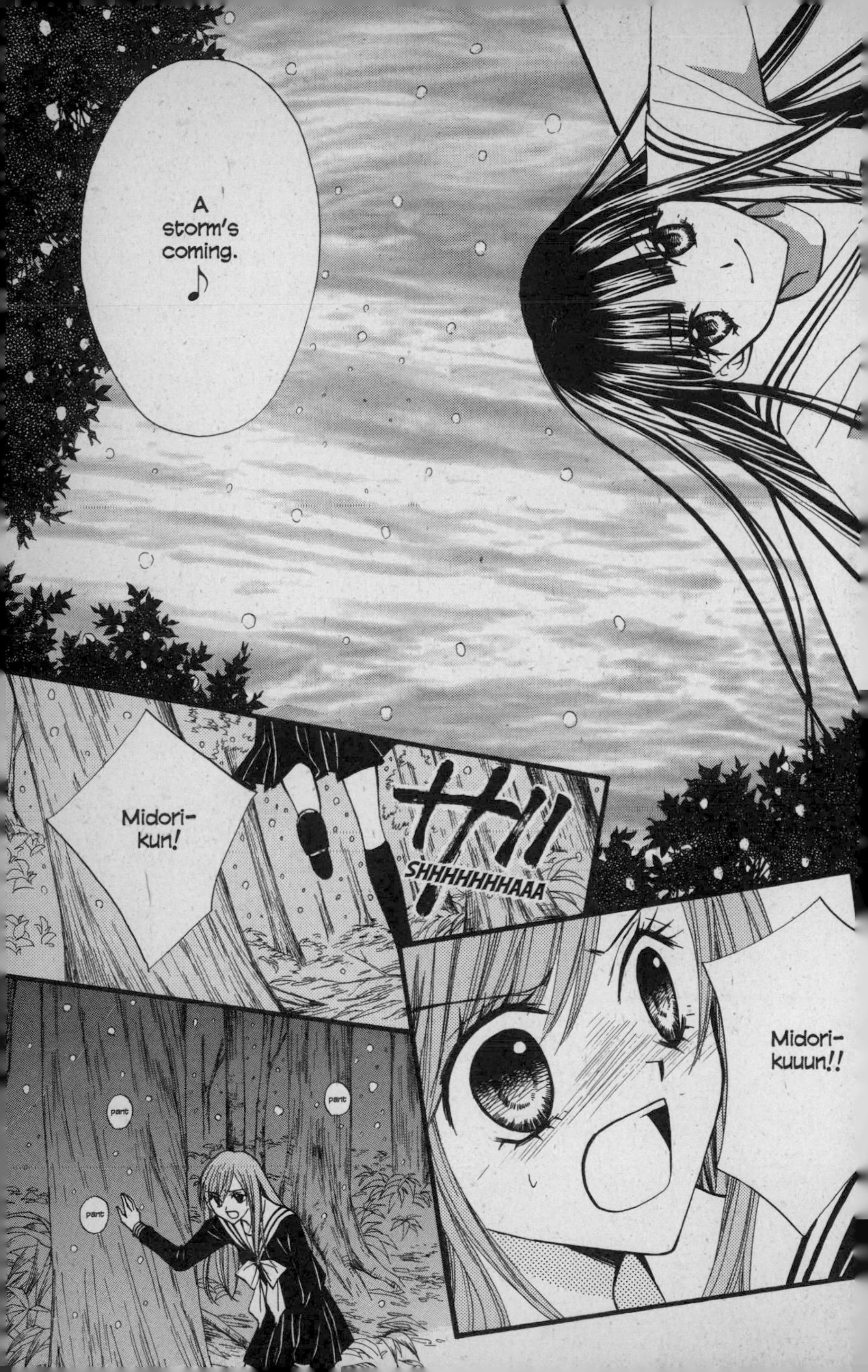
A storm's coming. ♪
SHHHHHHHAAA
Midori-kun!
Midori-kuuun!!
pant
pant

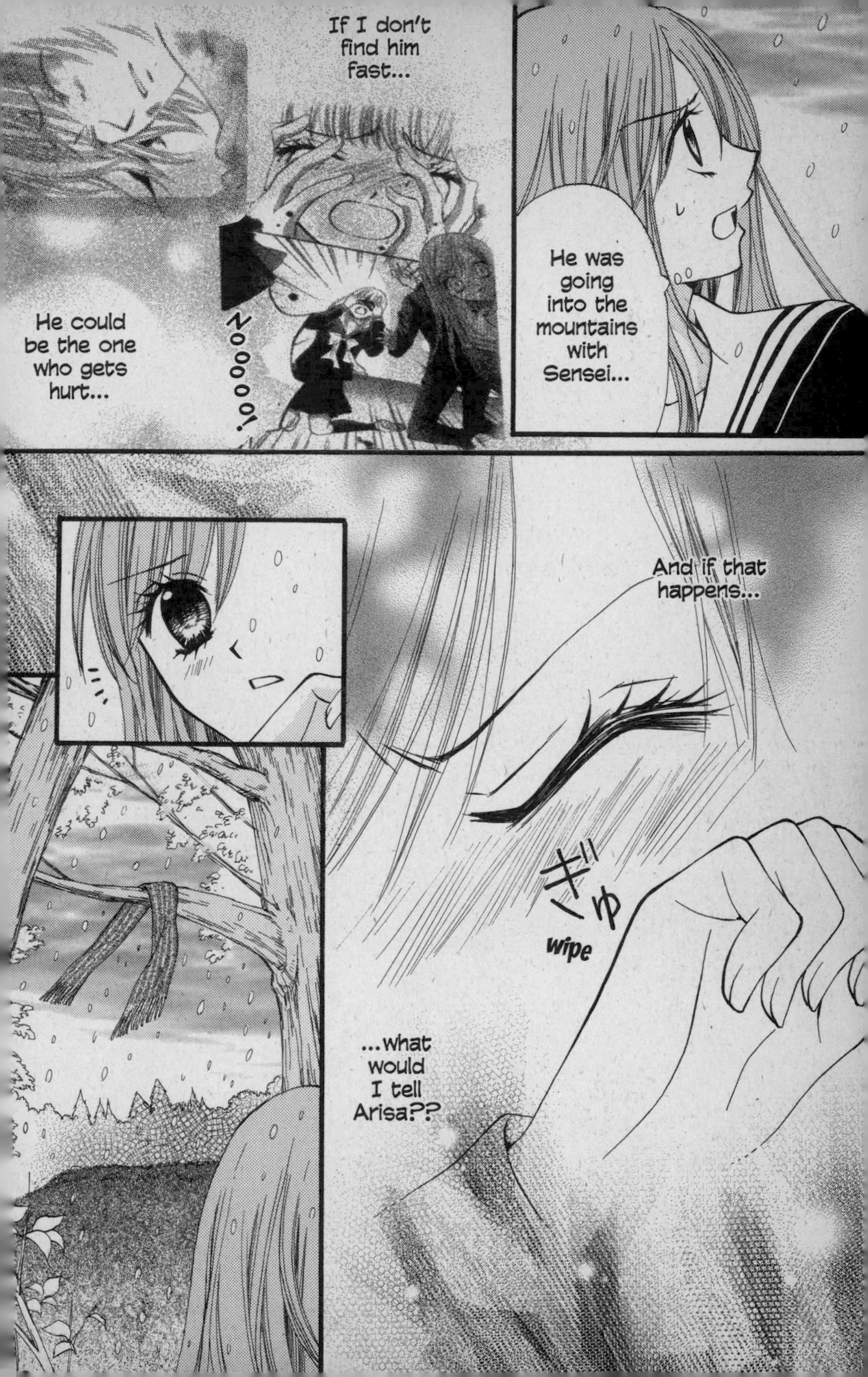
He was going into the mountains with Sensei...
If I don't find him fast...
Nooooo!
He could be the one who gets hurt...
And if that happens...
ぎゅ
wipe
...what would I tell Arisa??

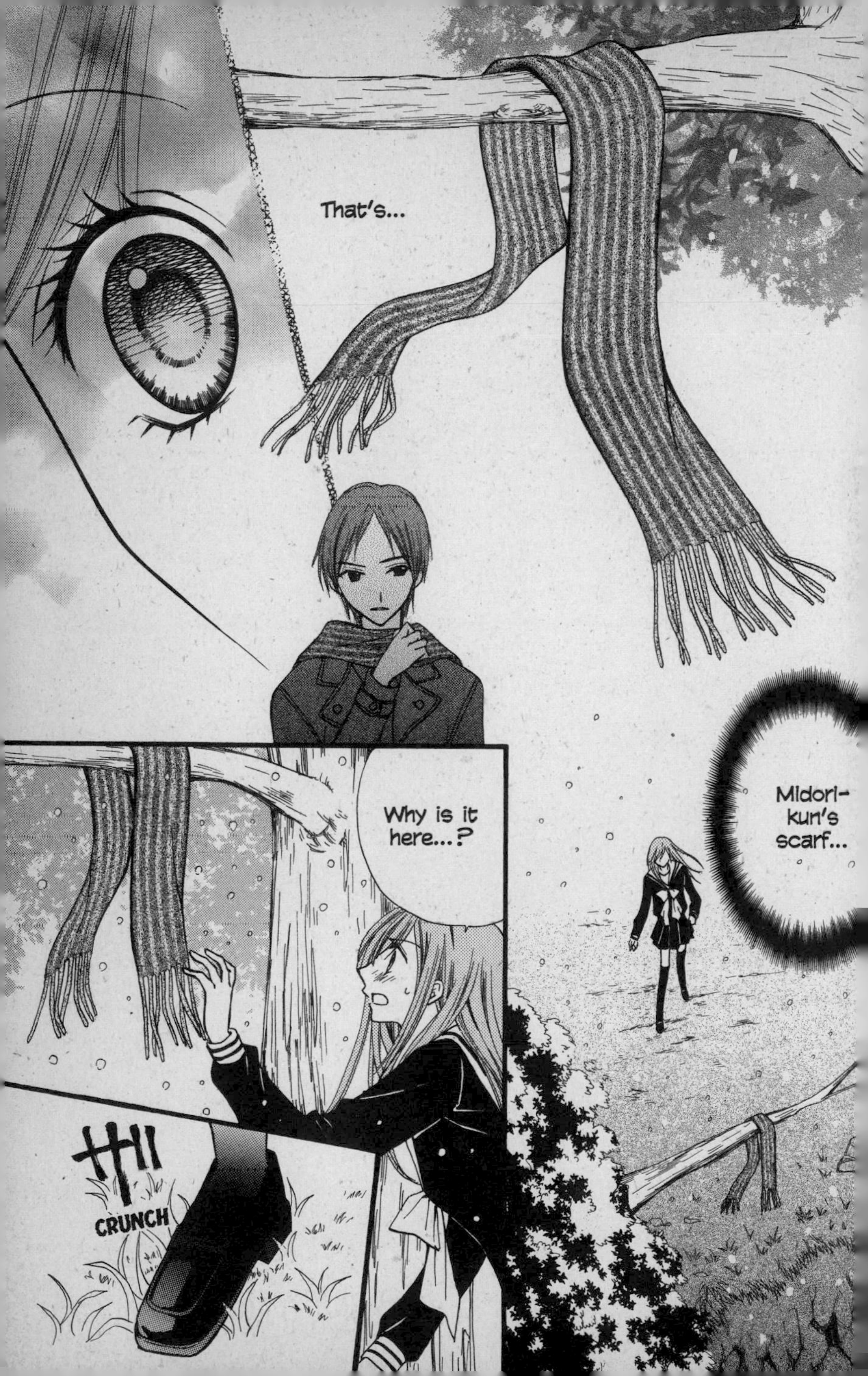
That's...
Midori-kun's scarf...
Why is it here...?
CRUNCH

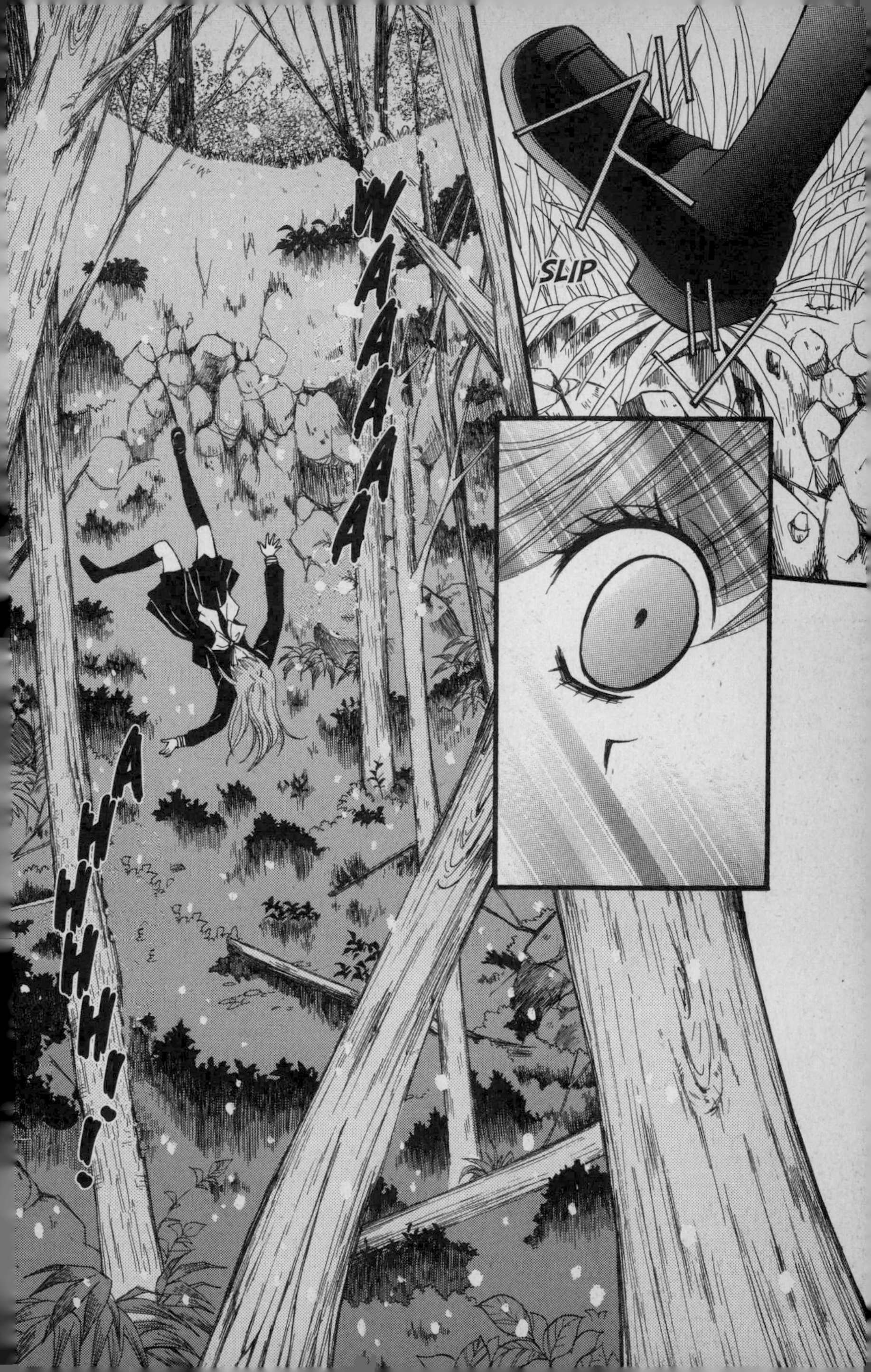
SLIP
WAAAAAAA
AHHHHHH!!

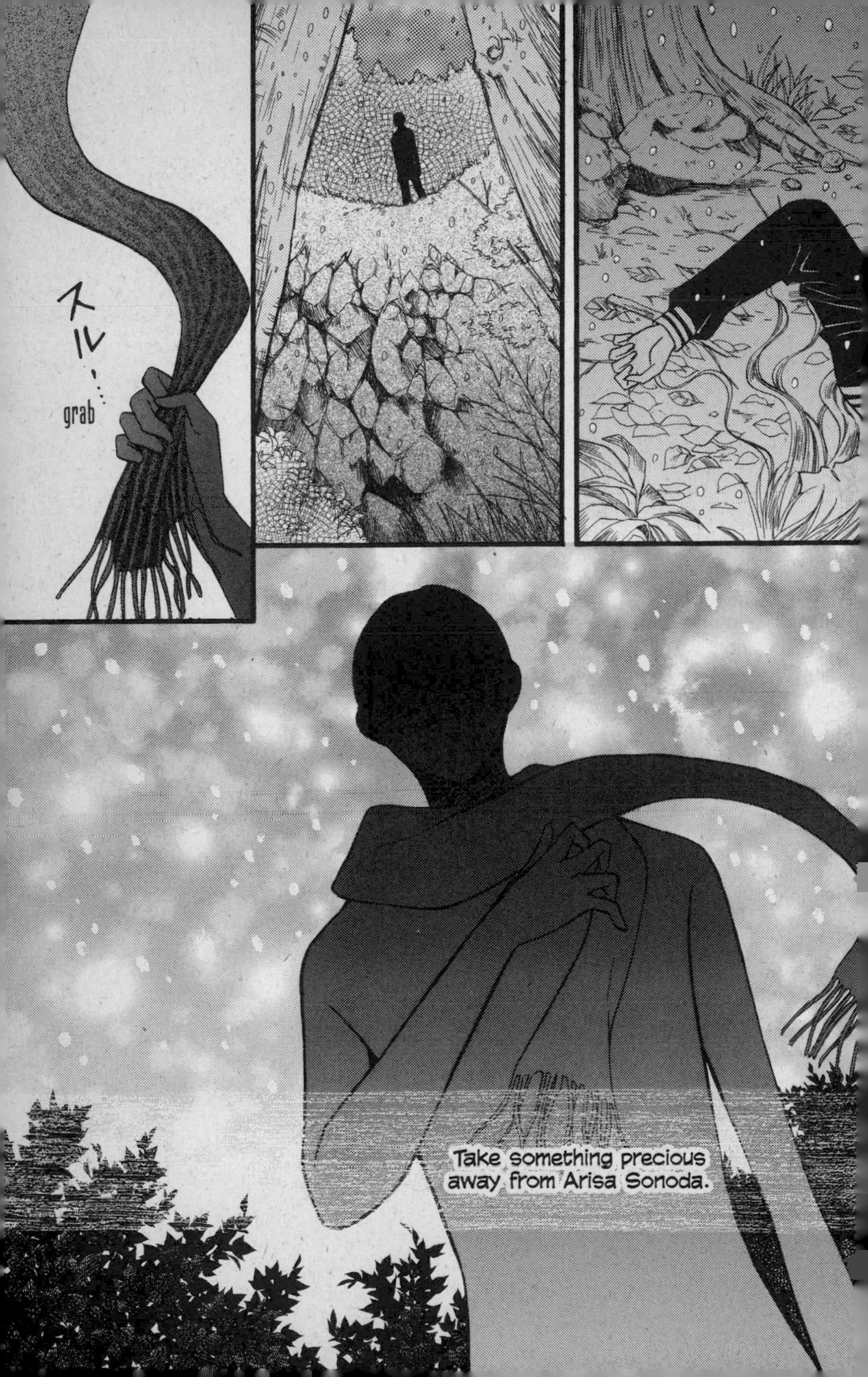
スル……
grab
Take something precious away from Arisa Sonoda.

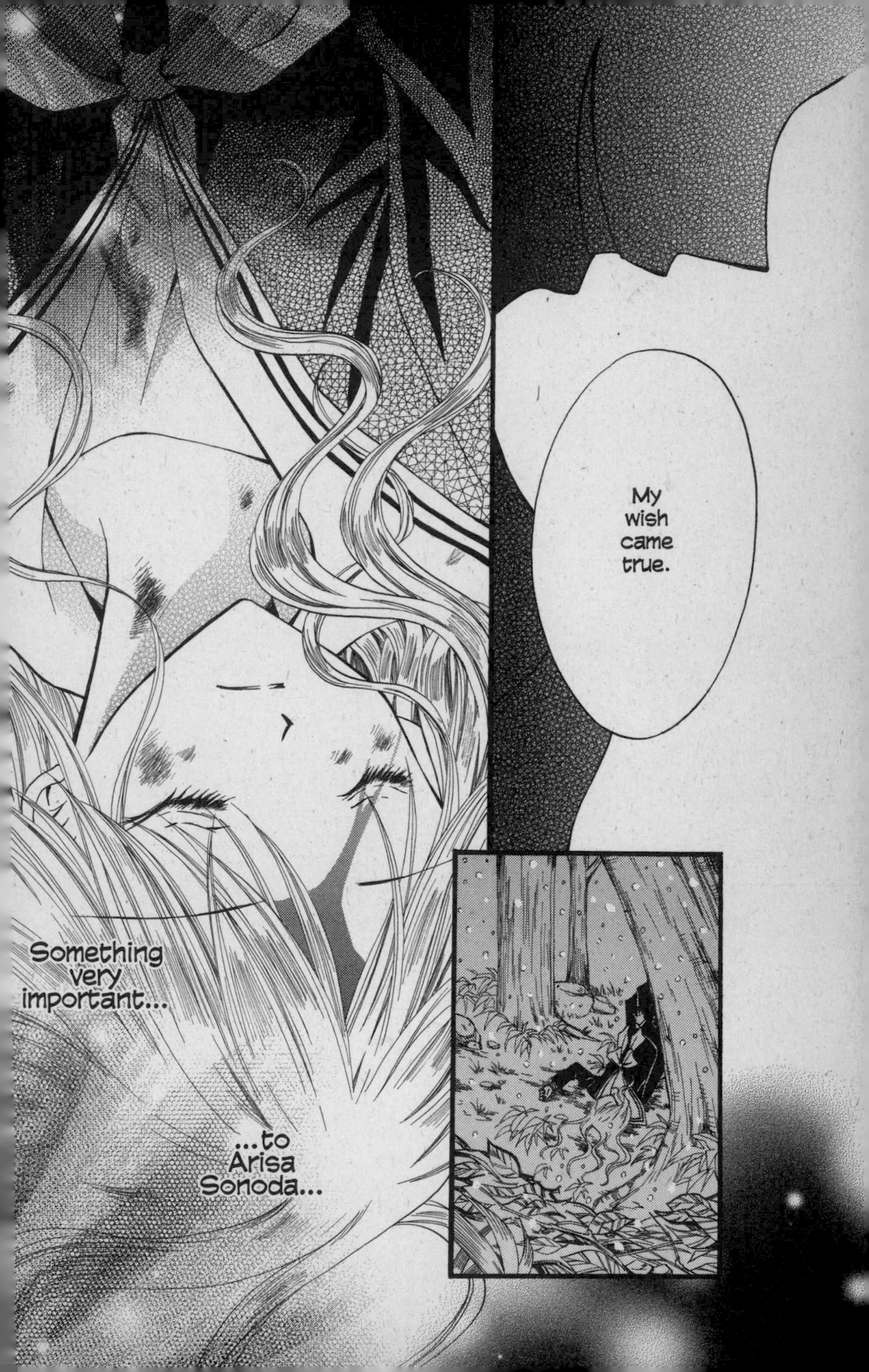
My wish came true.
Something very important...
...to Arisa Sonoda...

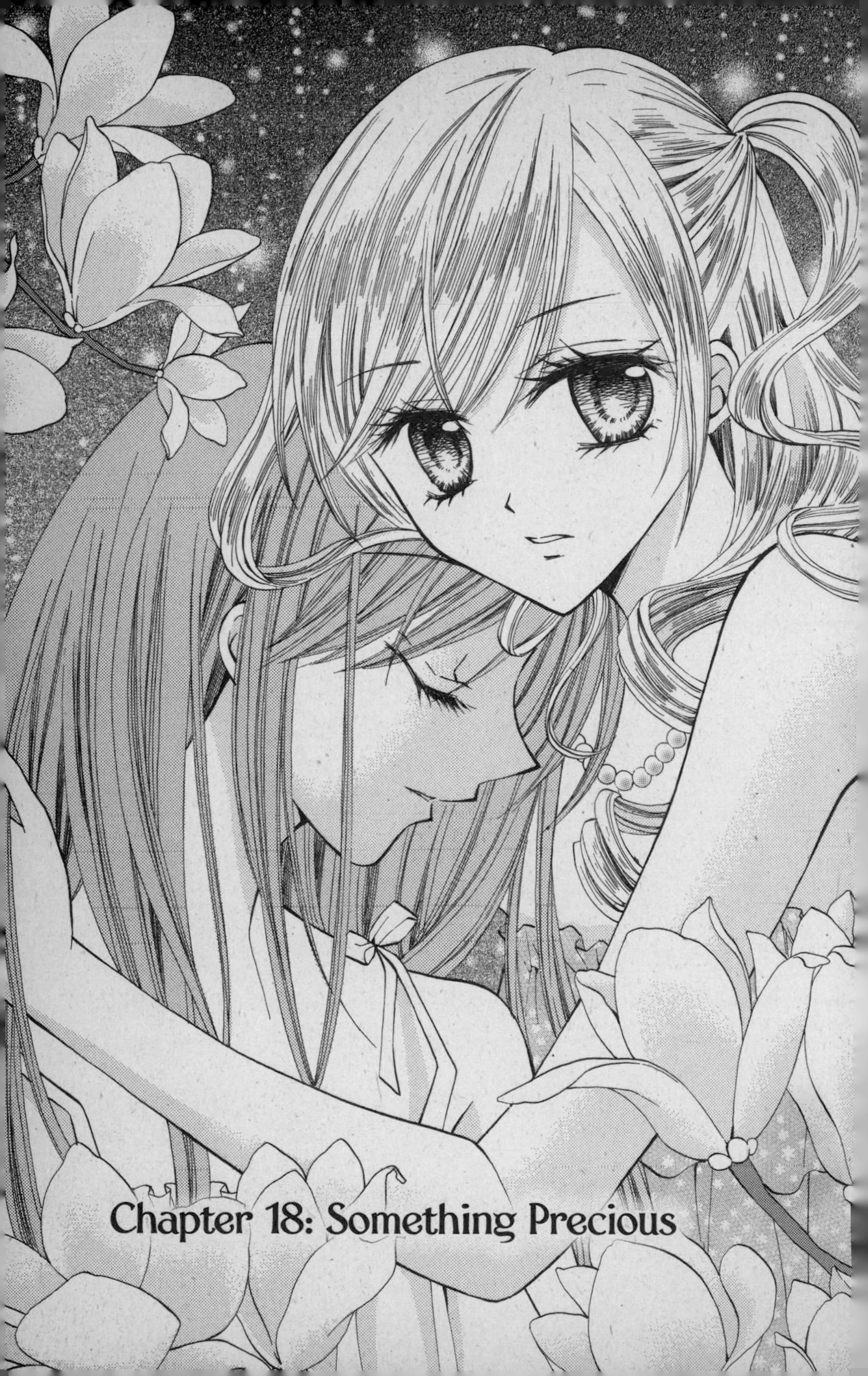
Chapter 18: Something Precious

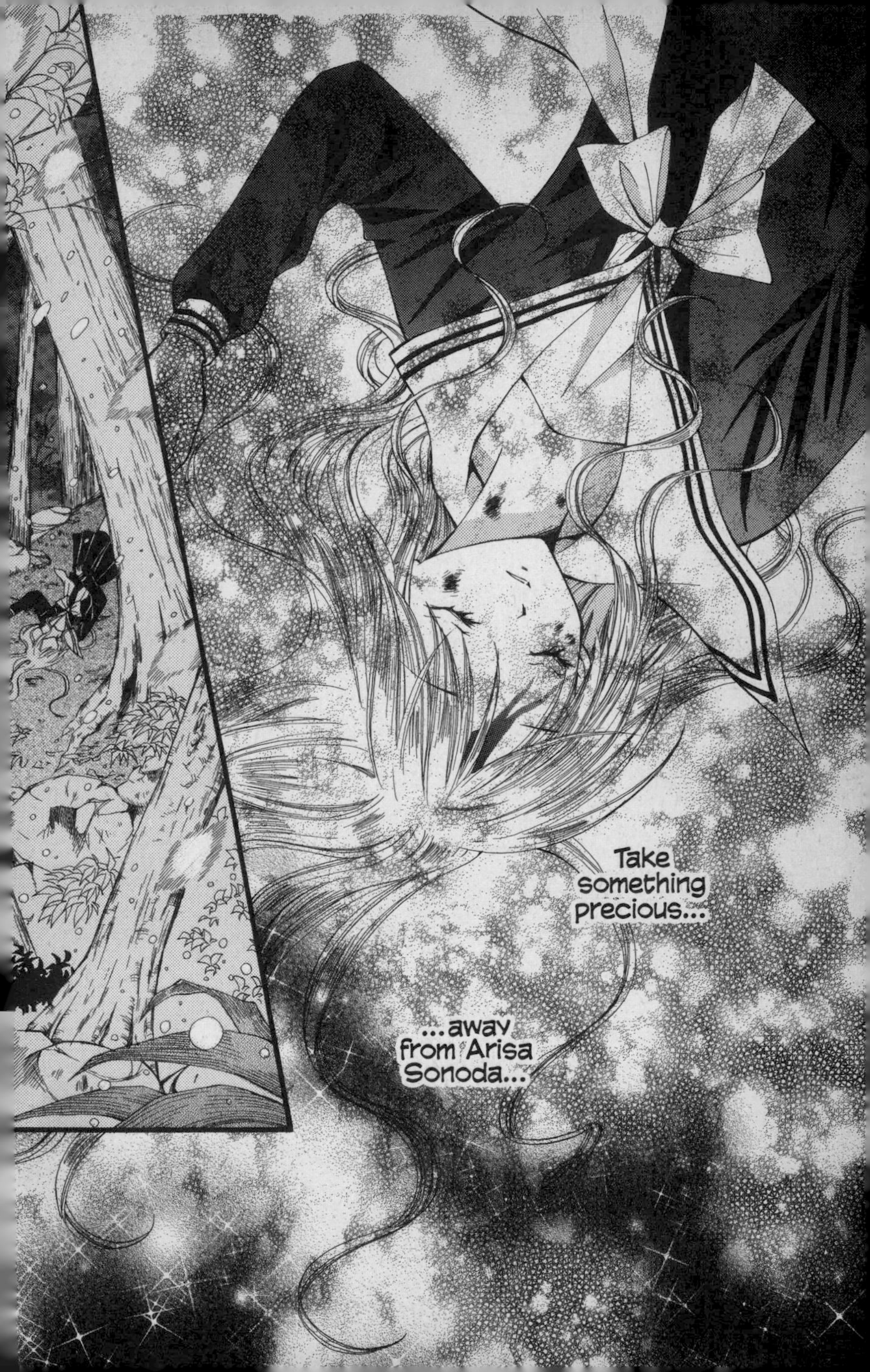
Take something precious...
...away from Arisa Sonoda...

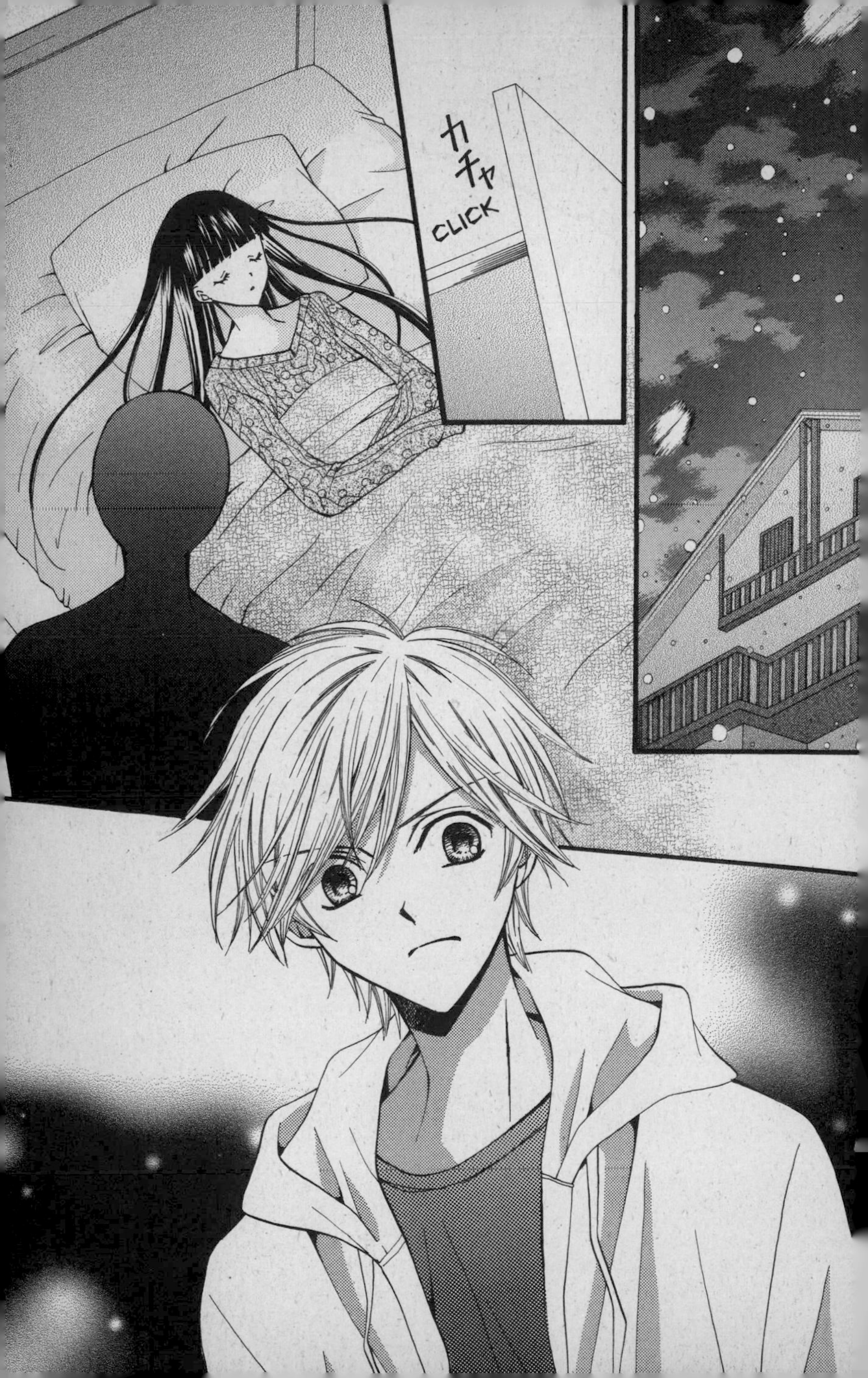
カチャ
CLICK

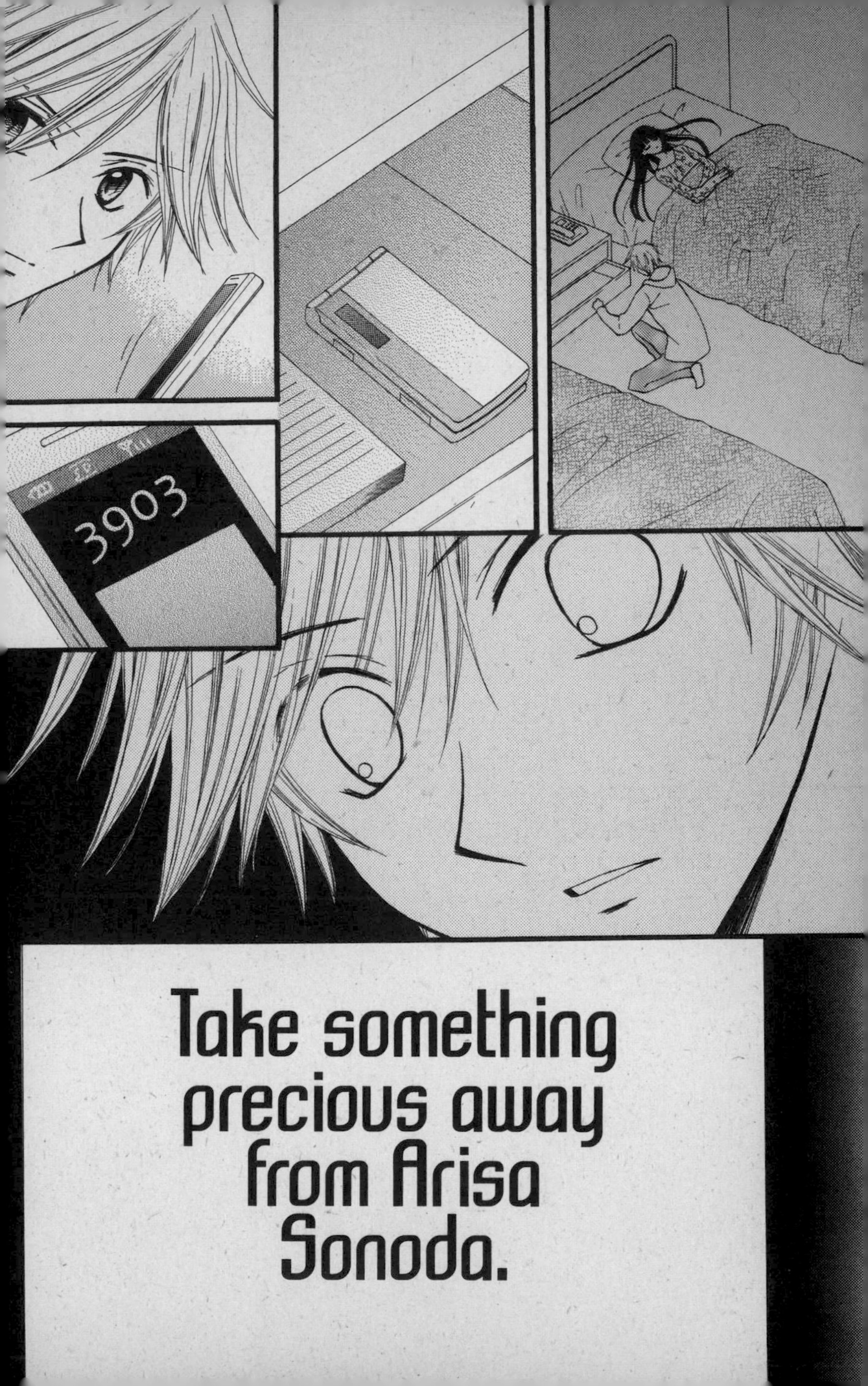
3903
Take something precious away from Arisa Sonoda.

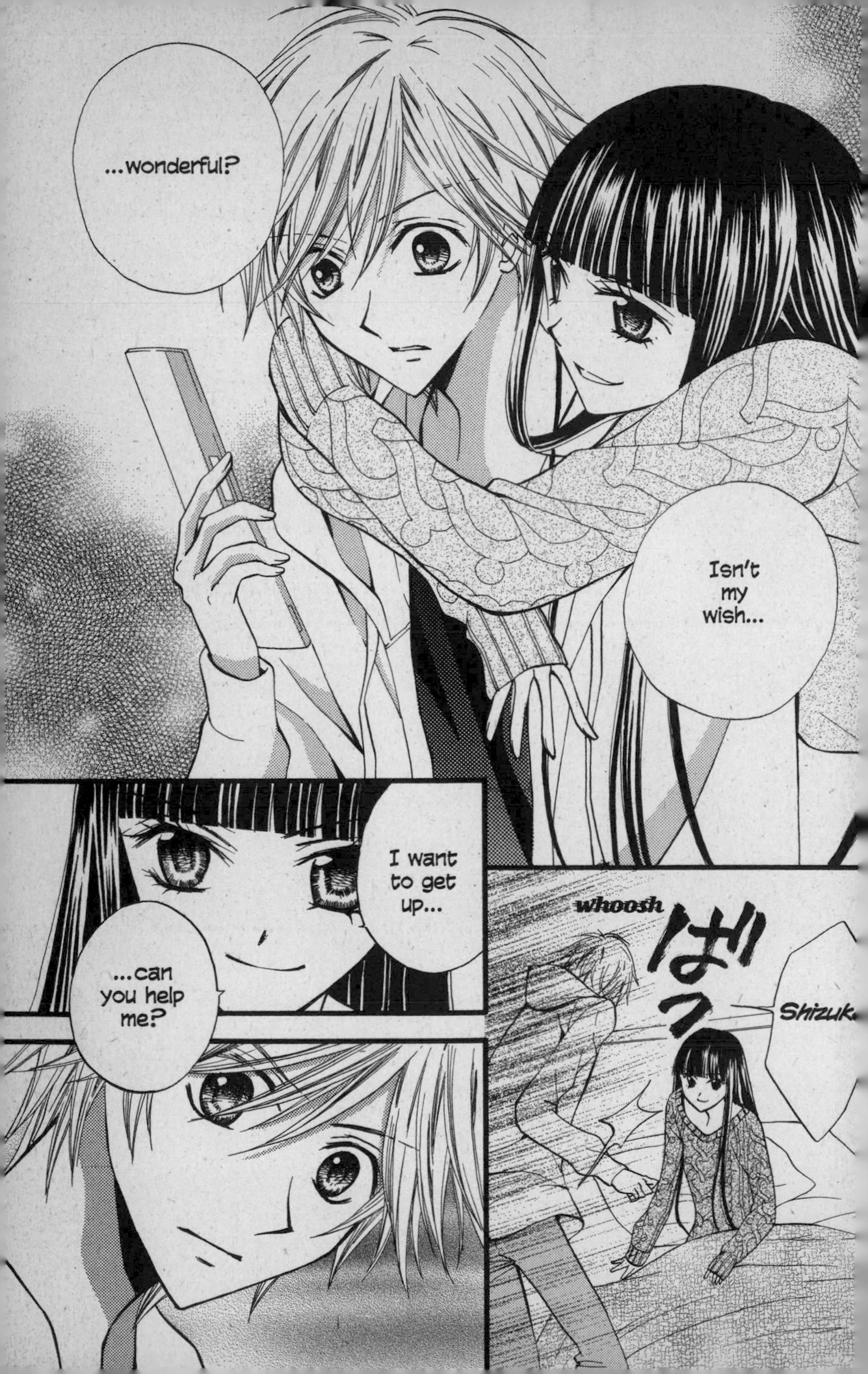
Isn't my wish...
...wonderful?
I want to get up...
...can you help me?
whoosh
ぱっ
Shizuk.

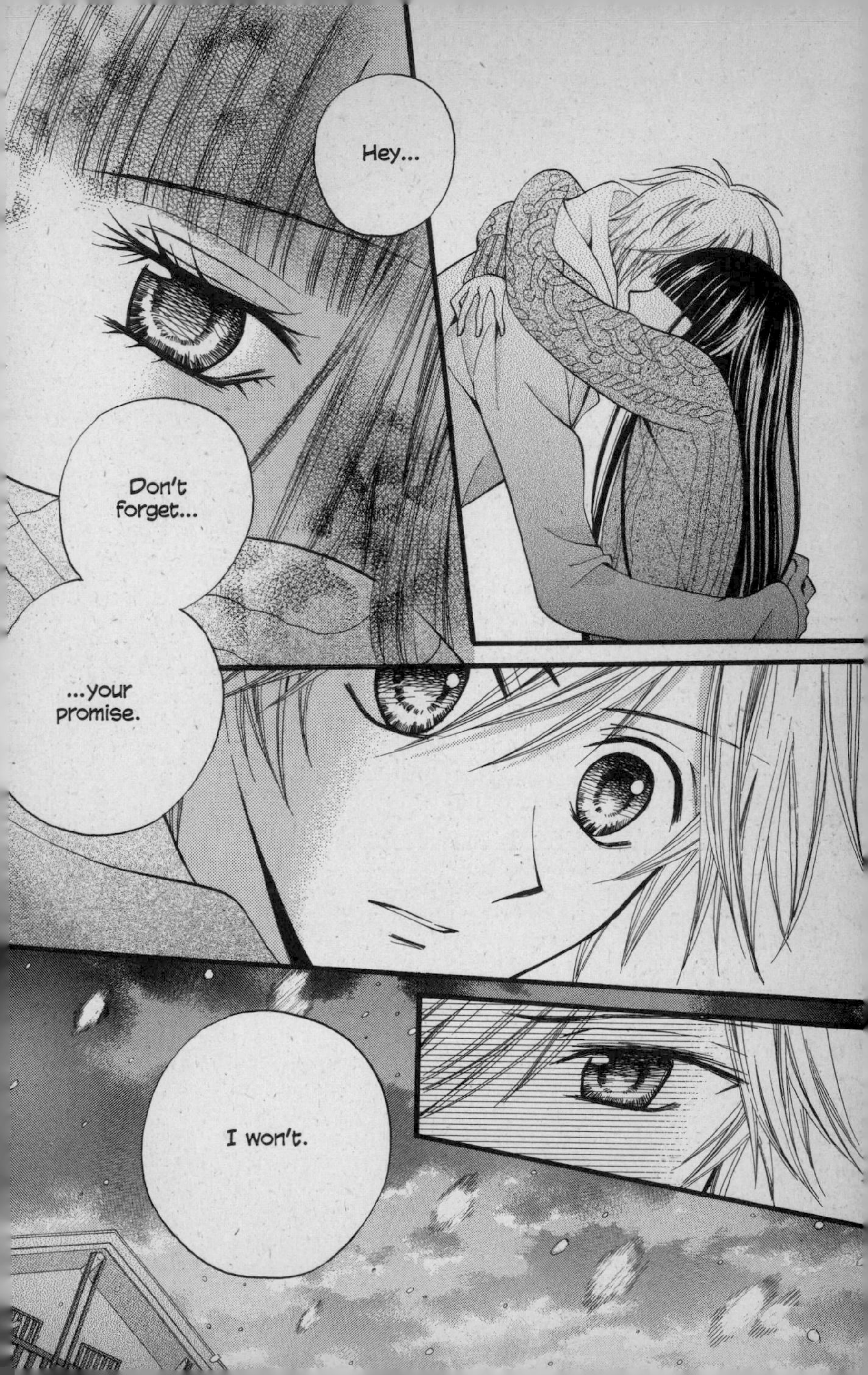
Hey...
Don't forget...
...your promise.
I won't.

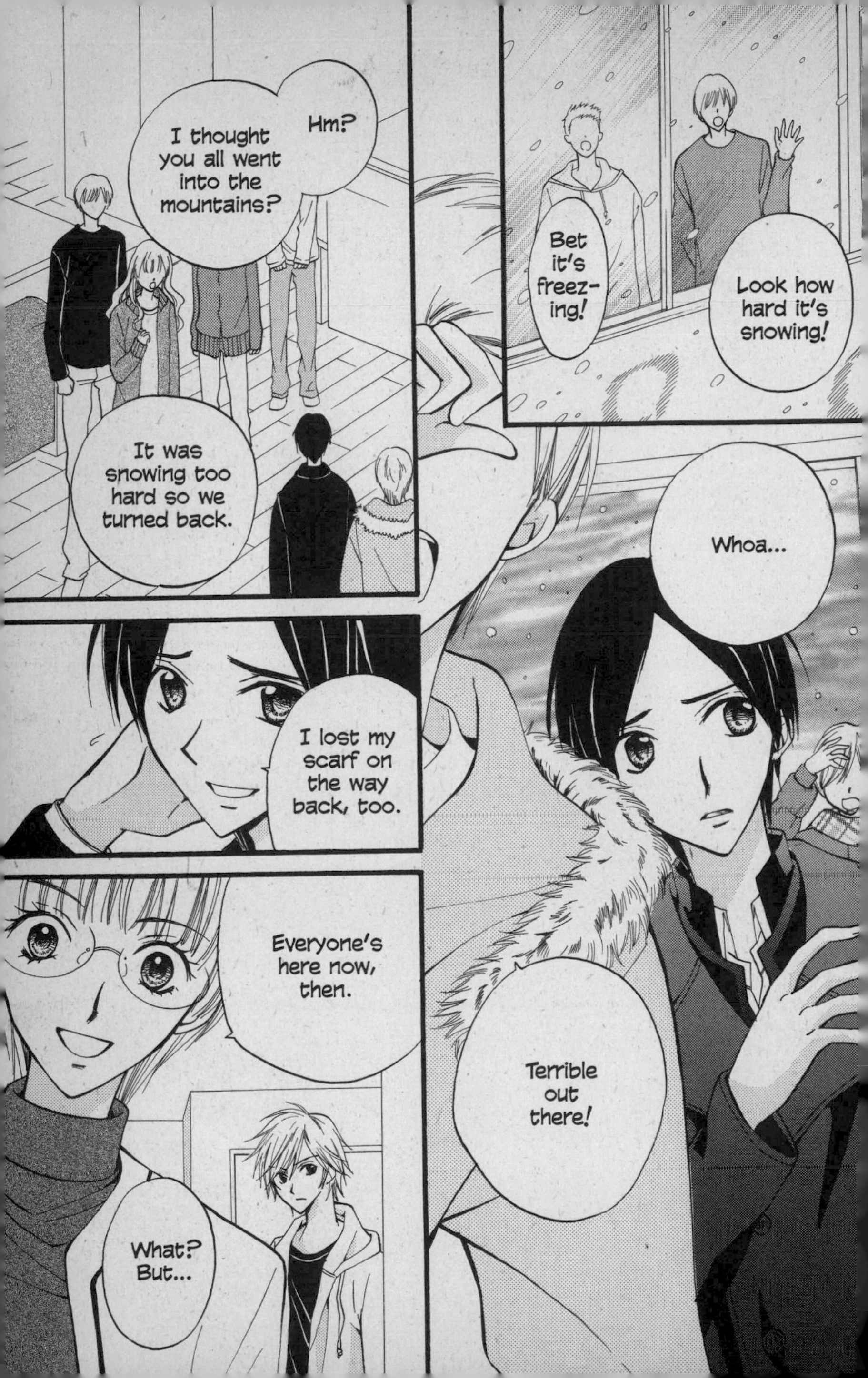

Look how hard it's snowing!
Bet it's freezing!
Hm?
I thought you all went into the mountains?
It was snowing too hard so we turned back.
Whoa...
Terrible out there!
I lost my scarf on the way back, too.
Everyone's here now, then.
What? But...

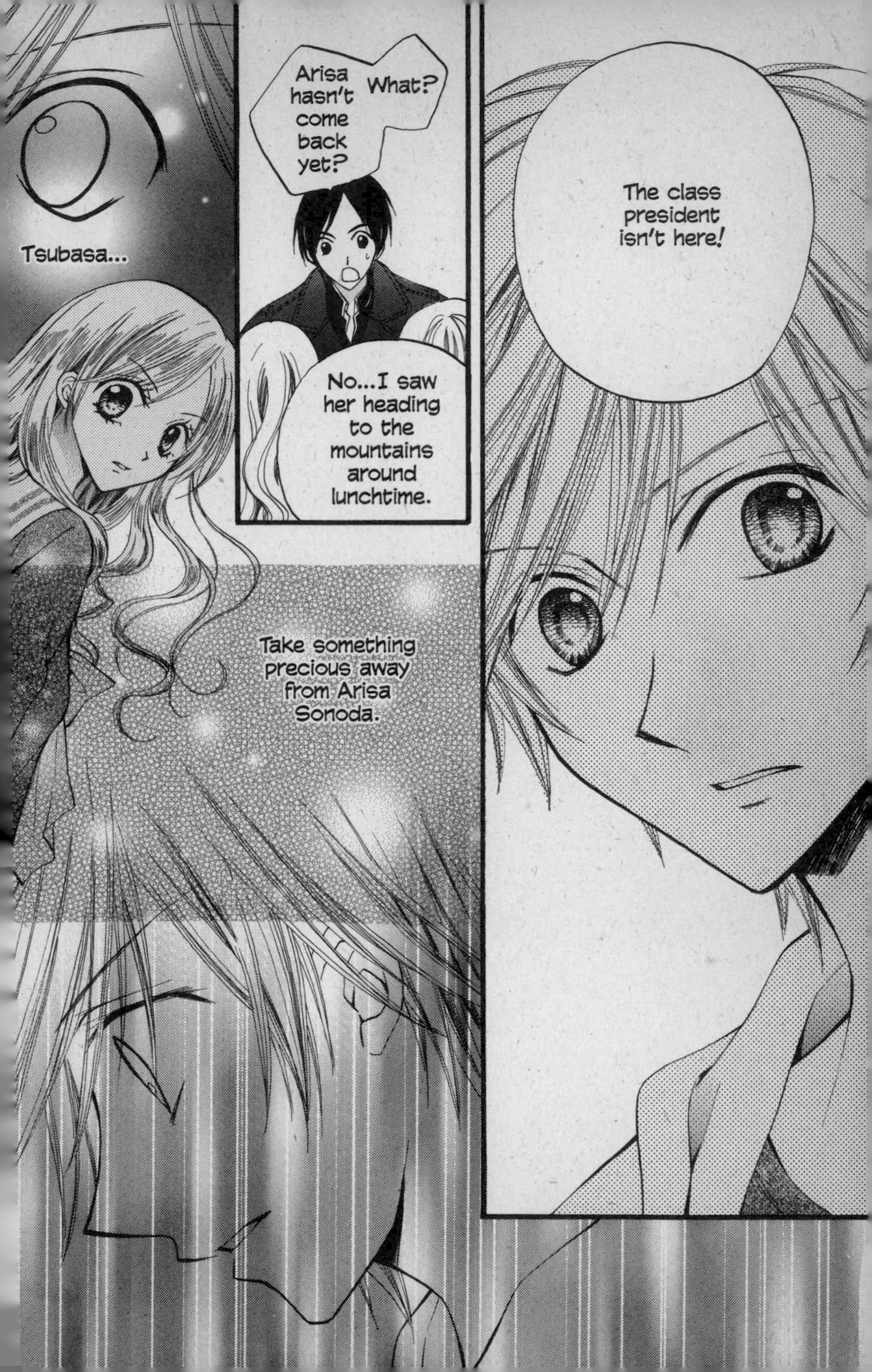
The class president isn't here!
What?
Arisa hasn't come back yet?
No...I saw her heading to the mountains around lunchtime.
Tsubasa...
Take something precious away from Arisa Sonoda.

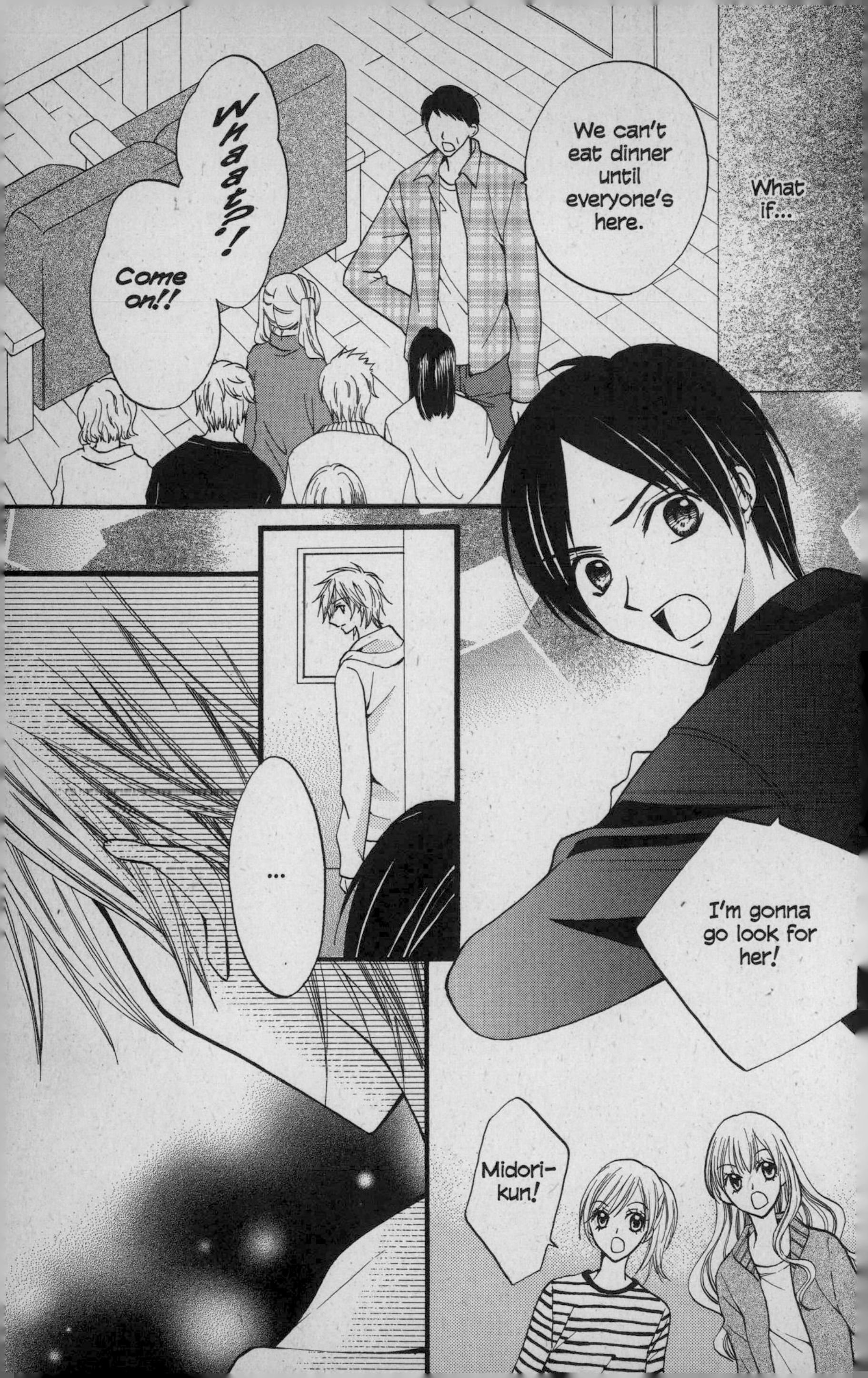
What if...
We can't eat dinner until everyone's here.
Whaaat?!!
Come on!!
I'm gonna go look for her!
...
Midori-kun!

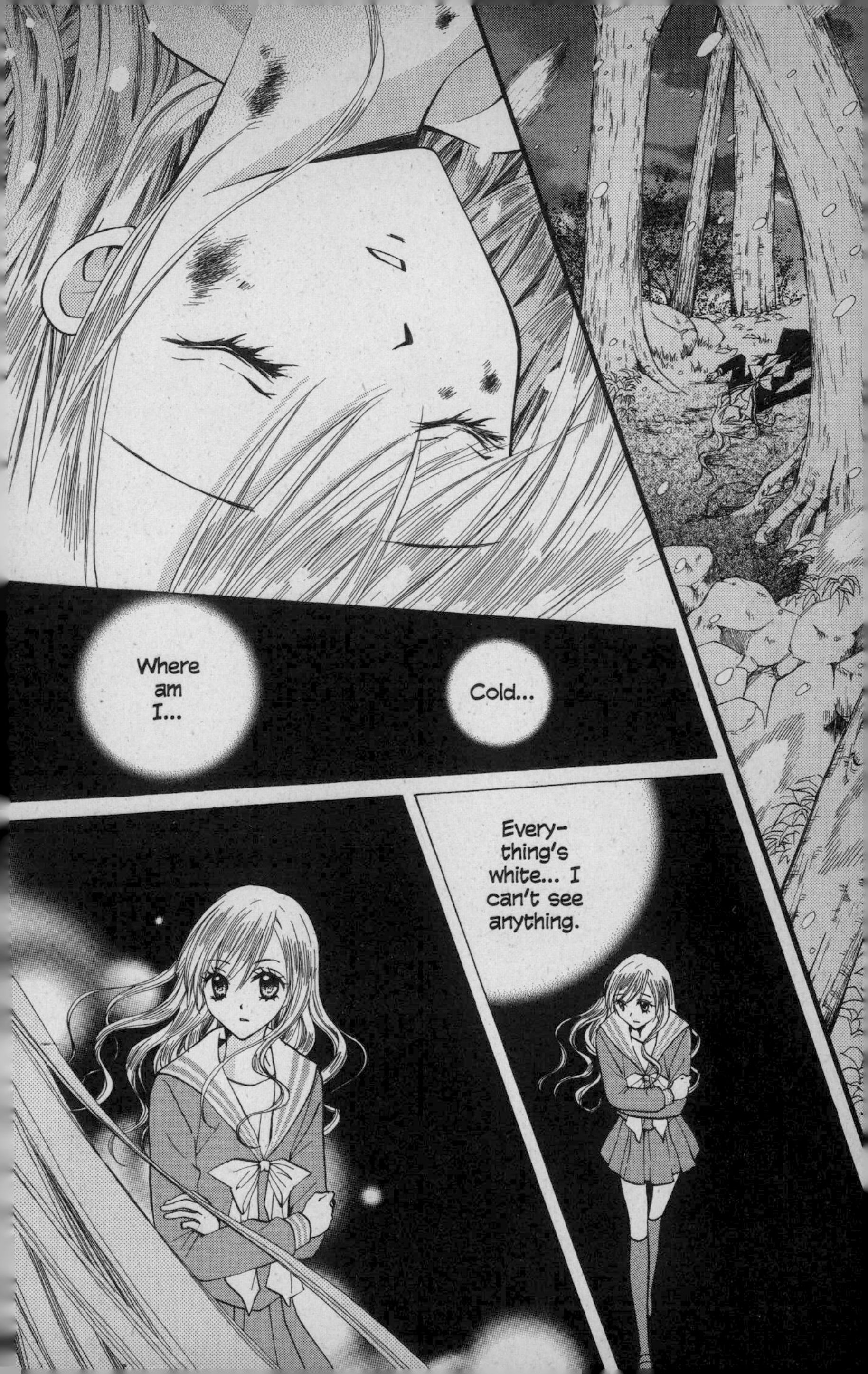
Cold...
Where am I...
Every-thing's white... I can't see anything.

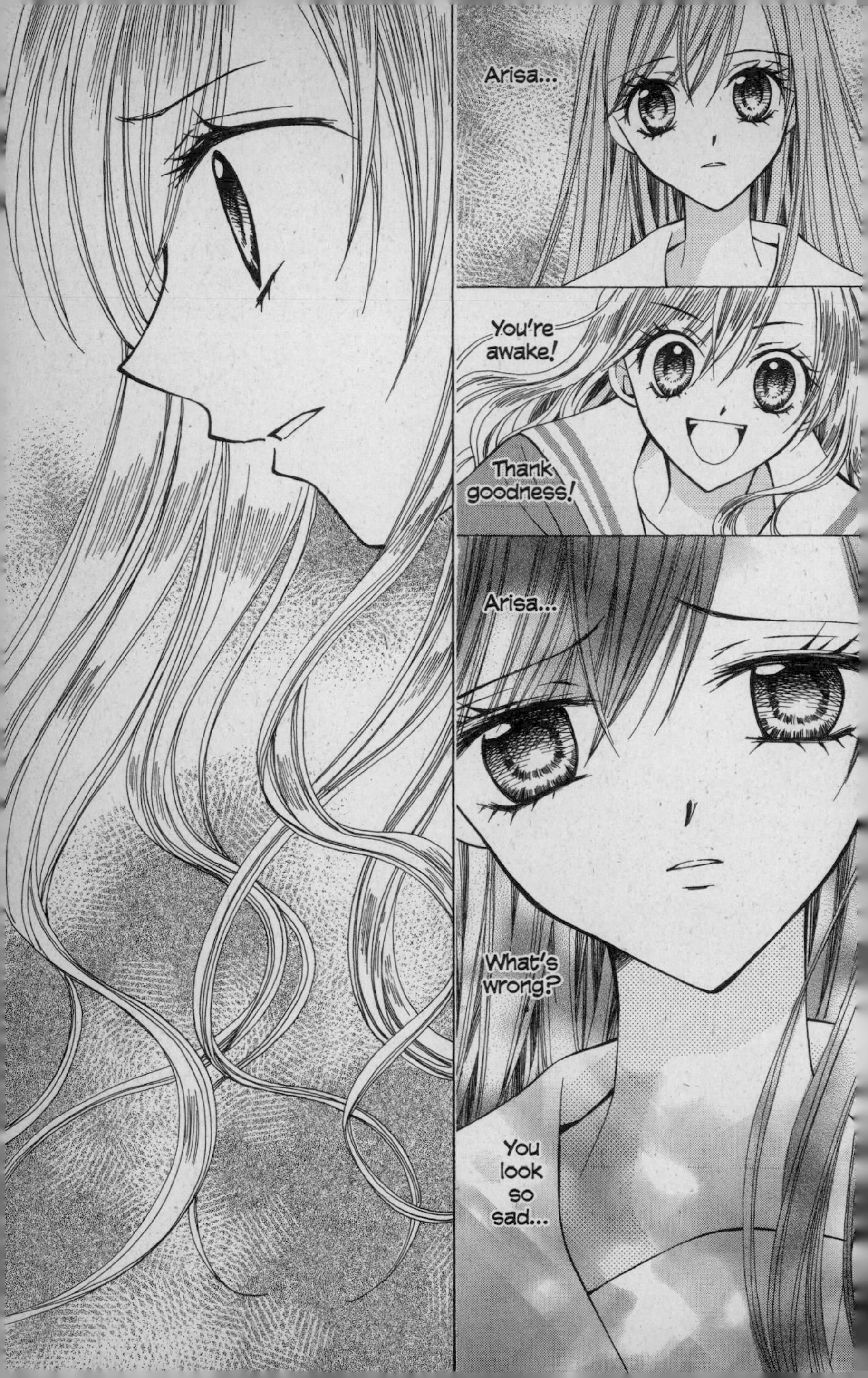
Arisa...
You're awake!
Thank goodness!
Arisa...
What's wrong?
You look so sad...

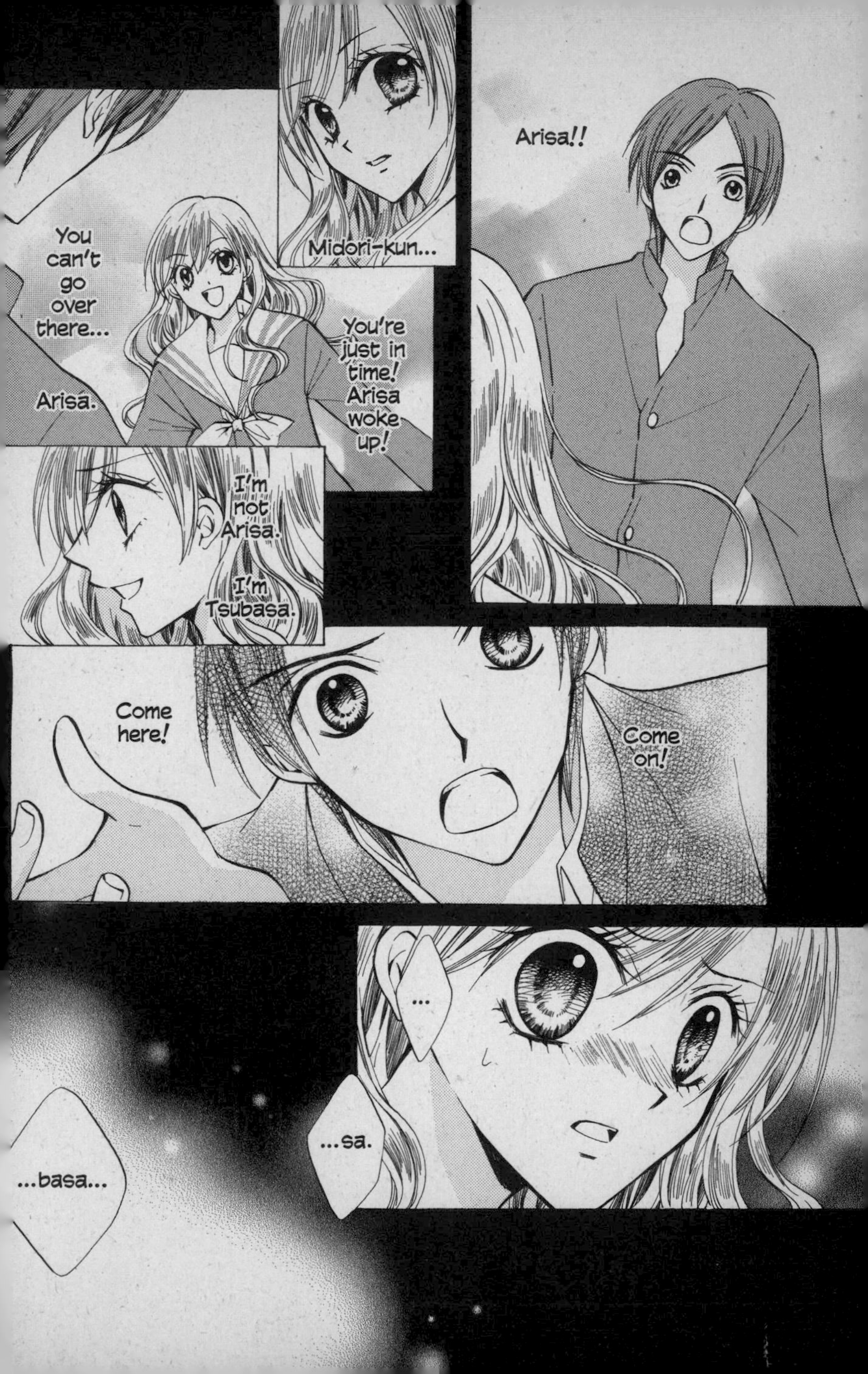
Arisa!!
Midori-kun...
You're just in time! Arisa woke up!
You can't go over there...
Arisa.
I'm not Arisa.
I'm Tsubasa.
Come on!
Come here!
...
...sa.
...basa...

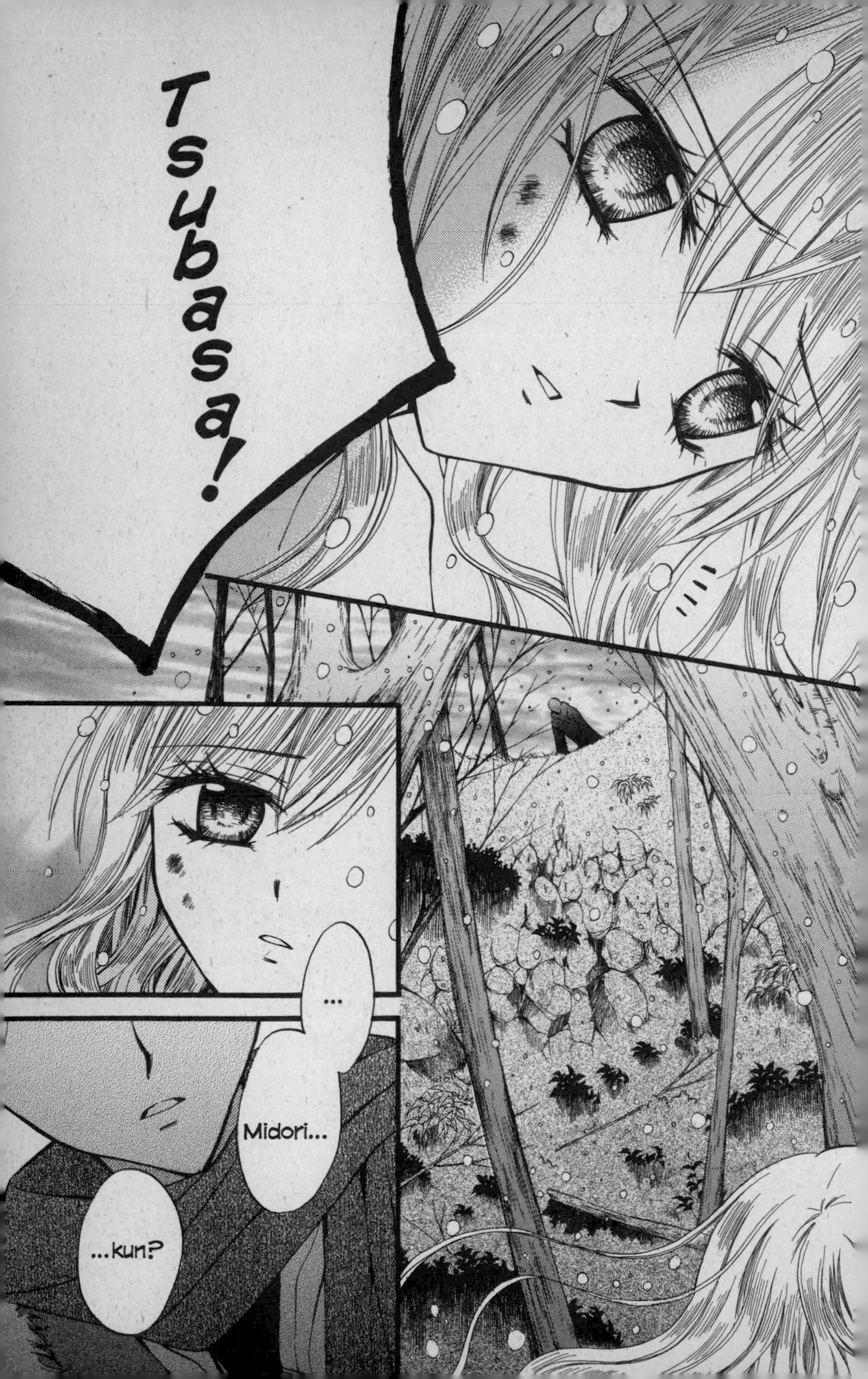
Tsubasa!
...
Midori...
...kun?

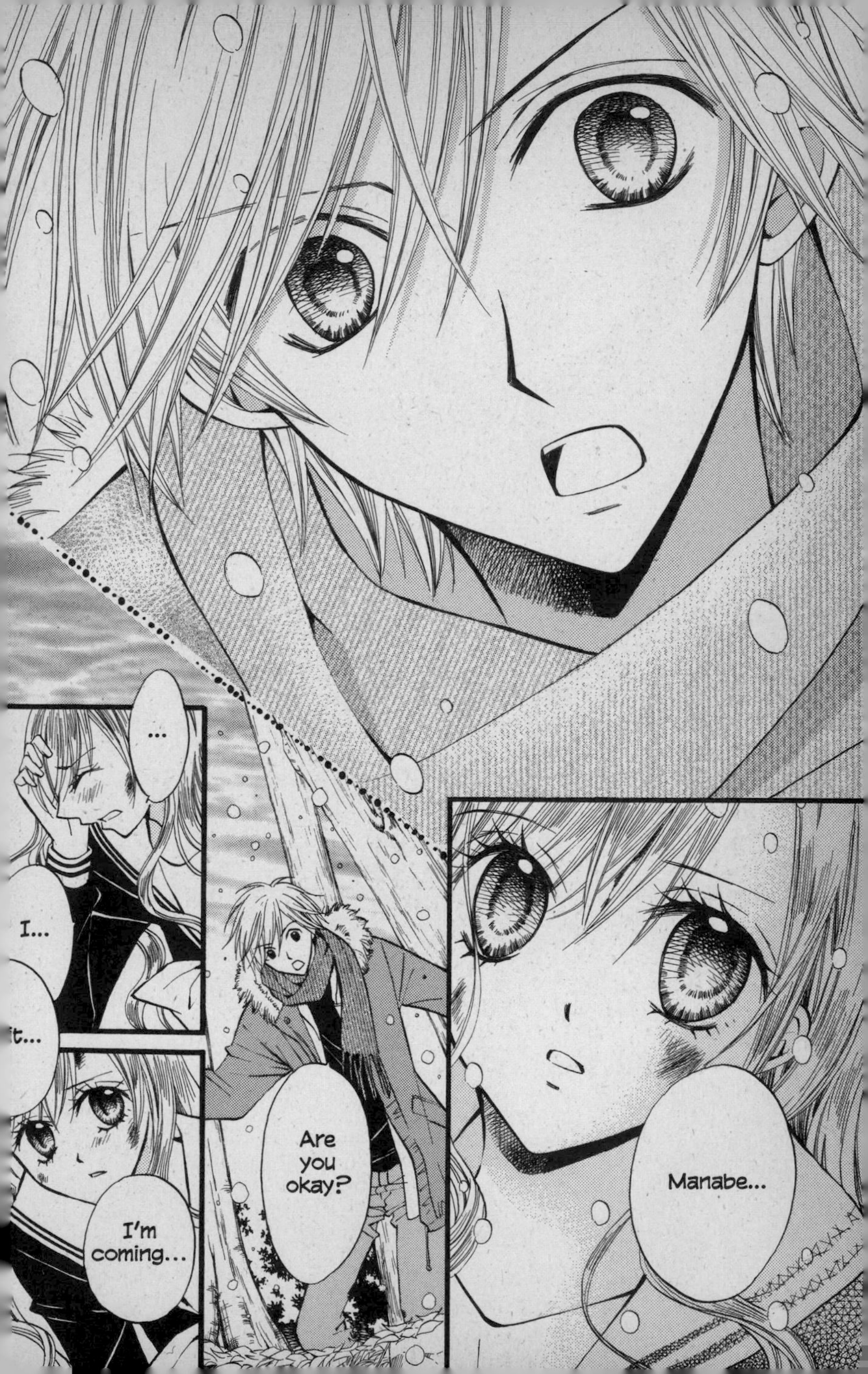
Manabe...
Are you okay?
...
I...
it...
I'm coming...

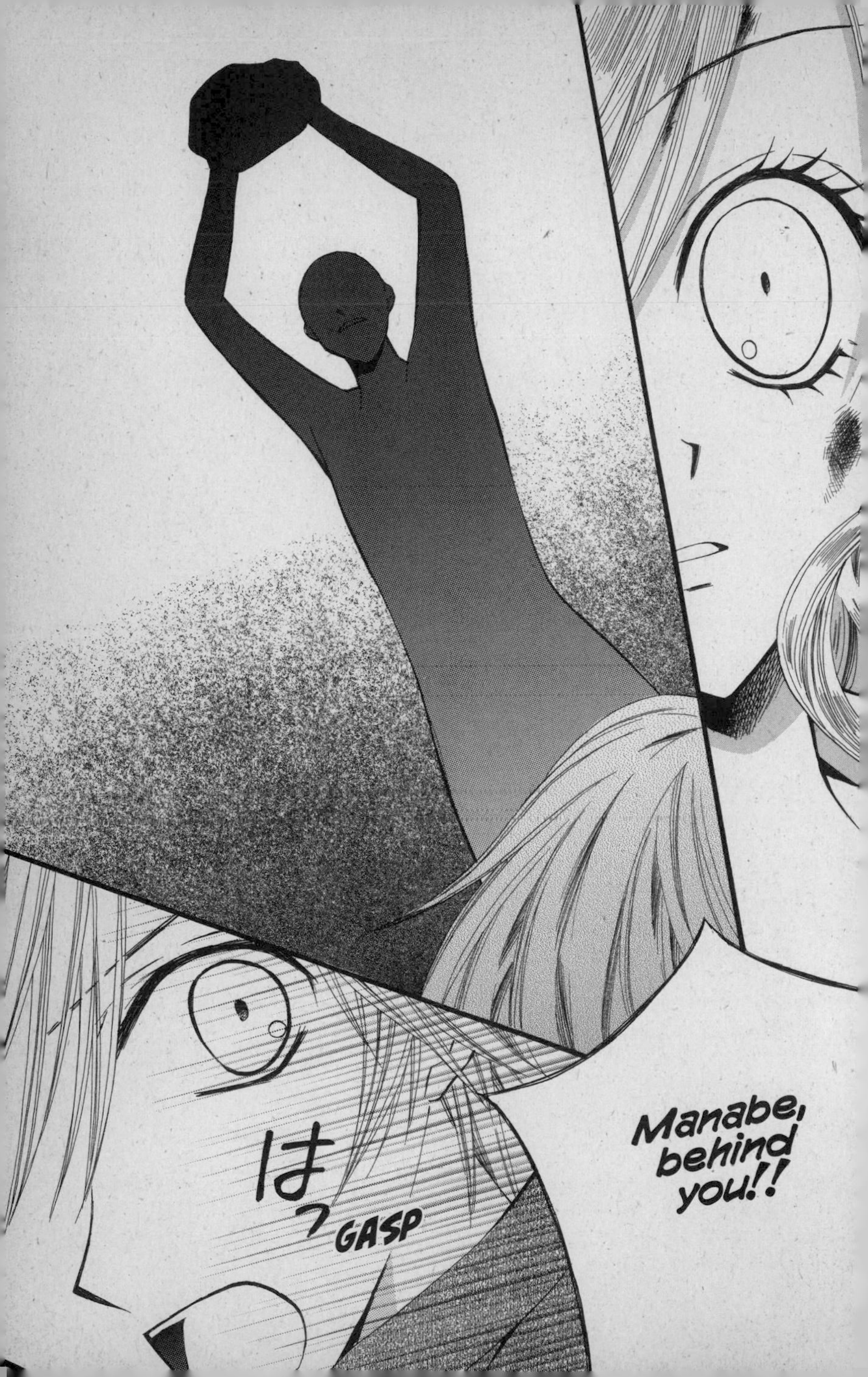
Manabe, behind you!!
はっ
GASP

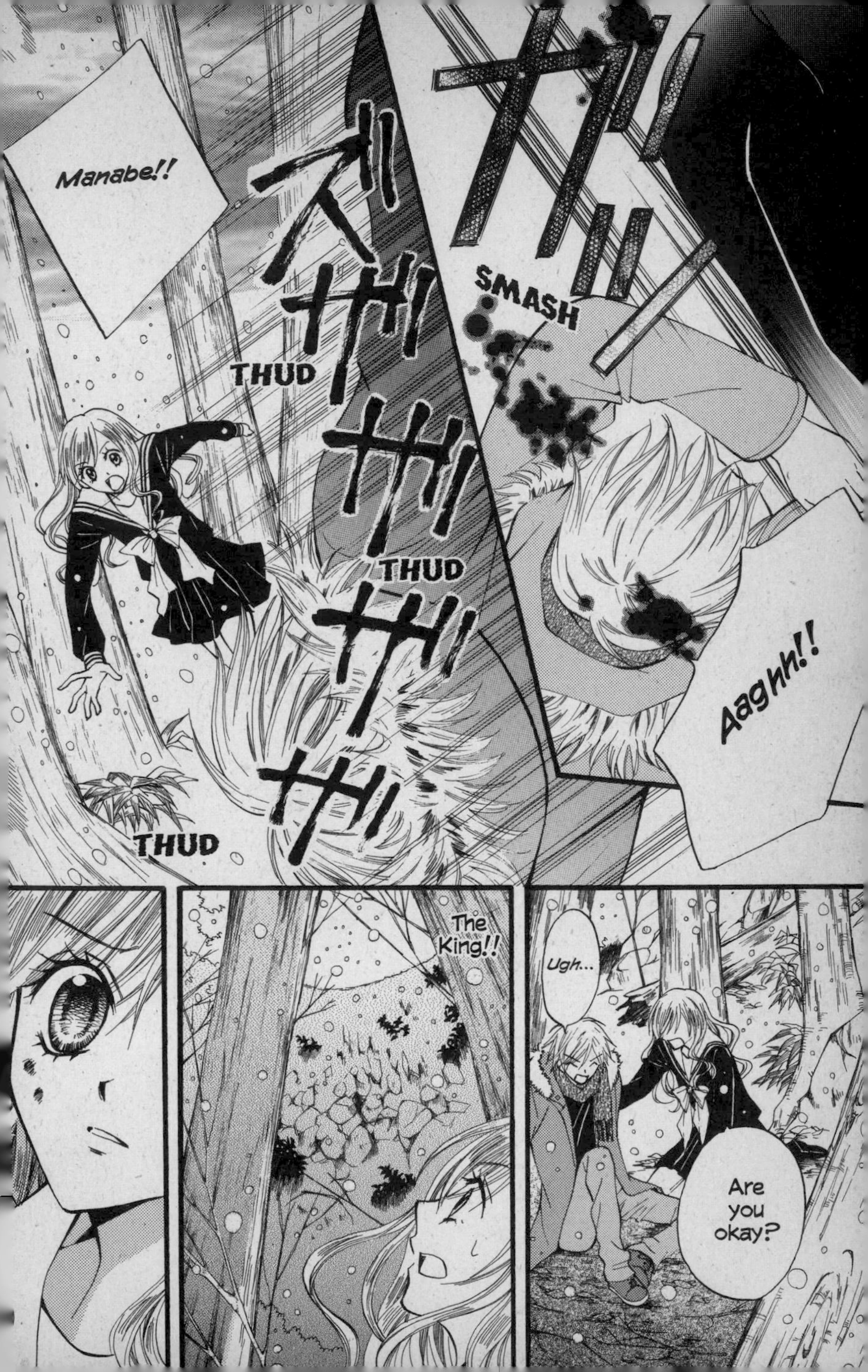
SMASH
Aaghh!!
THUD
THUD
Manabe!!
THUD
Ugh...
Are you okay?
The King!!

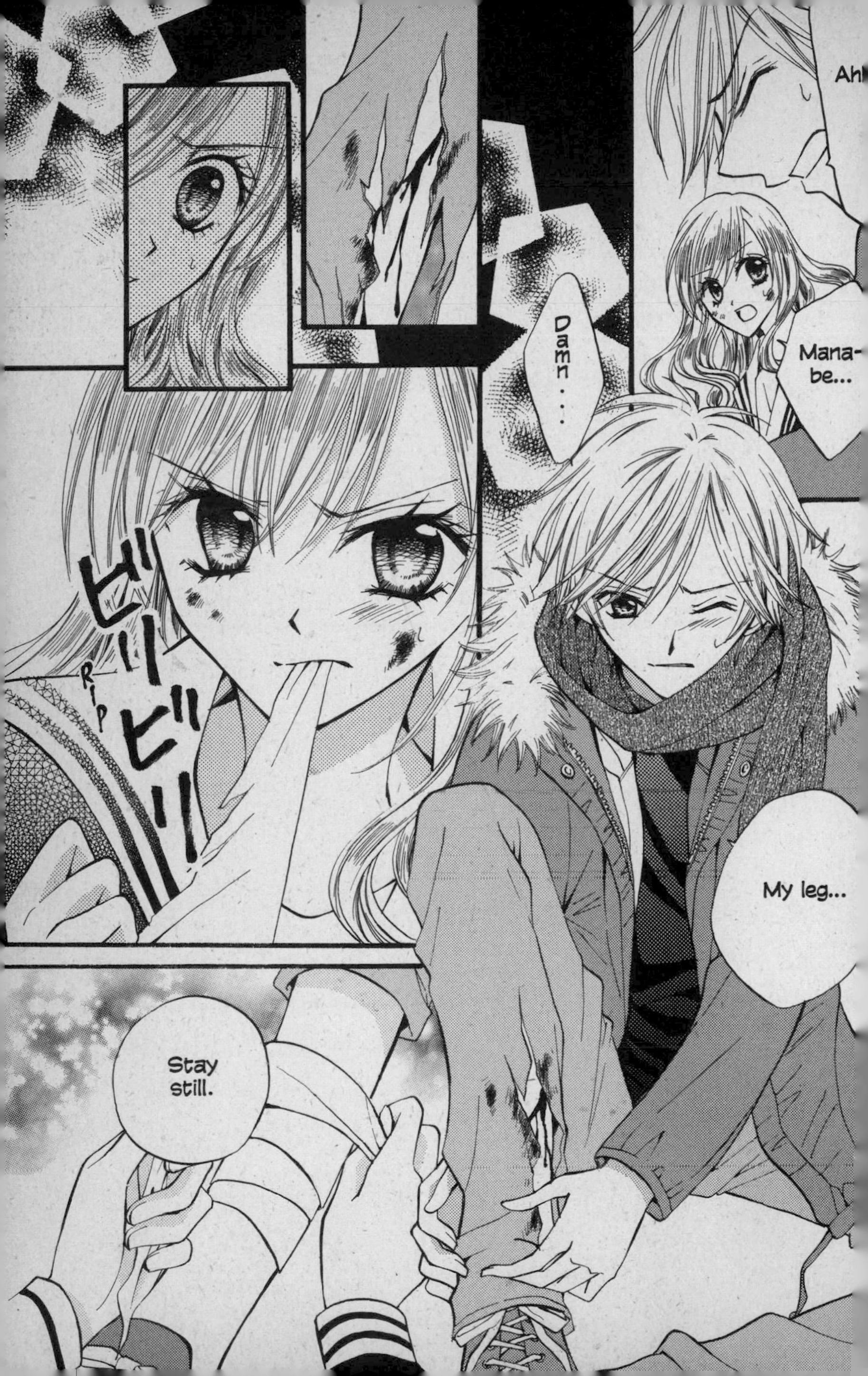
Ah
Mana-be...
Damn...
My leg...
ビリビリ
RIP
Stay still.

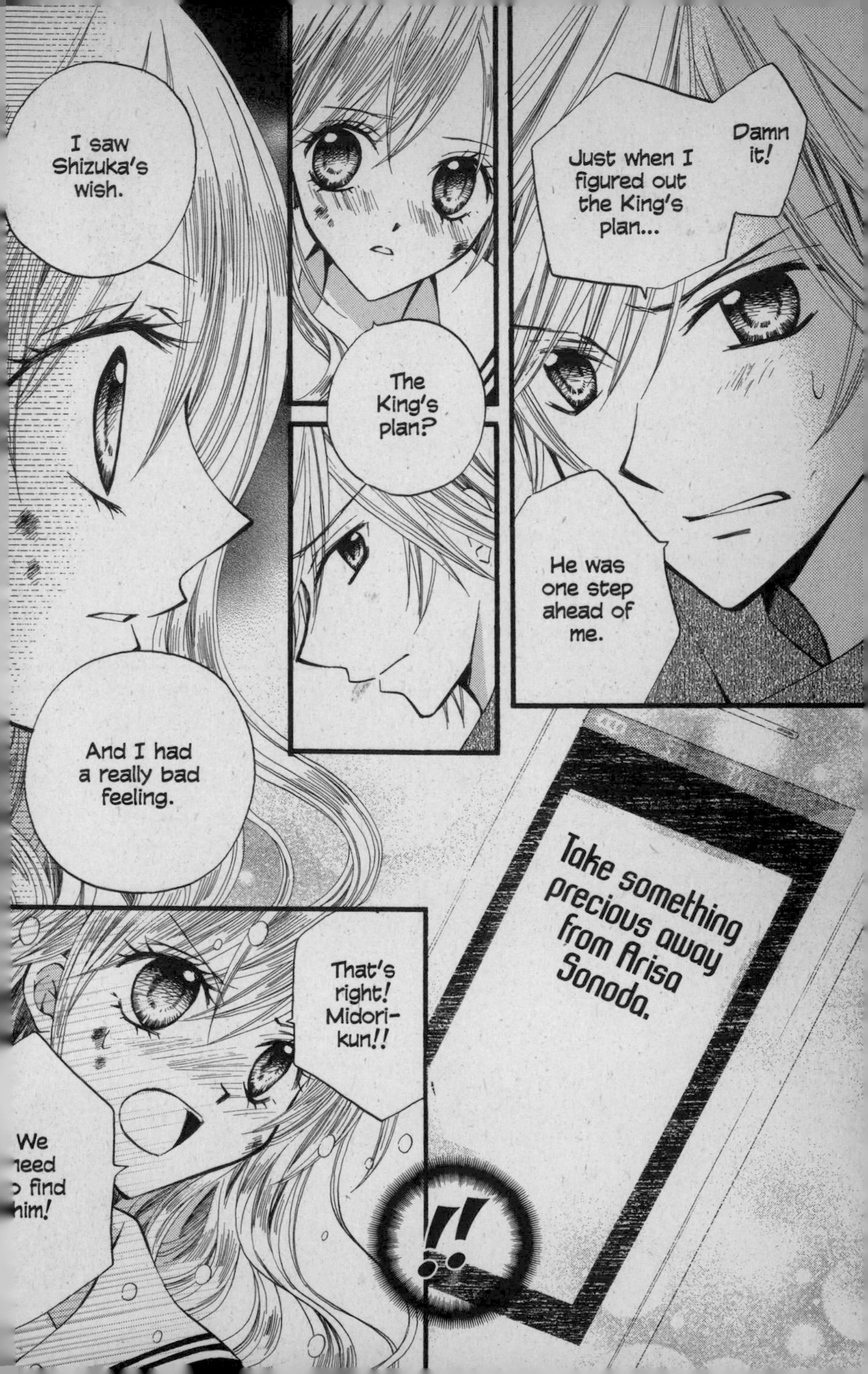

Damn it!
Just when I figured out the King's plan...
He was one step ahead of me.
The King's plan?
I saw Shizuka's wish.
And I had a really bad feeling.
Take something precious away from Arisa Sonoda.
!!
That's right! Midori-kun!!
We need to find him!

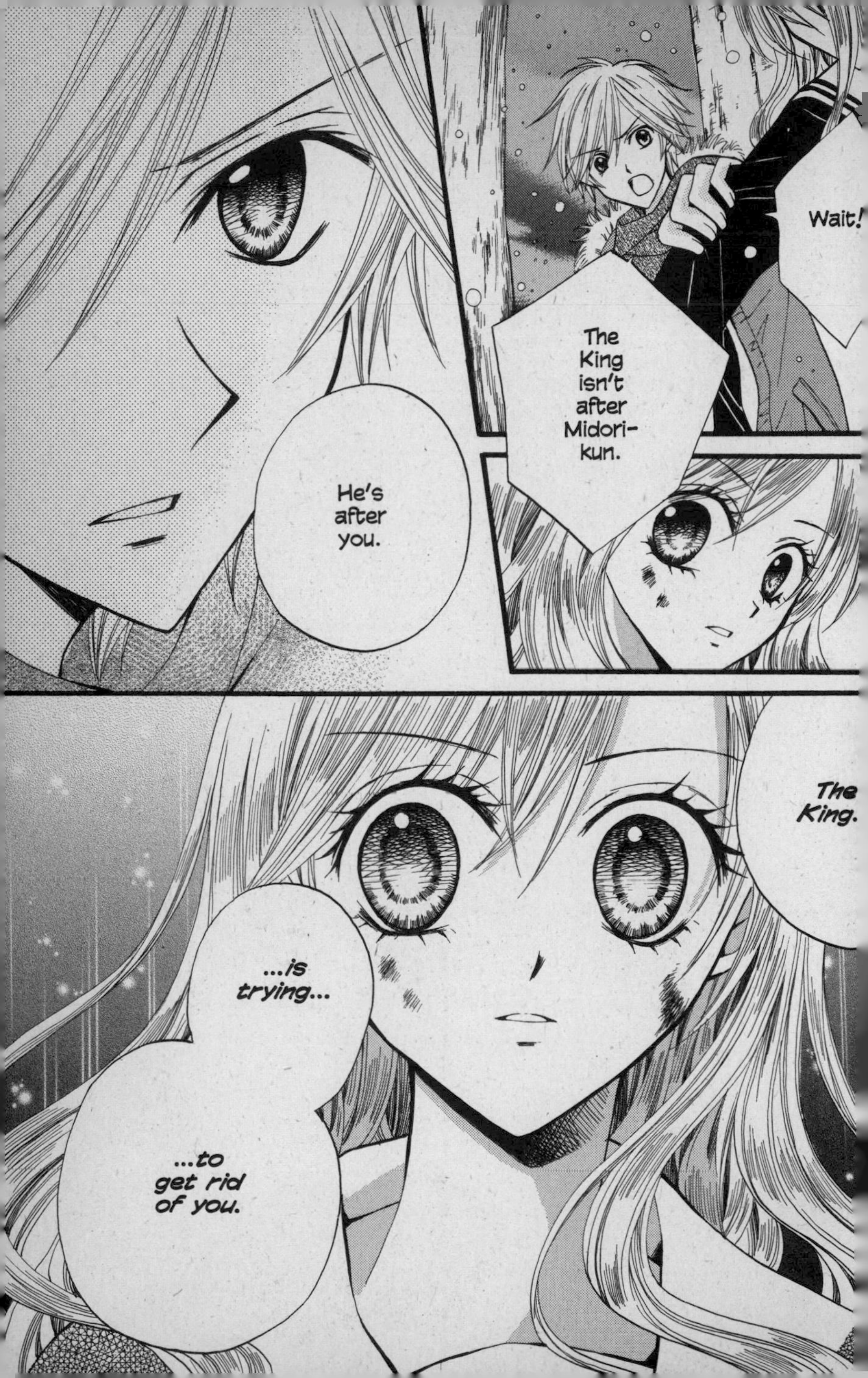
Wait!
The King isn't after Midori-kun.
He's after you.
The King.
...is trying...
...to get rid of you.

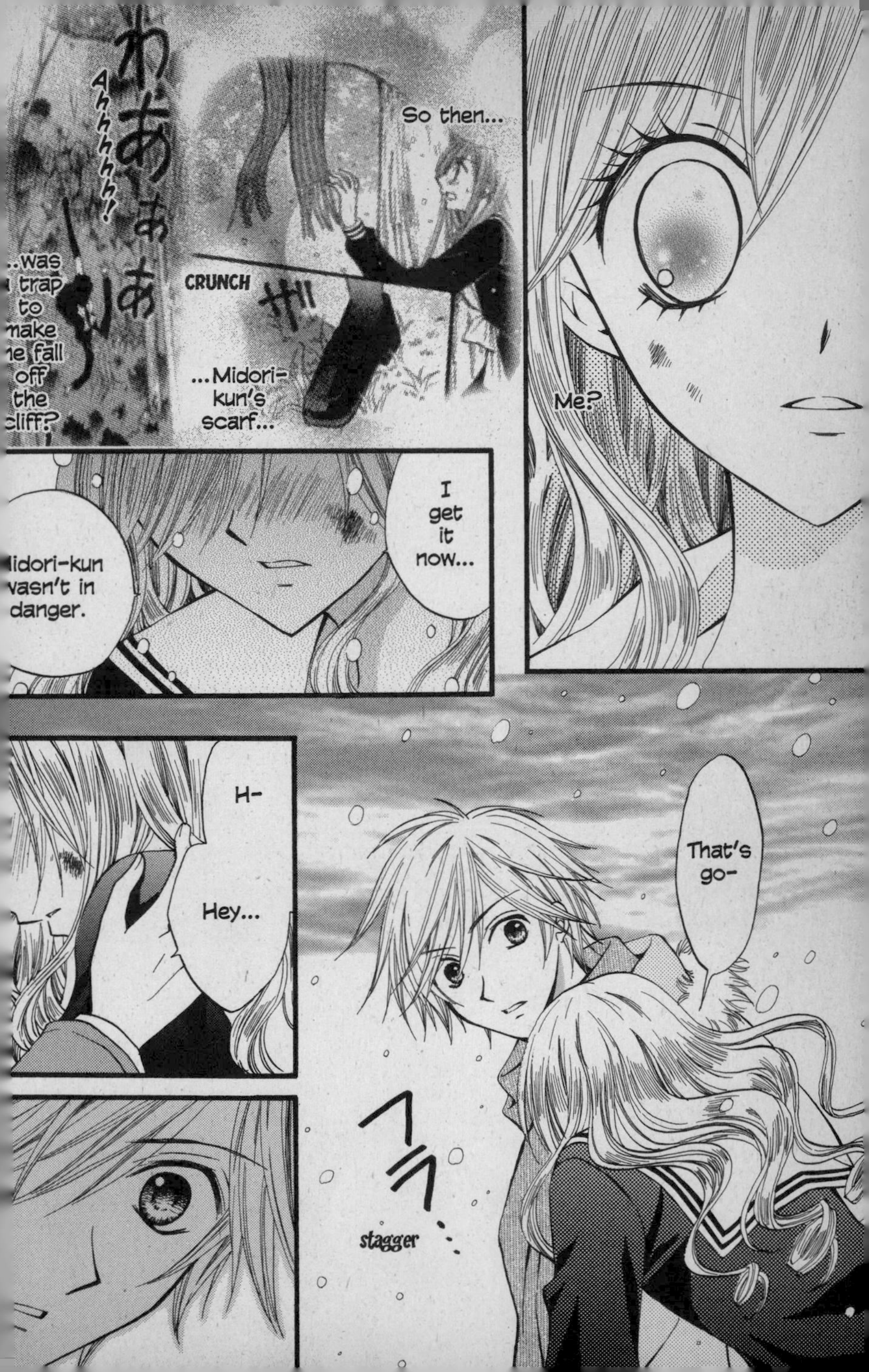
Me?
So then...
わあああ
Ahhhhh!
CRUNCH
ザ!!
...Midori-kun's scarf...
..was trap to make e fall off the cliff?
I get it now...
idori-kun vasn't in danger.
That's go-
stagger
H-
Hey...

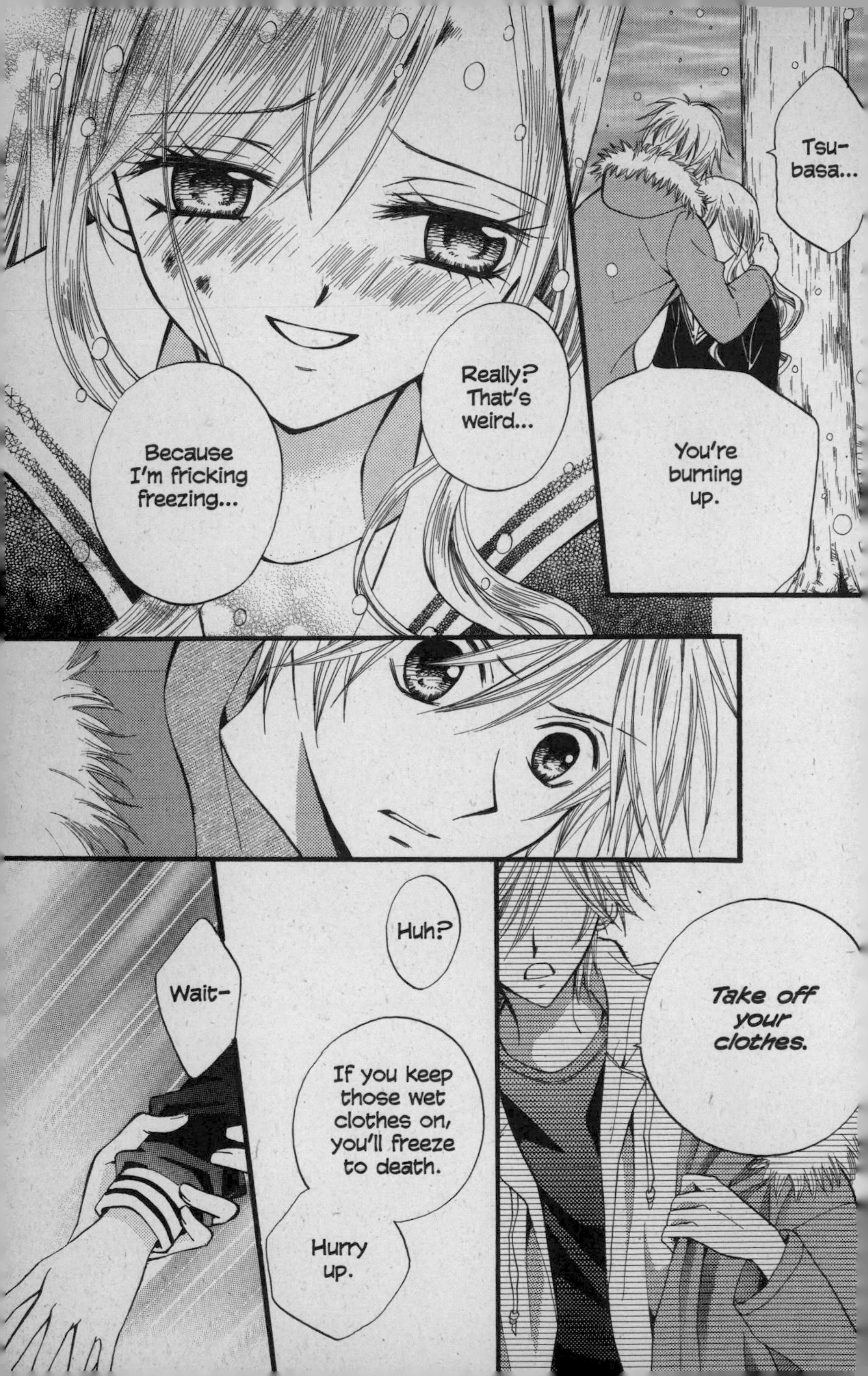
Tsu-basa...
You're burning up.
Really? That's weird...
Because I'm fricking freezing...
Take off your clothes.
Huh?
If you keep those wet clothes on, you'll freeze to death.
Hurry up.
Wait-

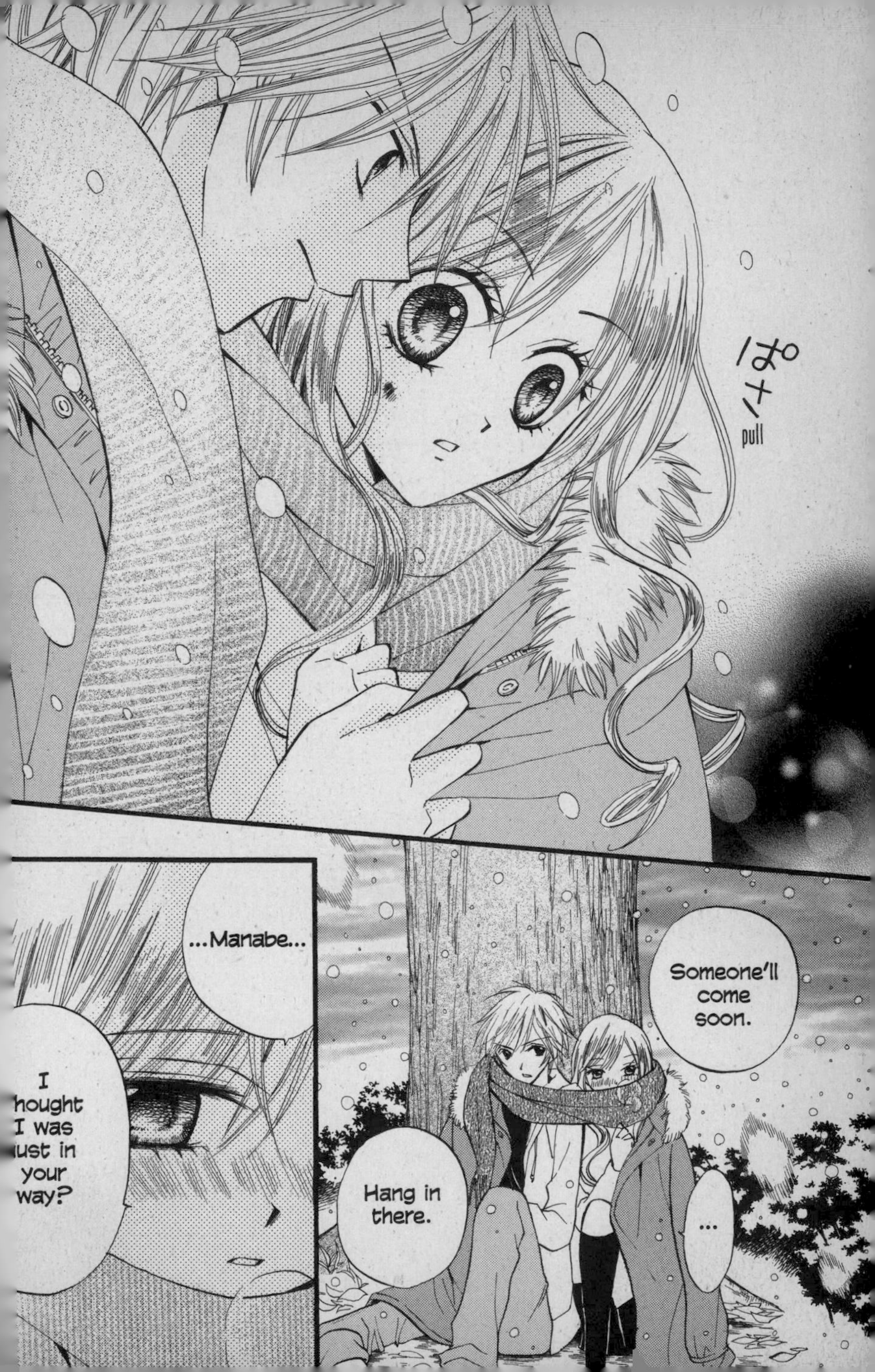
ぱさ
pull
Someone'll come soon.
Hang in there.
...
...Manabe...
I hought I was ust in your way?

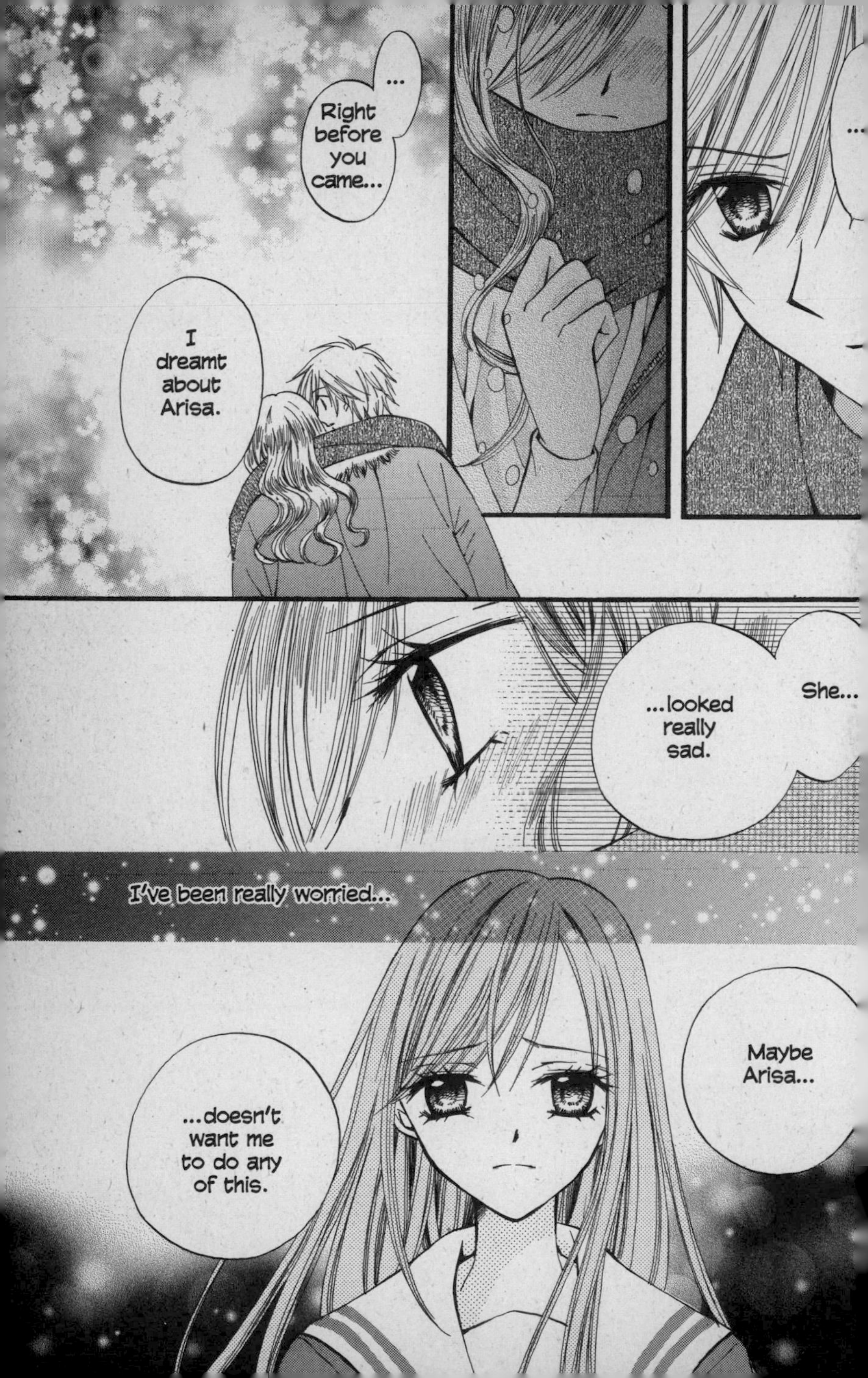
...
... Right before you came...
I dreamt about Arisa.
She...
...looked really sad.
I've been really worried...
Maybe Arisa...
...doesn't want me to do any of this.

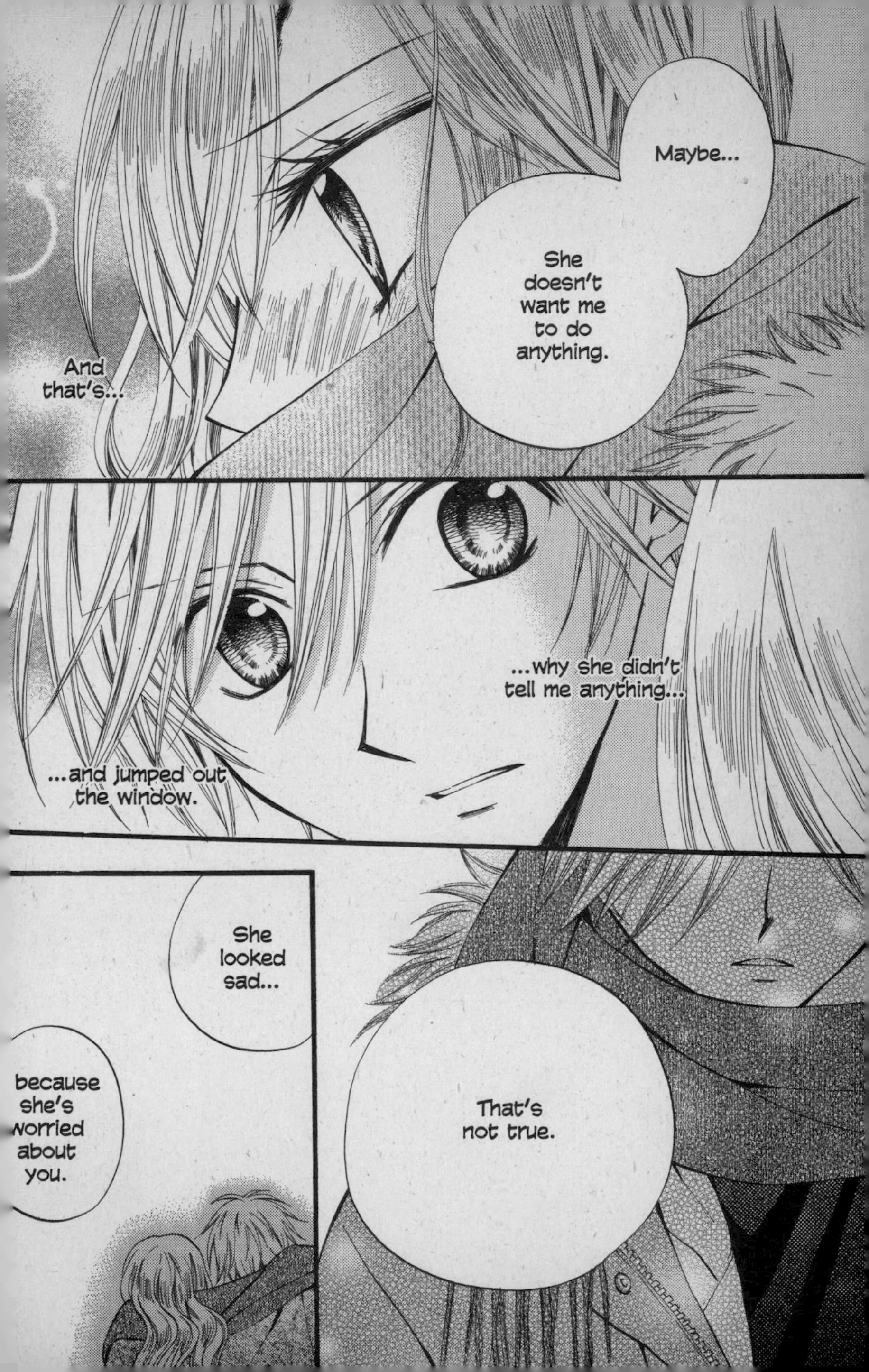
Maybe...
She doesn't want me to do anything.
And that's...
...why she didn't tell me anything...
...and jumped out the window.
That's not true.
She looked sad...
because she's worried about you.

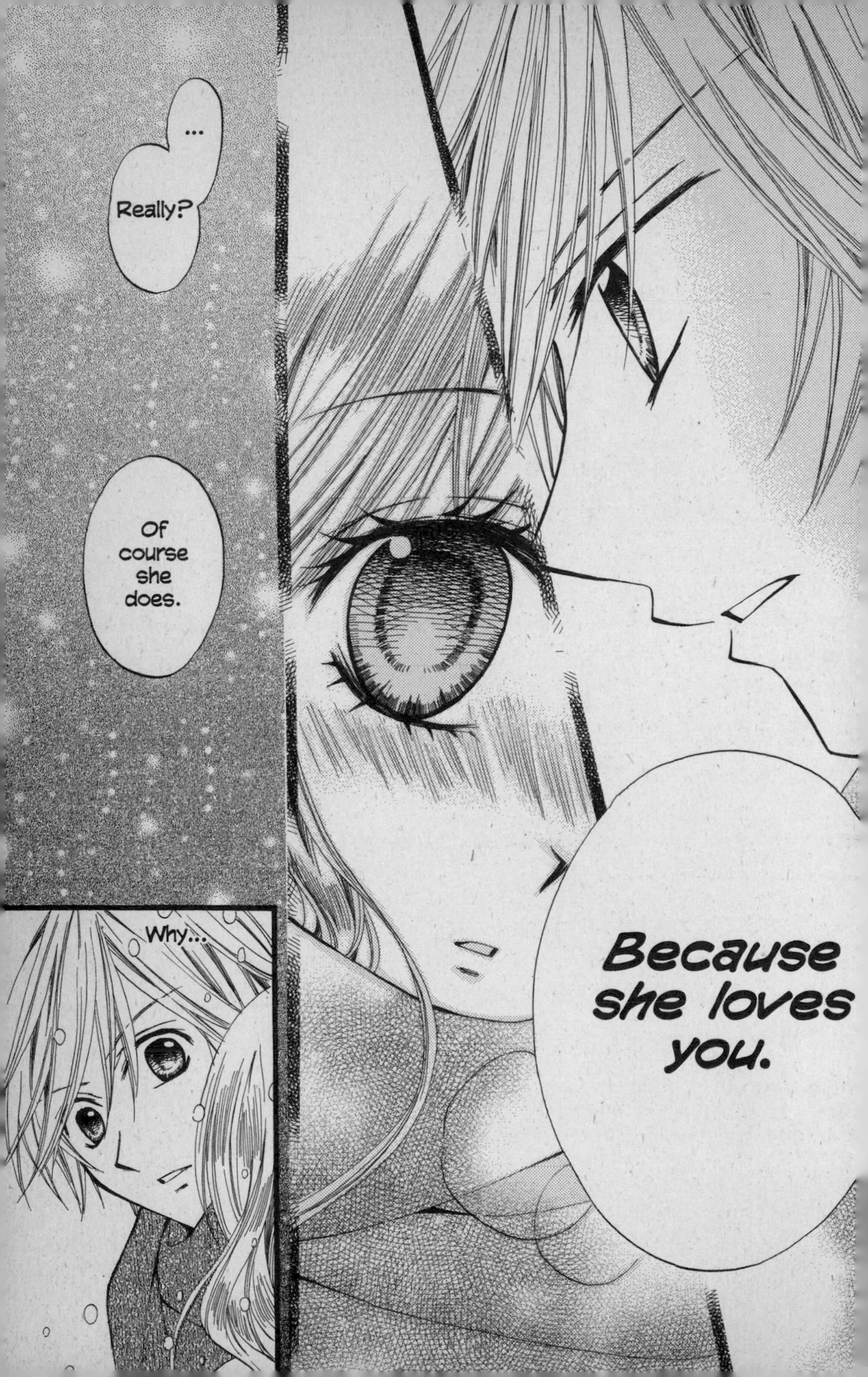
Because she loves you.
...
Really?
Of course she does.
Why...

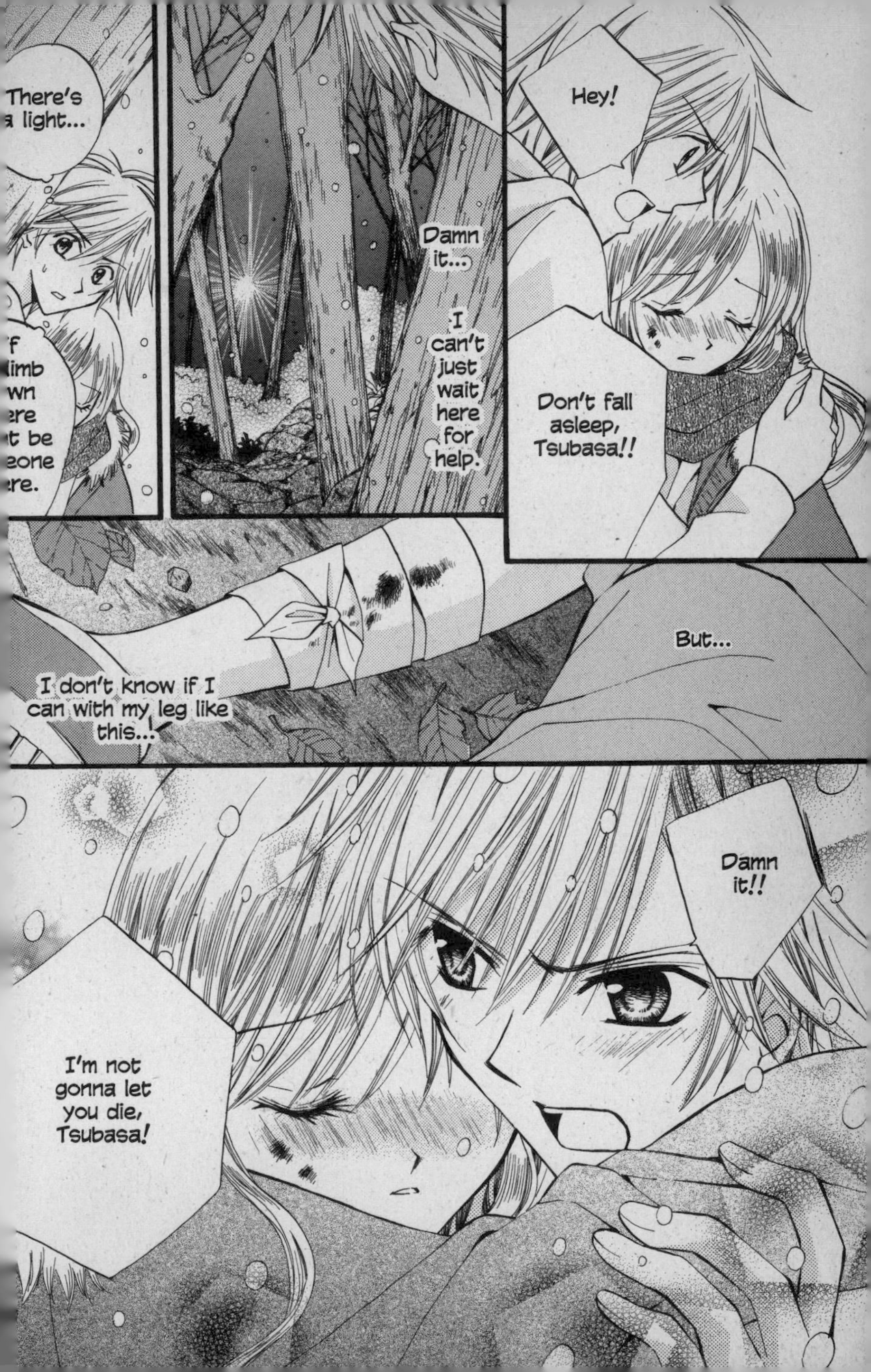
Hey!
Don't fall asleep, Tsubasa!!
Damn it...
I can't just wait here for help.
There's a light...
f limb wn ere t be eone ere.
But...
I don't know if I can with my leg like this...!
Damn it!!
I'm not gonna let you die, Tsubasa!

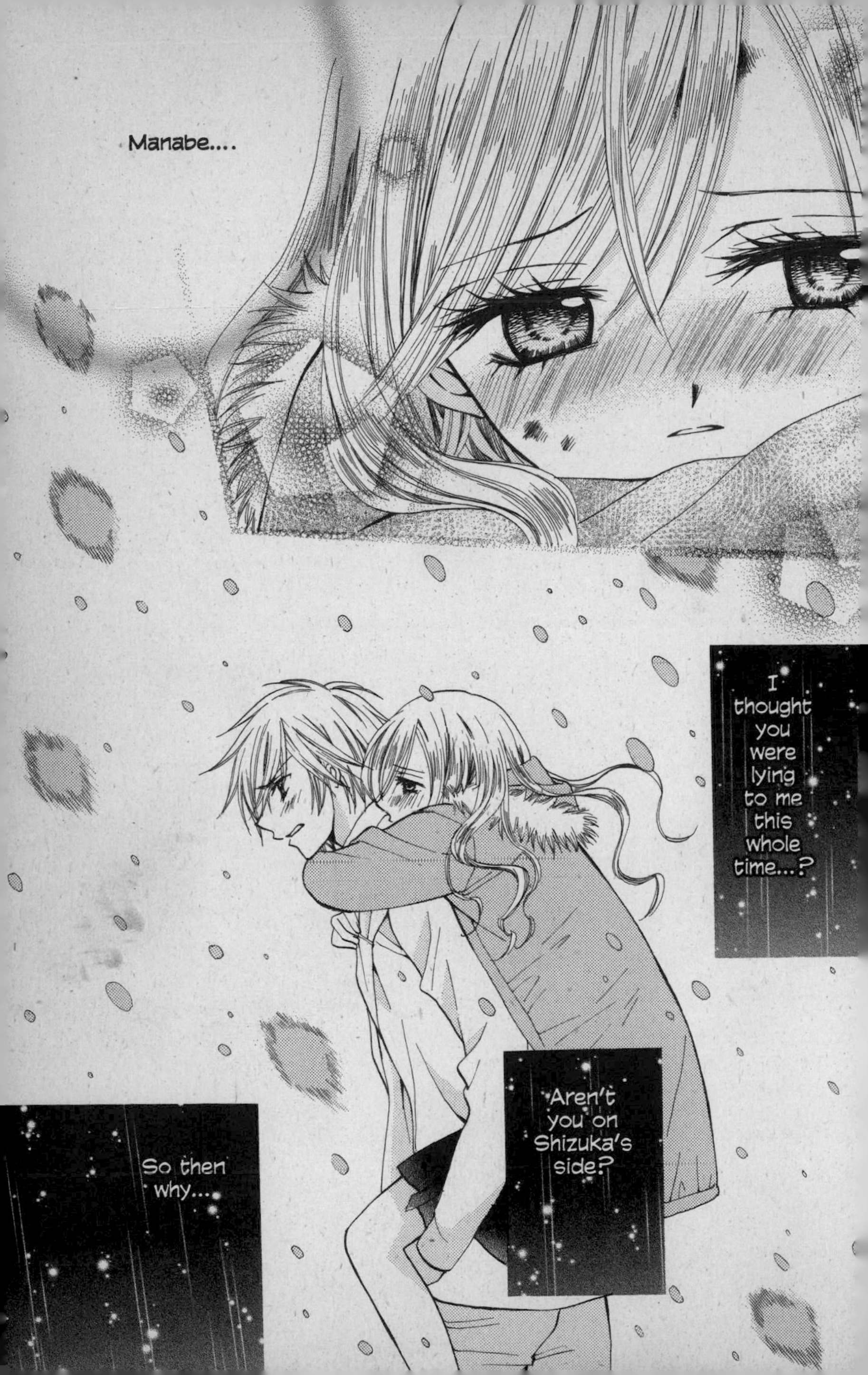
Manabe....
I thought you were lying to me this whole time...?
Aren't you on Shizuka's side?
So then why...

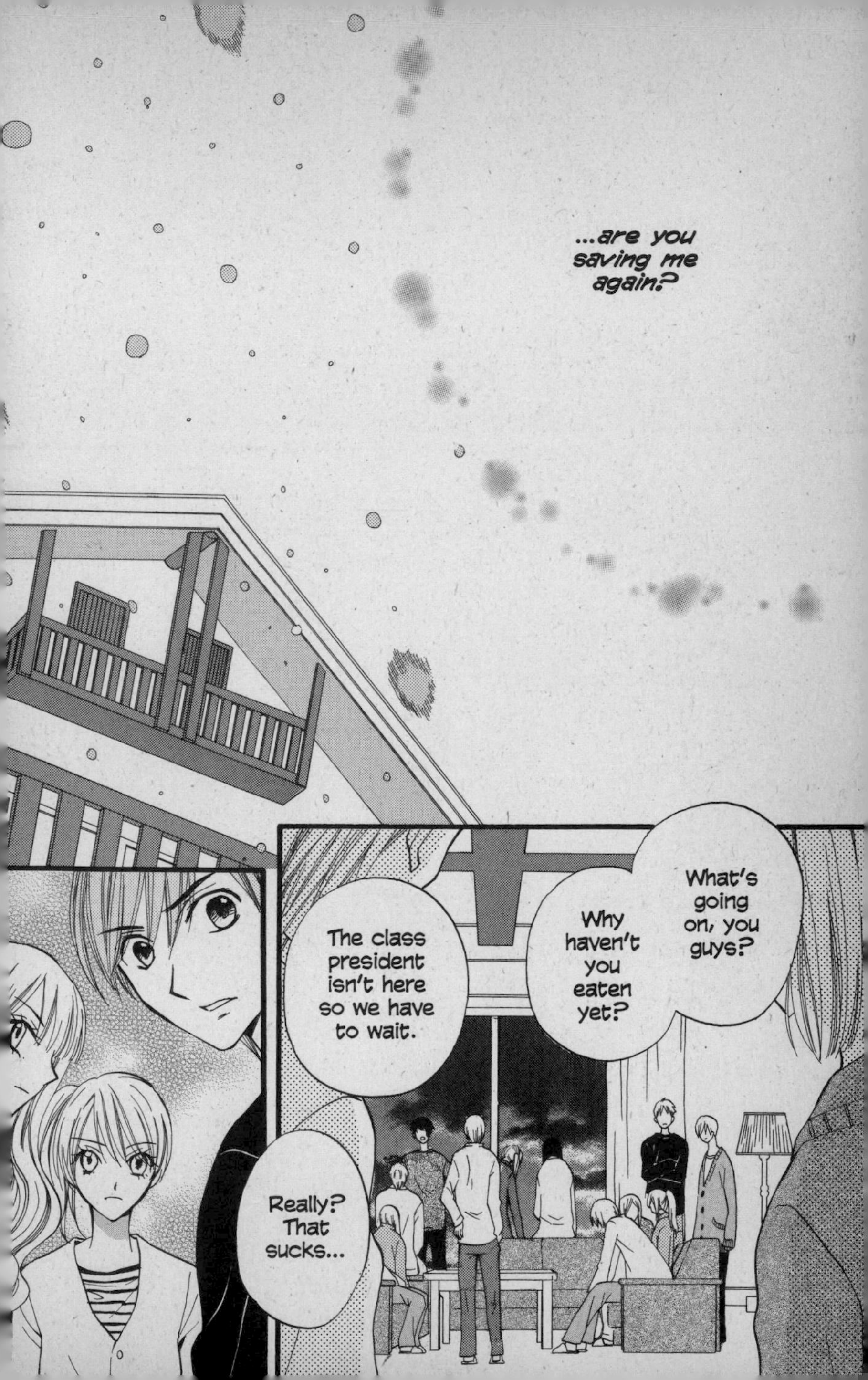
...are you saving me again?
What's going on, you guys?
Why haven't you eaten yet?
The class president isn't here so we have to wait.
Really? That sucks...

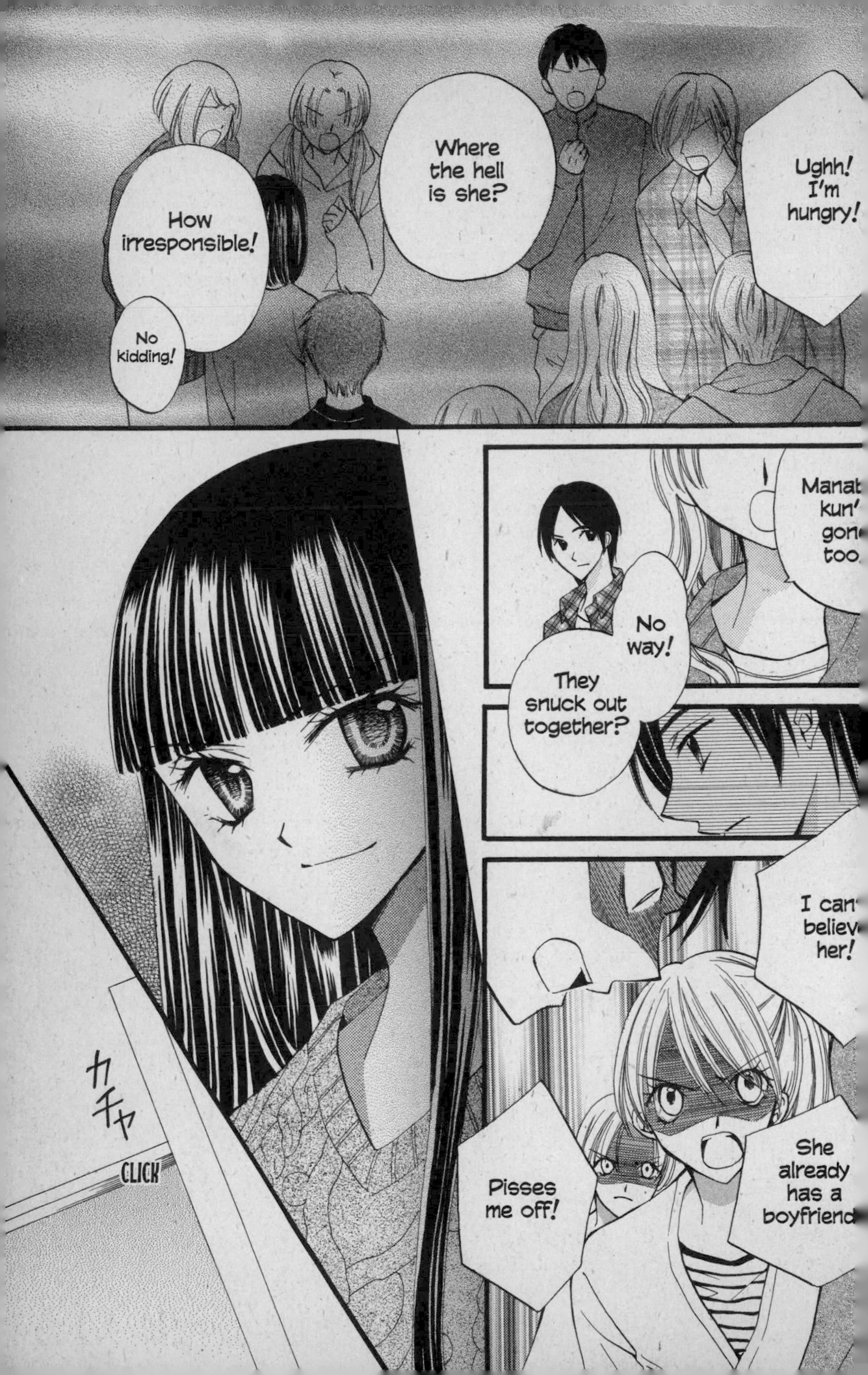
Ughh! I'm hungry!
Where the hell is she?
How irresponsible!
No kidding!
Manat kun' gon too,
No way!
They snuck out together?
I can' believ her!
She already has a boyfriend
Pisses me off!
カチャ
CLICK

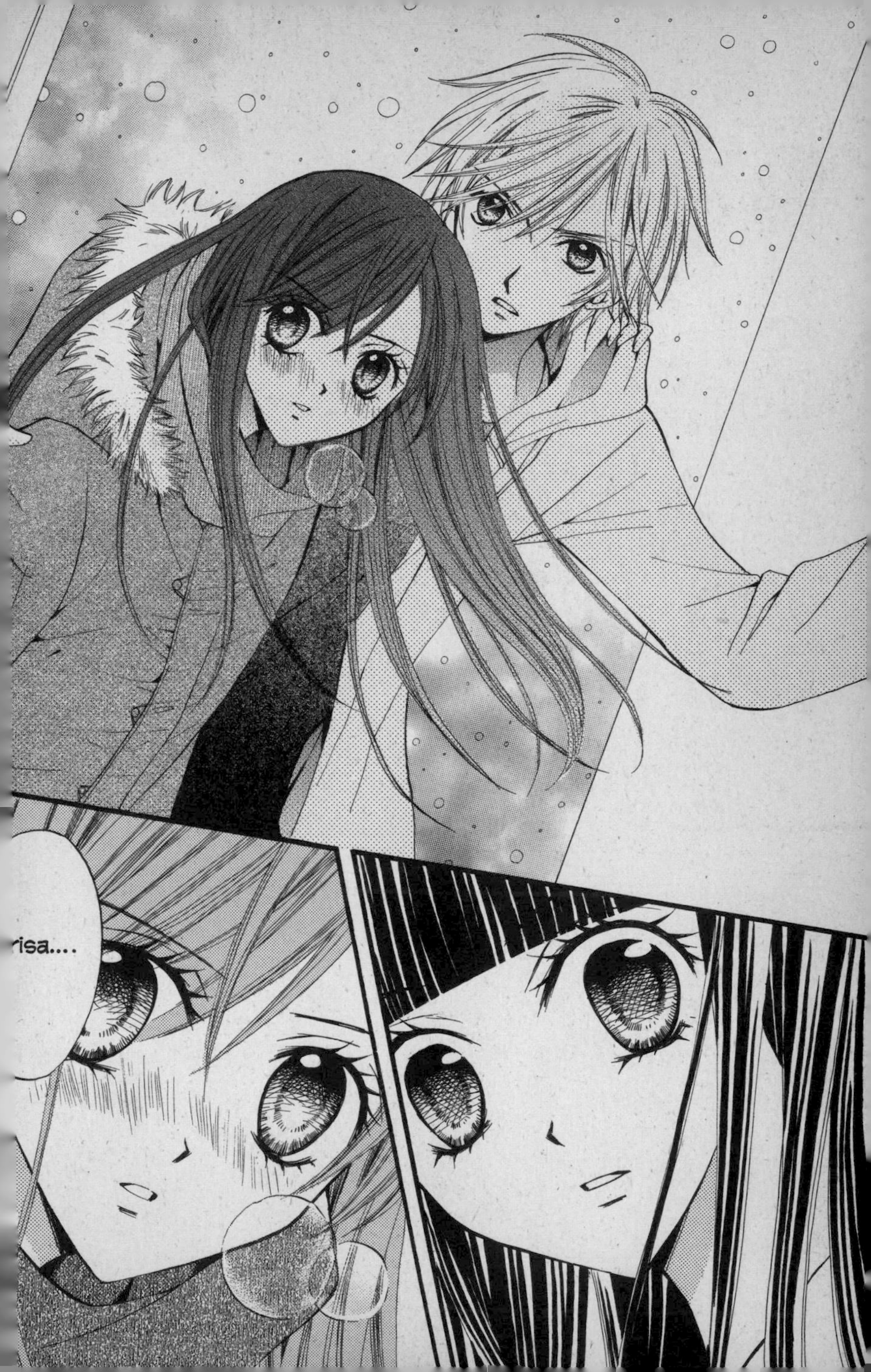
risa....

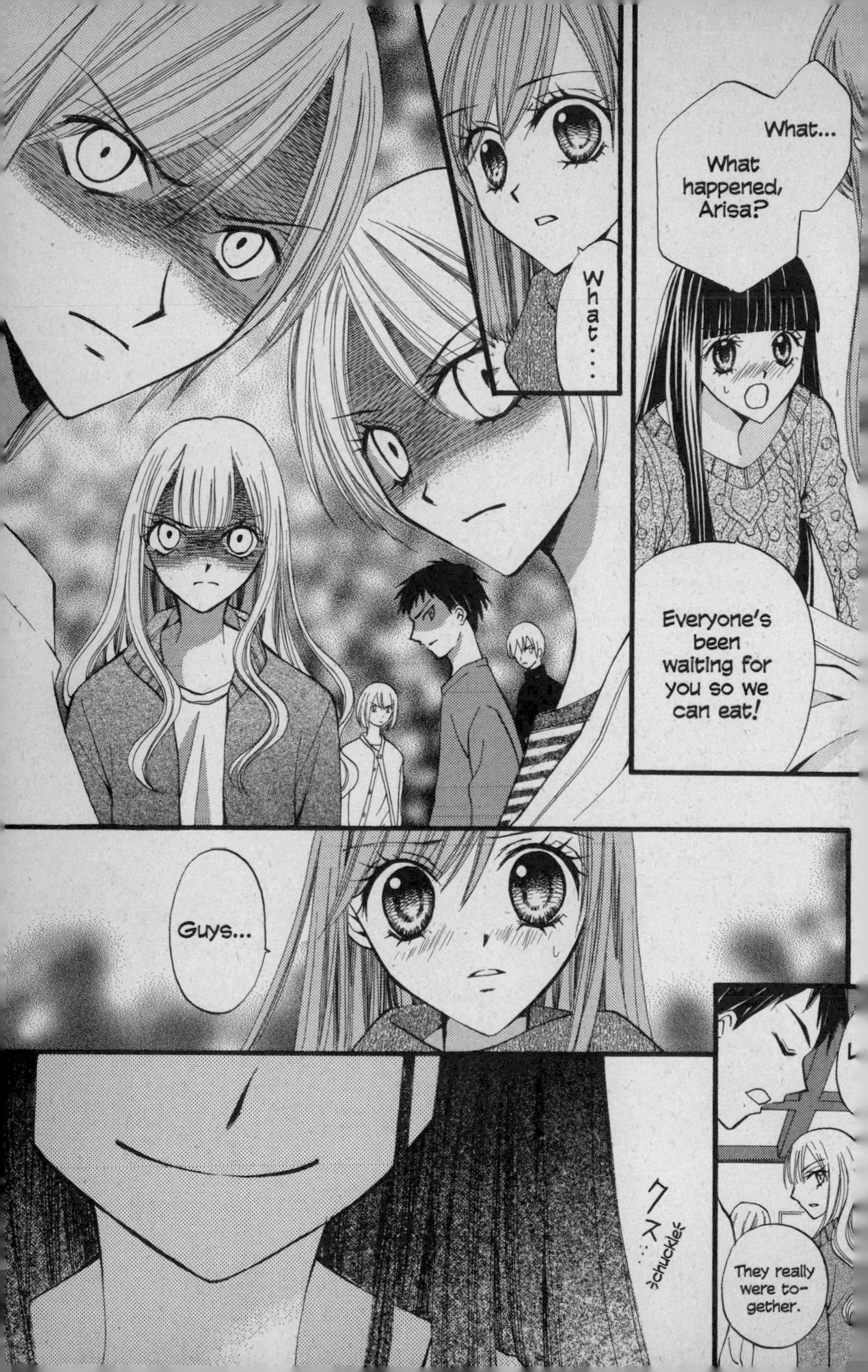
What... What happened, Arisa?
Everyone's been waiting for you so we can eat!
What...
Guys...
They really were to-gether.
クス
chuckle

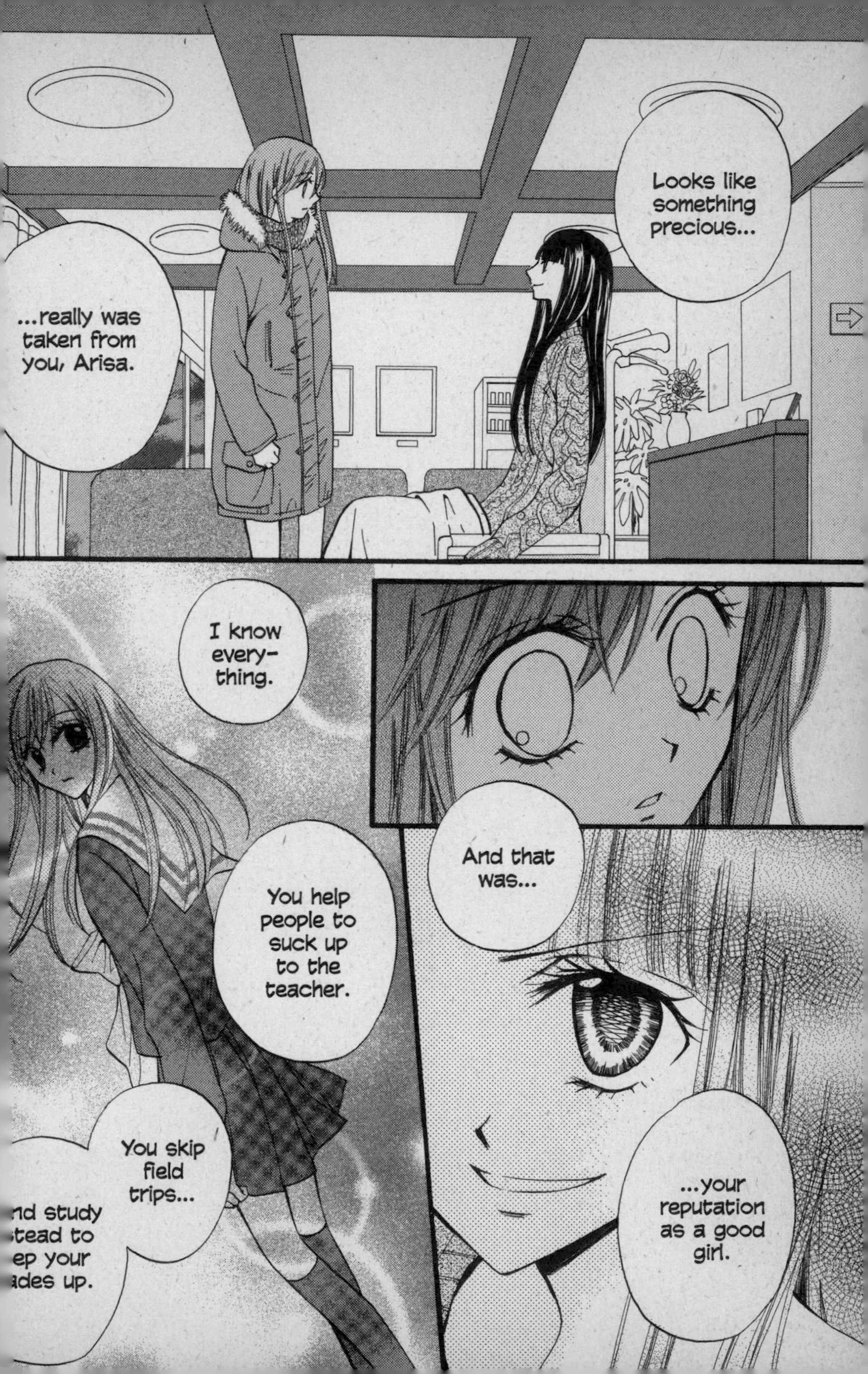
Looks like something precious...
...really was taken from you, Arisa.
And that was...
...your reputation as a good girl.
I know every-thing.
You help people to suck up to the teacher.
You skip field trips...
nd study stead to ep your ades up.

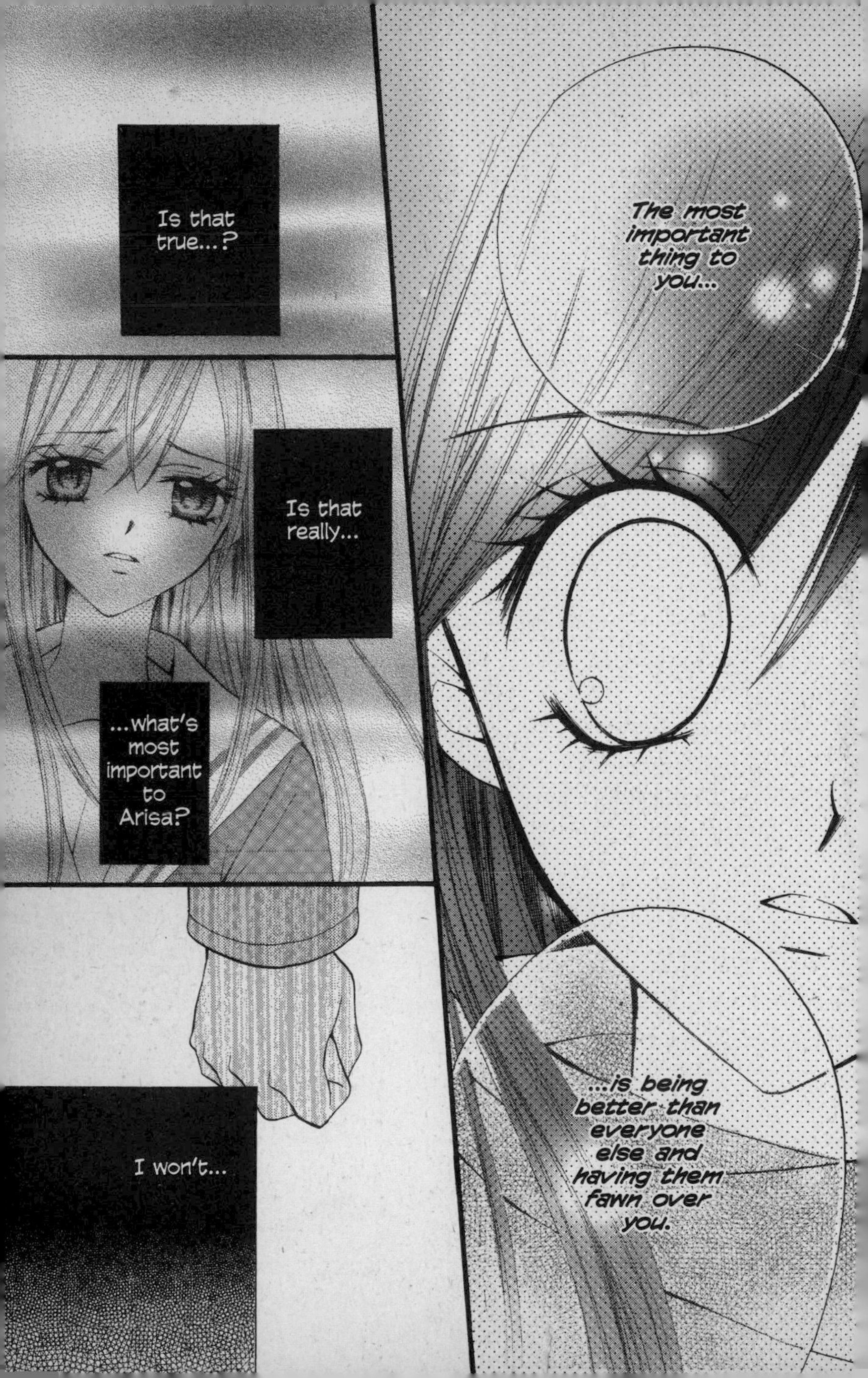
The most important thing to you...
...is being better than everyone else and having them fawn over you.
Is that true...?
Is that really...
...what's most important to Arisa?
I won't...

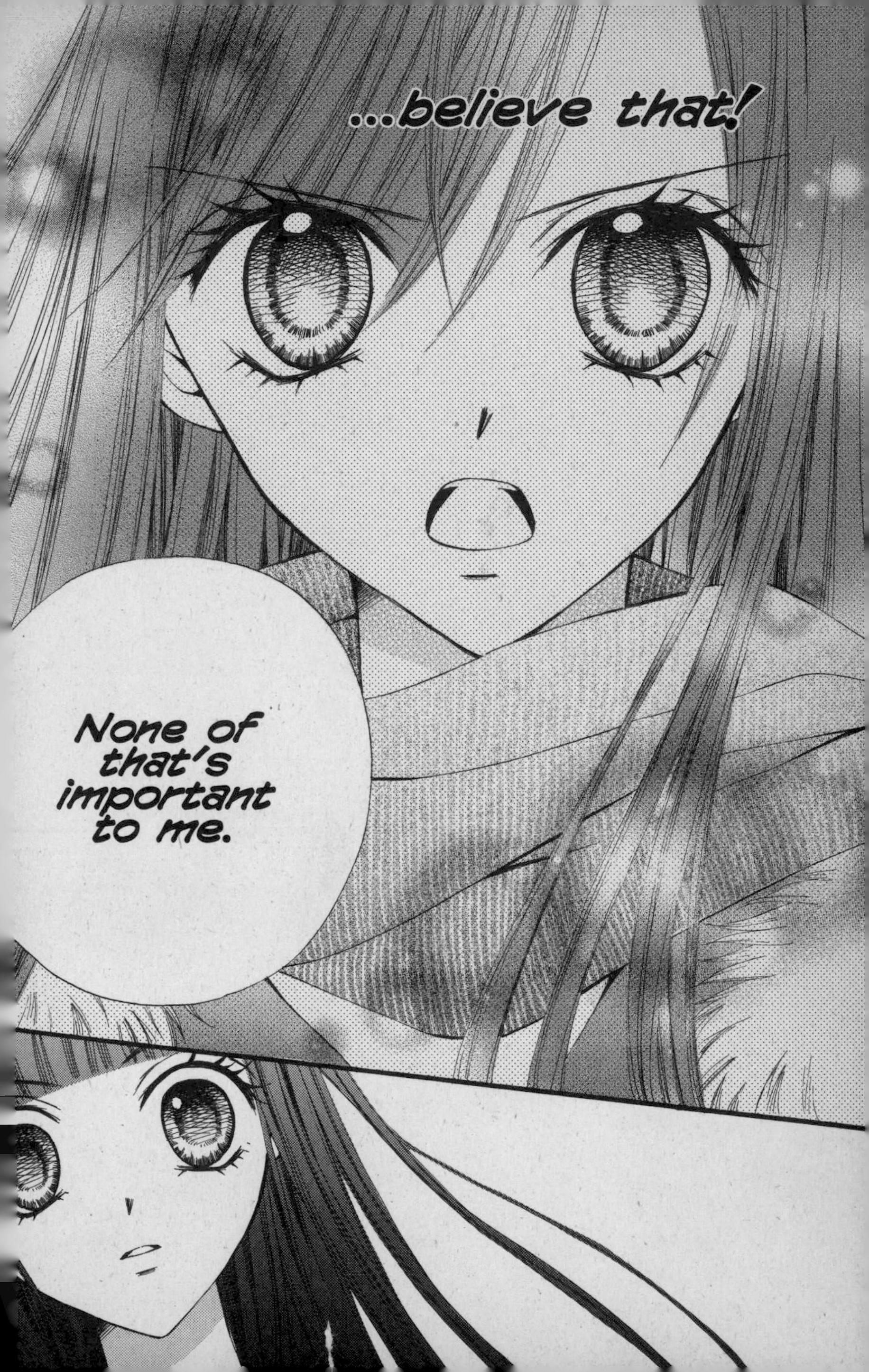
...believe that!
None of that's important to me.

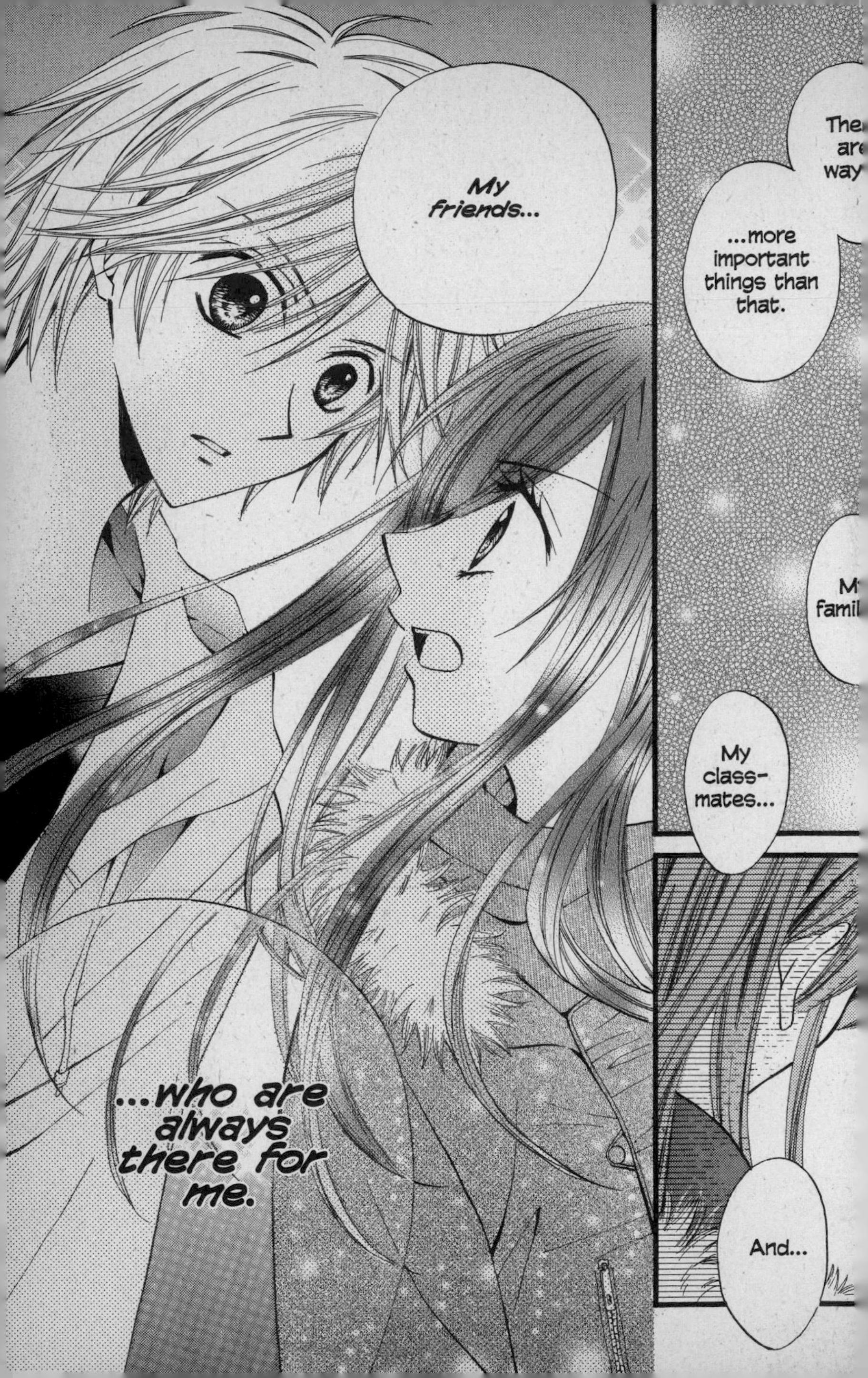
The are way
...more important things than that.
M famil
My class-mates...
And...
My friends...
...who are always there for me.

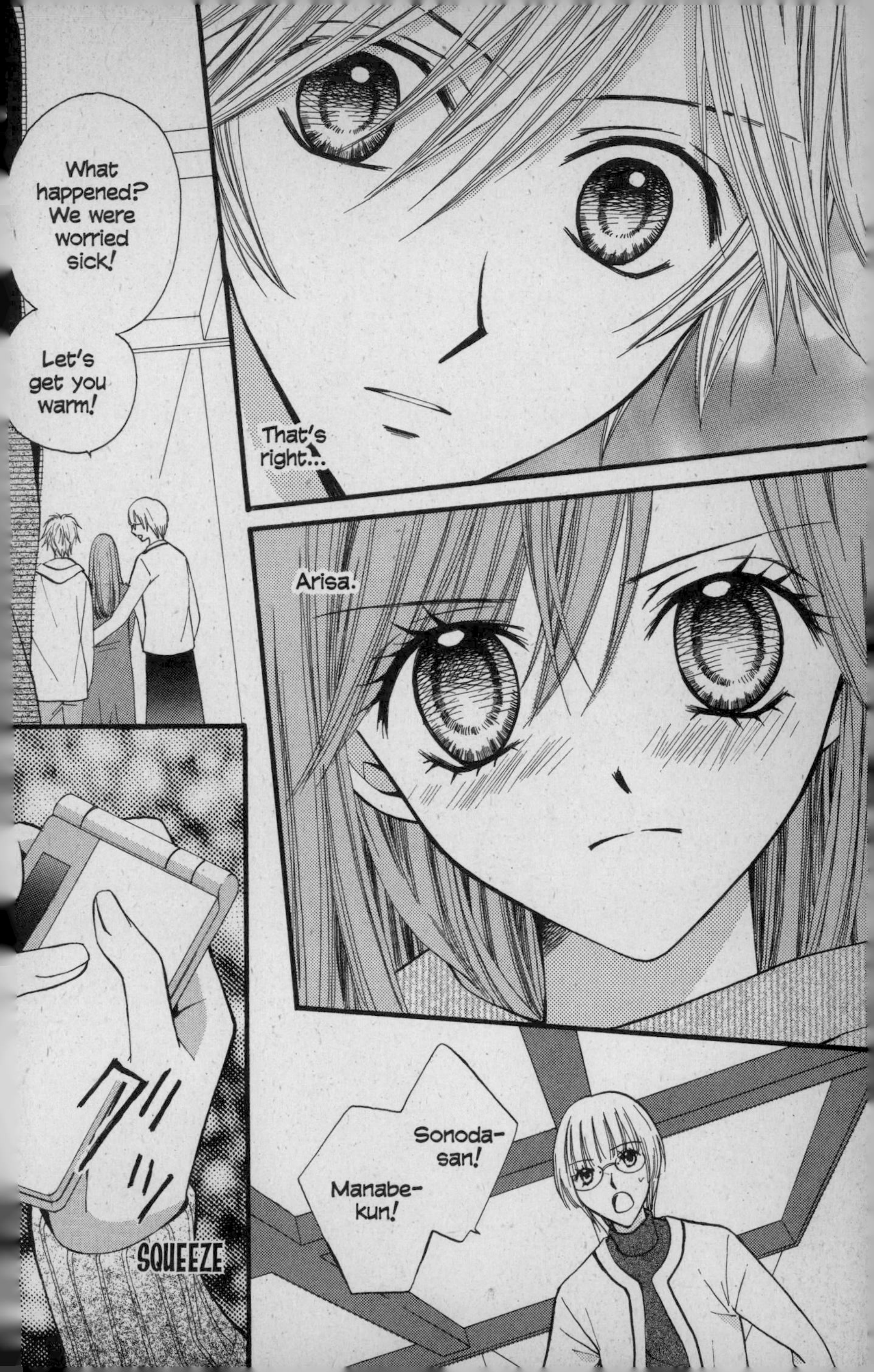
That's right...
Arisa.
What happened? We were worried sick!
Let's get you warm!
Sonoda-san!
Manabe-kun!
SQUEEZE

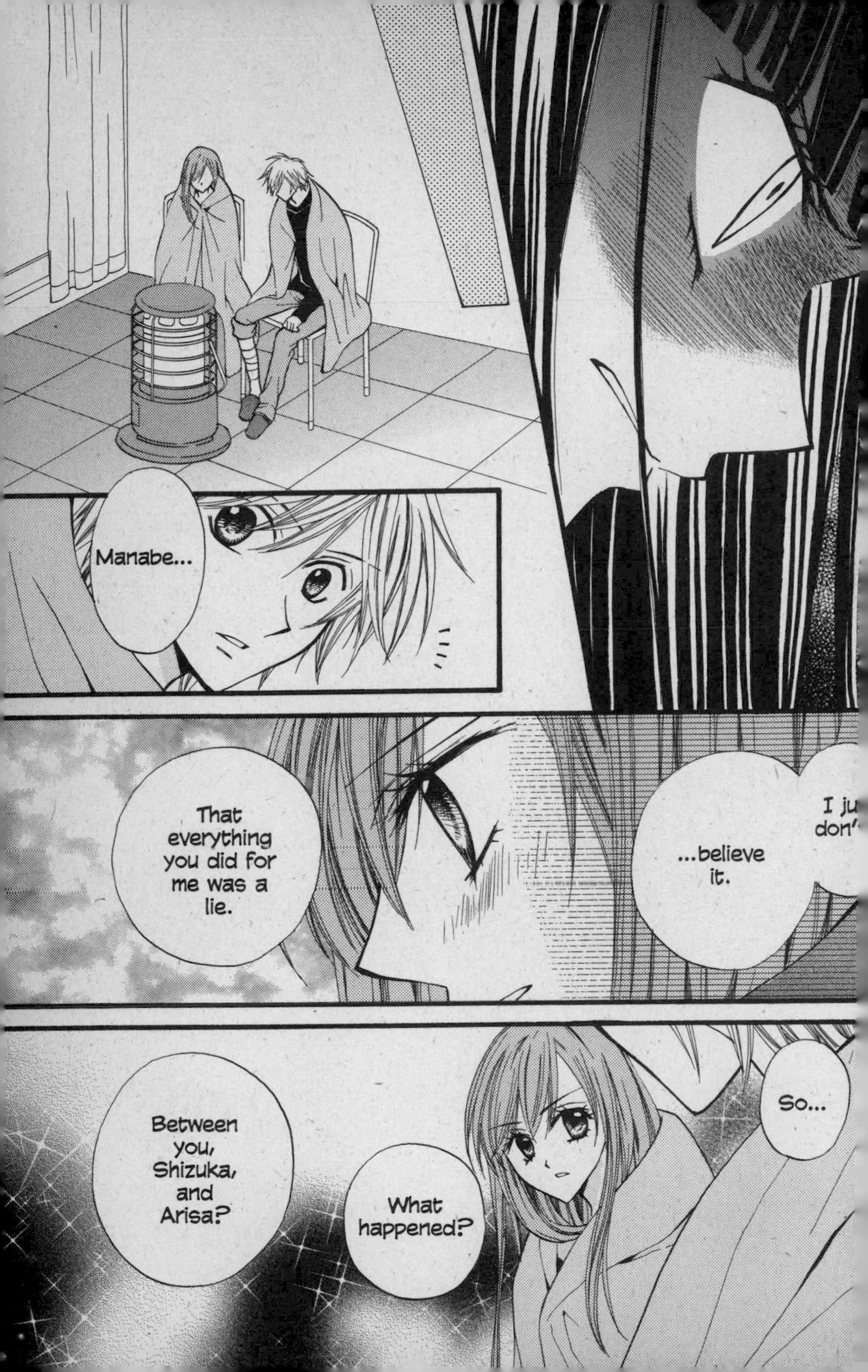
Manabe...
...believe it.
That everything you did for me was a lie.
So...
What happened?
Between you, Shizuka, and Arisa?

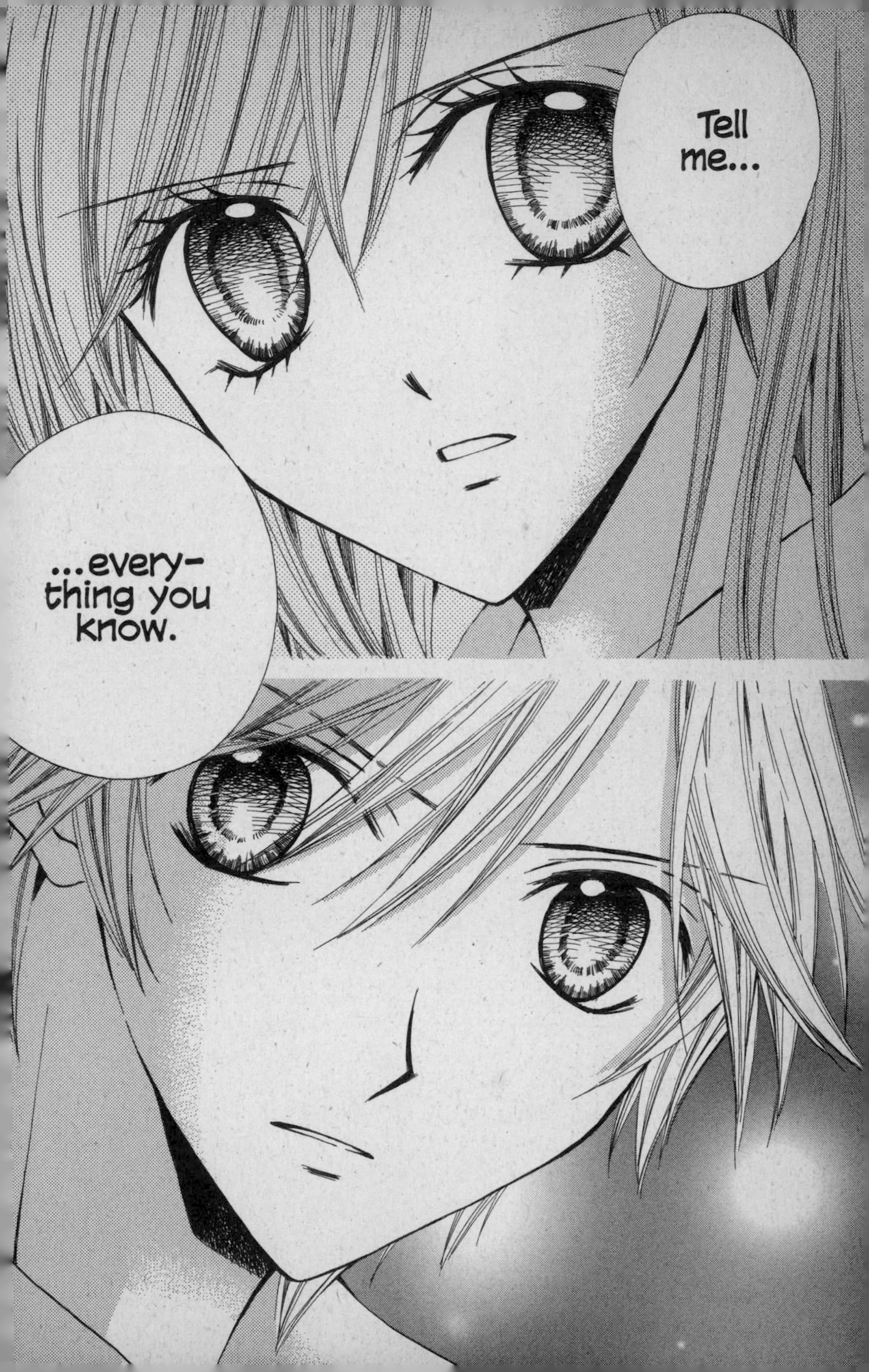
Tell me...
...every-thing you know.

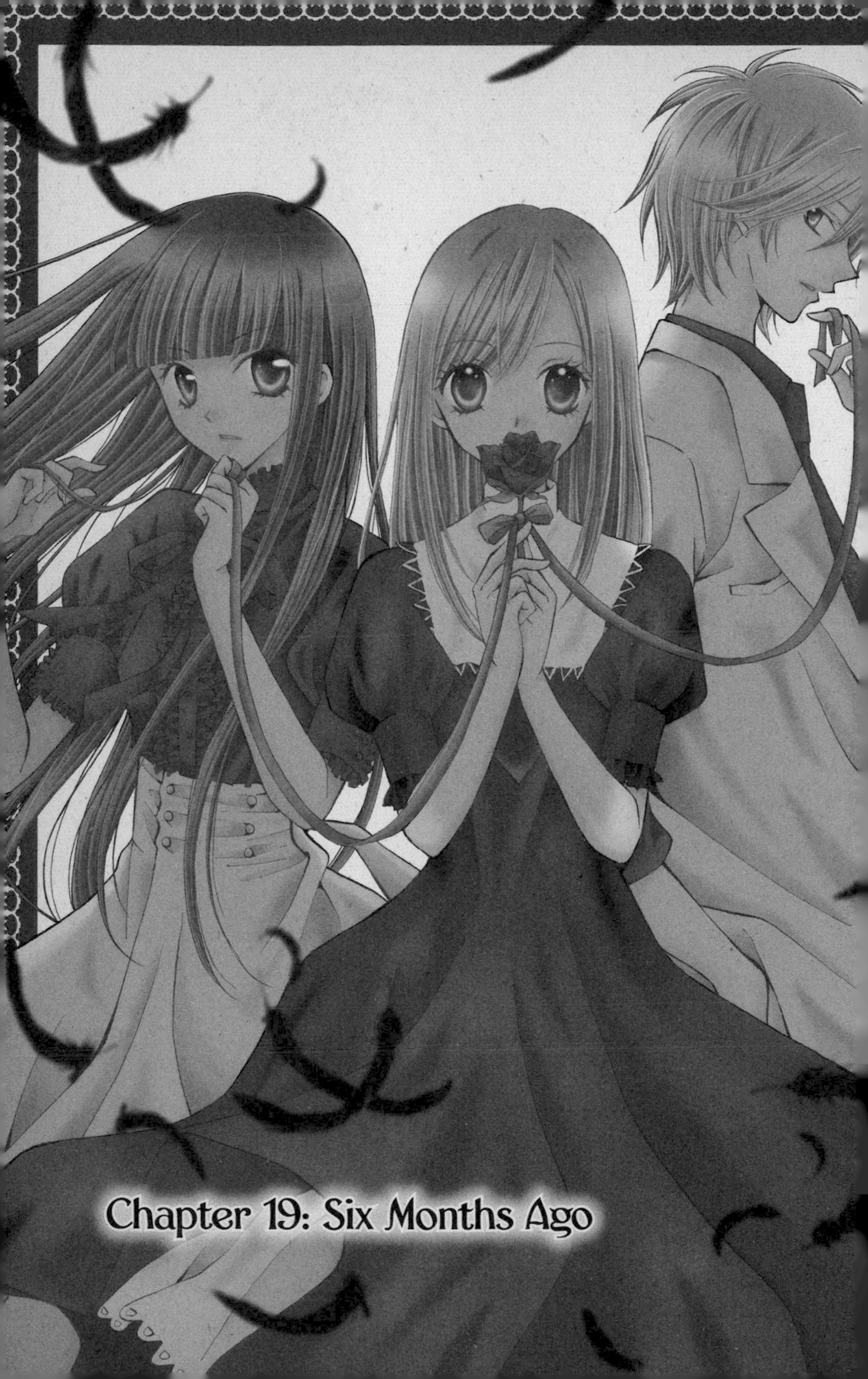
Chapter 19: Six Months Ago

ARISA

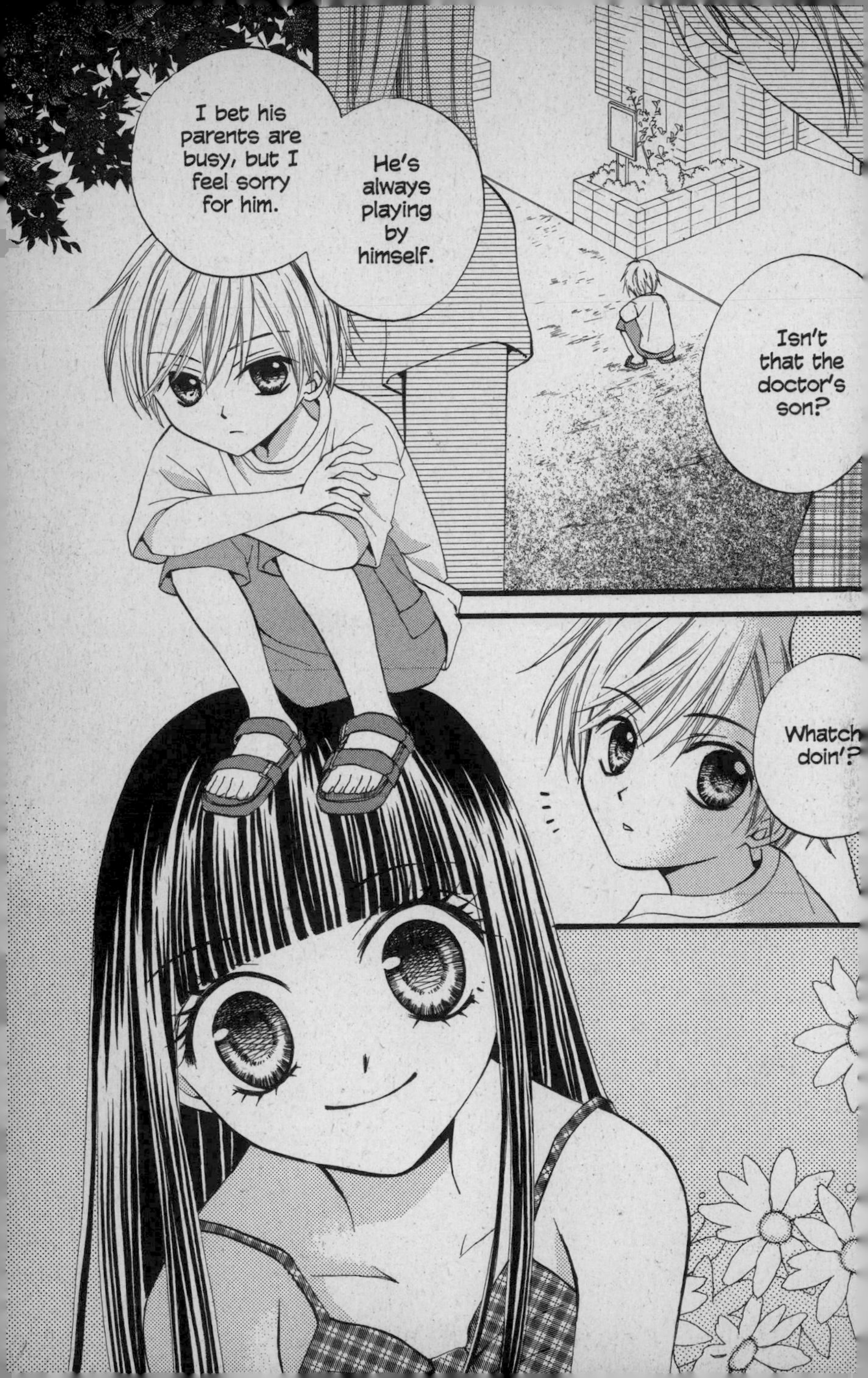
Isn't that the doctor's son?
He's always playing by himself.
I bet his parents are busy, but I feel sorry for him.
Whatch doin'?

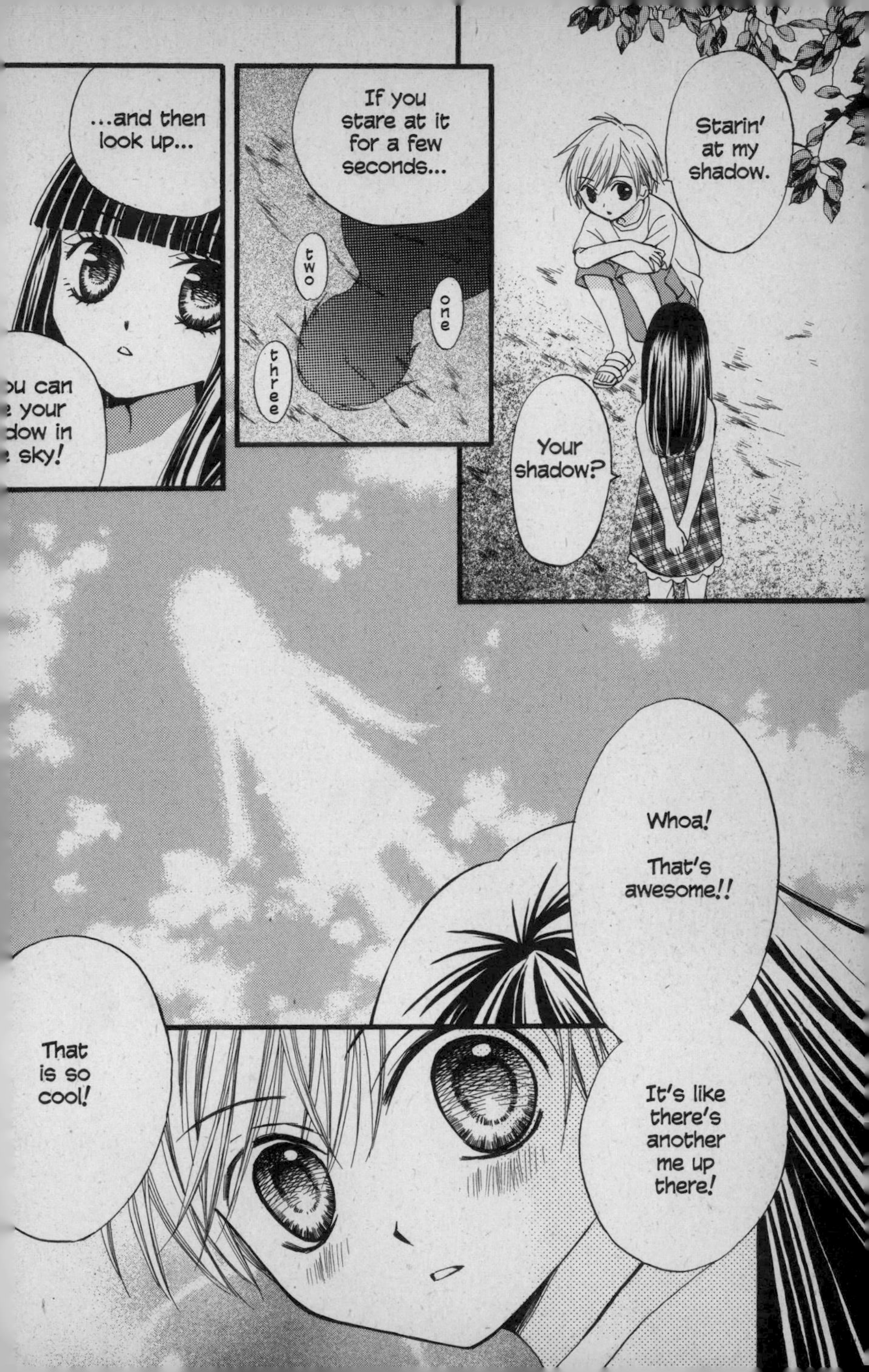

Starin' at my shadow.
Your shadow?
If you stare at it for a few seconds...
one
two
three
...and then look up...
ou can e your dow in e sky!
Whoa! That's awesome!!
It's like there's another me up there!
That is so cool!

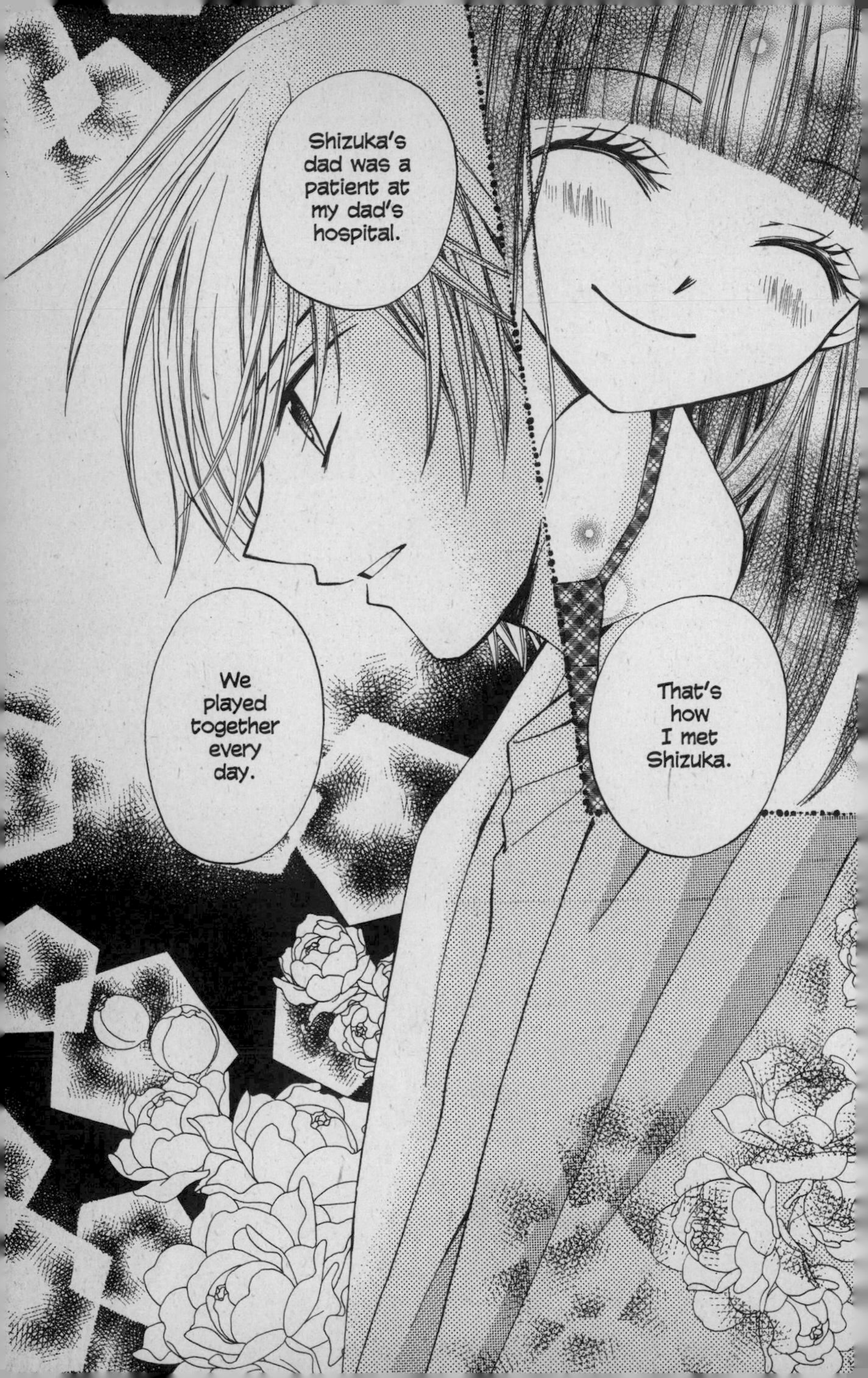
Shizuka's dad was a patient at my dad's hospital.
That's how I met Shizuka.
We played together every day.

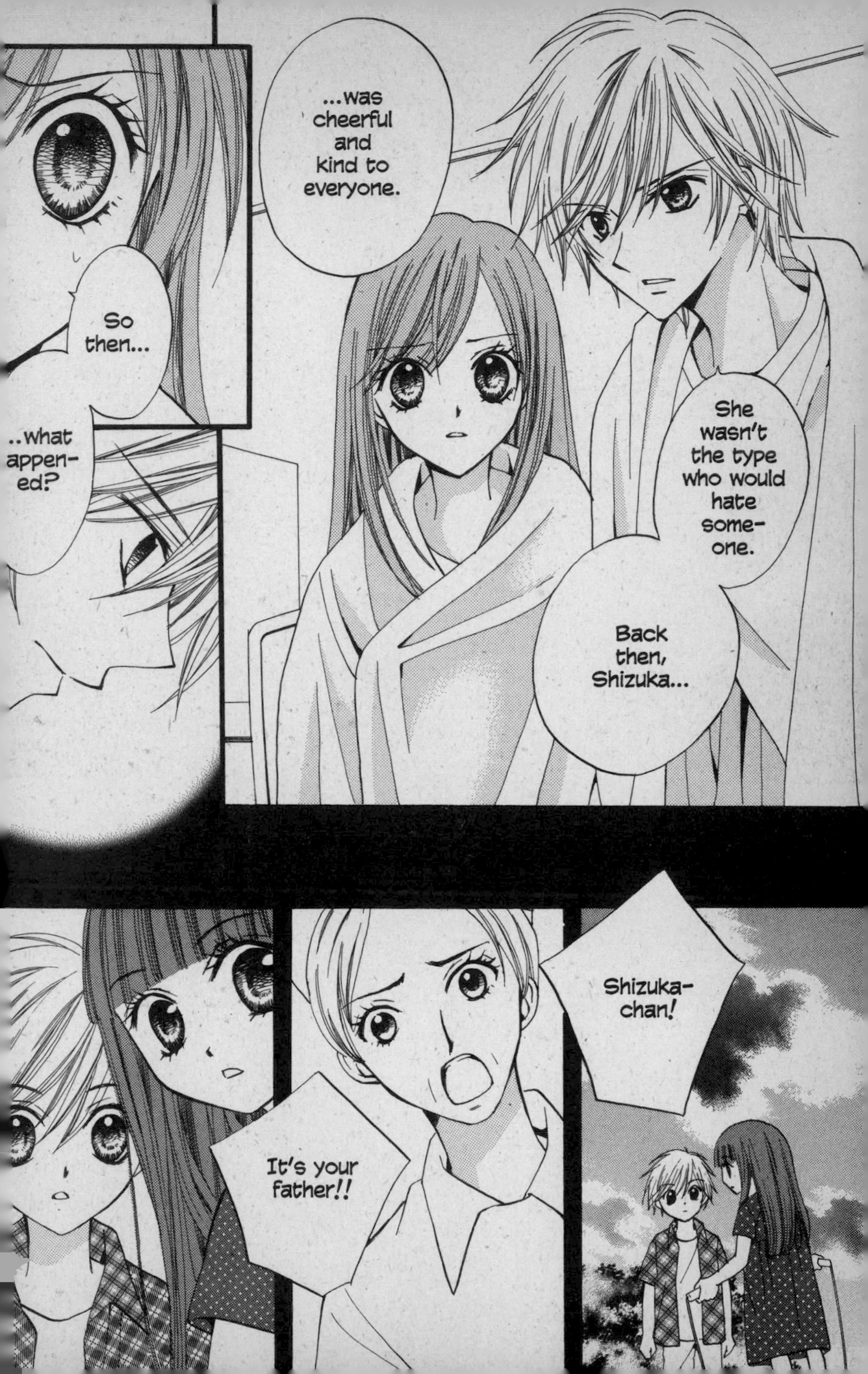
Back then, Shizuka...
...was cheerful and kind to everyone.
She wasn't the type who would hate some-one.
So then...
..what appen-ed?
Shizuka-chan!
It's your father!!

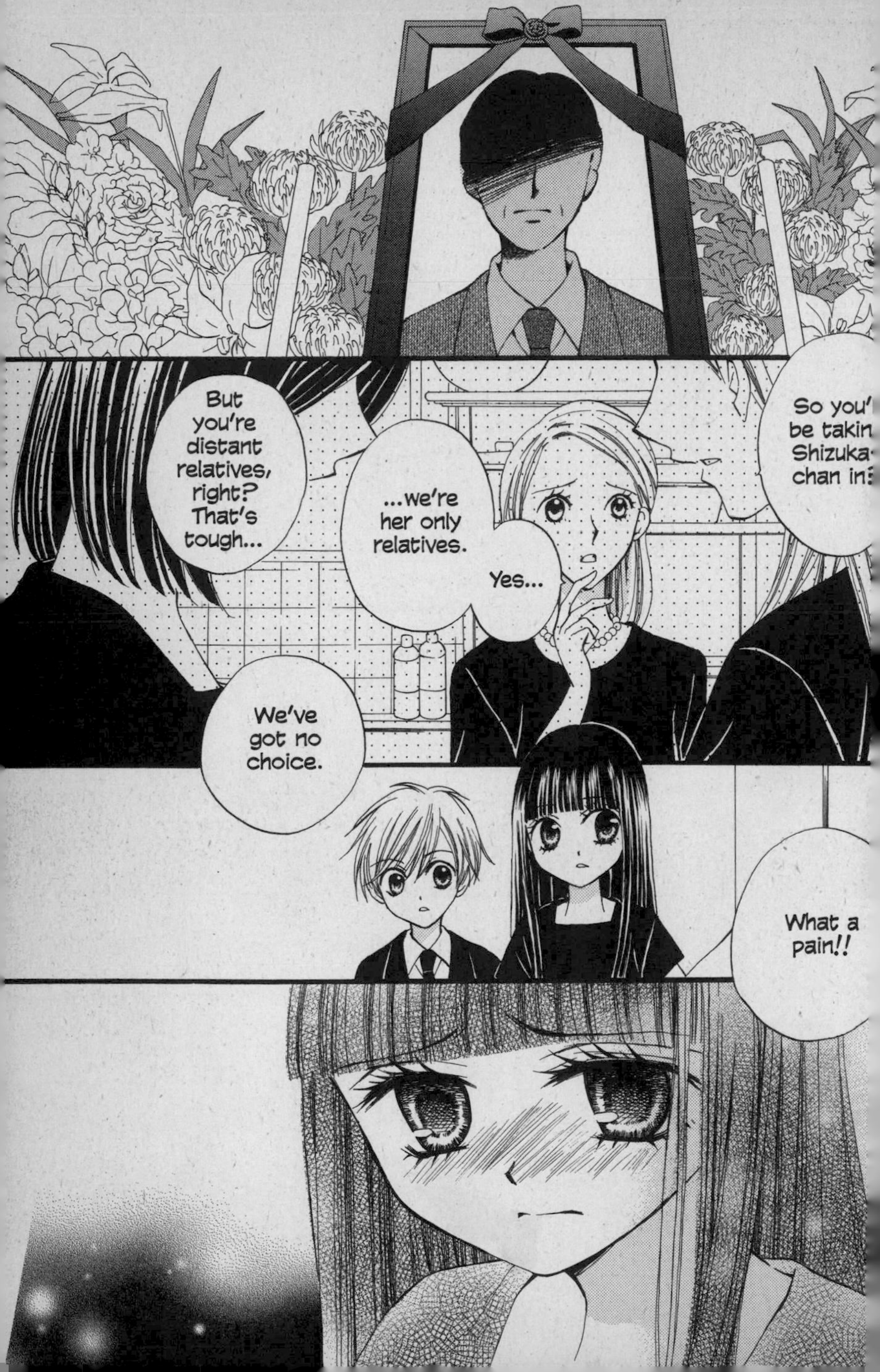

So you' be takin Shizuka-chan in?
Yes...
...we're her only relatives.
But you're distant relatives, right? That's tough...
We've got no choice.
What a pain!!

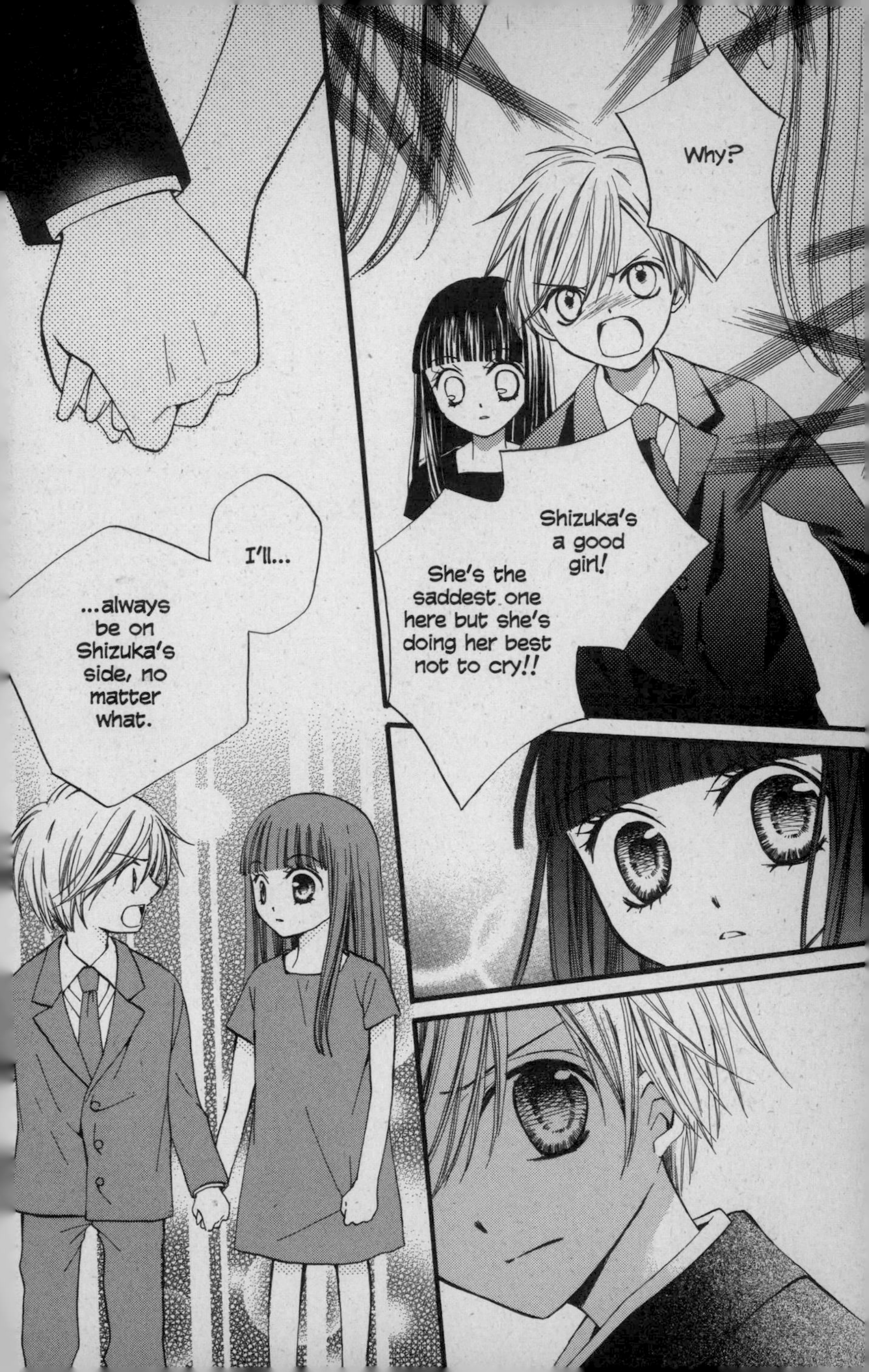

Why?
Shizuka's a good girl!
She's the saddest one here but she's doing her best not to cry!!
I'll...
...always be on Shizuka's side, no matter what.

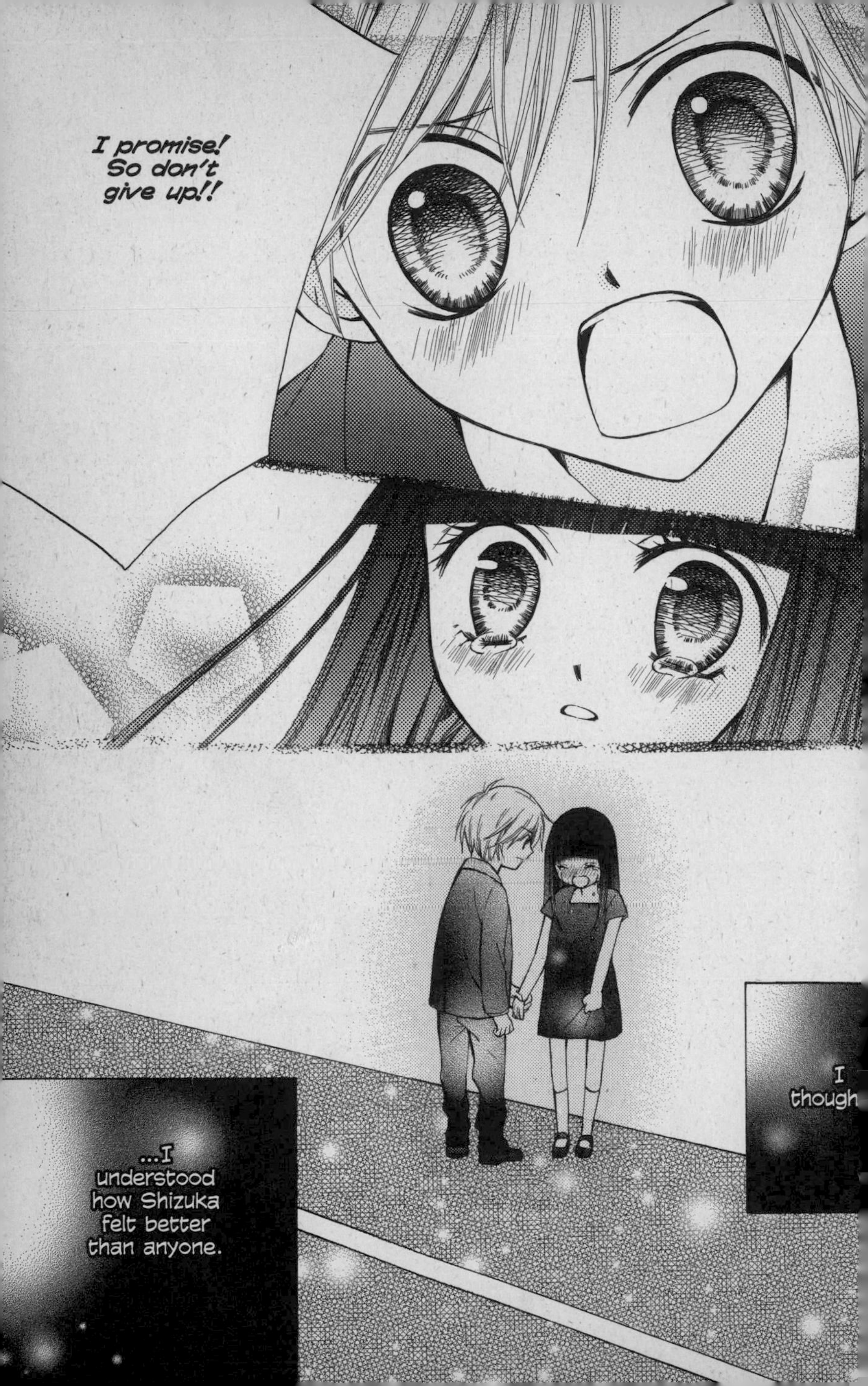
I promise! So don't give up!!
I though
...I understood how Shizuka felt better than anyone.

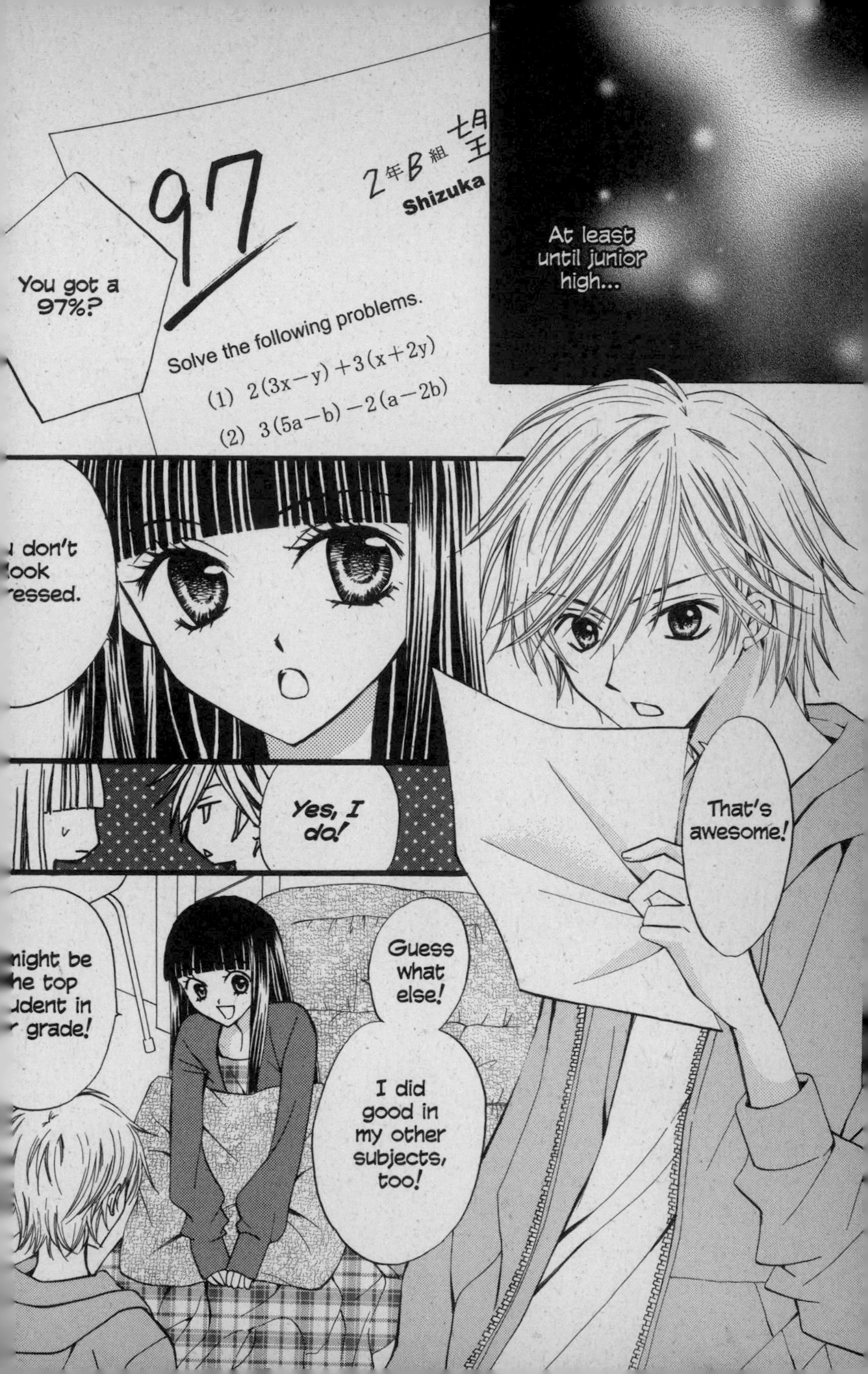

At least until junior high...
97
2年B組 望
Shizuka
You got a 97%?
Solve the following problems.
(1) 2(3x−y)+3(x+2y)
(2) 3(5a−b)−2(a−2b)
That's awesome!
u don't look ressed.
Yes, I do!
Guess what else!
I did good in my other subjects, too!
might be the top udent in r grade!

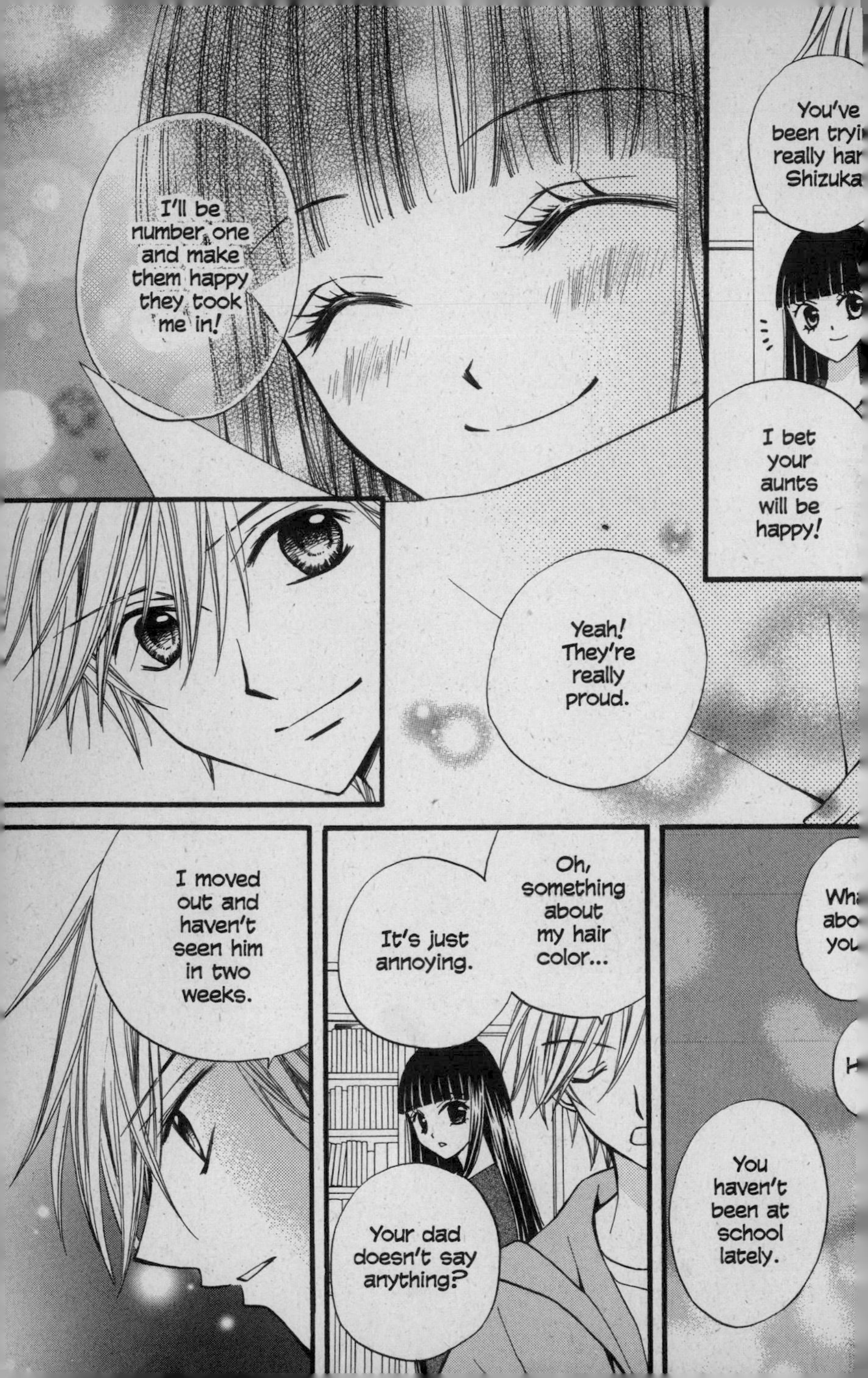
You've been tryi really har Shizuka
I bet your aunts will be happy!
I'll be number one and make them happy they took me in!
Yeah! They're really proud.
Wha abo you
H
You haven't been at school lately.
Oh, something about my hair color...
It's just annoying.
Your dad doesn't say anything?
I moved out and haven't seen him in two weeks.

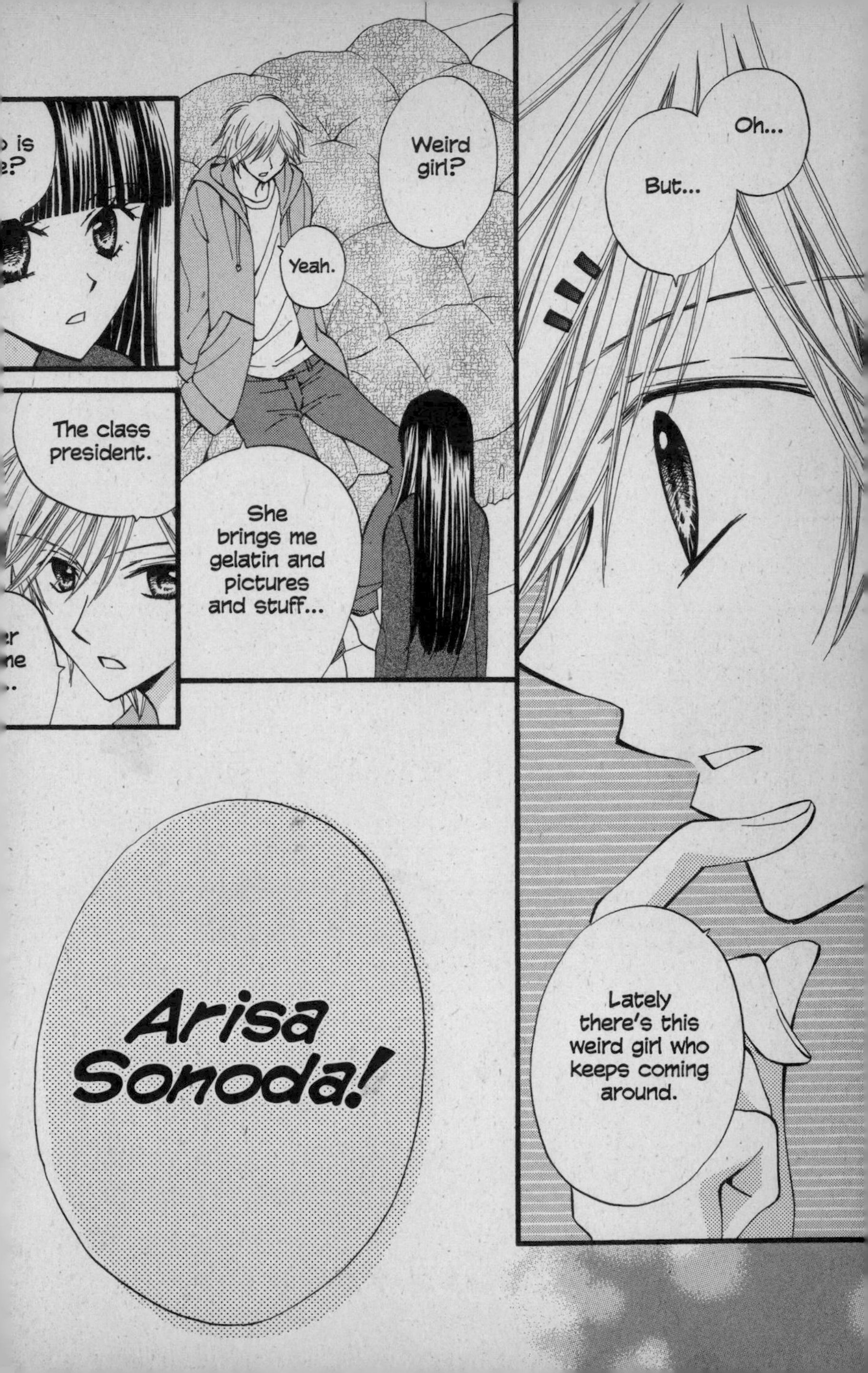
Oh...
But...
Lately there's this weird girl who keeps coming around.
Weird girl?
Yeah.
She brings me gelatin and pictures and stuff...
The class president.
Arisa Sonoda!

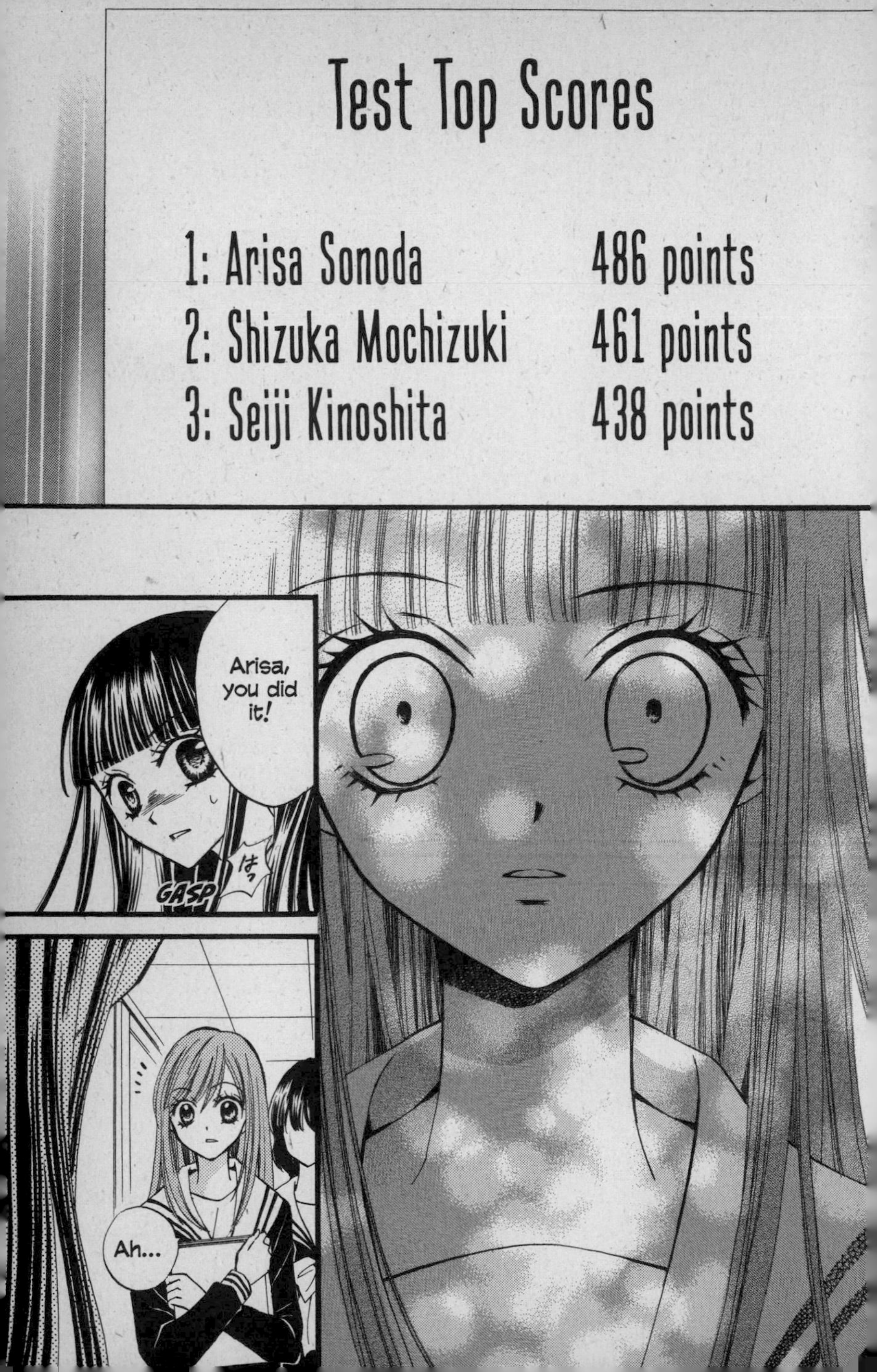
Test Top Scores
1: Arisa Sonoda 486 points
2: Shizuka Mochizuki 461 points
3: Seiji Kinoshita 438 points
Arisa, you did it!
はっ
GASP
Ah...

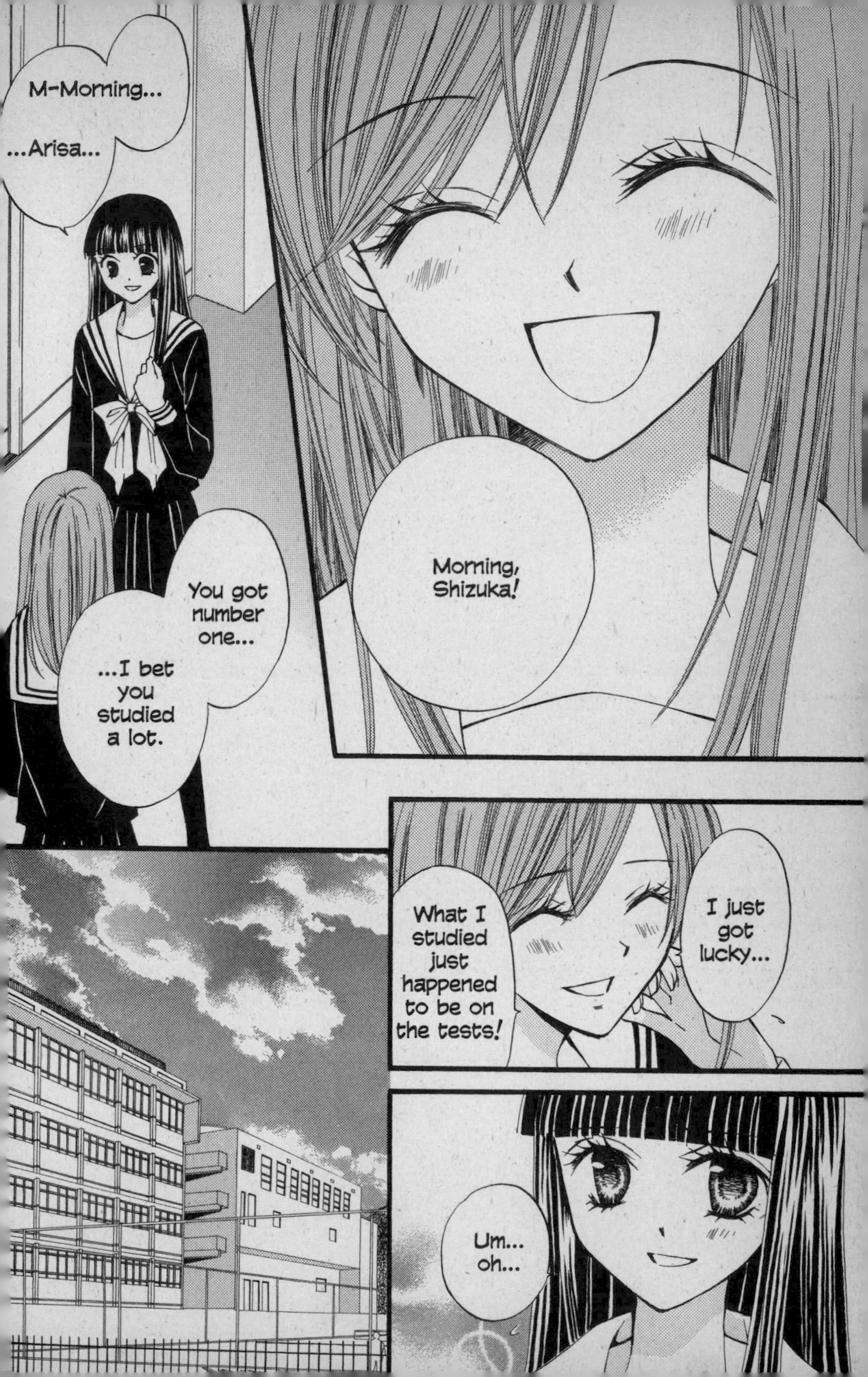
Morning, Shizuka!
M-Morning...
...Arisa...
You got number one...
...I bet you studied a lot.
I just got lucky...
What I studied just happened to be on the tests!
Um... oh...

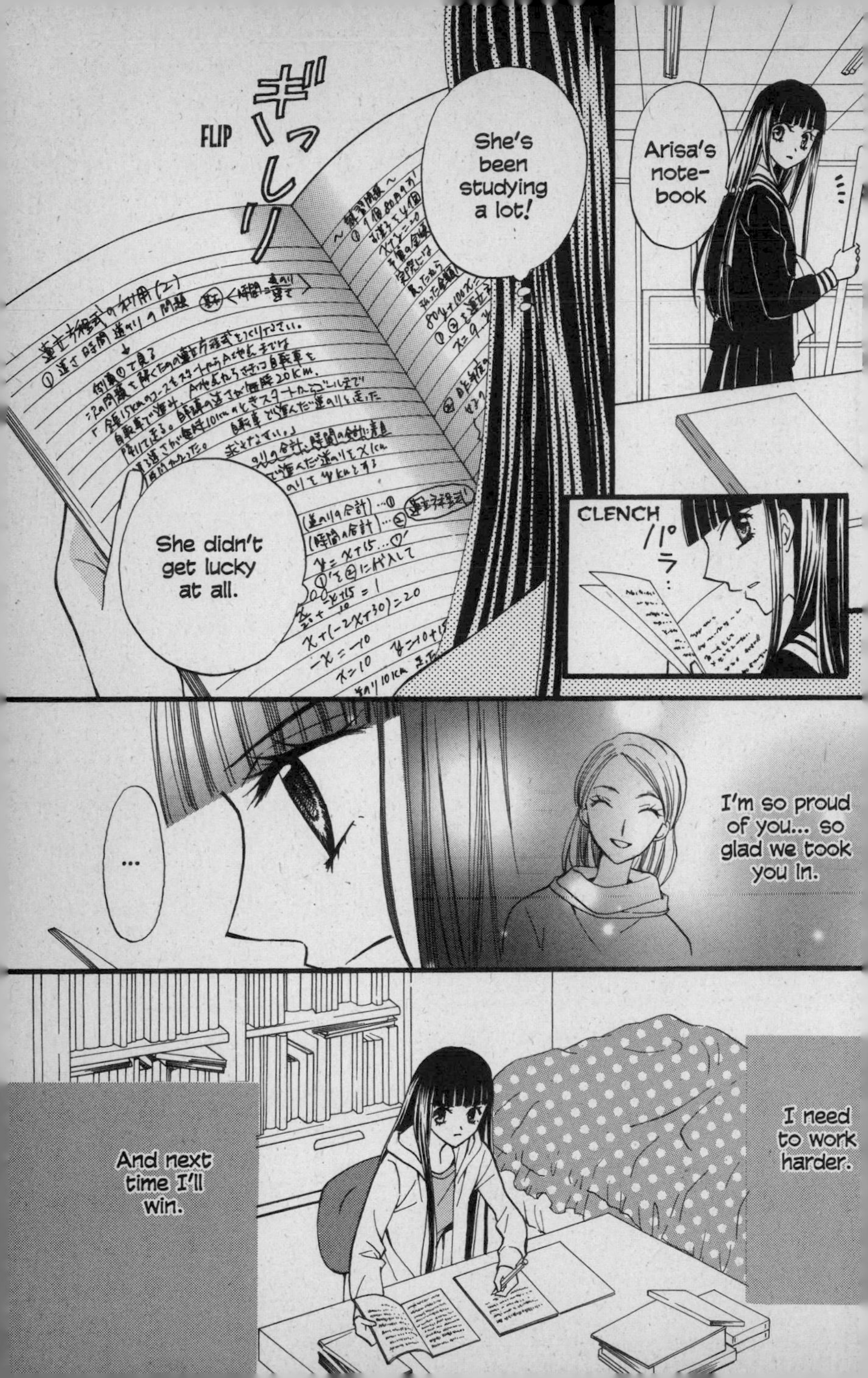
Arisa's notebook
CLENCH
パラ…
FLIP
ぎっしり
She's been studying a lot!
She didn't get lucky at all.
I'm so proud of you... so glad we took you in.
...
I need to work harder.
And next time I'll win.

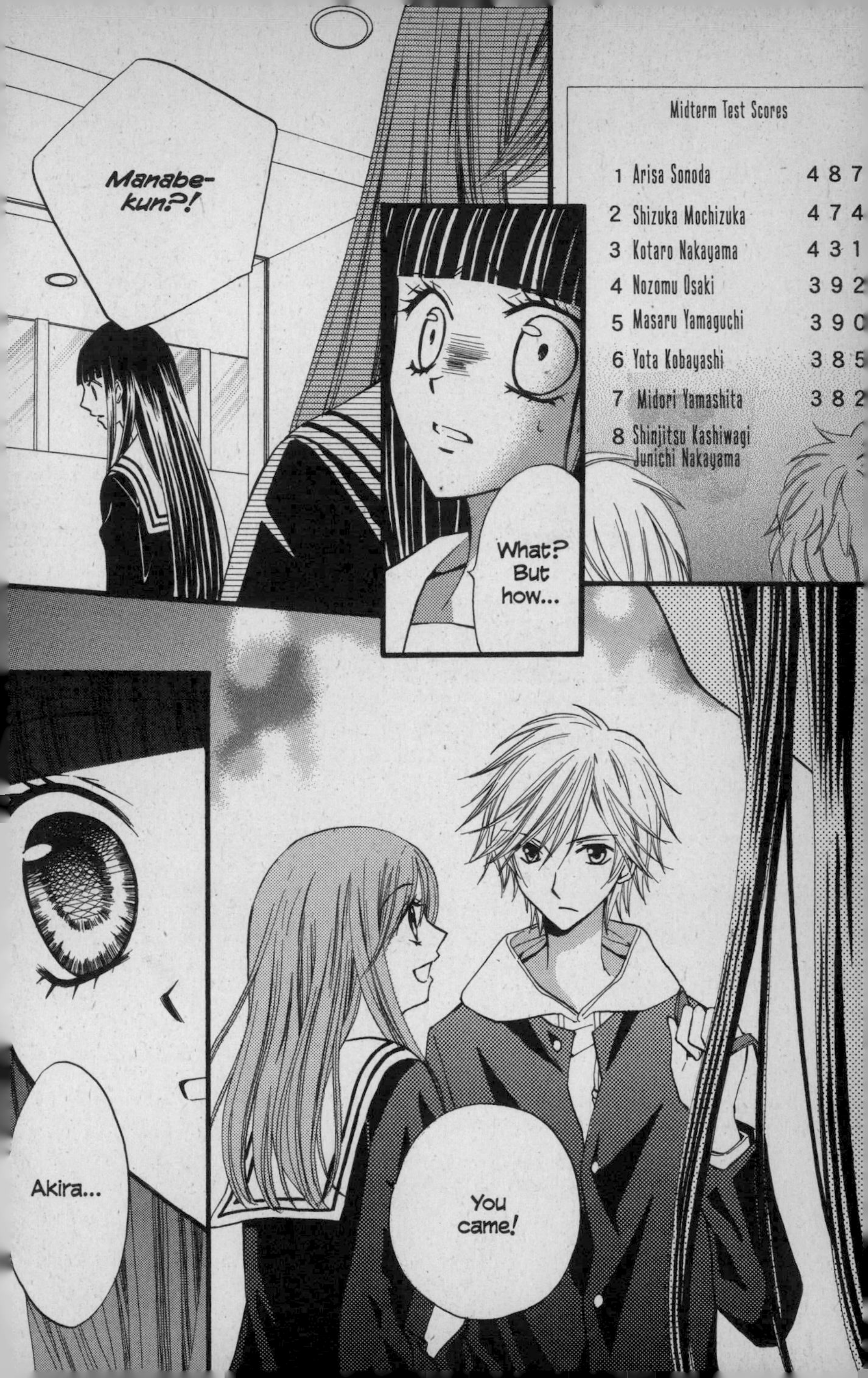
Midterm Test Scores
1 Arisa Sonoda 487
2 Shizuka Mochizuka 474
3 Kotaro Nakayama 431
4 Nozomu Osaki 392
5 Masaru Yamaguchi 390
6 Yota Kobayashi 385
7 Midori Yamashita 382
8 Shinjitsu Kashiwagi
Junichi Nakayama
What? But how...
Manabe-kun?!
You came!
Akira...

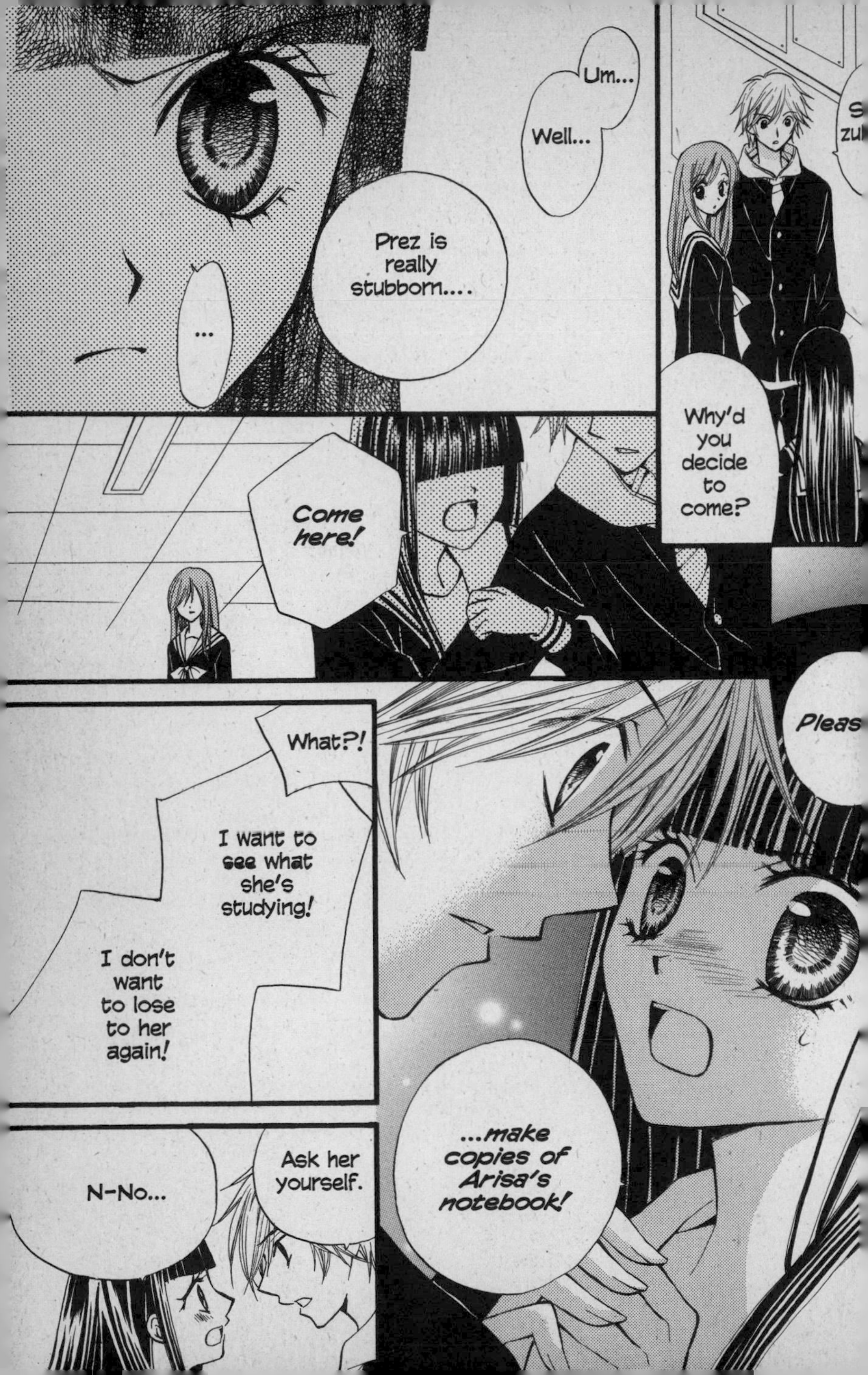

Why'd you decide to come?
Um...
Well...
Prez is really stubborn....
...
Come here!
Pleas
...make copies of Arisa's notebook!
What?!
I want to see what she's studying!
I don't want to lose to her again!
Ask her yourself.
N-No...

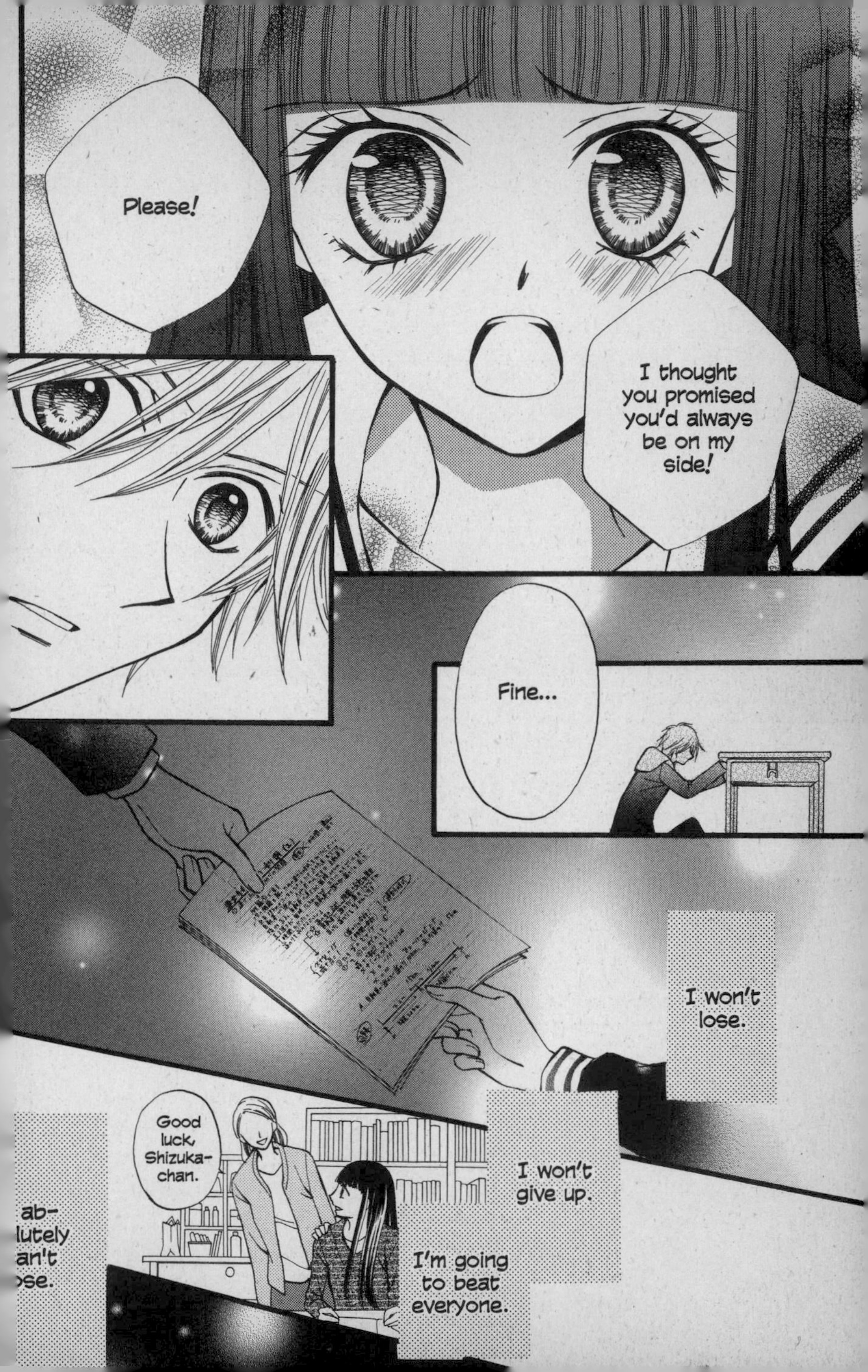
Please!
I thought you promised you'd always be on my side!
Fine...
I won't lose.
I won't give up.
Good luck, Shizuka-chan.
I'm going to beat everyone.
ab- lutely an't ose.

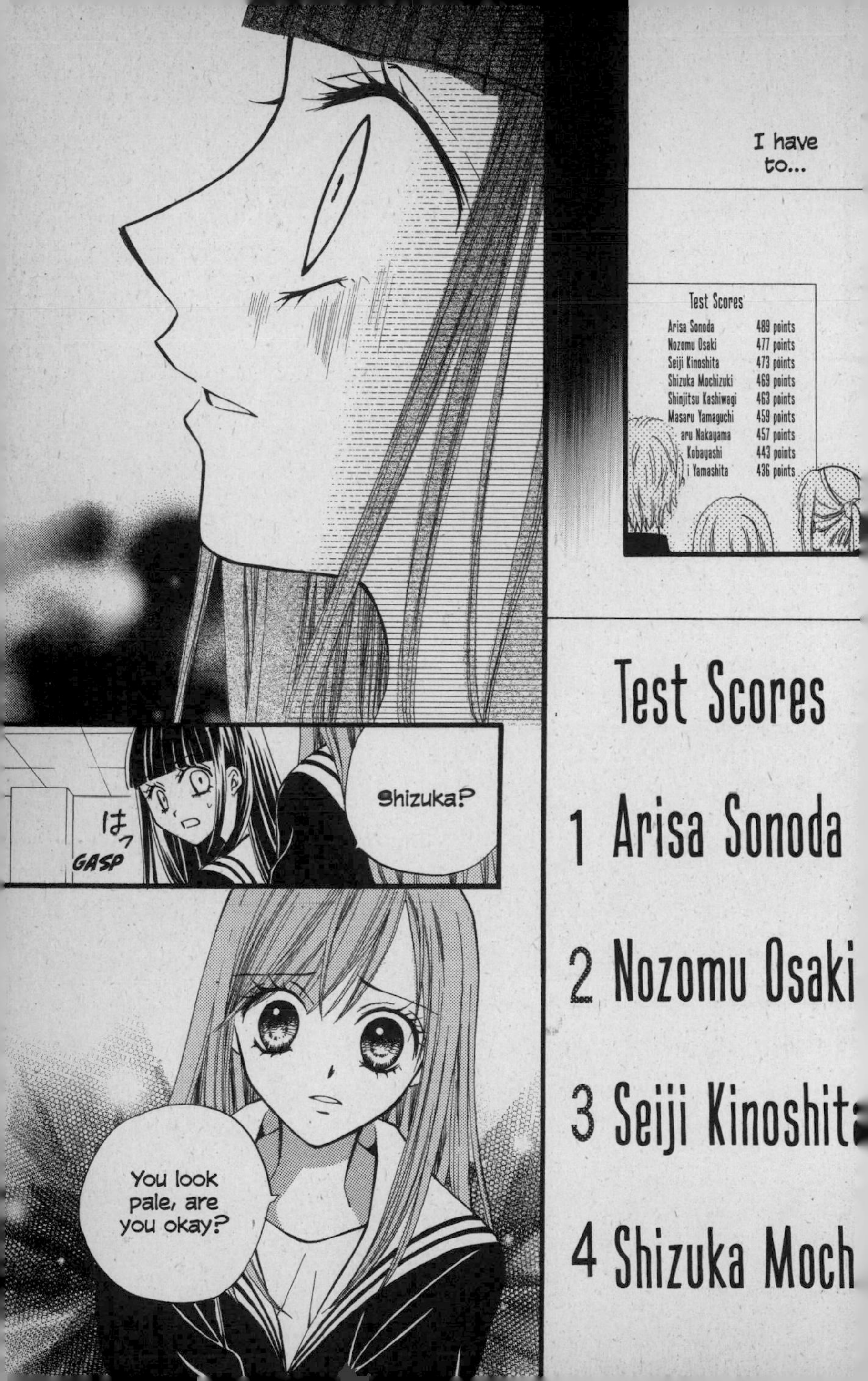
I have to...
Test Scores
Arisa Sonoda 489 points
Nozomu Osaki 477 points
Seiji Kinoshita 473 points
Shizuka Mochizuki 469 points
Shinjitsu Kashiwagi 463 points
Masaru Yamaguchi 459 points
aru Nakayama 457 points
Kobayashi 443 points
i Yamashita 436 points
Test Scores
1 Arisa Sonoda
2 Nozomu Osaki
3 Seiji Kinoshit
4 Shizuka Moch
Shizuka?
はっ
GASP
You look pale, are you okay?

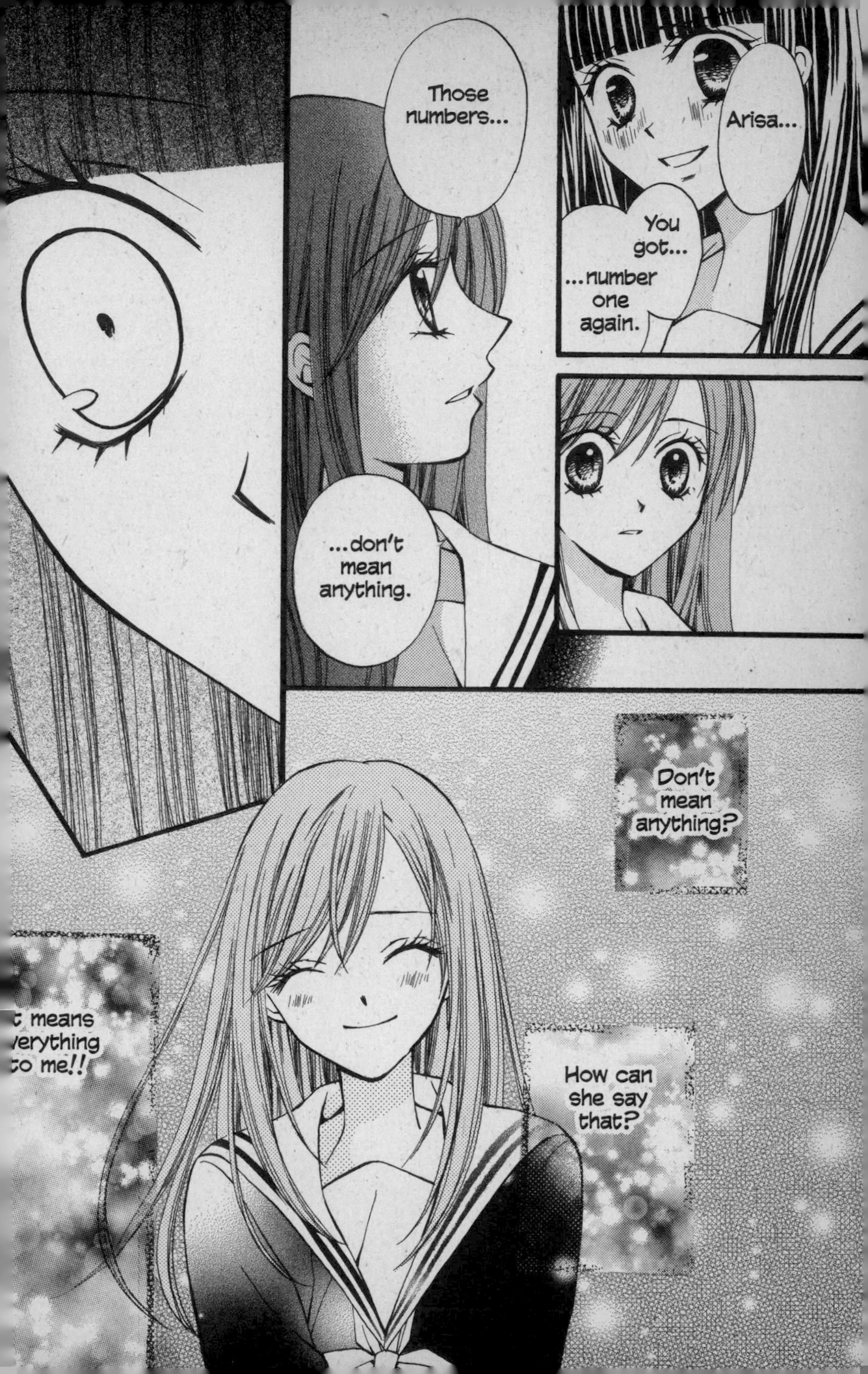

Arisa...
You got... ...number one again.
Those numbers...
...don't mean anything.
Don't mean anything?
How can she say that?
t means verything to me!!

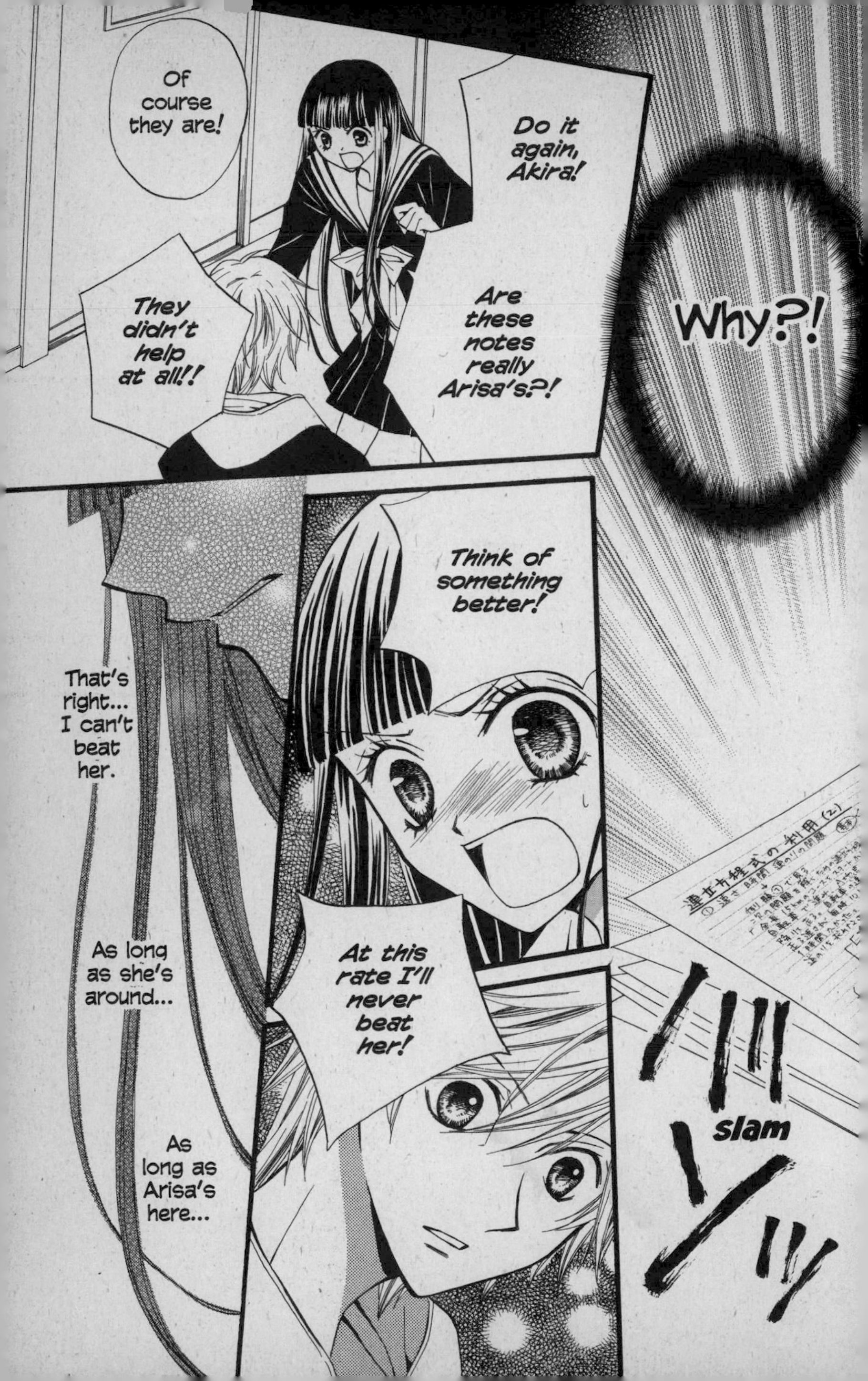
Do it again, Akira!
Are these notes really Arisa's?!
Of course they are!
They didn't help at all!!
Why?!
slam
Think of something better!
At this rate I'll never beat her!
That's right... I can't beat her.
As long as she's around...
As long as Arisa's here...

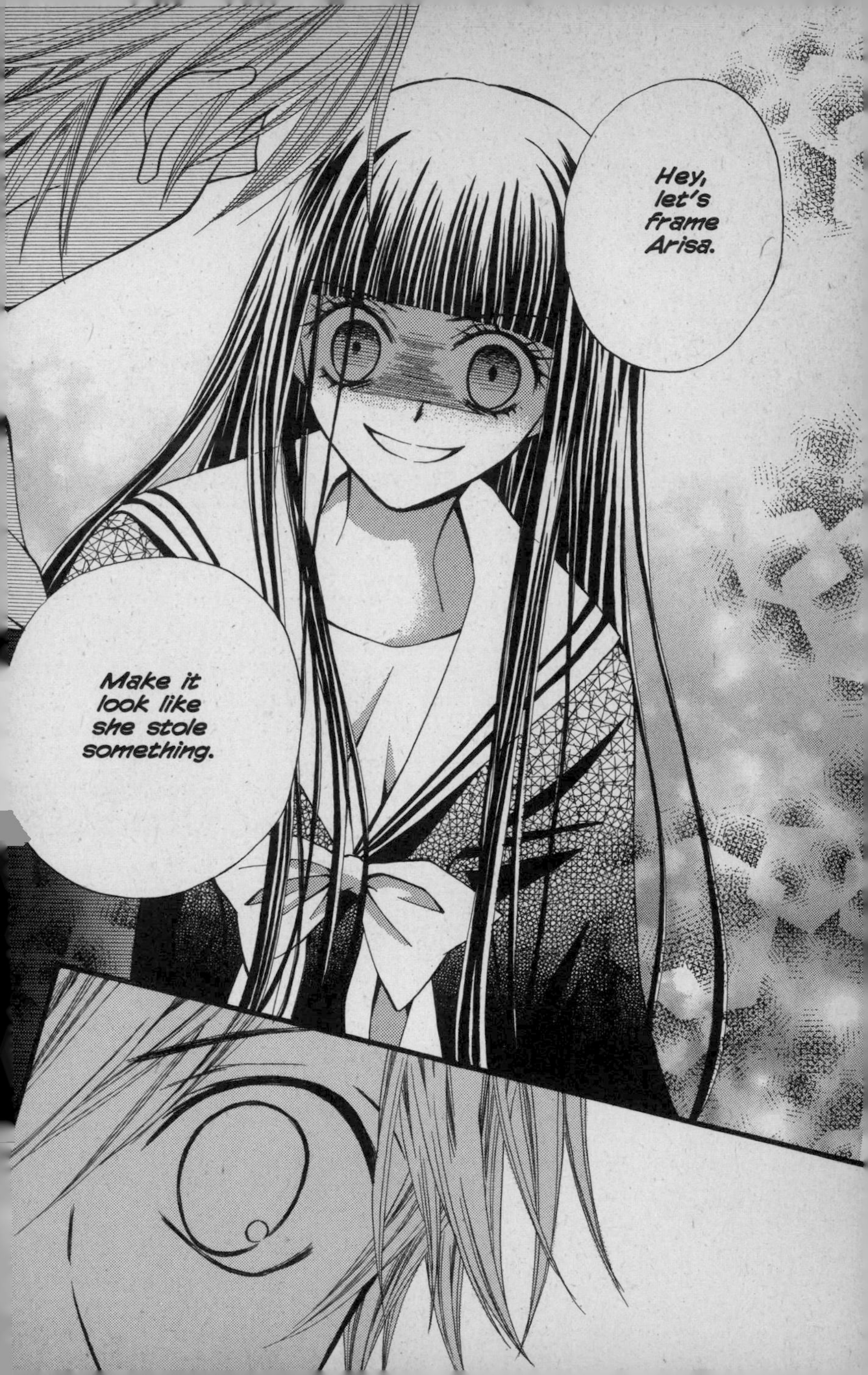
Hey, let's frame Arisa.
Make it look like she stole something.

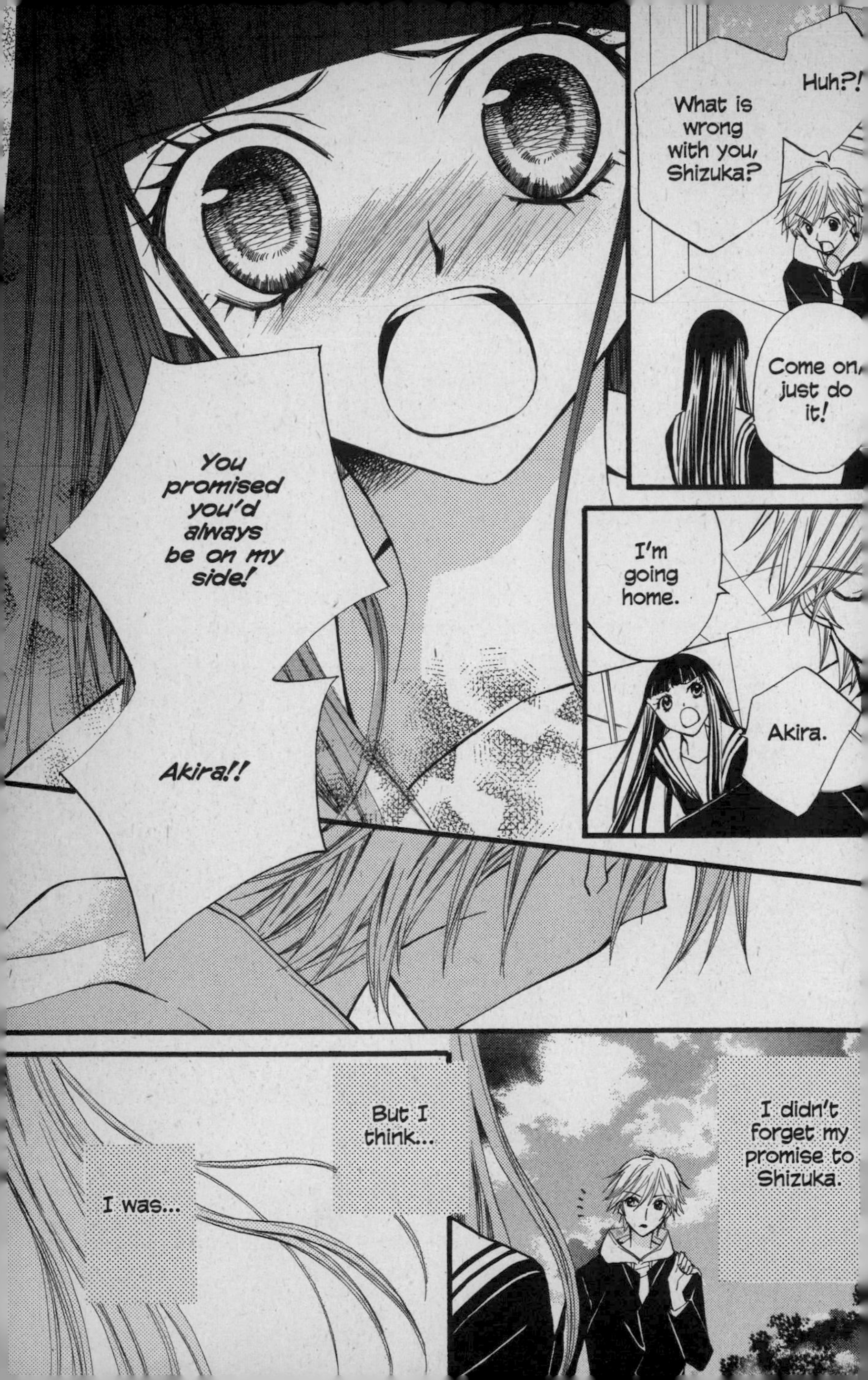
Huh?!
What is wrong with you, Shizuka?
Come on, just do it!
I'm going home.
Akira.
You promised you'd always be on my side!
Akira!!
I didn't forget my promise to Shizuka.
But I think...
I was...

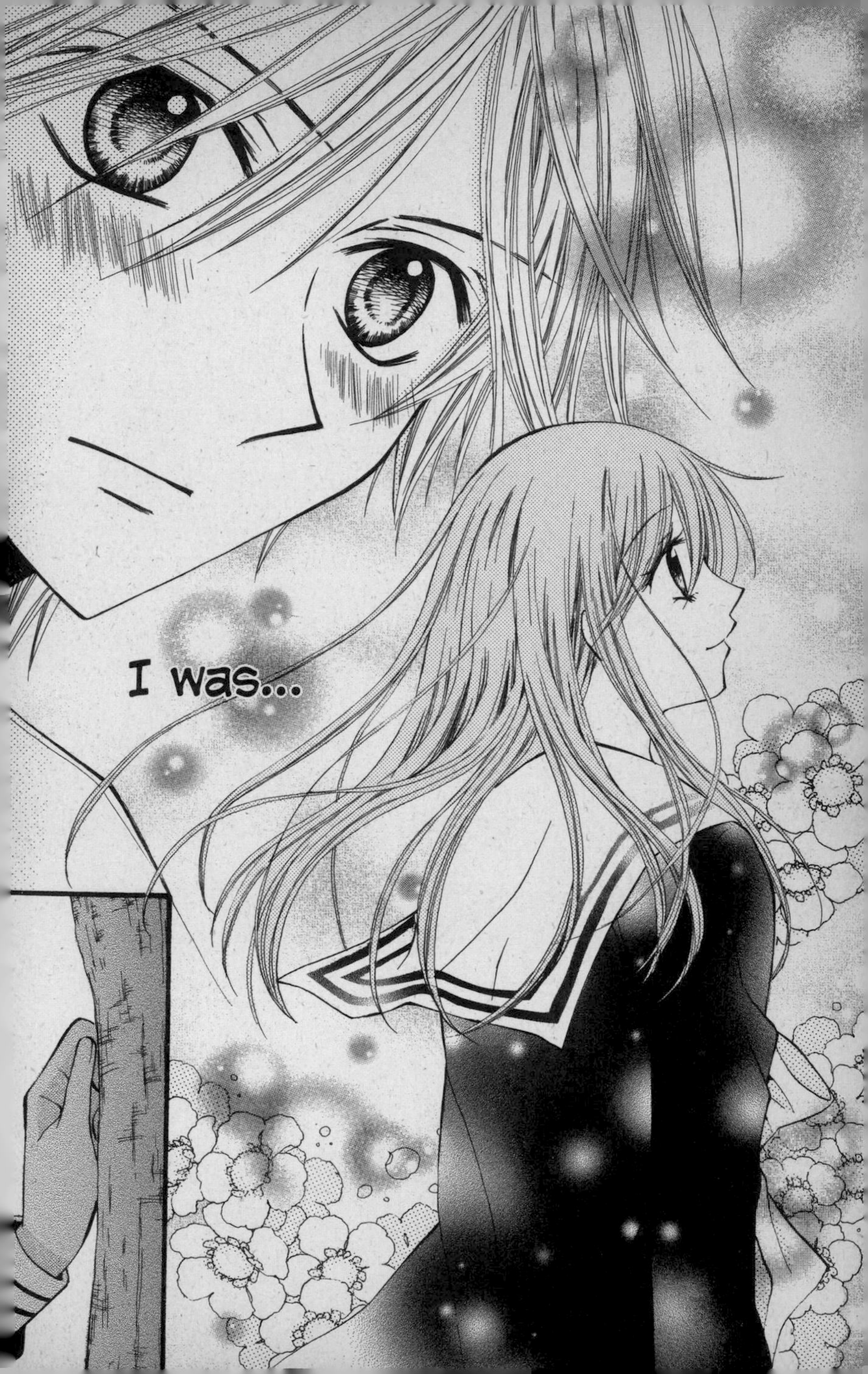
I was...

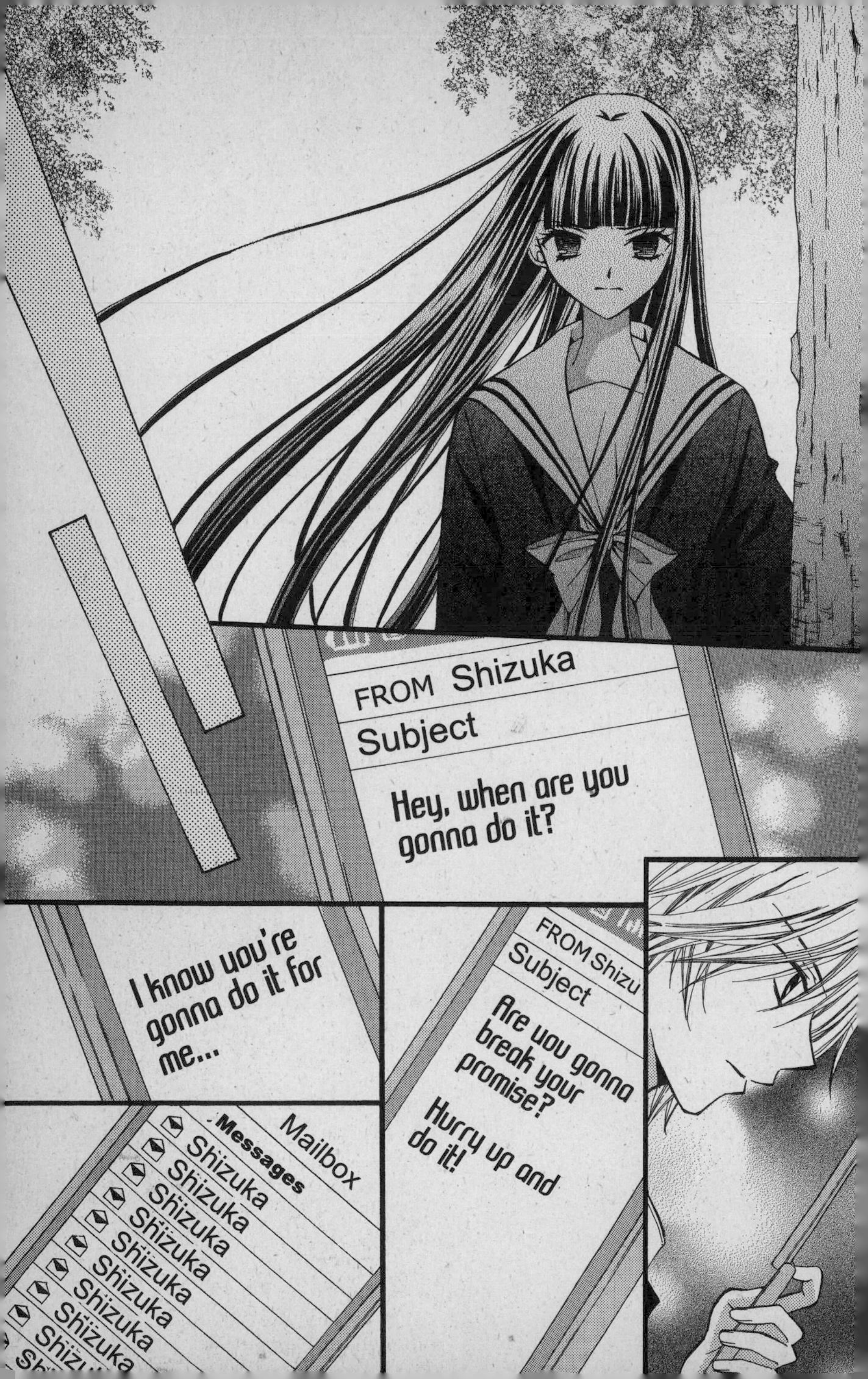
FROM Shizuka
Subject
Hey, when are you gonna do it?
FROM Shizu
Subject
Are you gonna break your promise?
Hurry up and do it!
I know you're gonna do it for me...
Mailbox
Messages
Shizuka
Shizuka
Shizuka
Shizuka
Shizuka
Shizuka
Shizuka
Shizuka

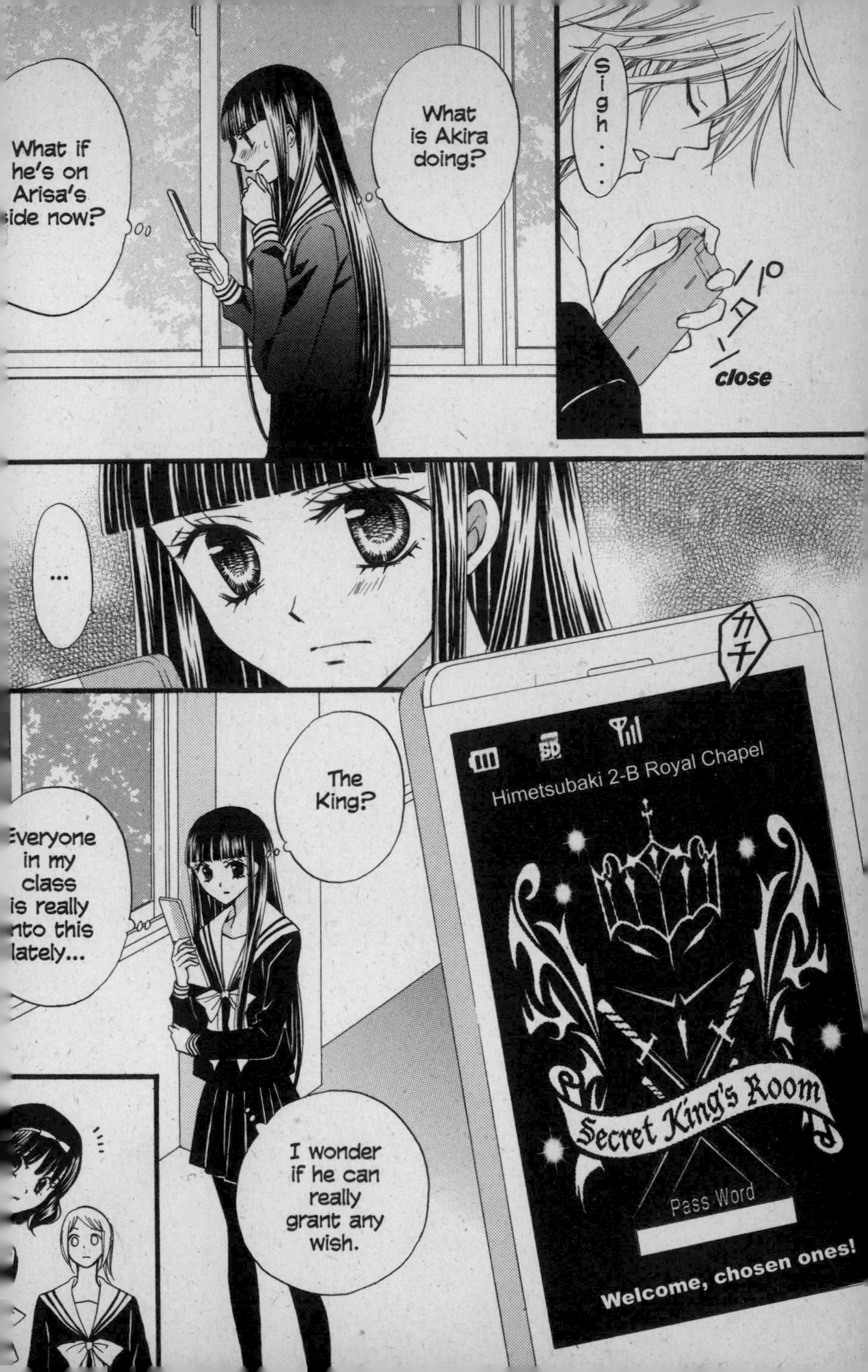
Sigh...
パタン
close
What is Akira doing?
What if he's on Arisa's ide now?
...
カチ
Himetsubaki 2-B Royal Chapel
Secret King's Room
Pass Word
Welcome, chosen ones!
The King?
Everyone in my class is really nto this lately...
I wonder if he can really grant any wish.

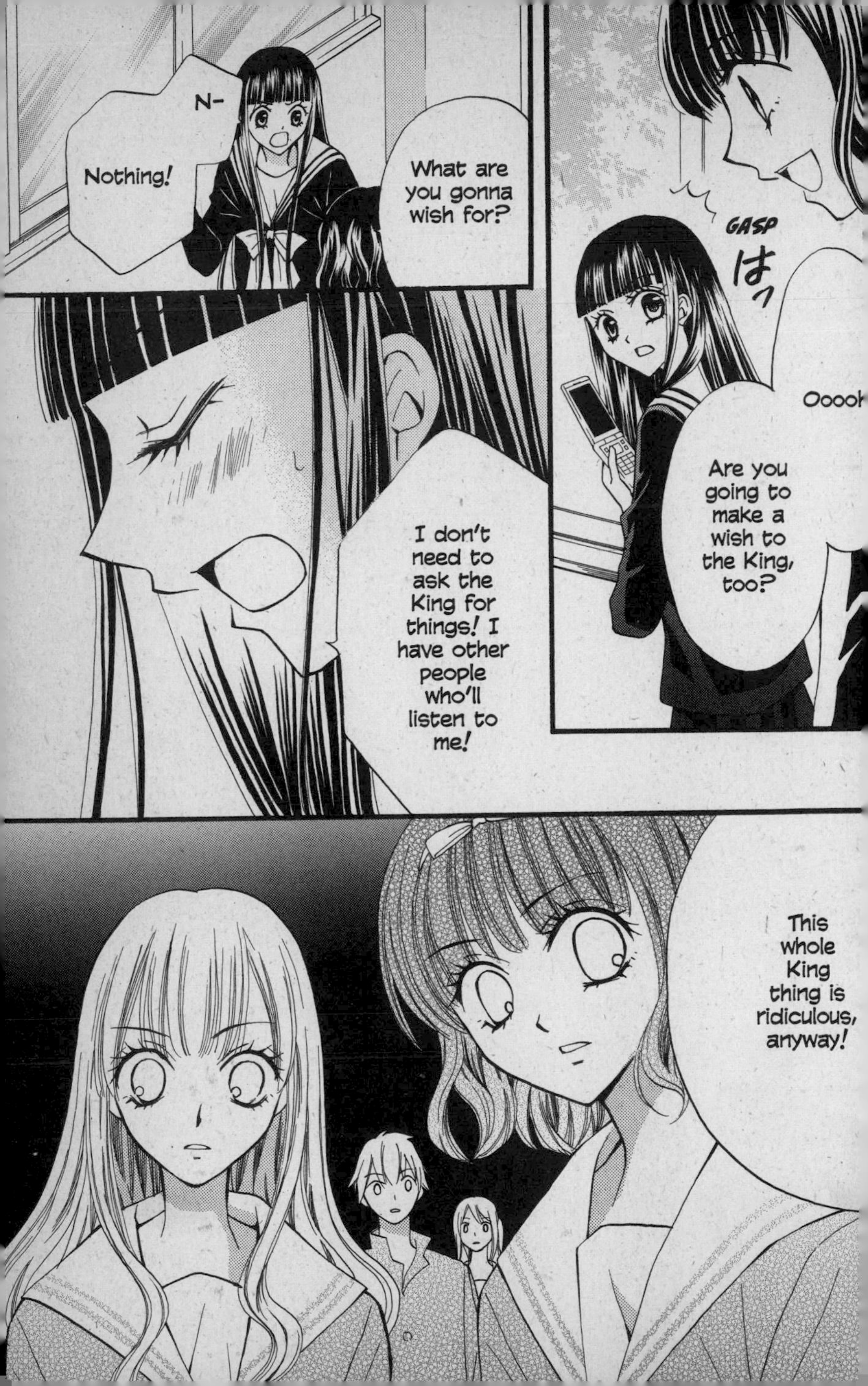
GASP
は
Oooo
Are you going to make a wish to the King, too?
What are you gonna wish for?
N-
Nothing!
I don't need to ask the King for things! I have other people who'll listen to me!
This whole King thing is ridiculous, anyway!

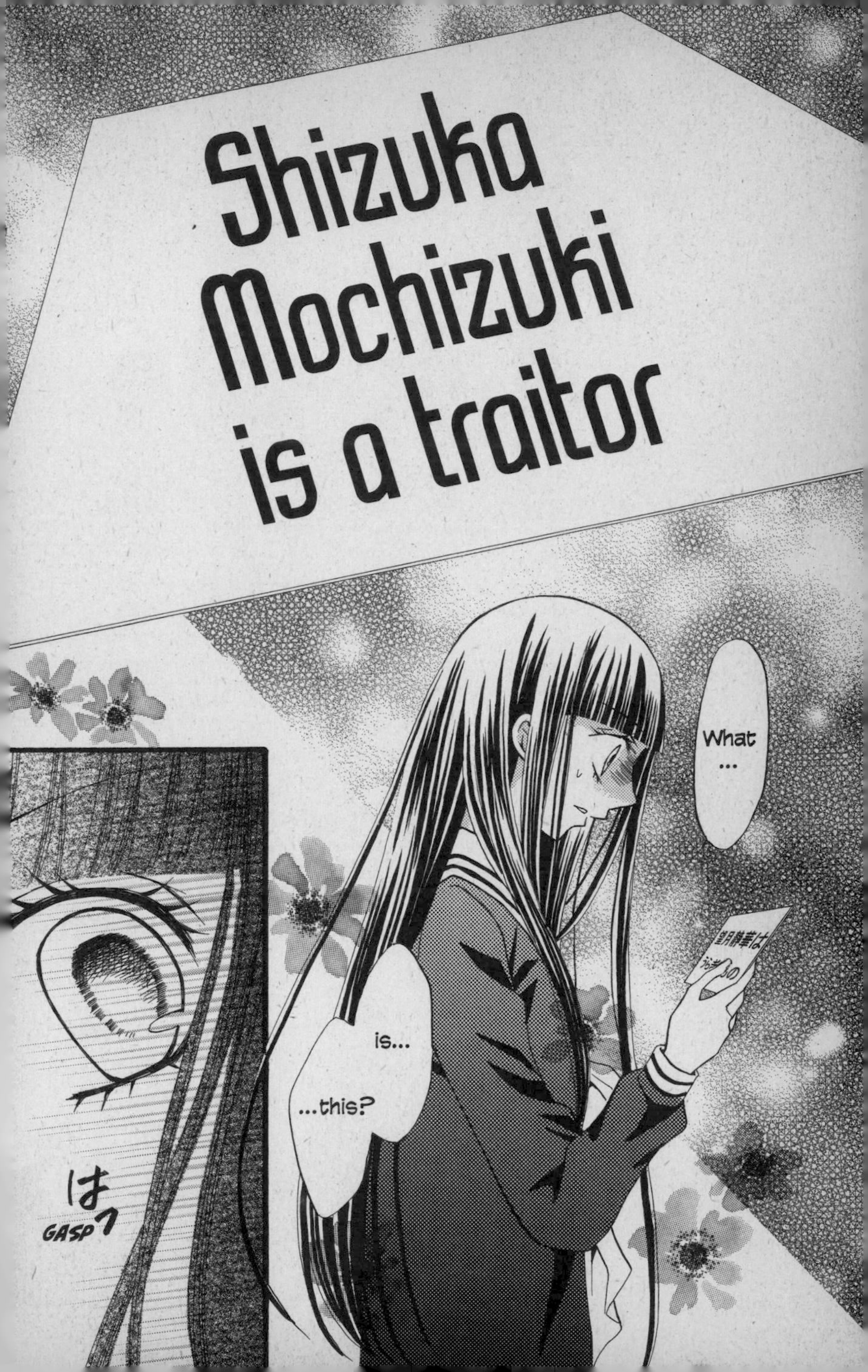
Shizuka Mochizuki is a traitor
What...
is...
...this?
はっ
GASP

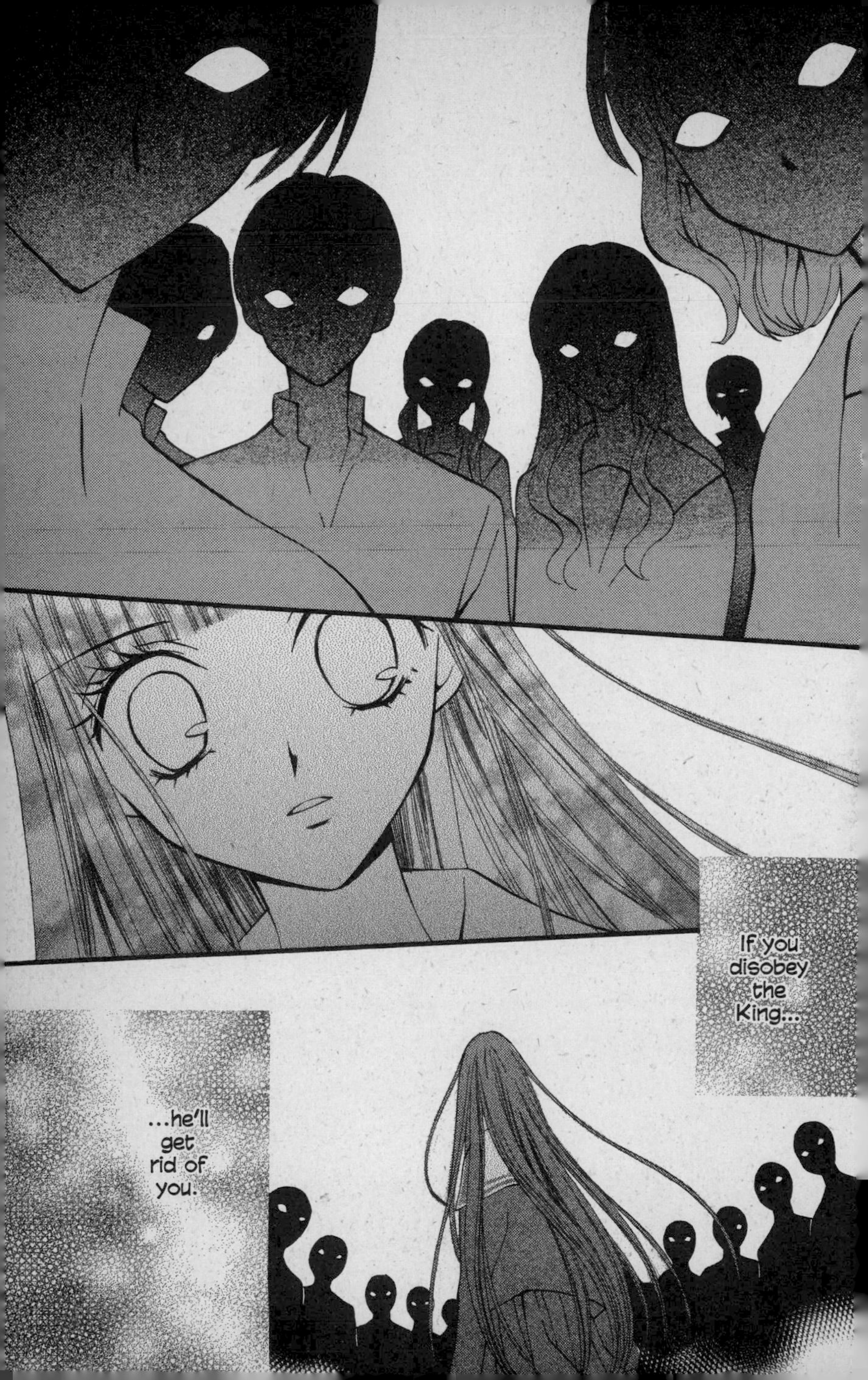
If you disobey the King...
...he'll get rid of you.

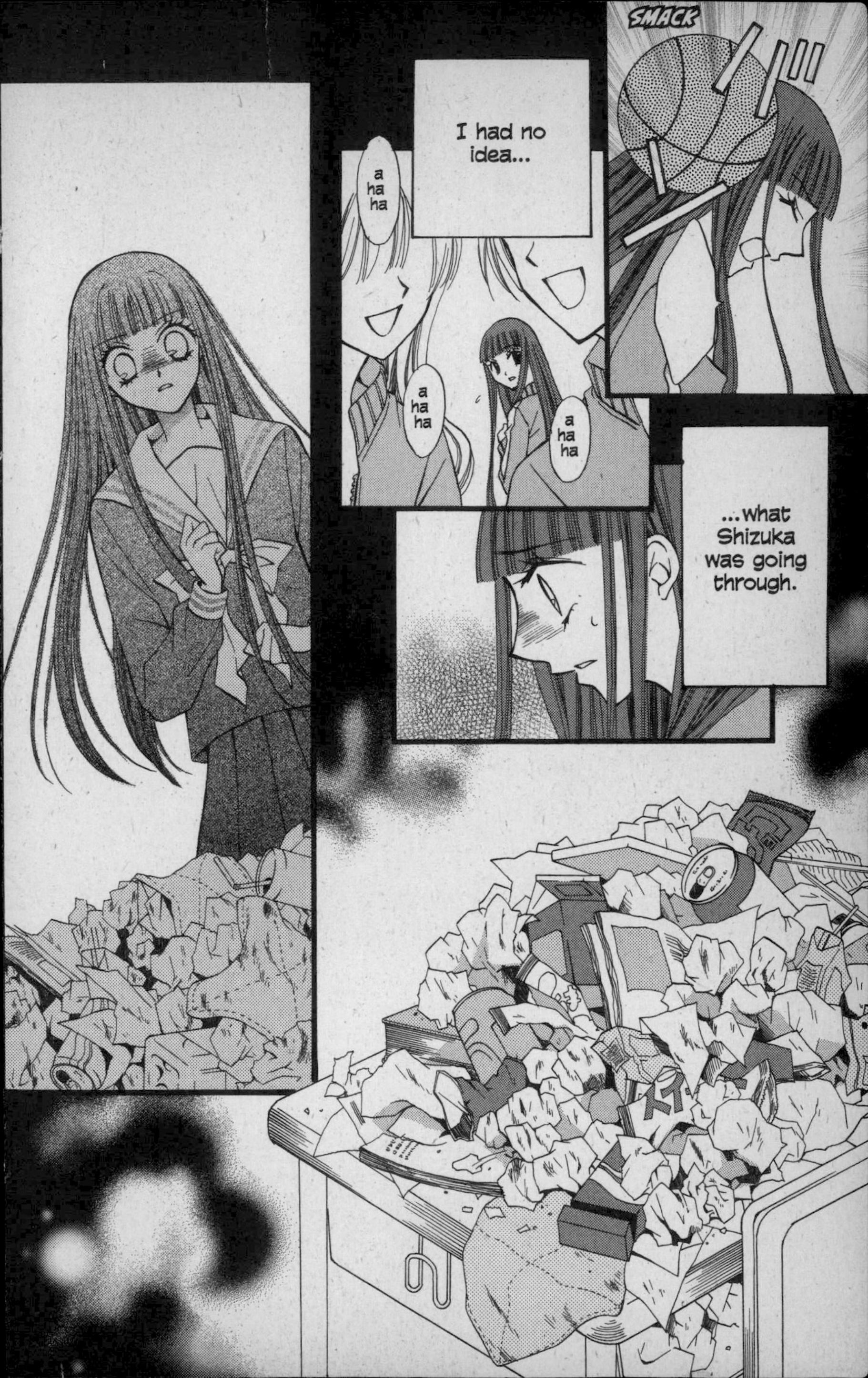
SMACK
I had no idea...
a ha ha
a ha ha
a ha ha
...what Shizuka was going through.

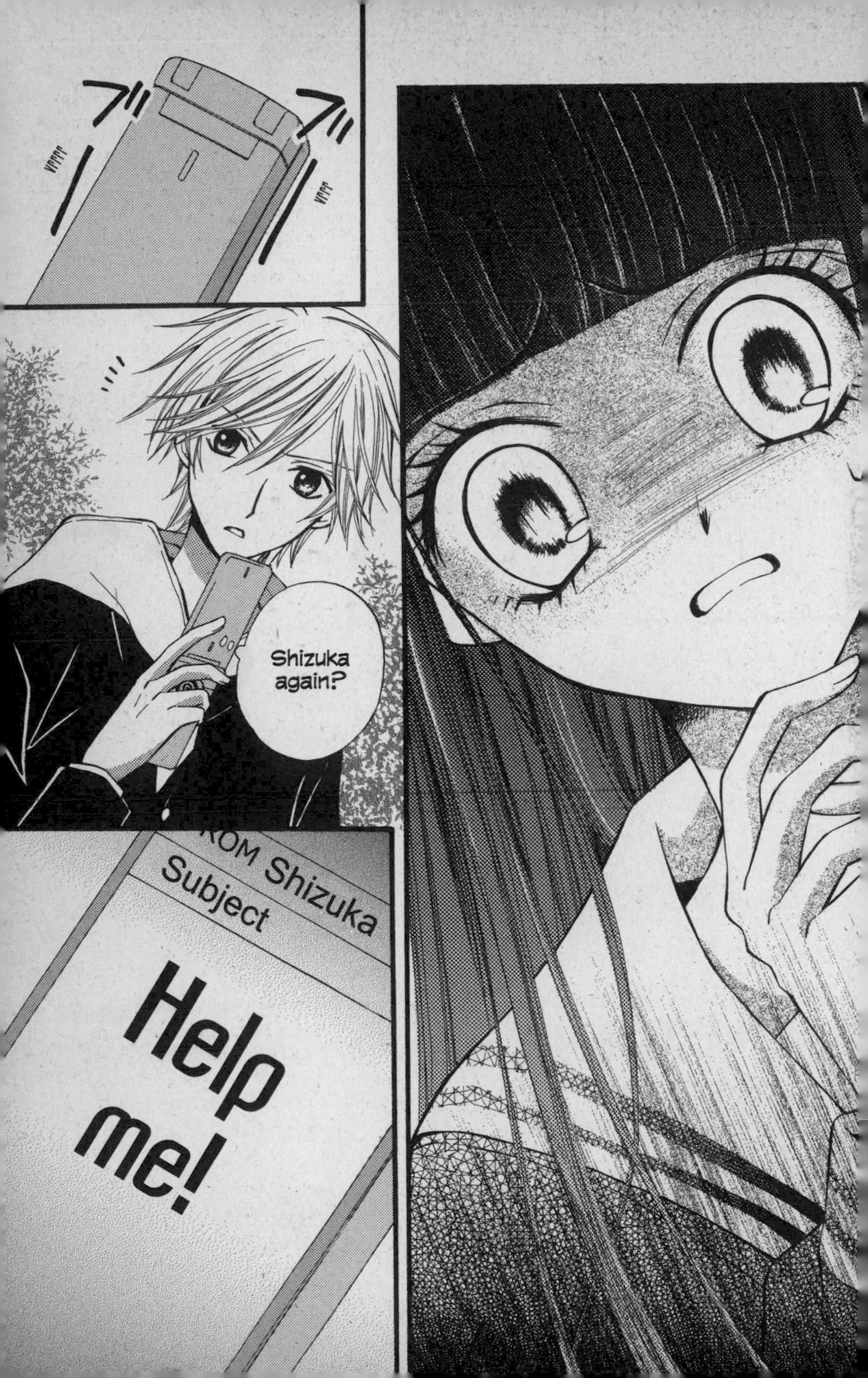
VRRR
VRRRR
Shizuka again?
ROM Shizuka
Subject
Help me!

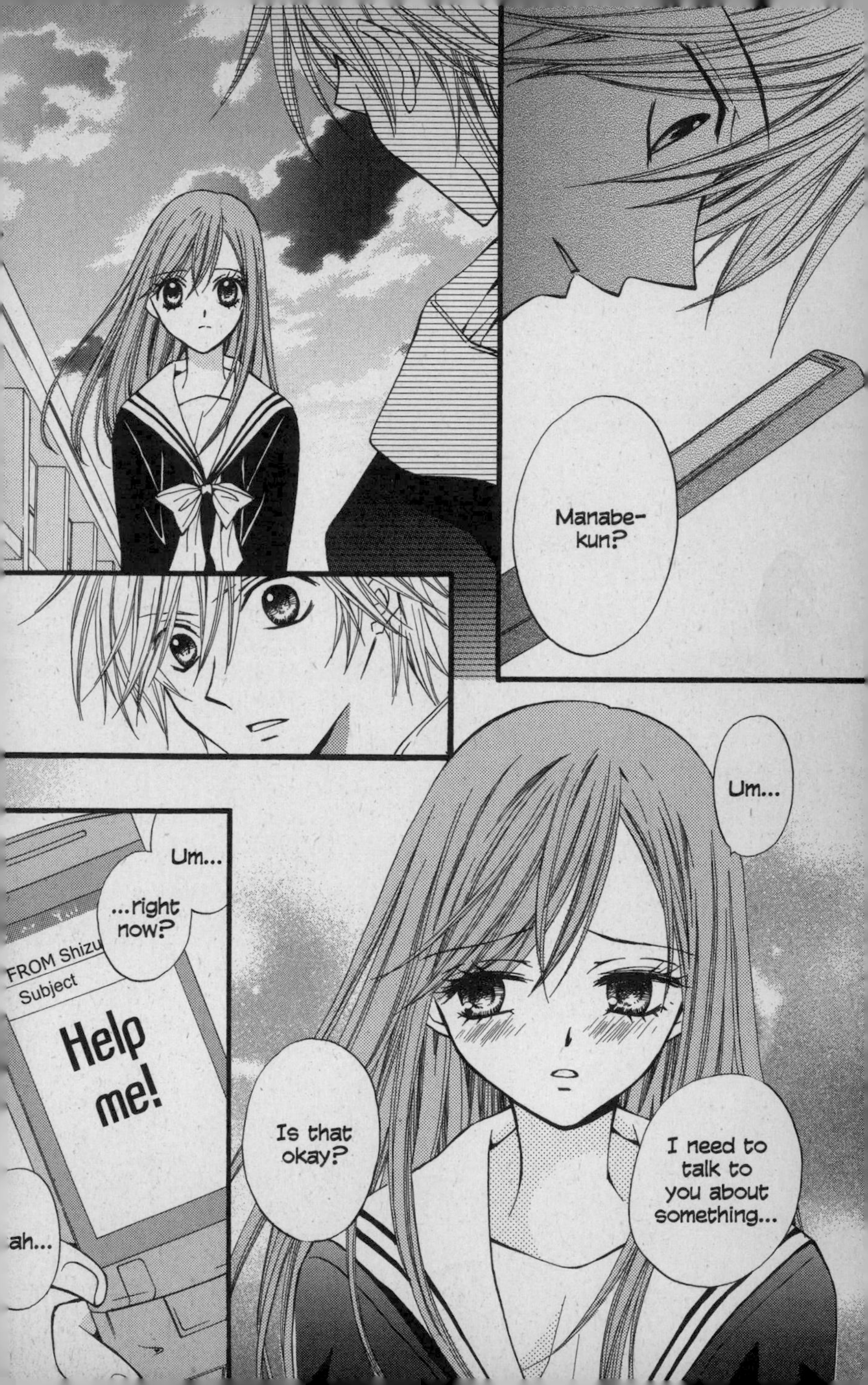

Manabe-kun?
Um...
I need to talk to you about something...
Is that okay?
Um...
...right now?
FROM Shizu
Subject
Help me!
ah...

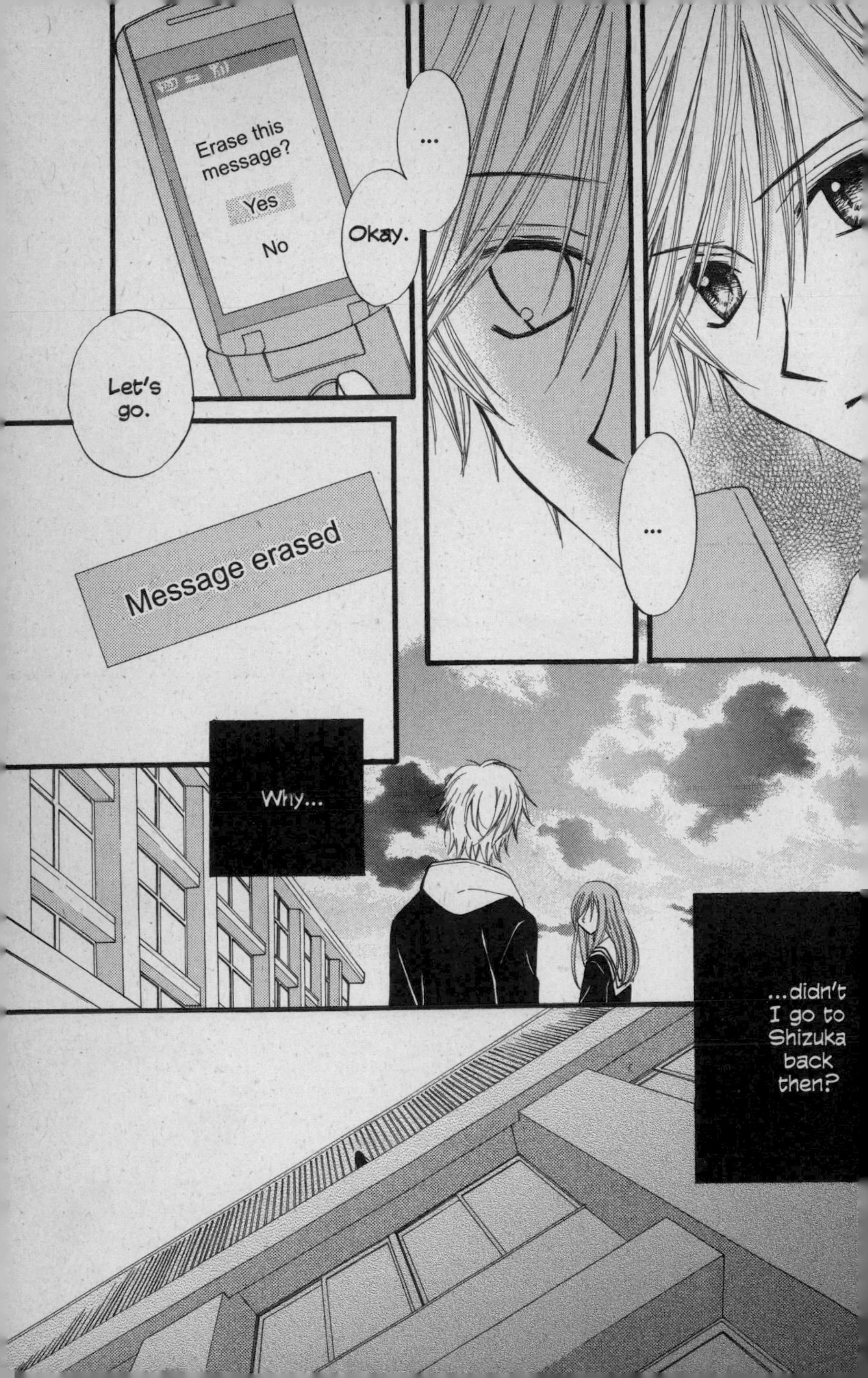
...
...
Okay.
Erase this message?
Yes
No
Let's go.
Message erased
Why...
...didn't I go to Shizuka back then?

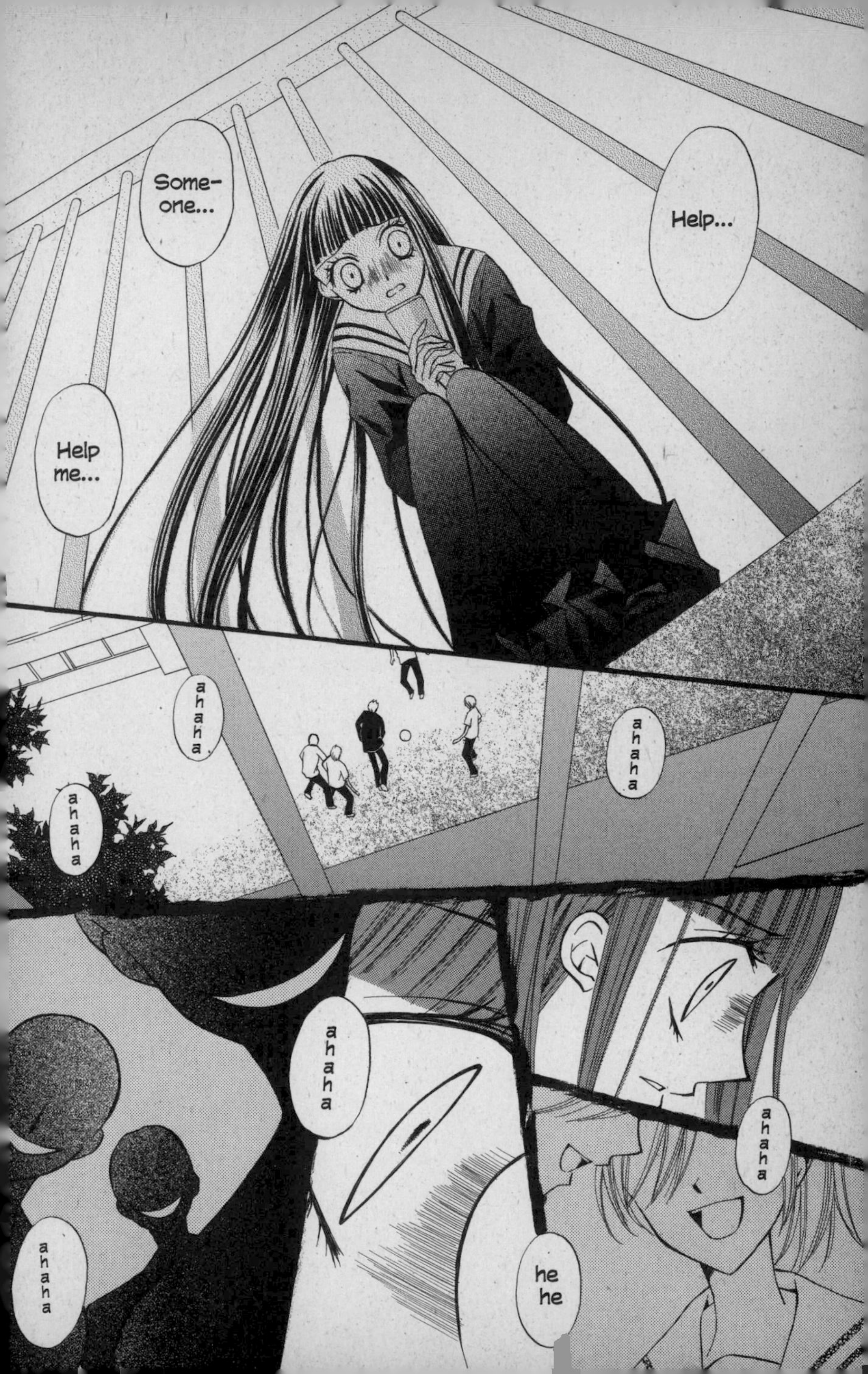
Help...
Some-one...
Help me...
ahaha
ahaha
ahaha
ahaha
ahaha
he he
ahaha

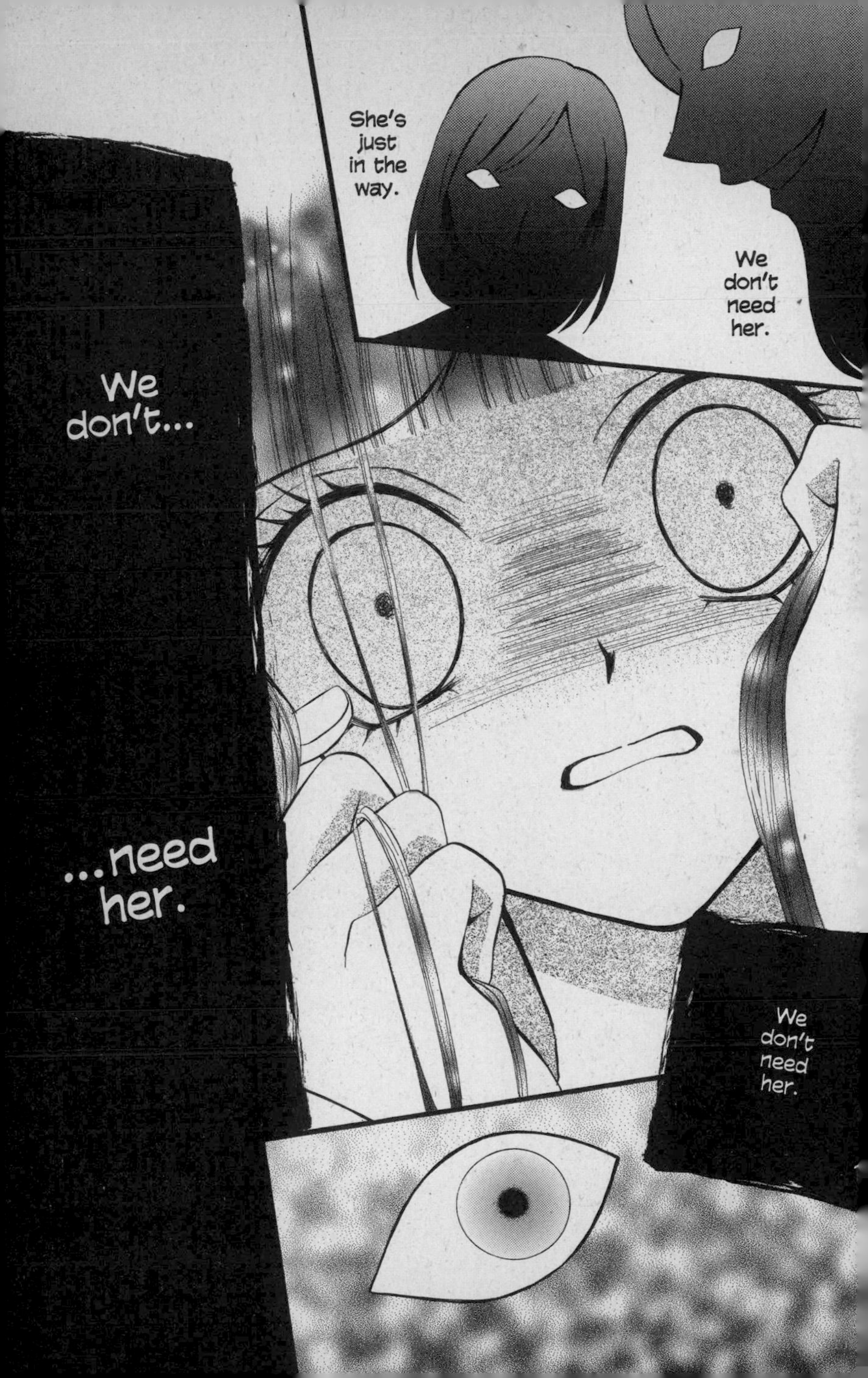
We don't need her.
She's just in the way.
We don't need her.
We don't...
...need her.

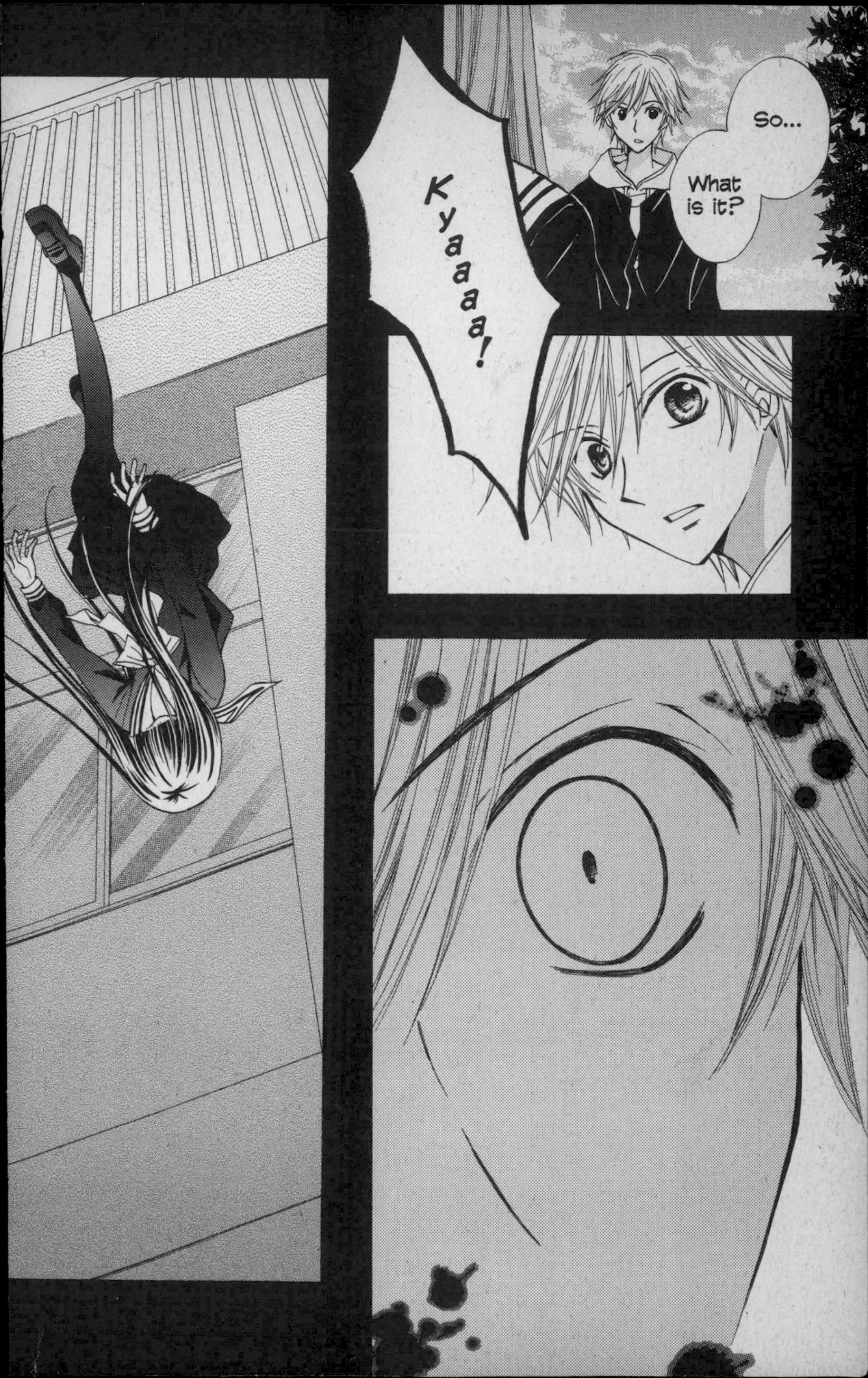
So...
What is it?
Kyaaaa!

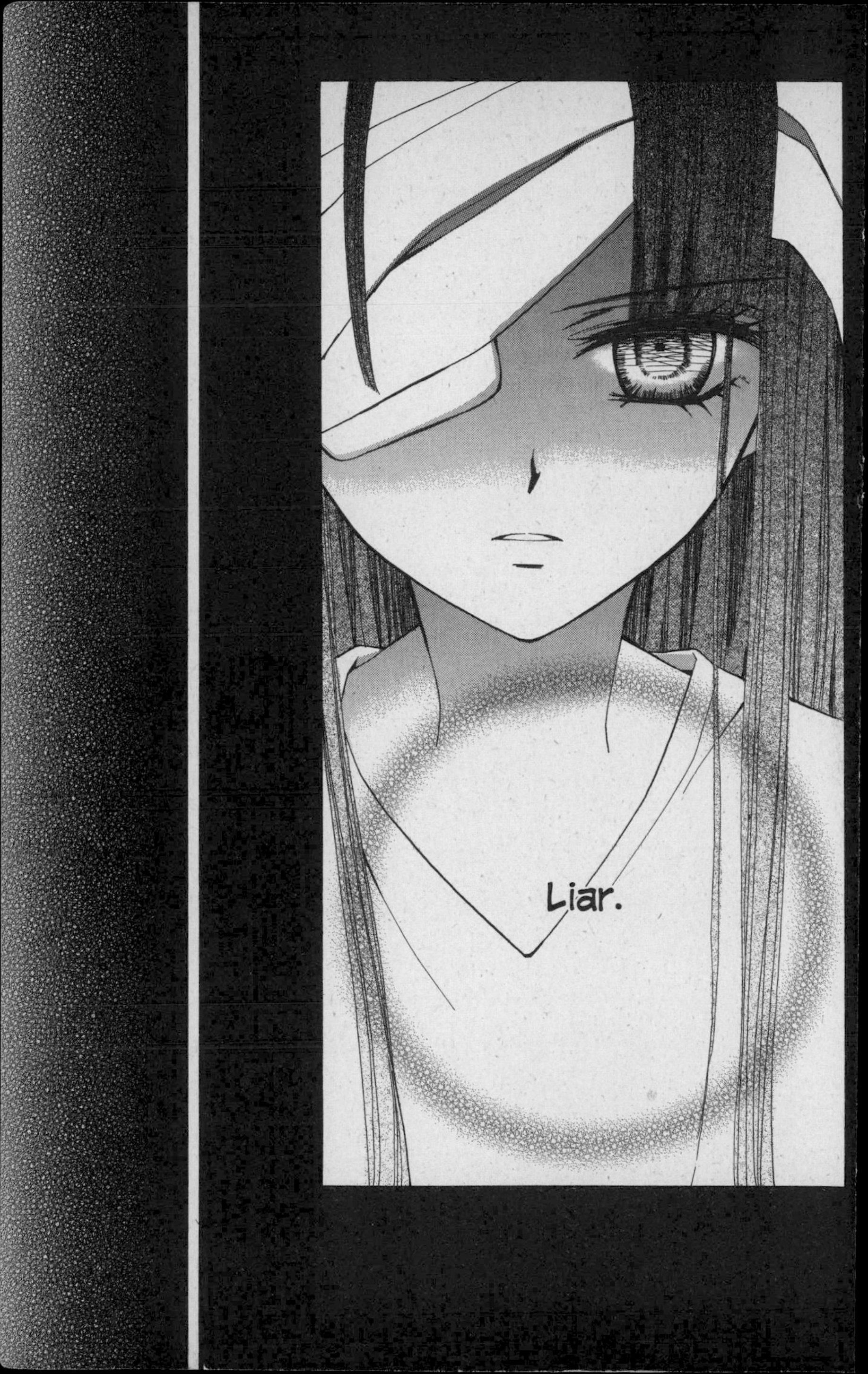
Liar.

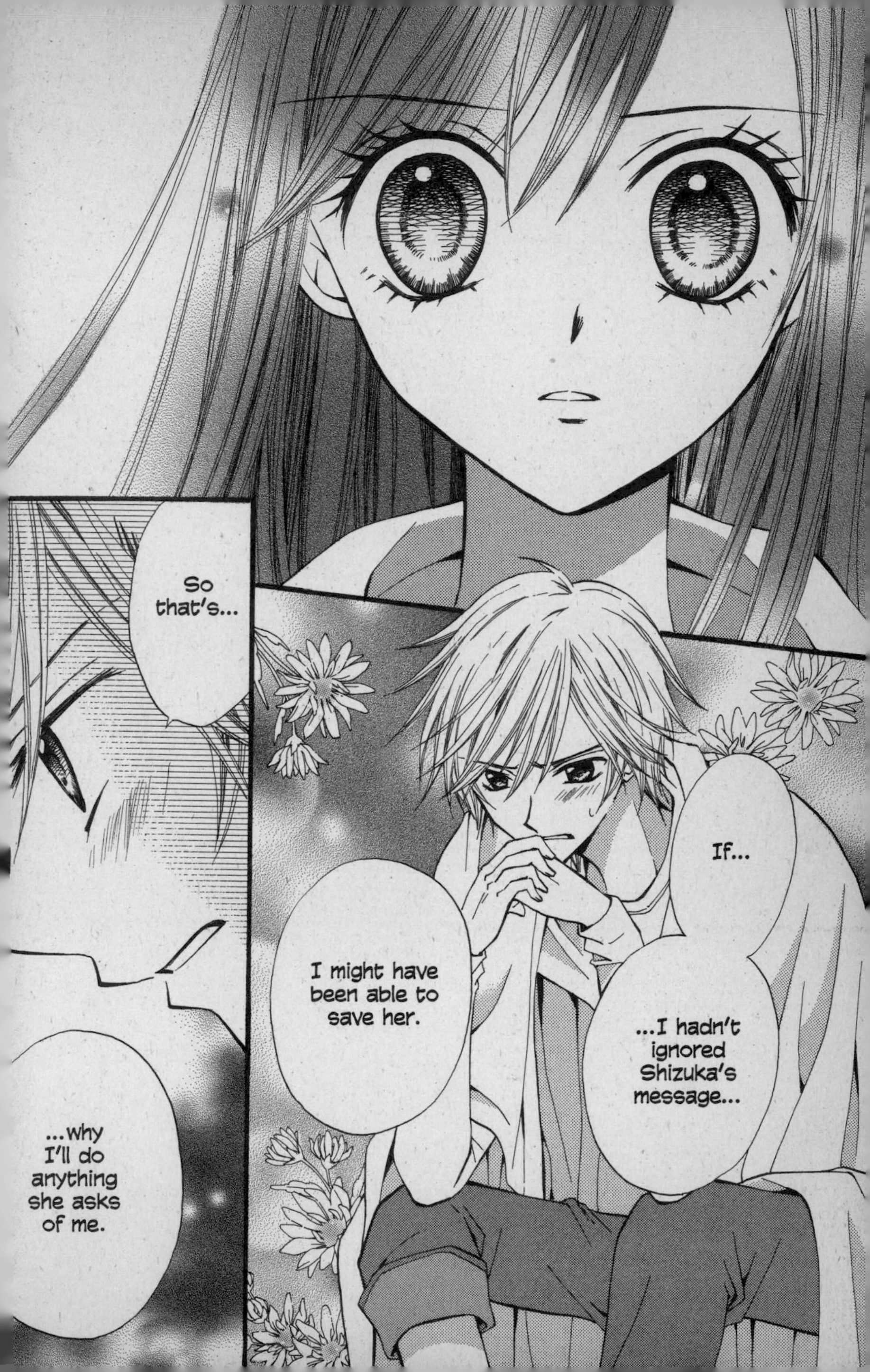
If...
...I hadn't ignored Shizuka's message...
I might have been able to save her.
So that's...
...why I'll do anything she asks of me.

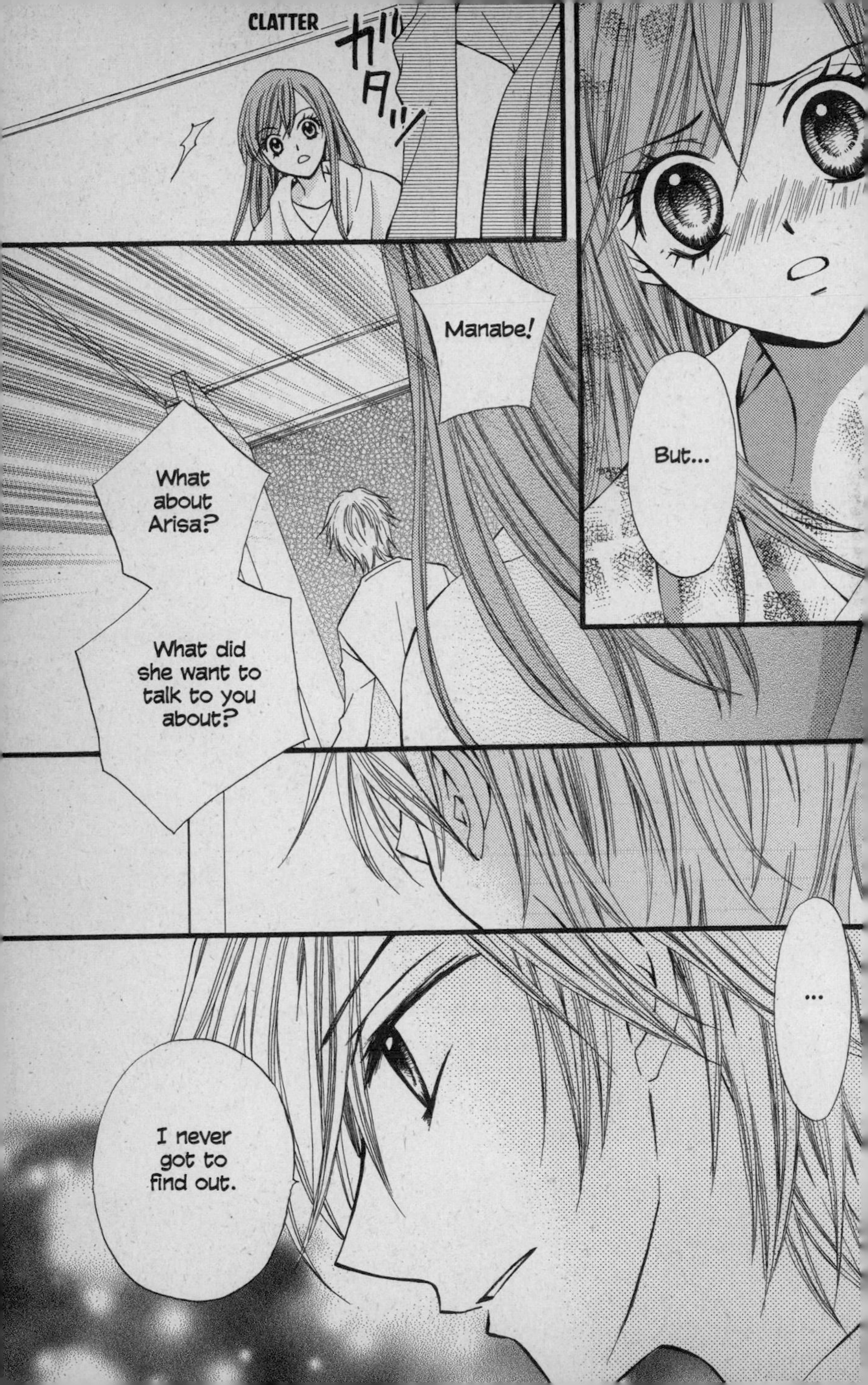
But...
CLATTER
ガタッ
Manabe!
What about Arisa?
What did she want to talk to you about?
...
I never got to find out.

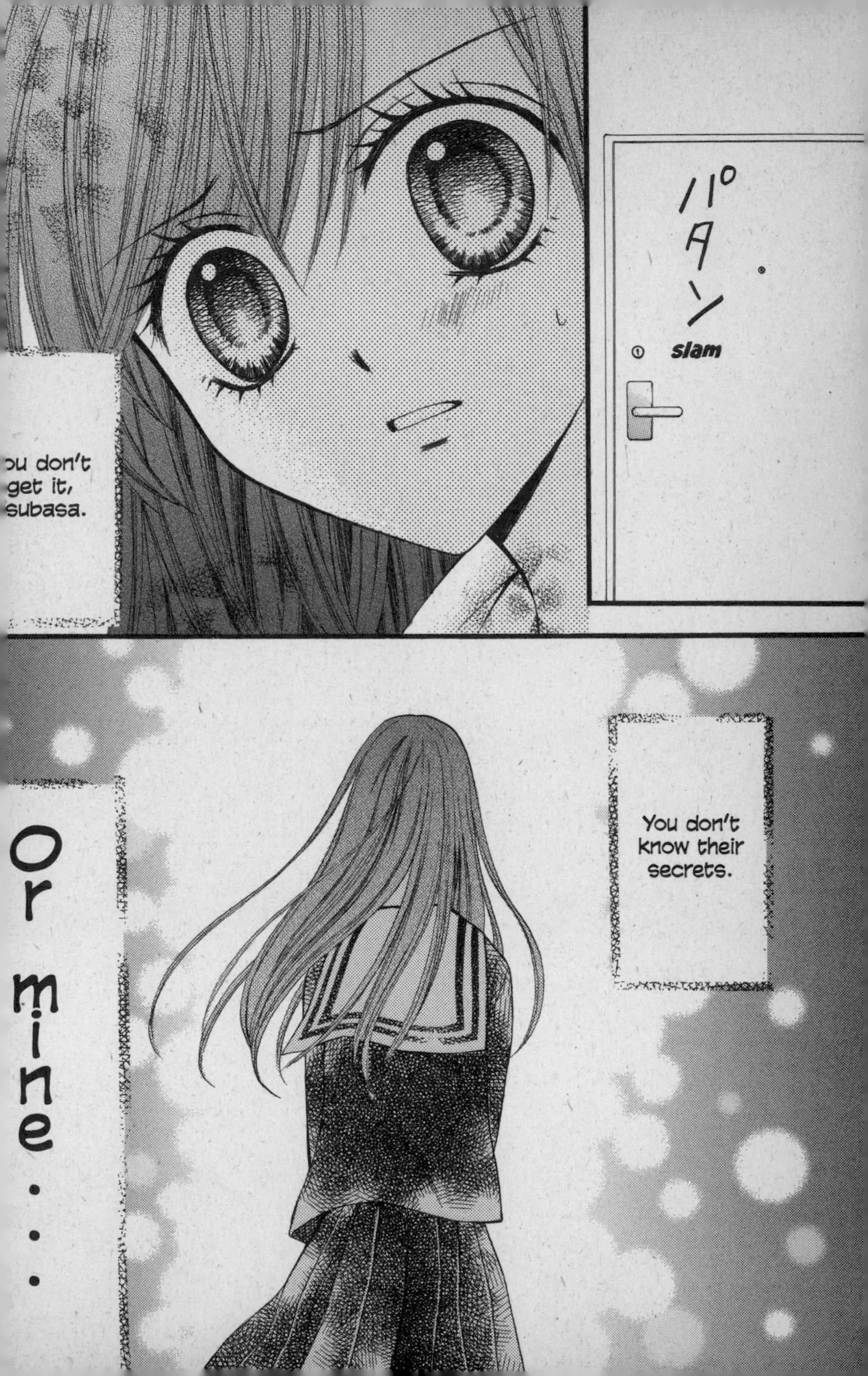
パタン
slam
ou don't get it, subasa.
You don't know their secrets.
Or mine...

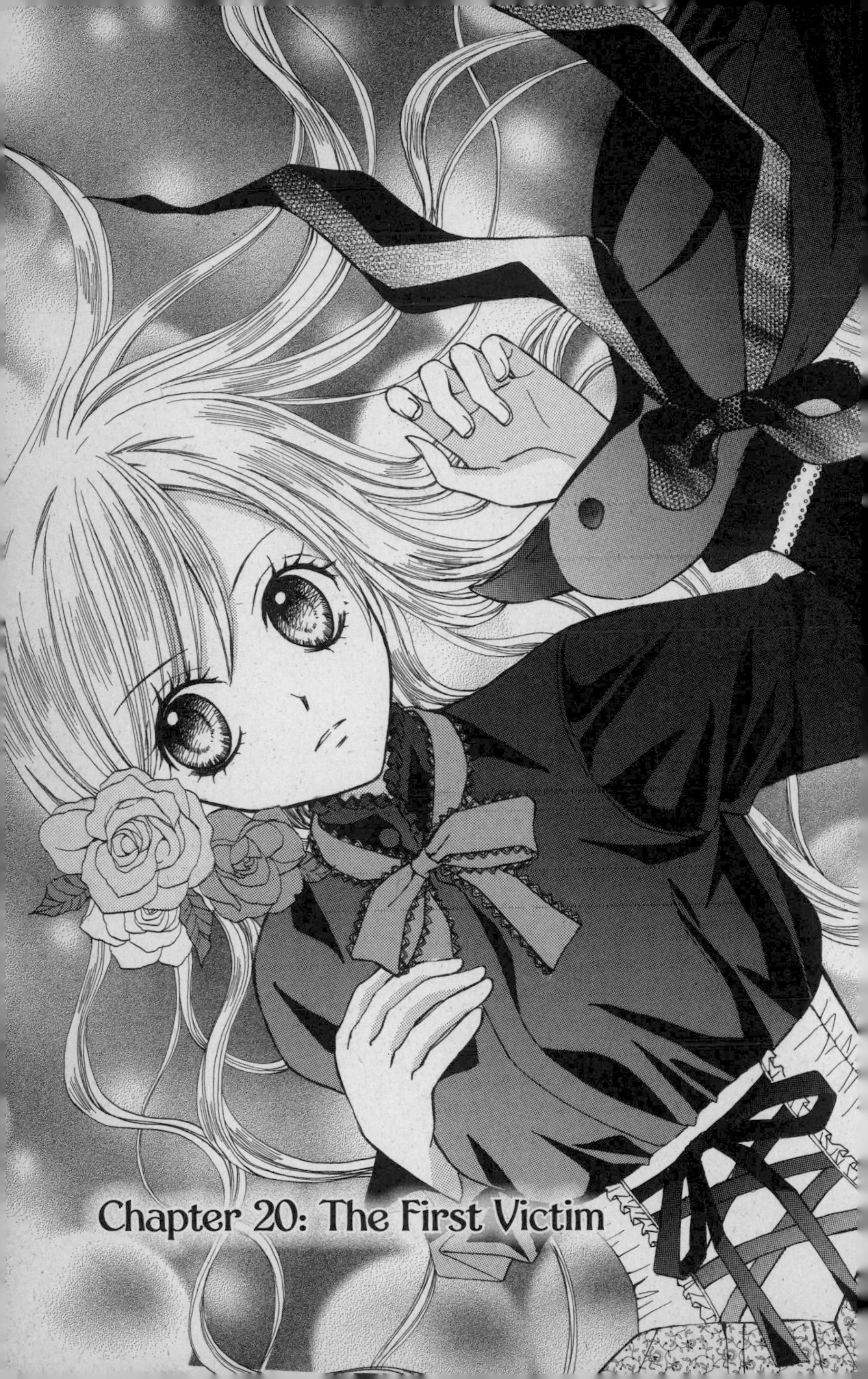

Chapter 20: The First Victim

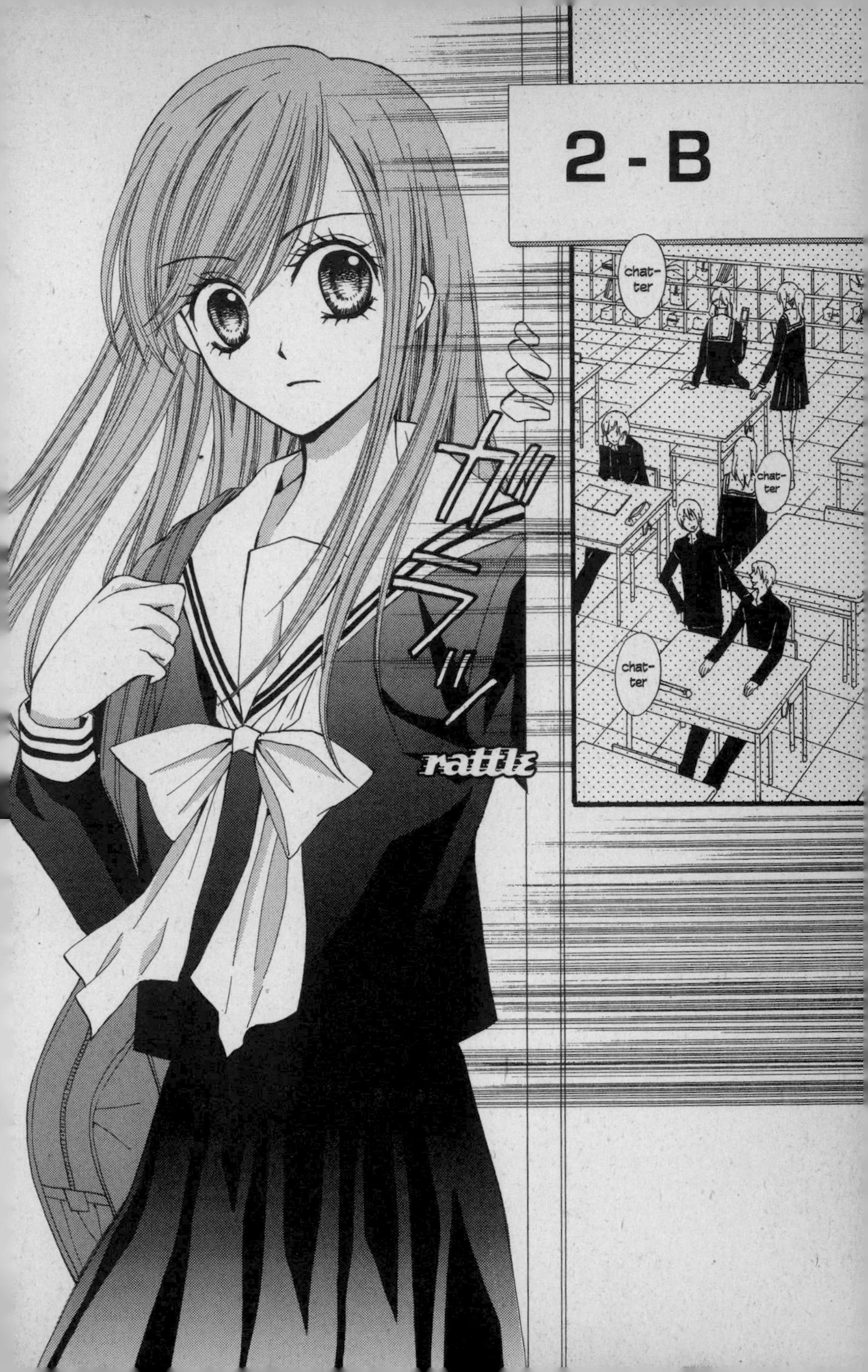
2 - B
chat-ter
chat-ter
chat-ter
rattle

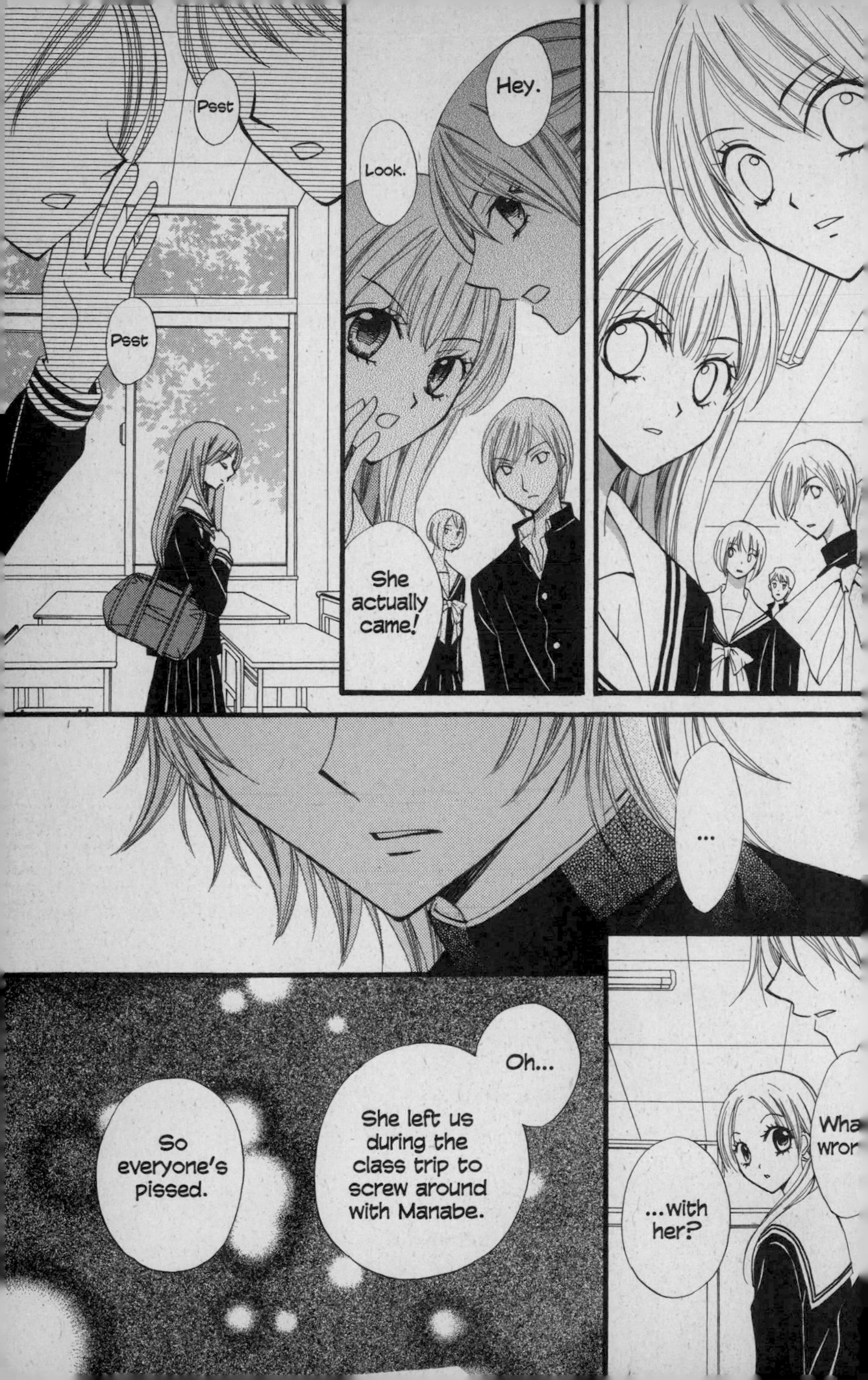

Hey.
Look.
She actually came!
Psst
Psst
...
...with her?
Oh...
She left us during the class trip to screw around with Manabe.
So everyone's pissed.

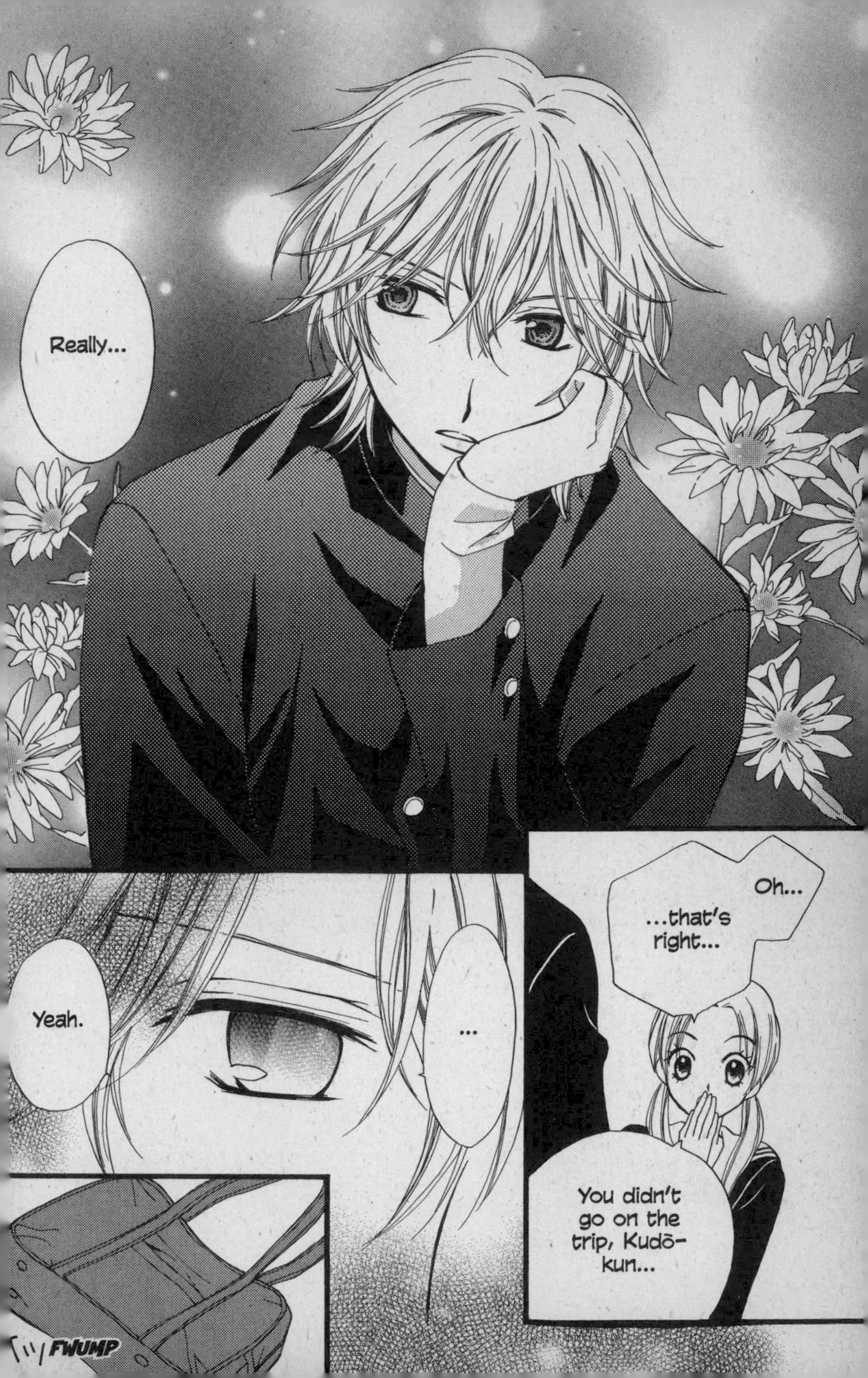
Really...
Oh...
...that's right...
You didn't go on the trip, Kudō-kun...
...
Yeah.
FWUMP

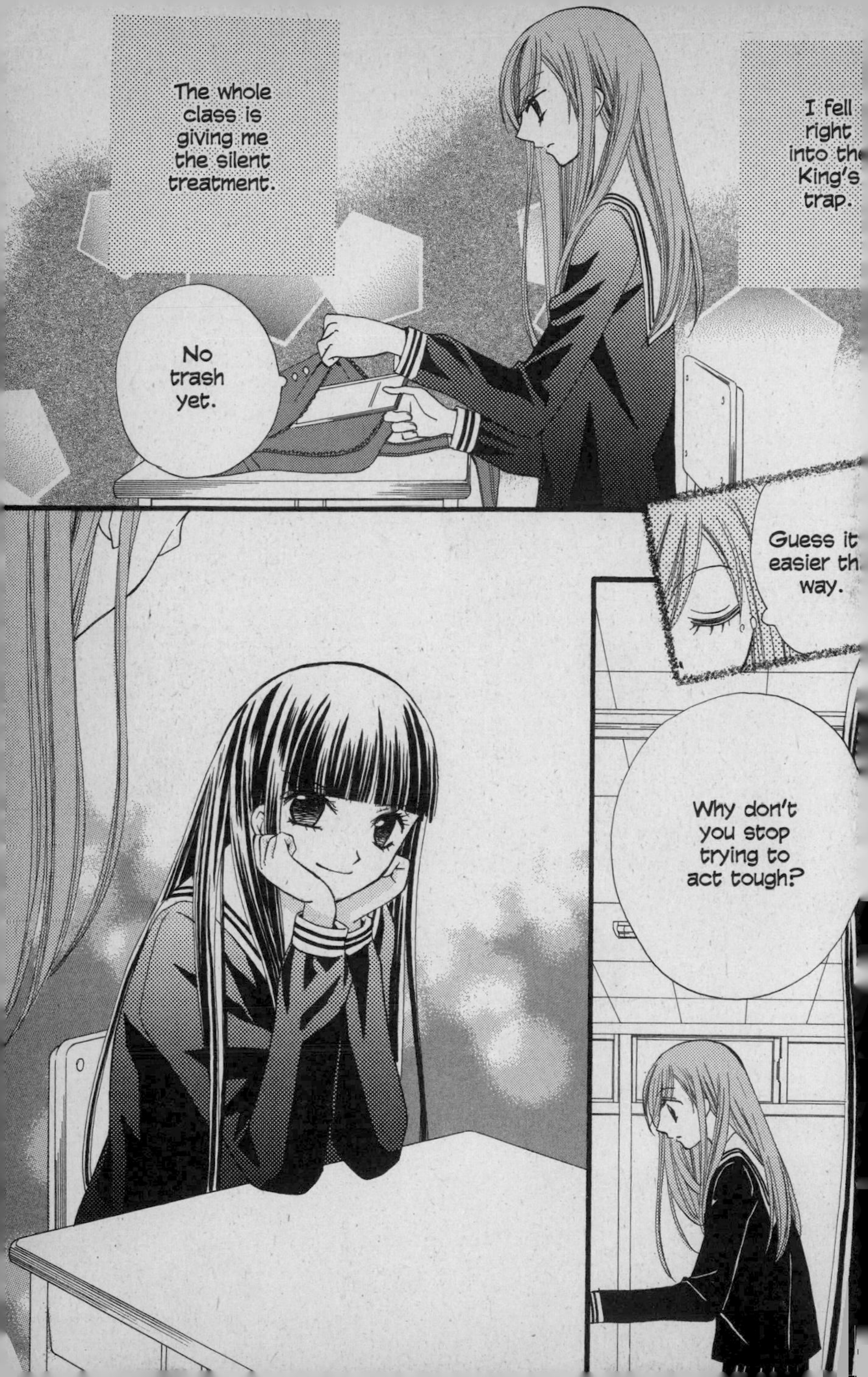
I fell right into th King's trap.
The whole class is giving me the silent treatment.
No trash yet.
Guess it easier th way.
Why don't you stop trying to act tough?

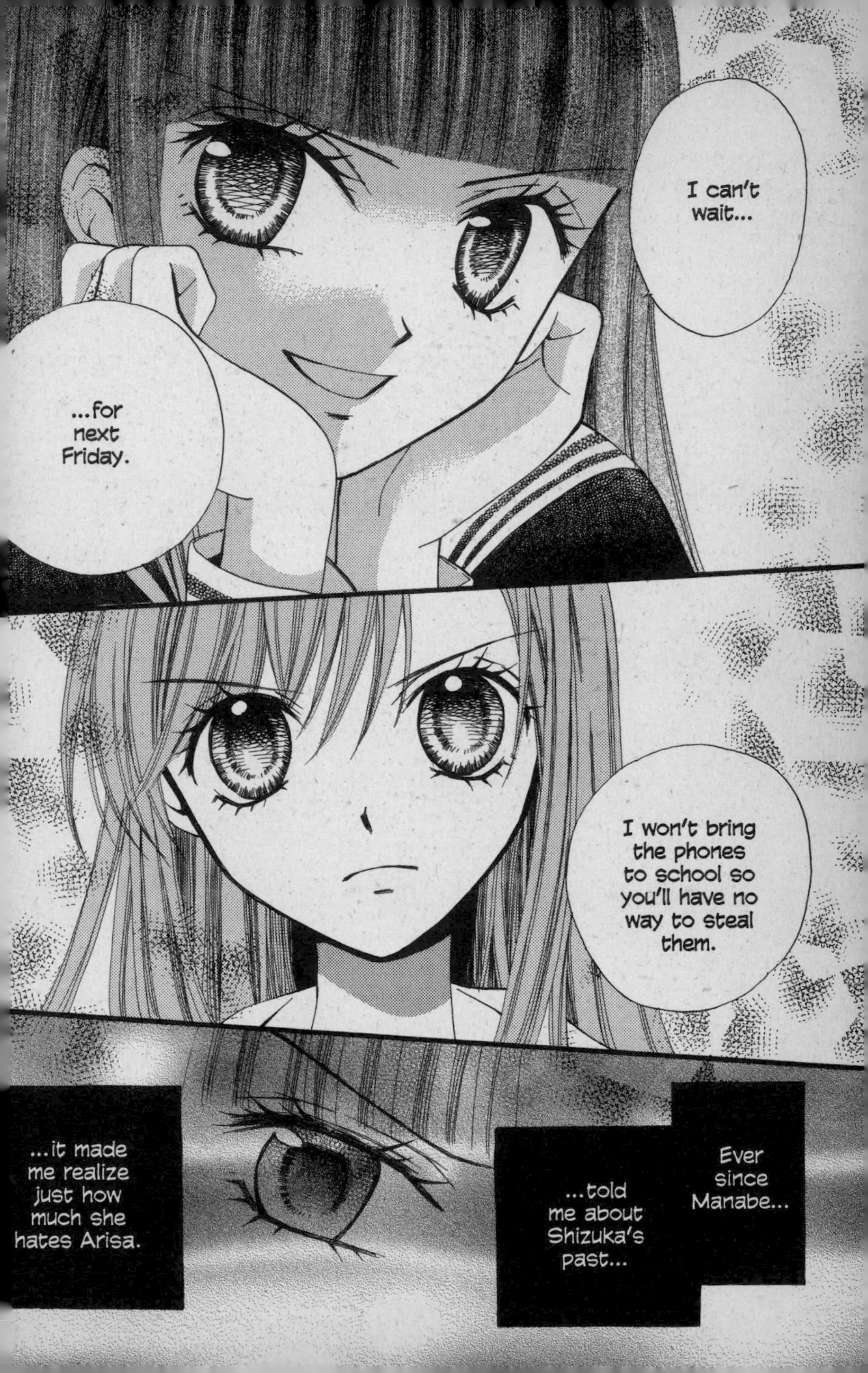
I can't wait...
...for next Friday.
I won't bring the phones to school so you'll have no way to steal them.
Ever since Manabe...
...told me about Shizuka's past...
...it made me realize just how much she hates Arisa.

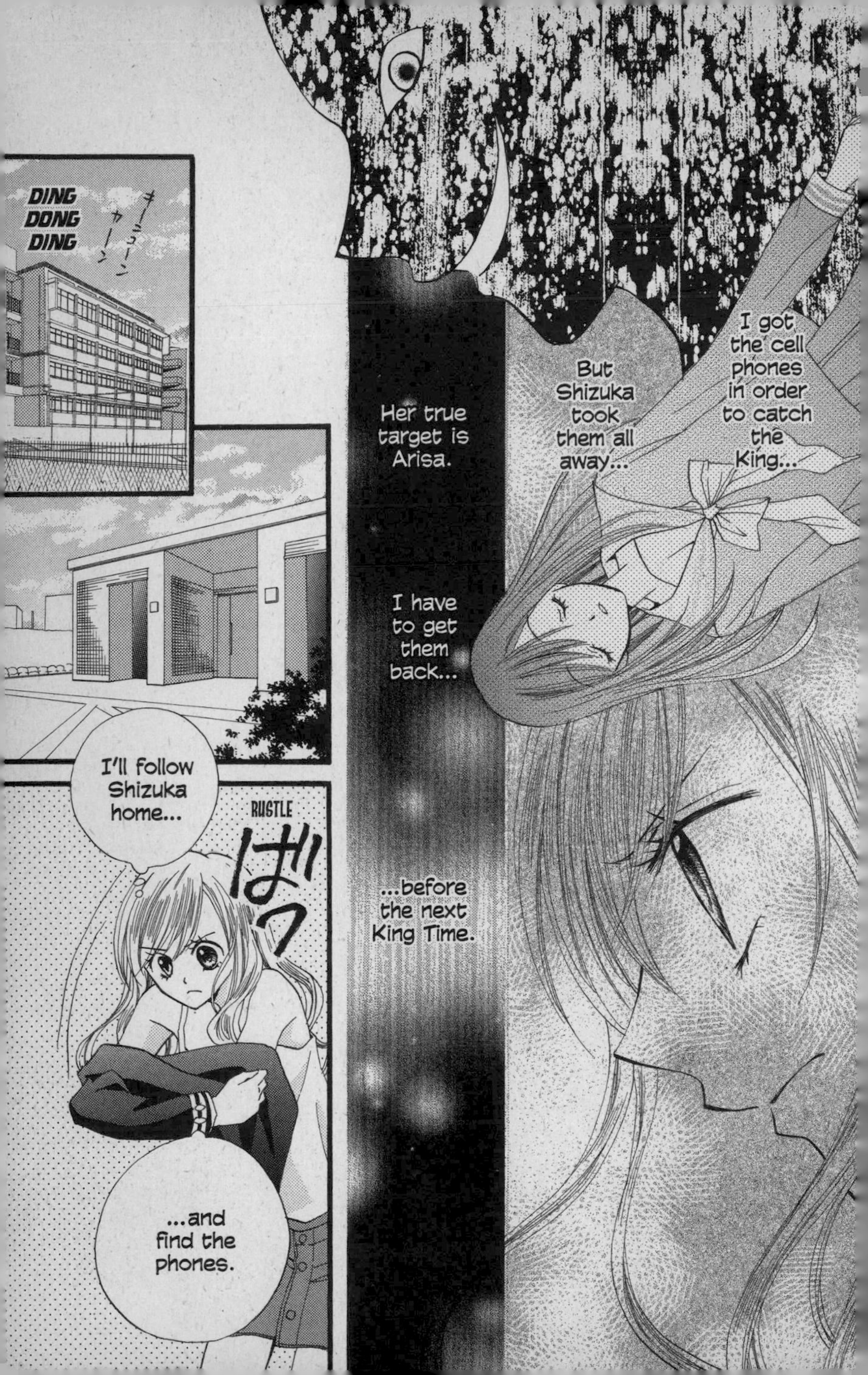
I got the cell phones in order to catch the King...
But Shizuka took them all away...
Her true target is Arisa.
I have to get them back...
...before the next King Time.
DING DONG DING
キーンコーンカーン
I'll follow Shizuka home...
RUSTLE
ばっ
...and find the phones.

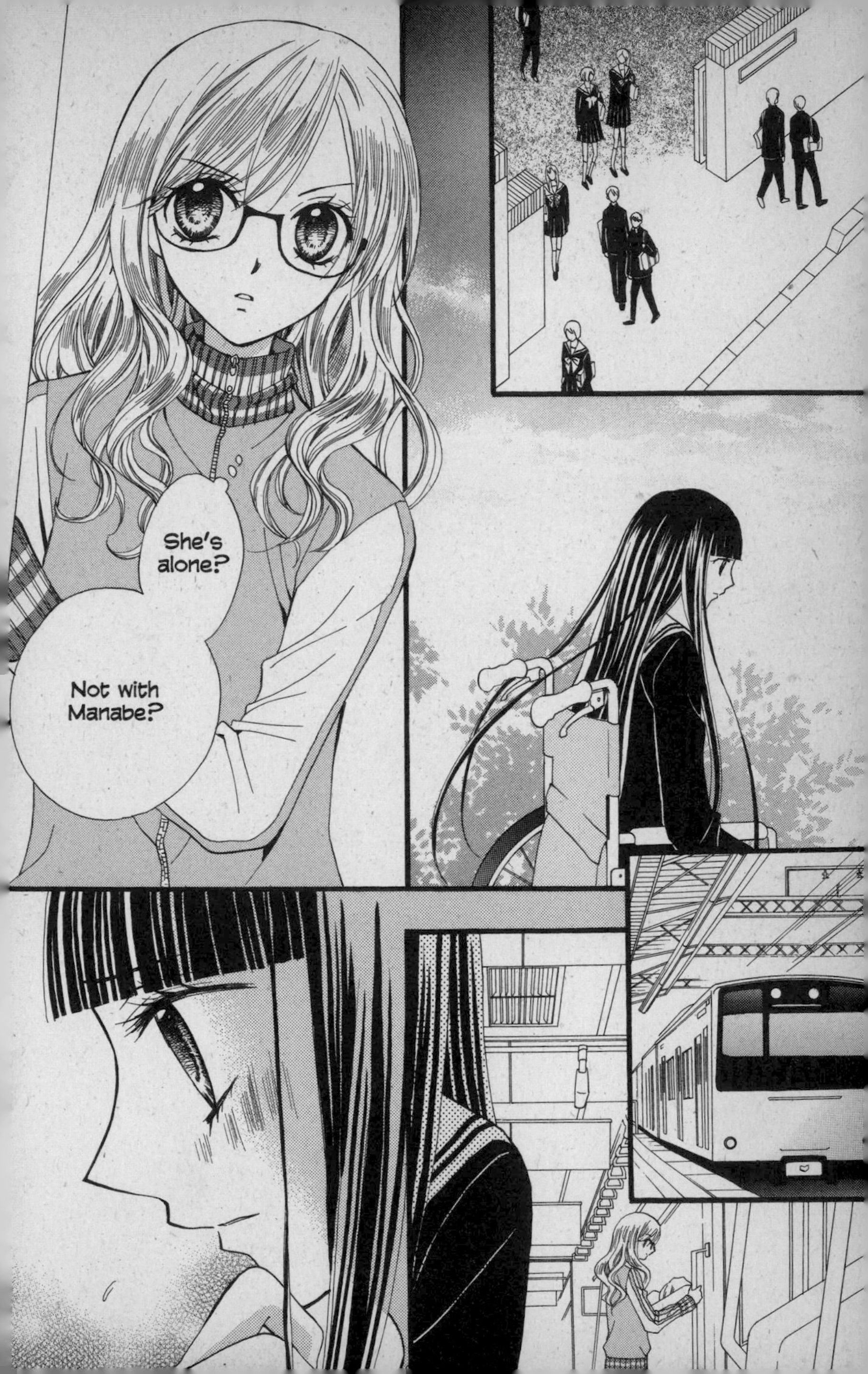
She's alone?
Not with Manabe?

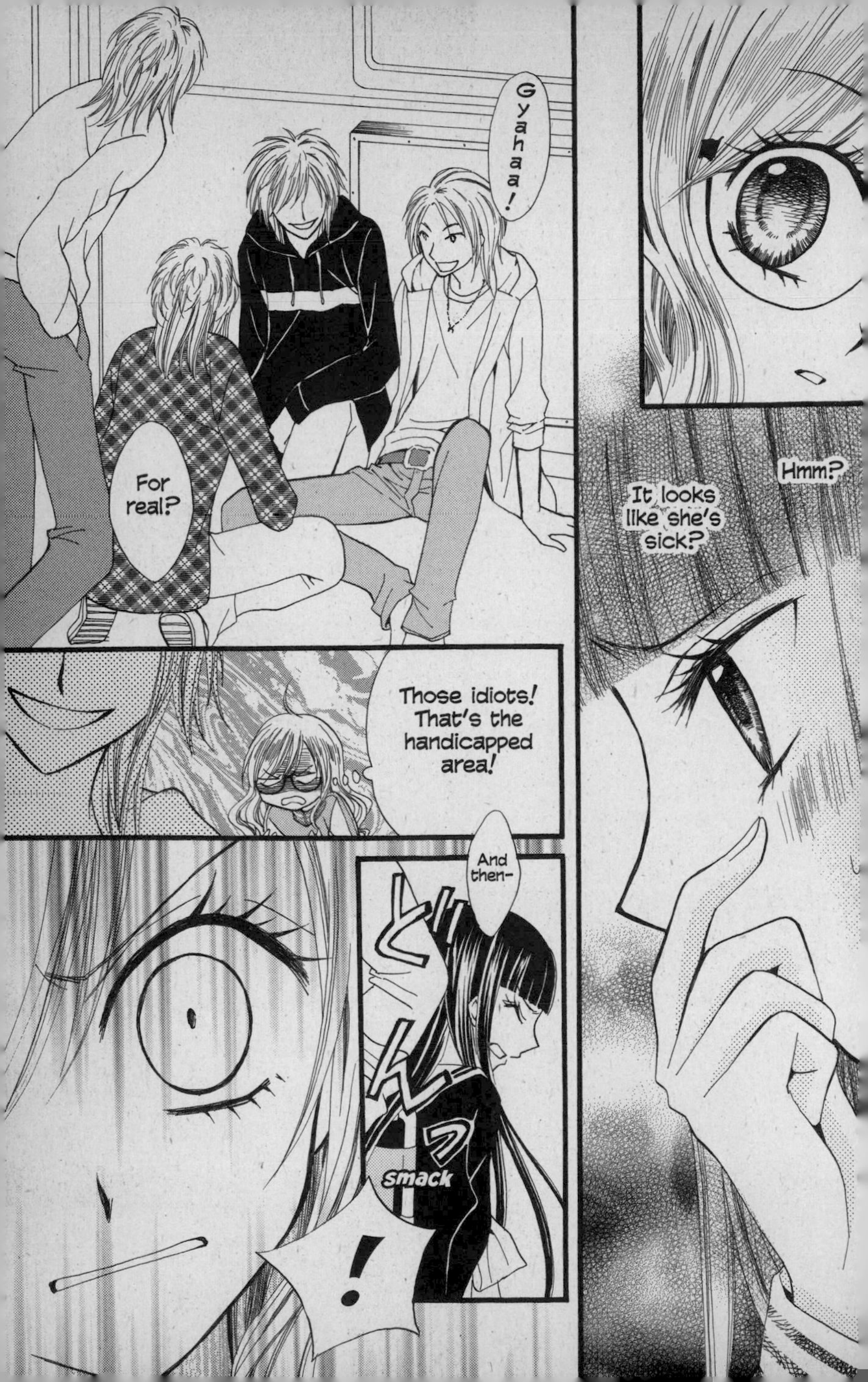
Hmm?
It looks like she's sick?
Gyahaa!
For real?
Those idiots! That's the handicapped area!
And then-
smack
!

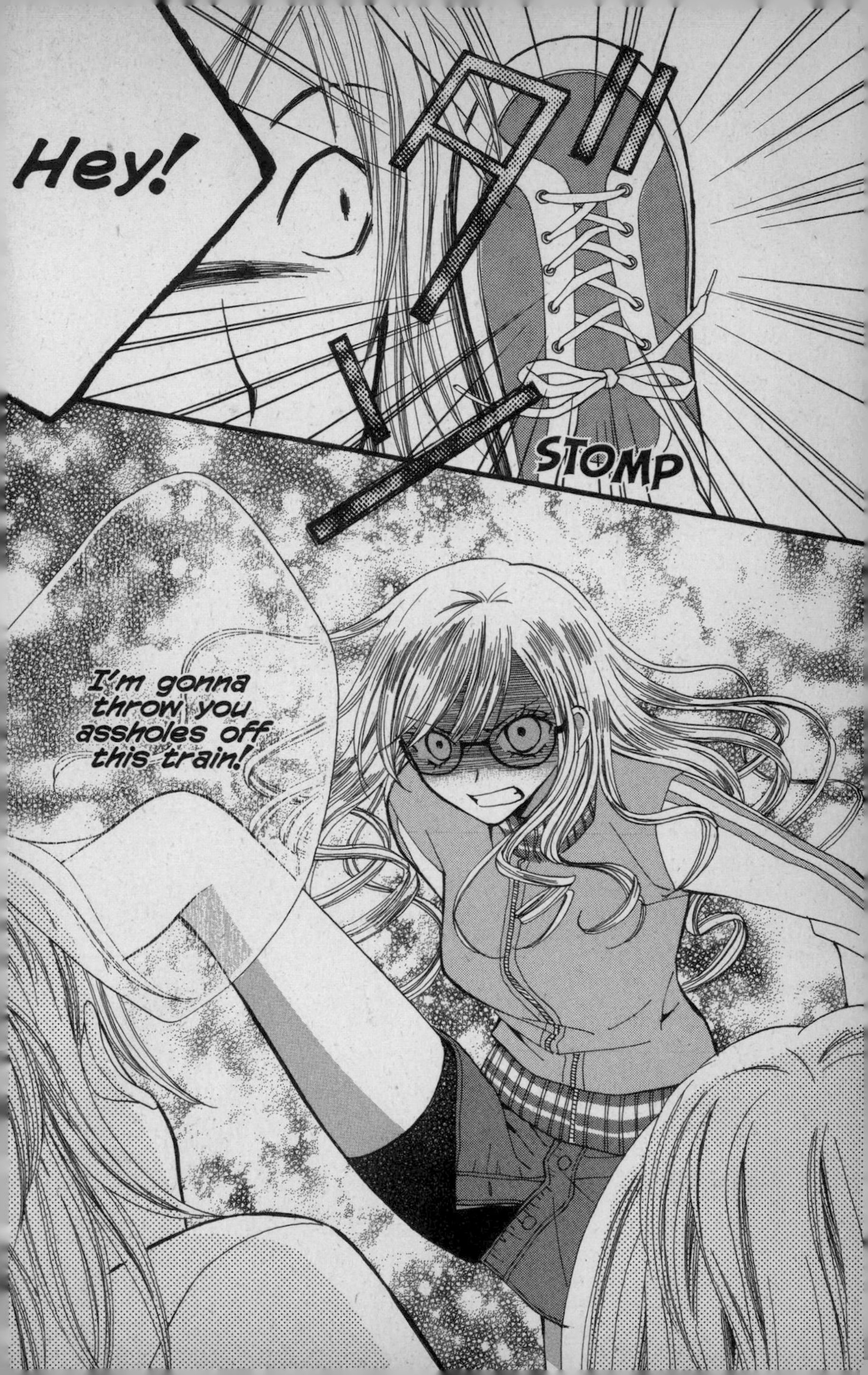
Hey!
STOMP
I'm gonna throw you assholes off this train!

Special Thanks:

T. Nakamura
H. Kishimoto
M. Nakata

My assistants and editors at Nakayoshi
Red Rooster
Takashi Shimoyama
GINNANSHA
Toriumi-sama

Please send mail to:

Natsumi Ando
c/o Kodansha Comics
451 Park Ave. South,
7th Fl.
New York, NY 10016

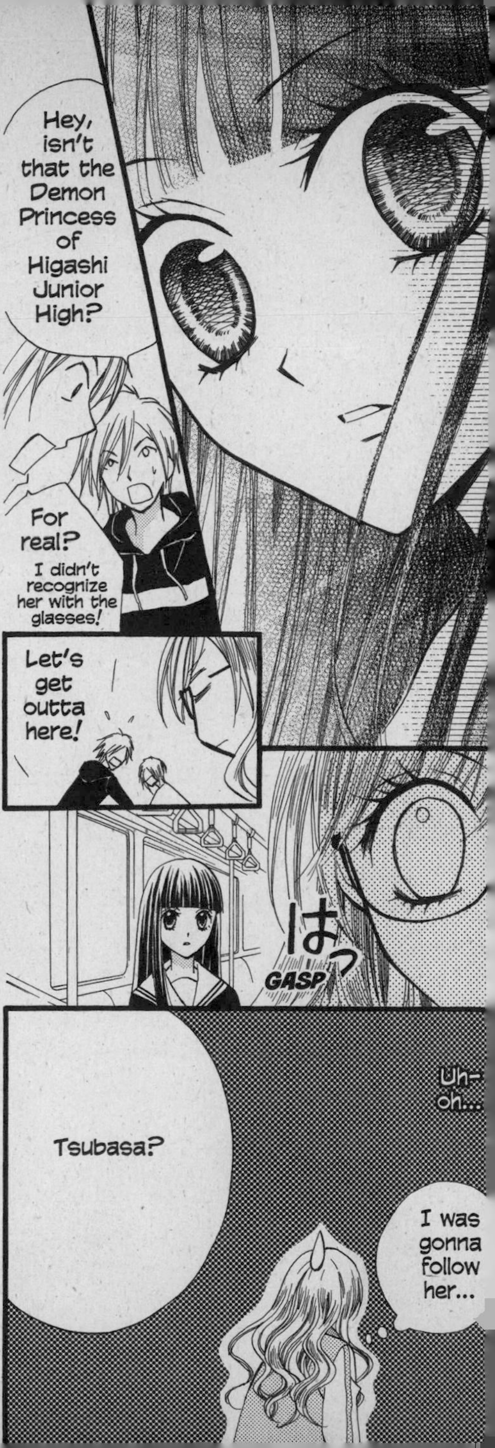
Hey, isn't that the Demon Princess of Higashi Junior High?
For real?
I didn't recognize her with the glasses!
Let's get outta here!
はっ
GASP
Uh-oh...
Tsubasa?
I was gonna follow her...

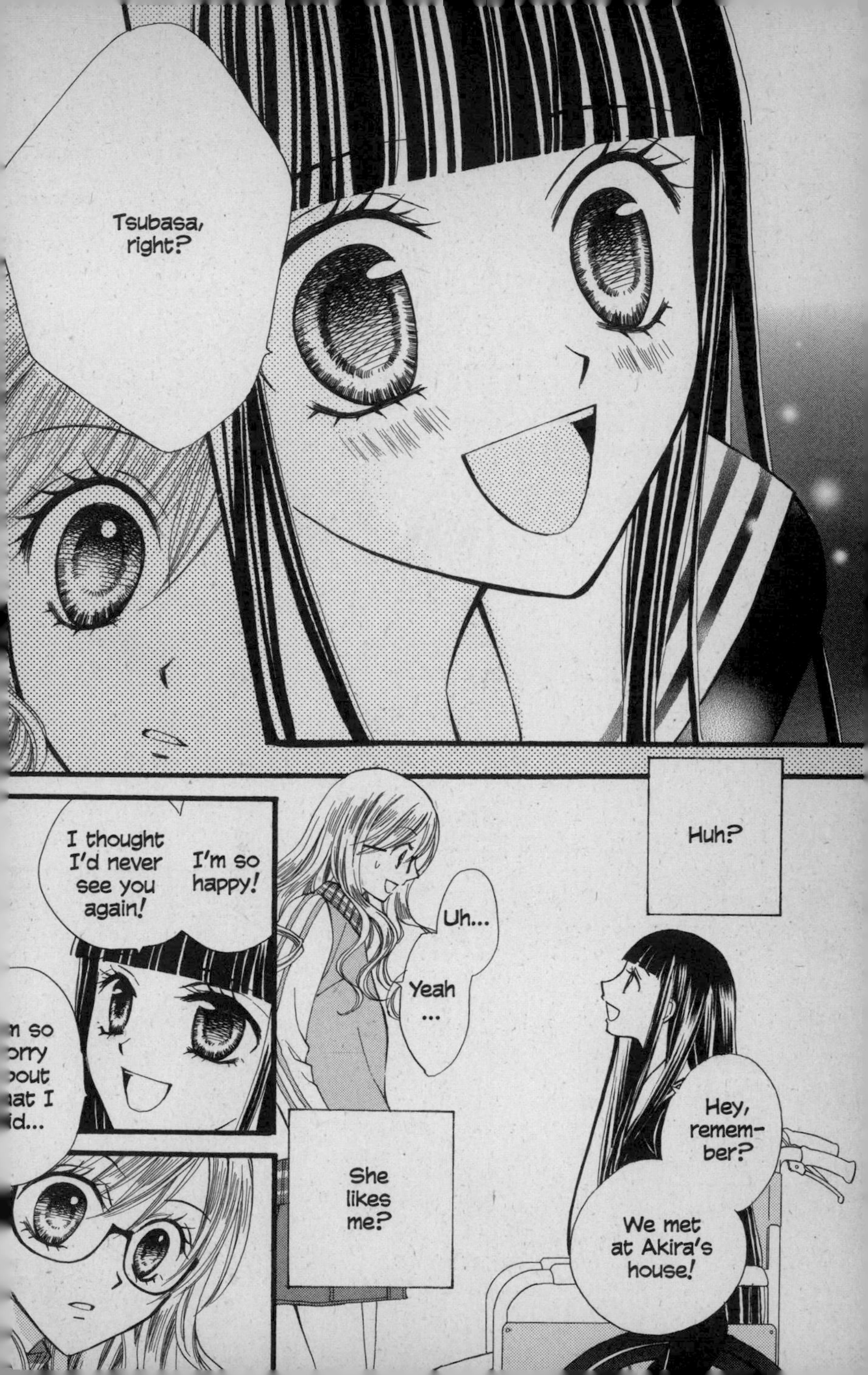

Tsubasa, right?
Huh?
Hey, remember?
We met at Akira's house!
Uh...
Yeah ...
She likes me?
I'm so happy!
I thought I'd never see you again!
m so orry bout at I id...

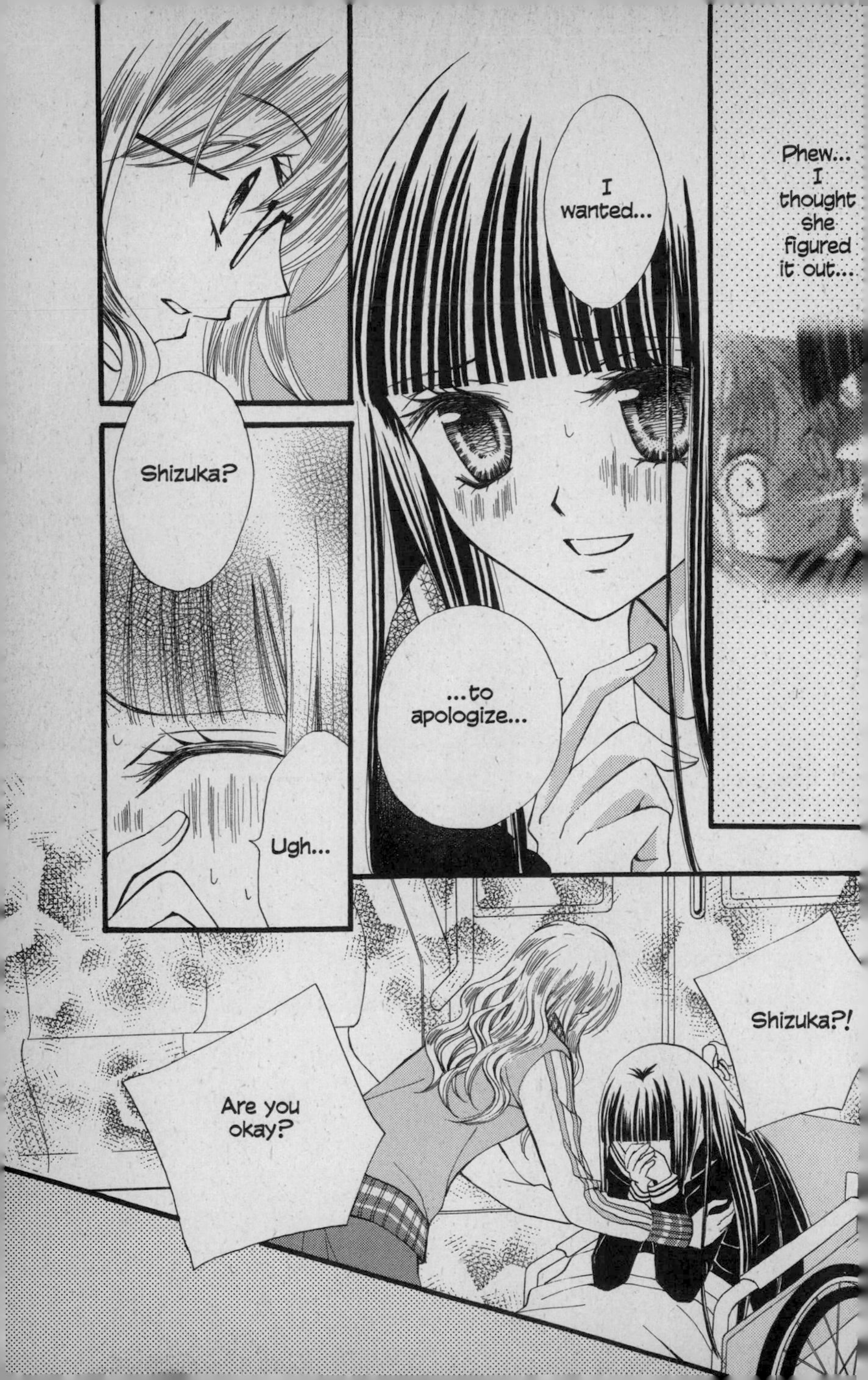
Phew... I thought she figured it out...
I wanted...
...to apologize...
Shizuka?
Ugh...
Shizuka?!
Are you okay?

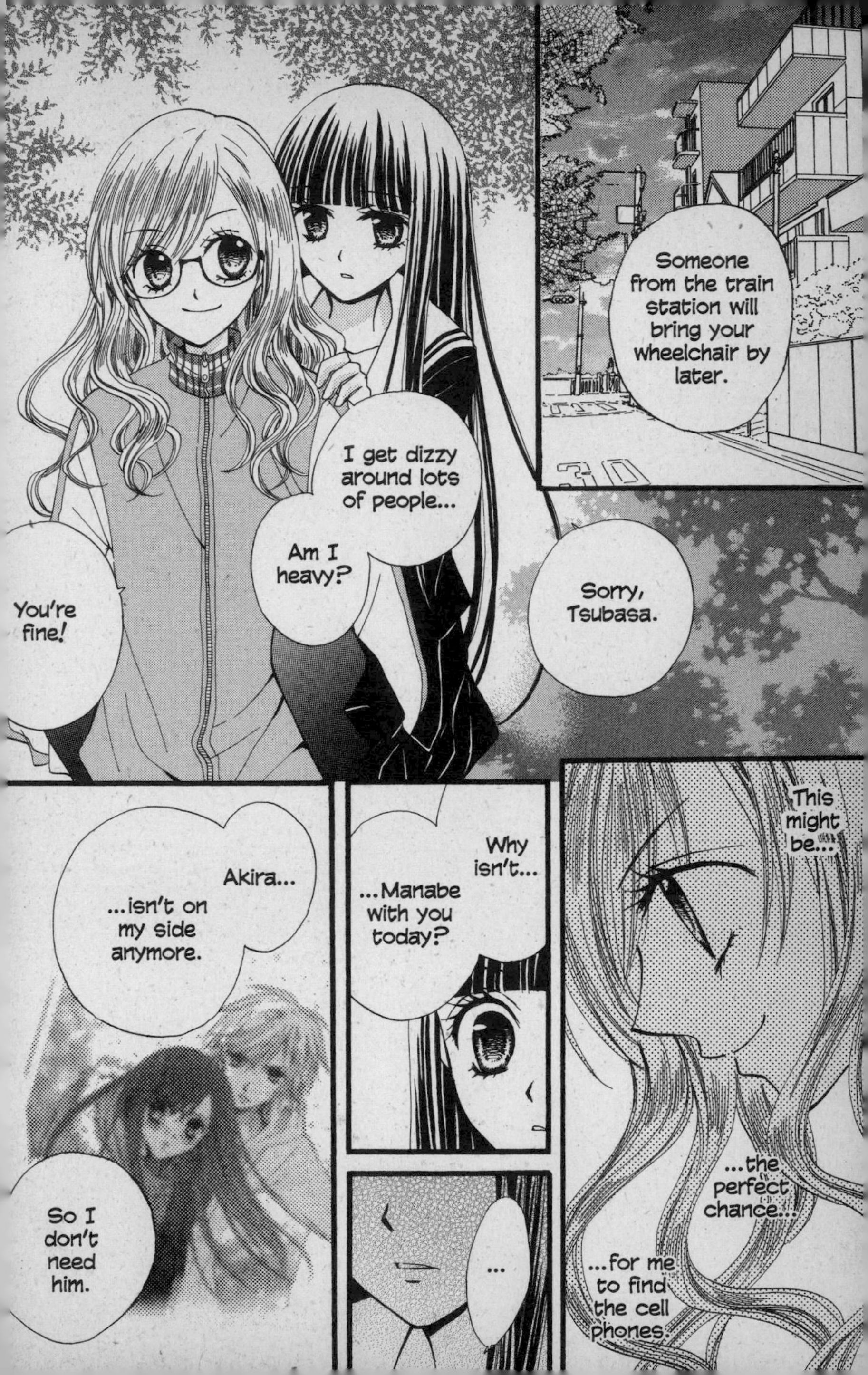
Someone from the train station will bring your wheelchair by later.
Sorry, Tsubasa.
I get dizzy around lots of people...
Am I heavy?
You're fine!
This might be...
...the perfect chance...
...for me to find the cell phones.
Why isn't...
...Manabe with you today?
...
Akira...
...isn't on my side anymore.
So I don't need him.

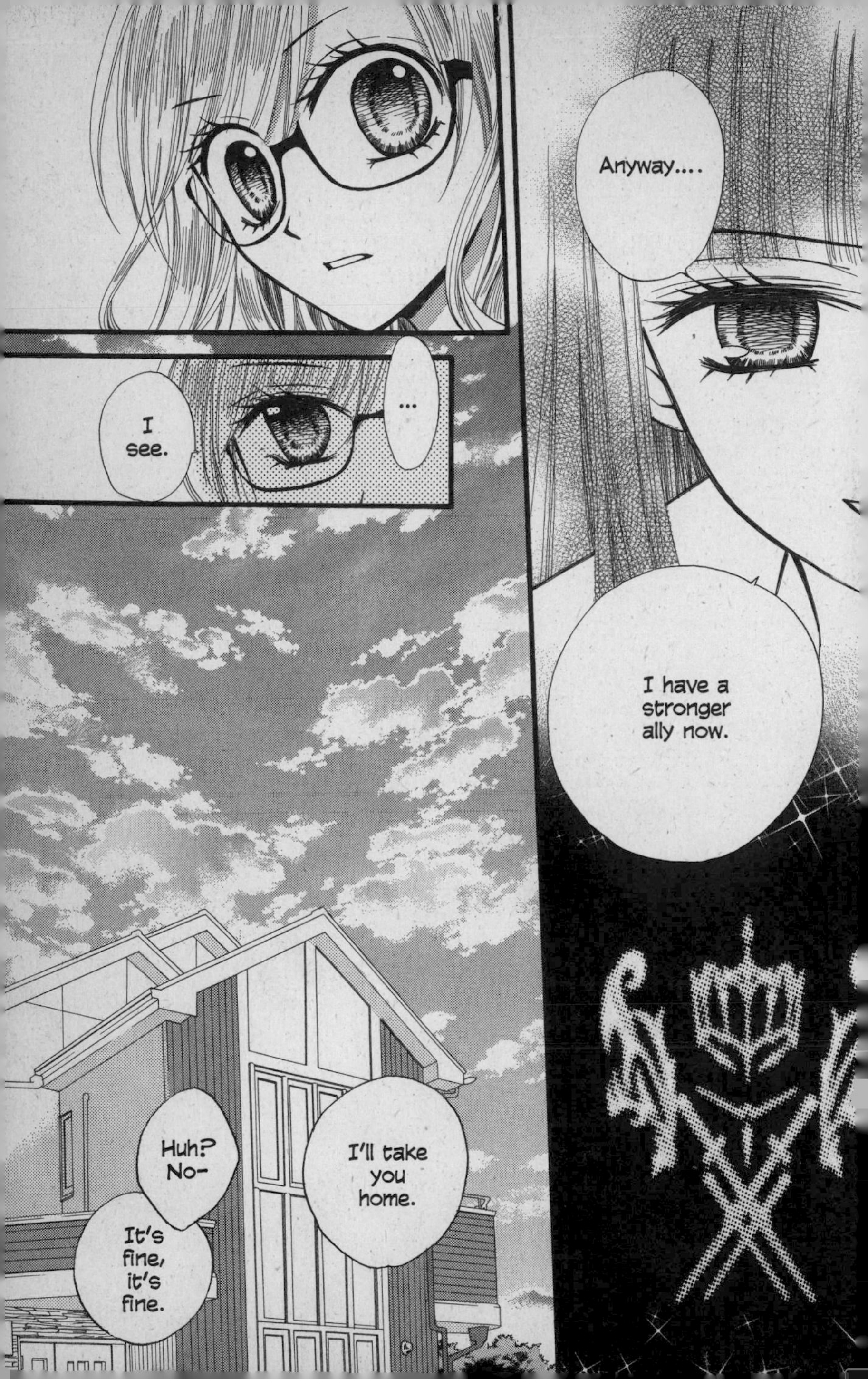
Anyway....
I have a stronger ally now.
...
I see.
I'll take you home.
Huh? No-
It's fine, it's fine.

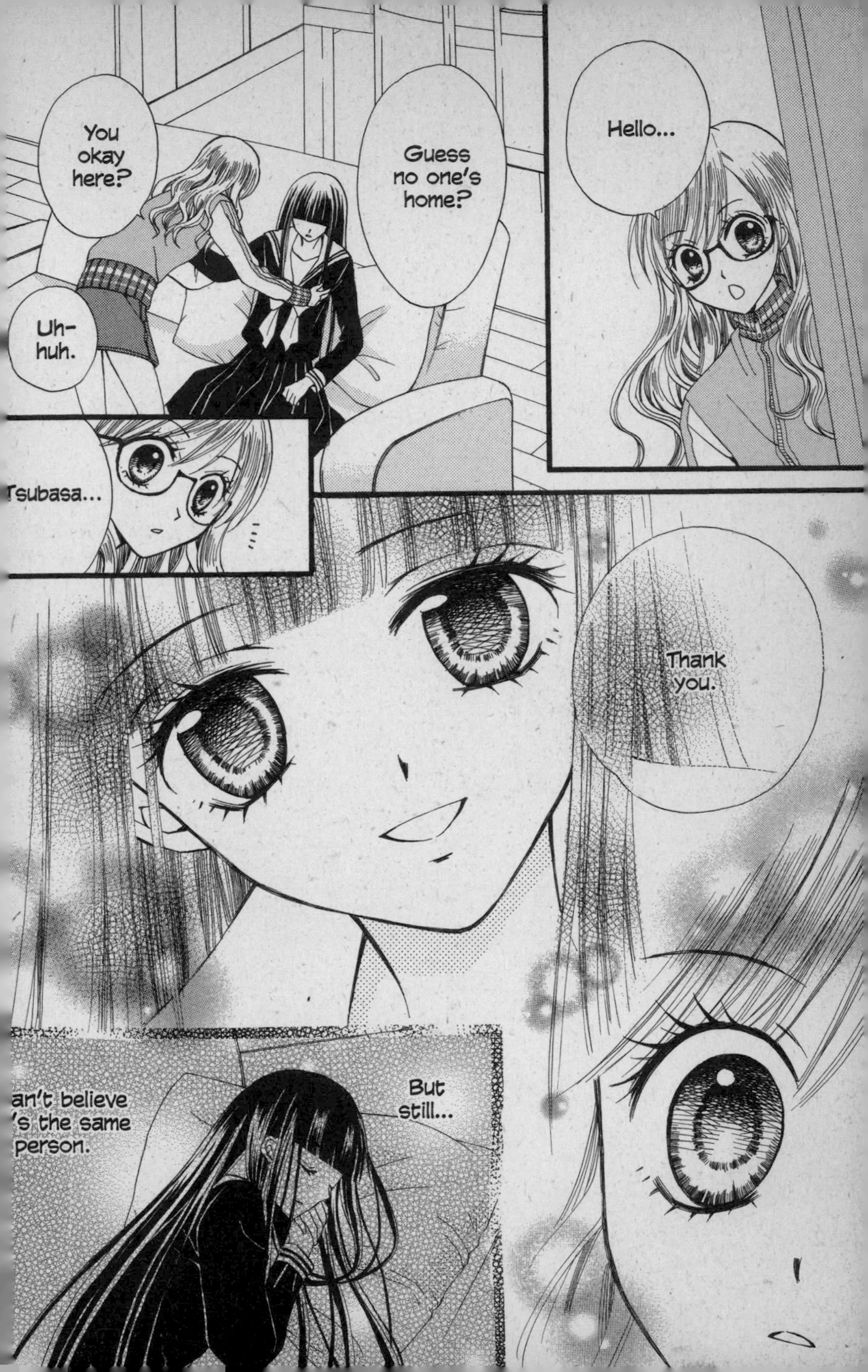
Hello...
Guess no one's home?
You okay here?
Uh-huh.
Tsubasa...
Thank you.
But still...
an't believe
's the same
person.

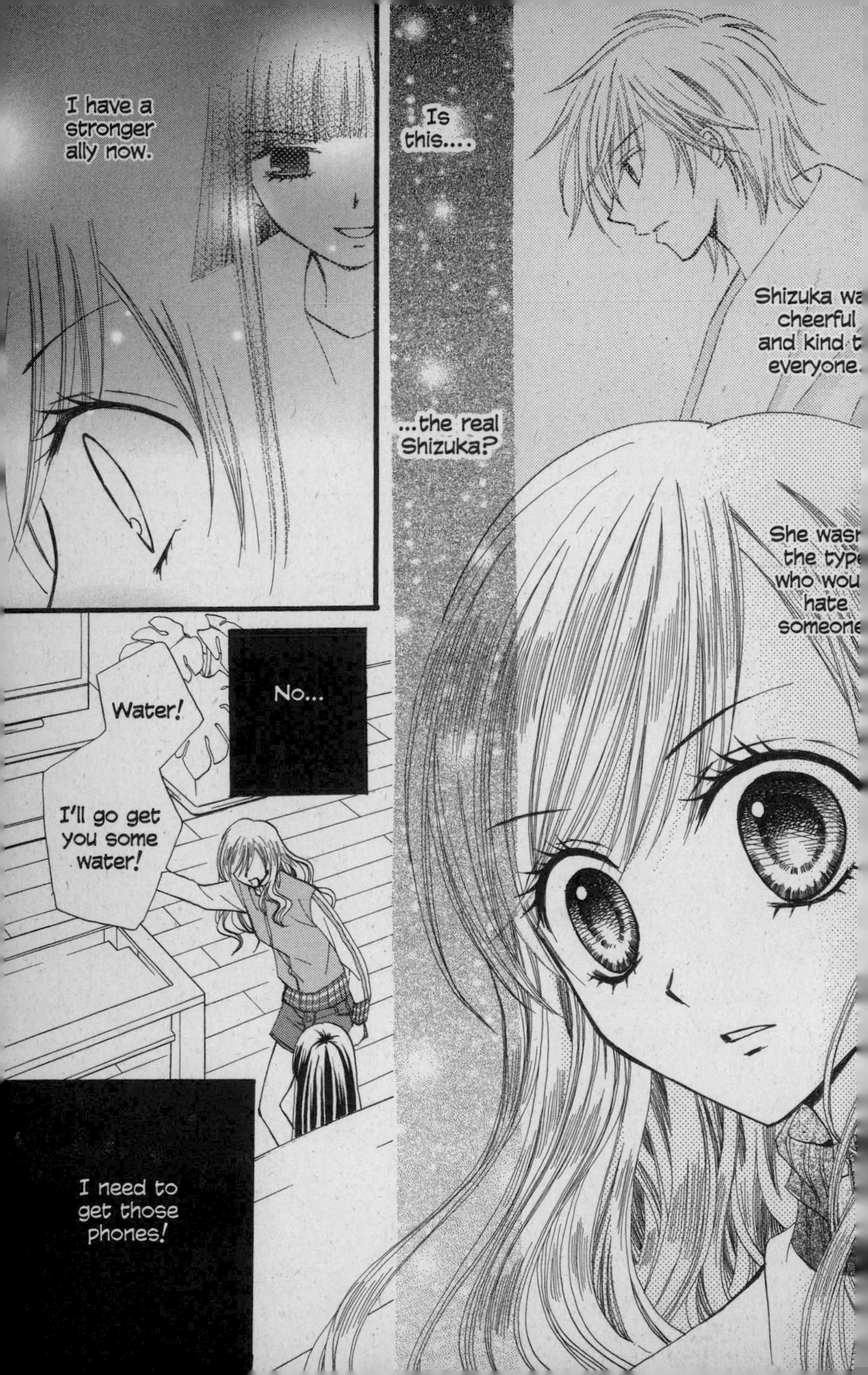
Shizuka wa
cheerful
and kind t
everyone.
She wasn
the type
who wou
hate
someone
Is this....
...the real Shizuka?
I have a stronger ally now.
No...
Water!
I'll go get you some water!
I need to get those phones!

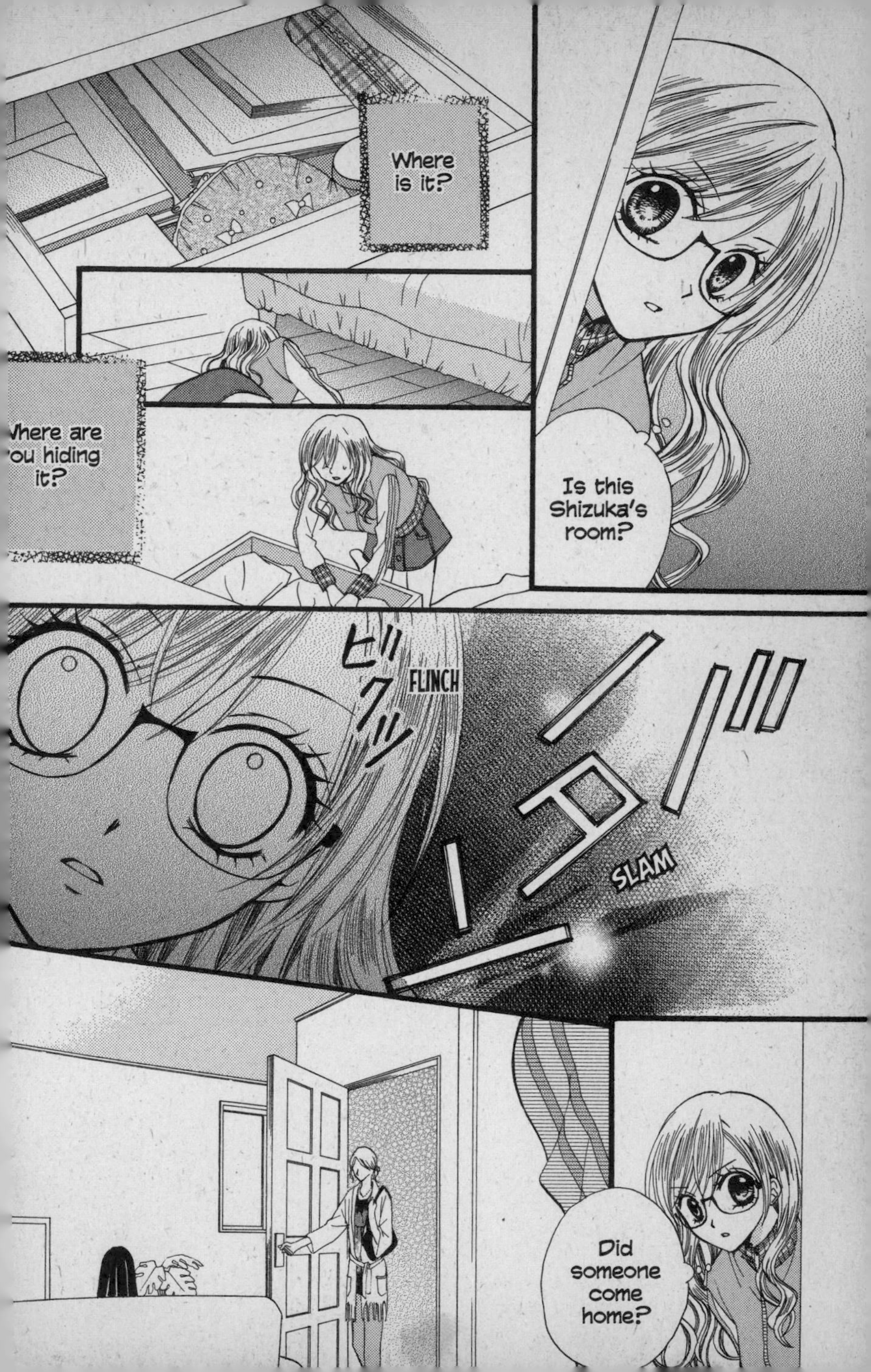

Is this Shizuka's room?
Where is it?
Where are you hiding it?
SLAM
ビクッ
FLINCH
Did someone come home?

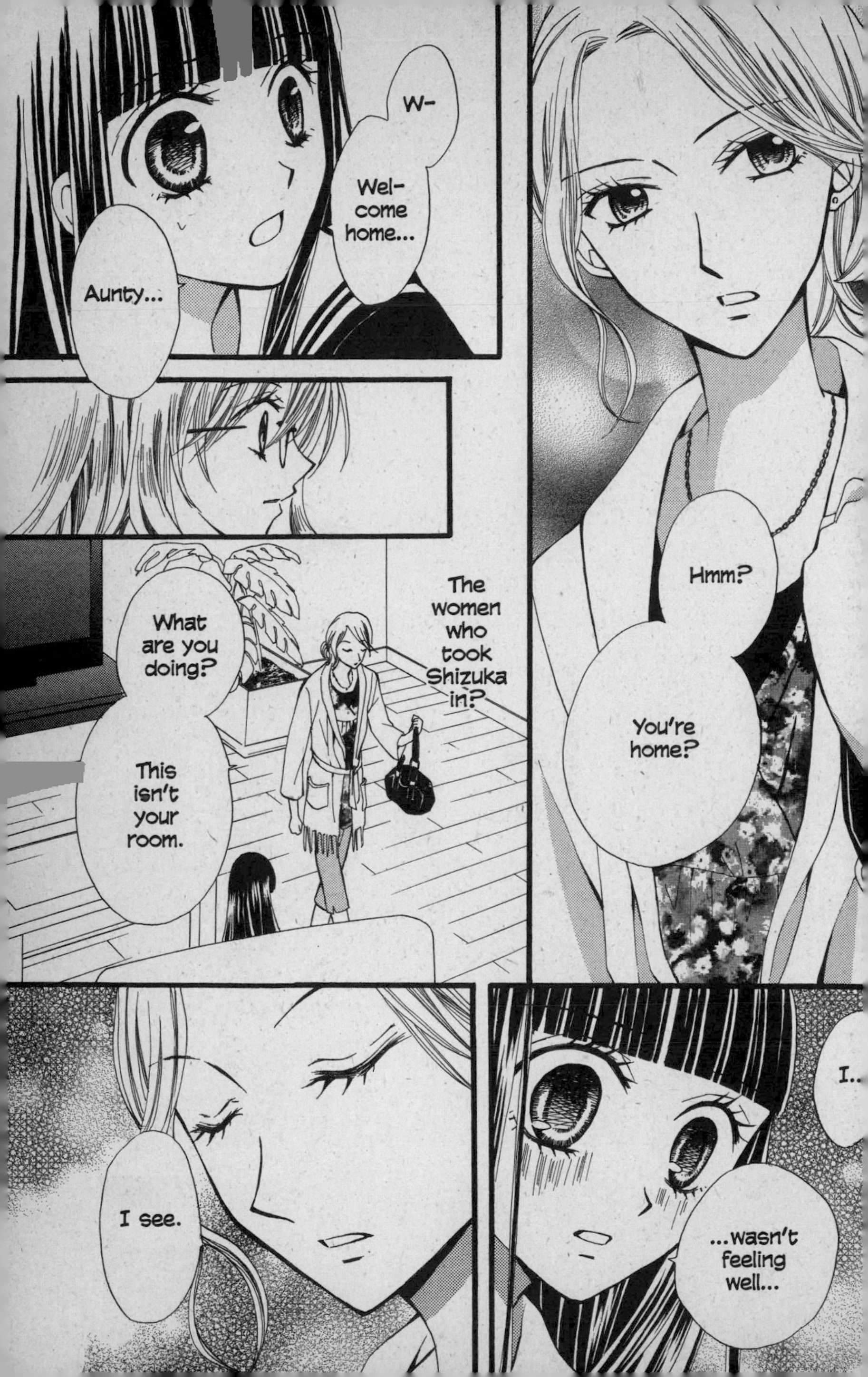
Hmm?
You're home?
W-
Wel-come home...
Aunty...
The women who took Shizuka in?
What are you doing?
This isn't your room.
I...
...wasn't feeling well...
I see.

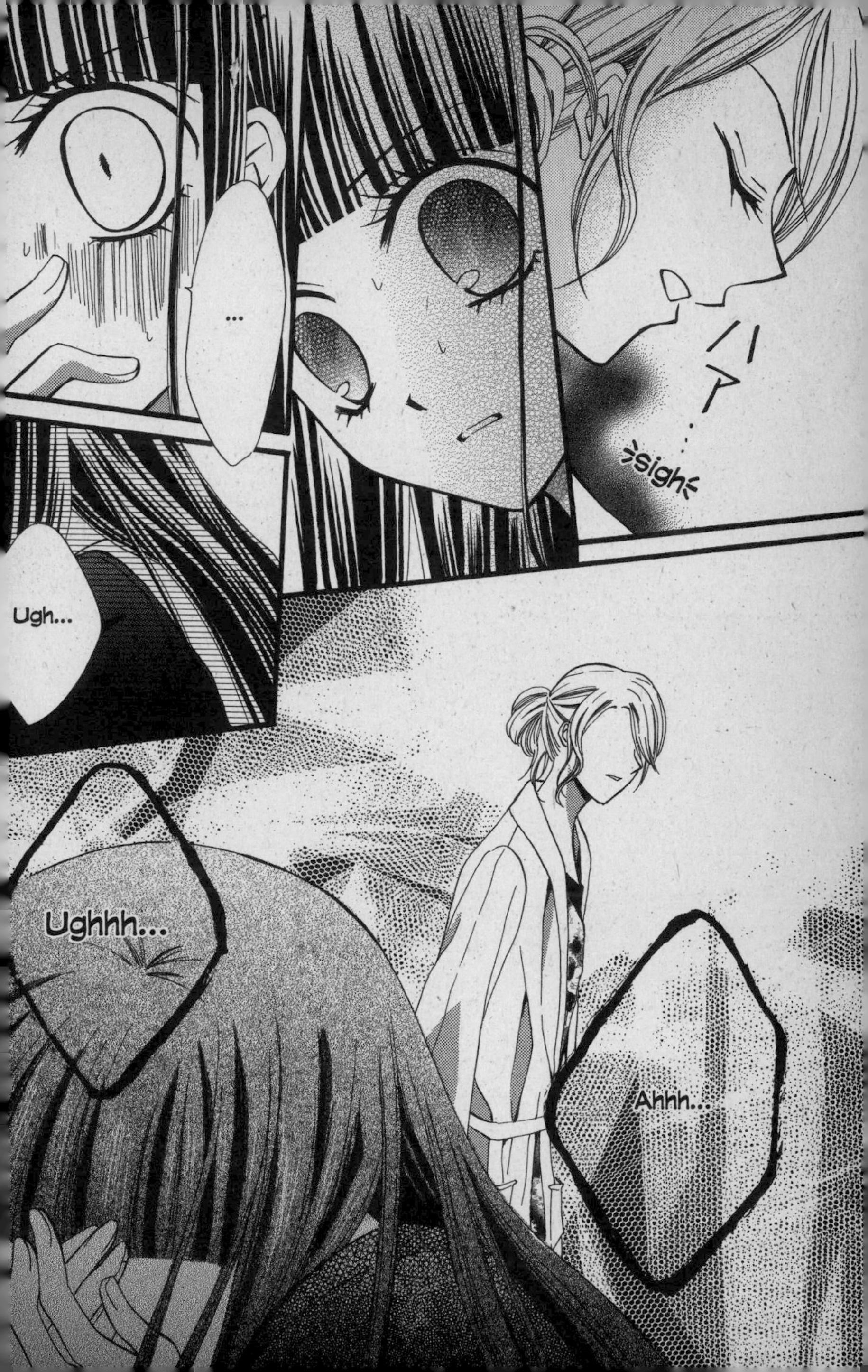
ハア
sigh
...
Ugh...
Ahhh...
Ughhh...

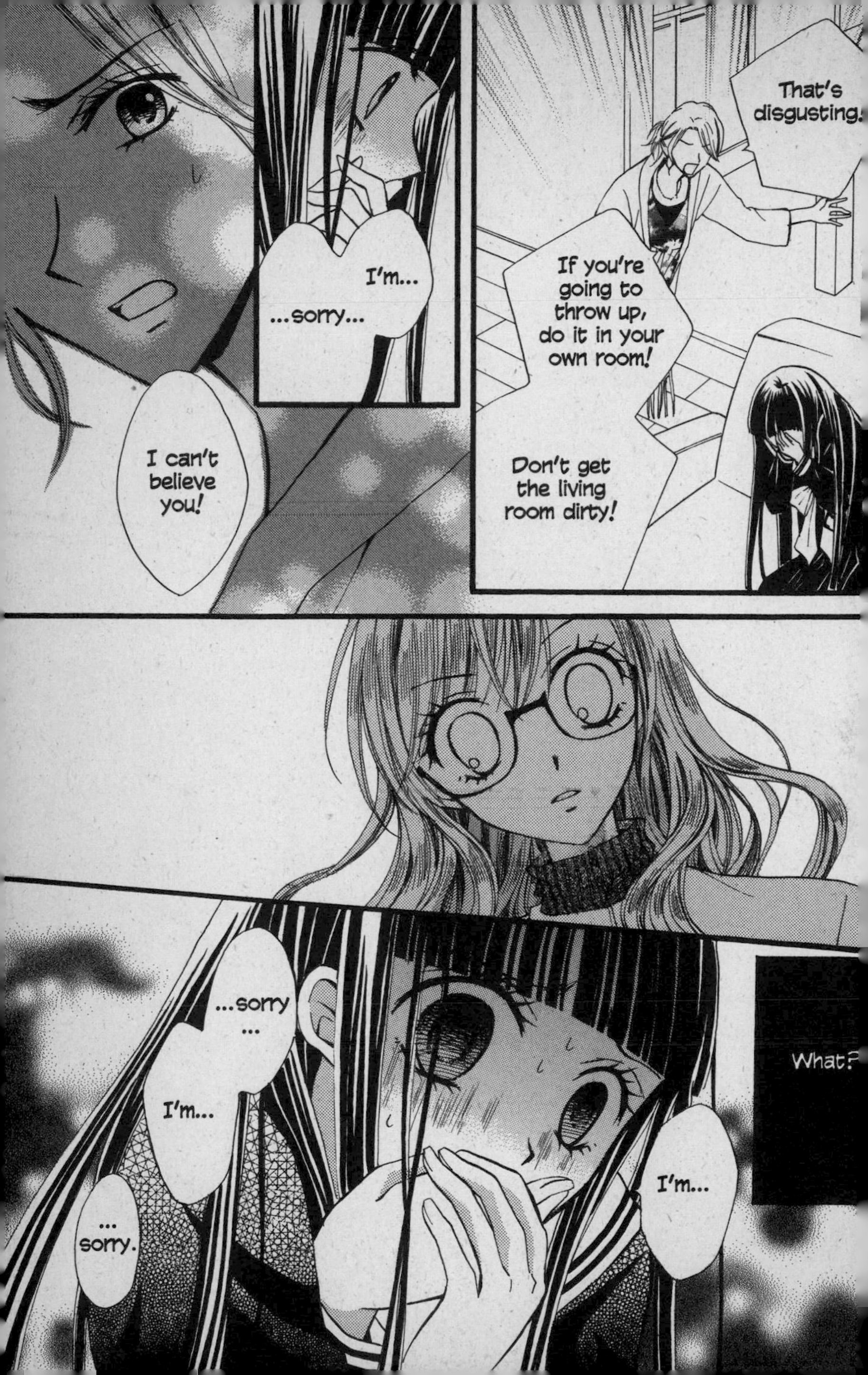
That's disgusting.
If you're going to throw up, do it in your own room!
Don't get the living room dirty!
I'm...
...sorry...
I can't believe you!
What?
I'm...
...sorry ...
I'm...
... sorry.

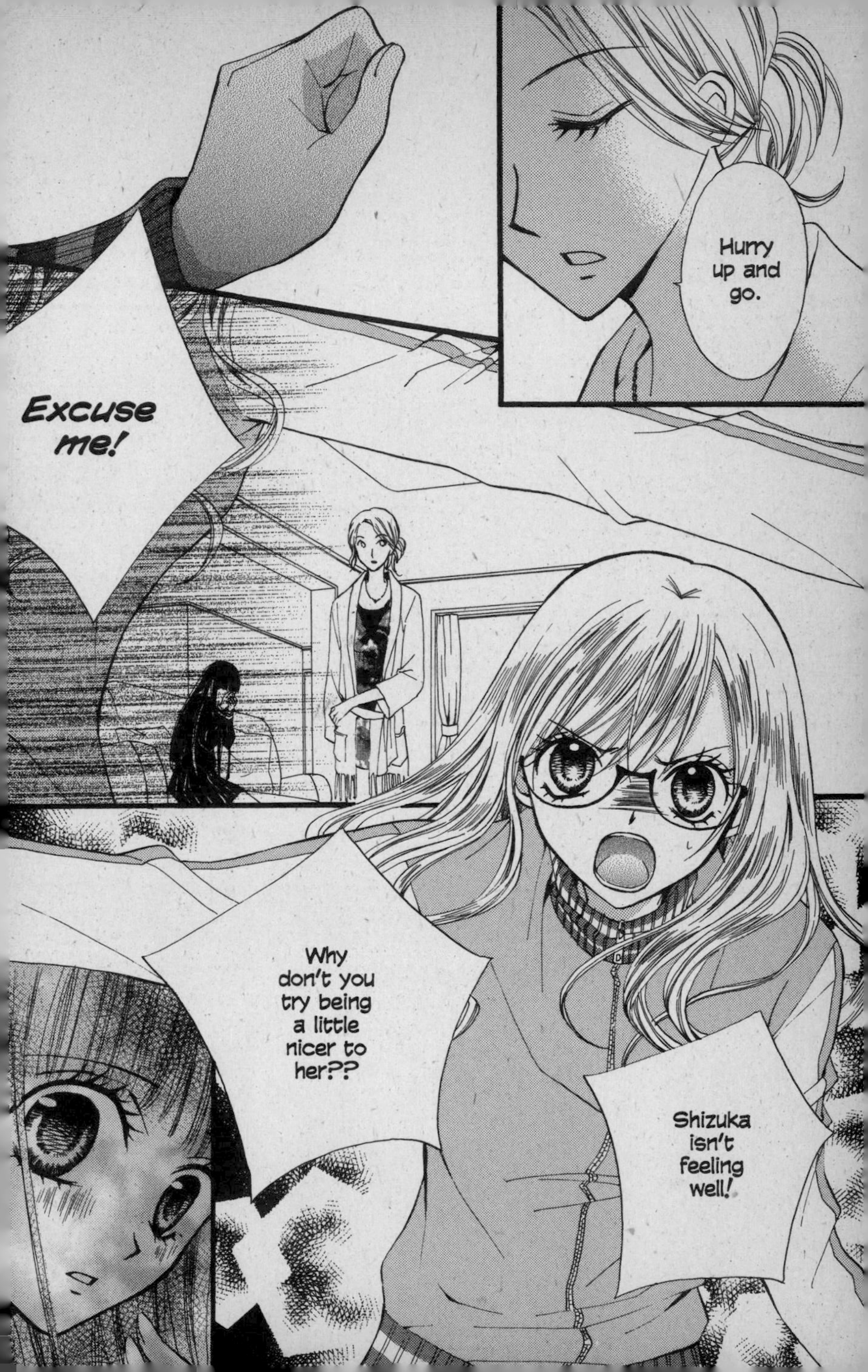
Hurry up and go.
Excuse me!
Shizuka isn't feeling well!
Why don't you try being a little nicer to her??

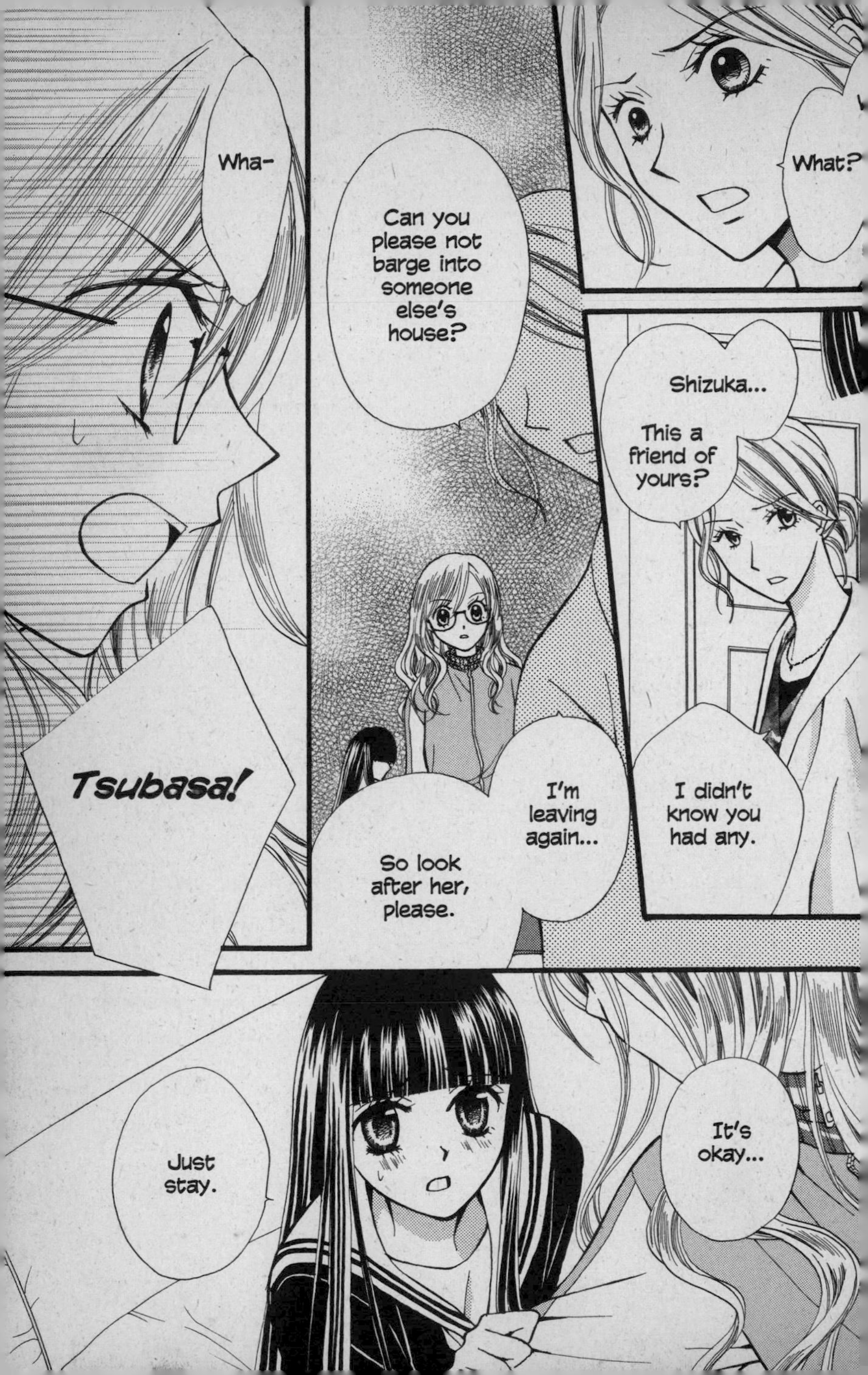
What?
Shizuka...
This a friend of yours?
I didn't know you had any.
Can you please not barge into someone else's house?
I'm leaving again...
So look after her, please.
Wha-
Tsubasa!
It's okay...
Just stay.

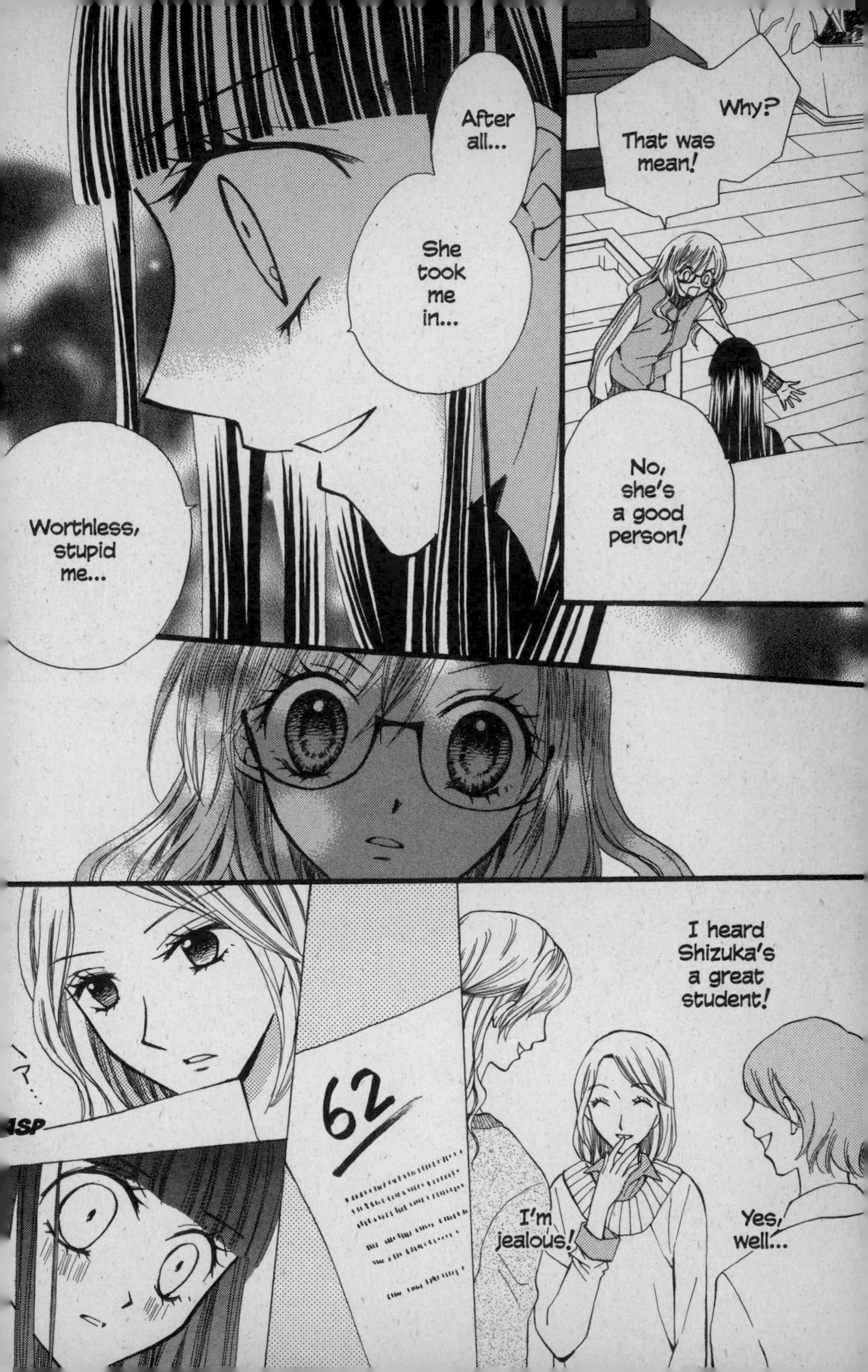
Why?
That was mean!
No, she's a good person!
After all...
She took me in...
Worthless, stupid me...
I heard Shizuka's a great student!
Yes, well...
I'm jealous!
62

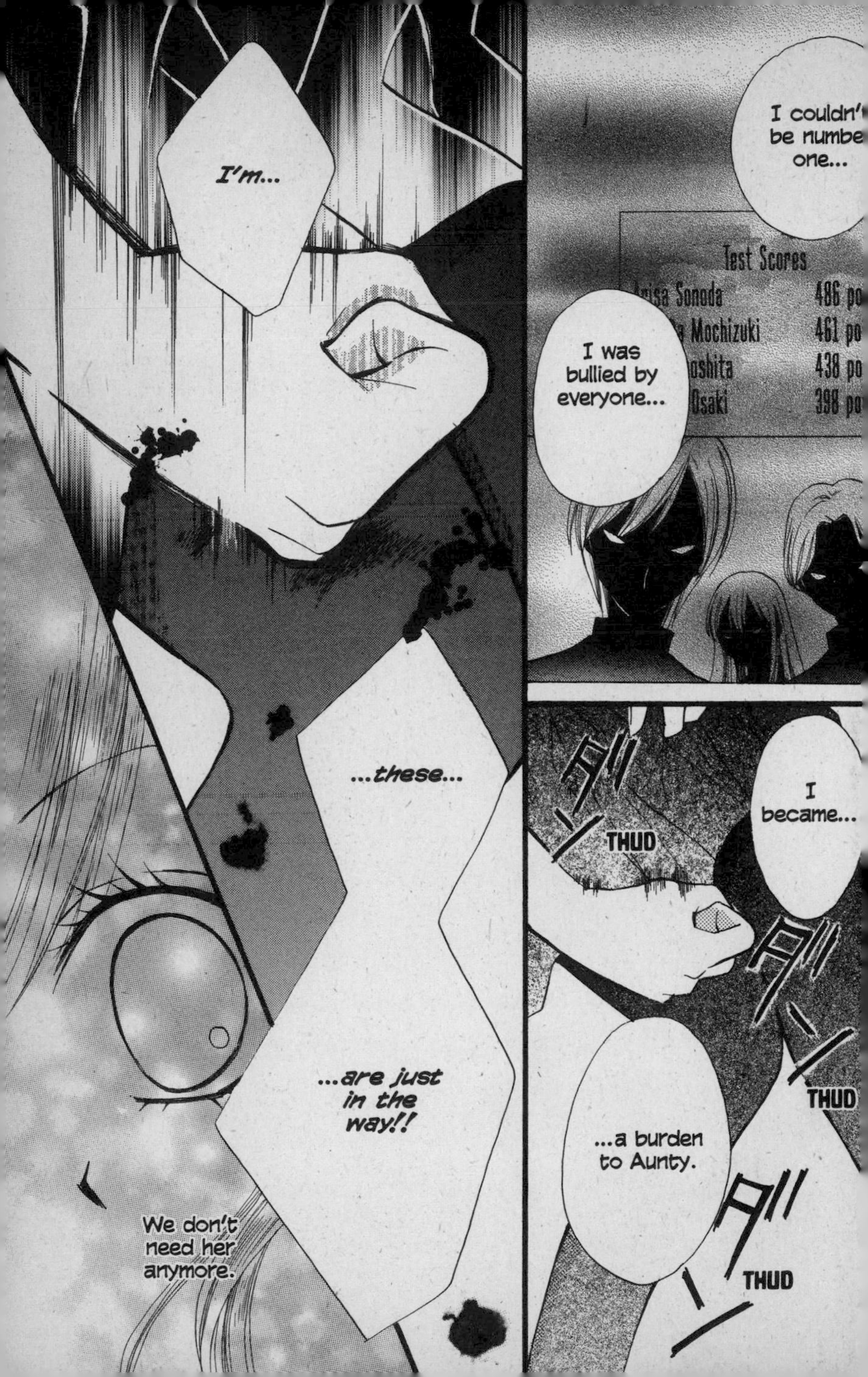
I couldn' be numbe one...
Test Scores
risa Sonoda 486 po
Mochizuki 461 po
oshita 438 po
Osaki 398 po
I was bullied by everyone...
I became...
THUD
...a burden to Aunty.
THUD
THUD
I'm...
...these...
...are just in the way!!
We don't need her anymore.

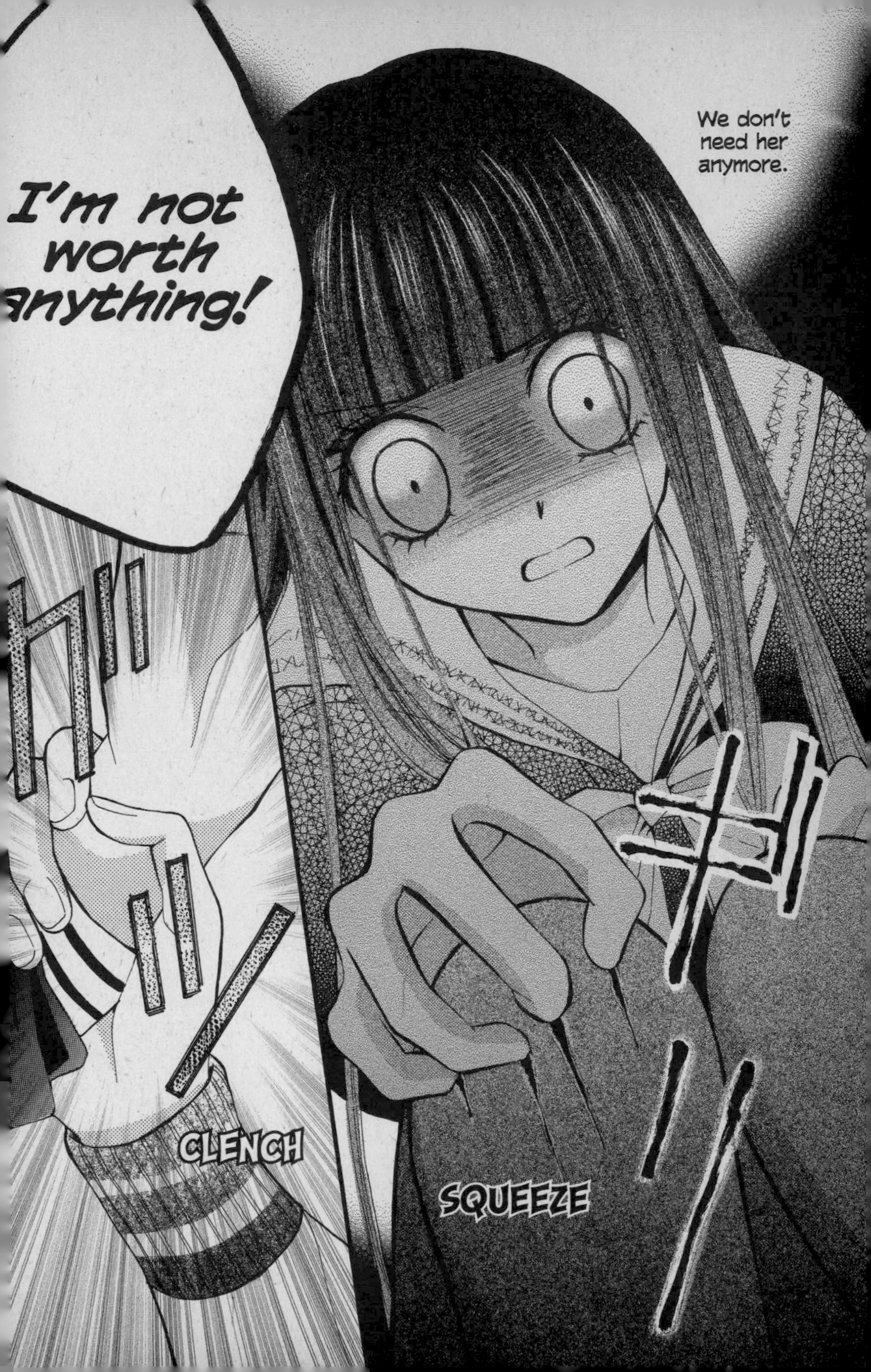
We don't need her anymore.
I'm not worth anything!
SQUEEZE
CLENCH

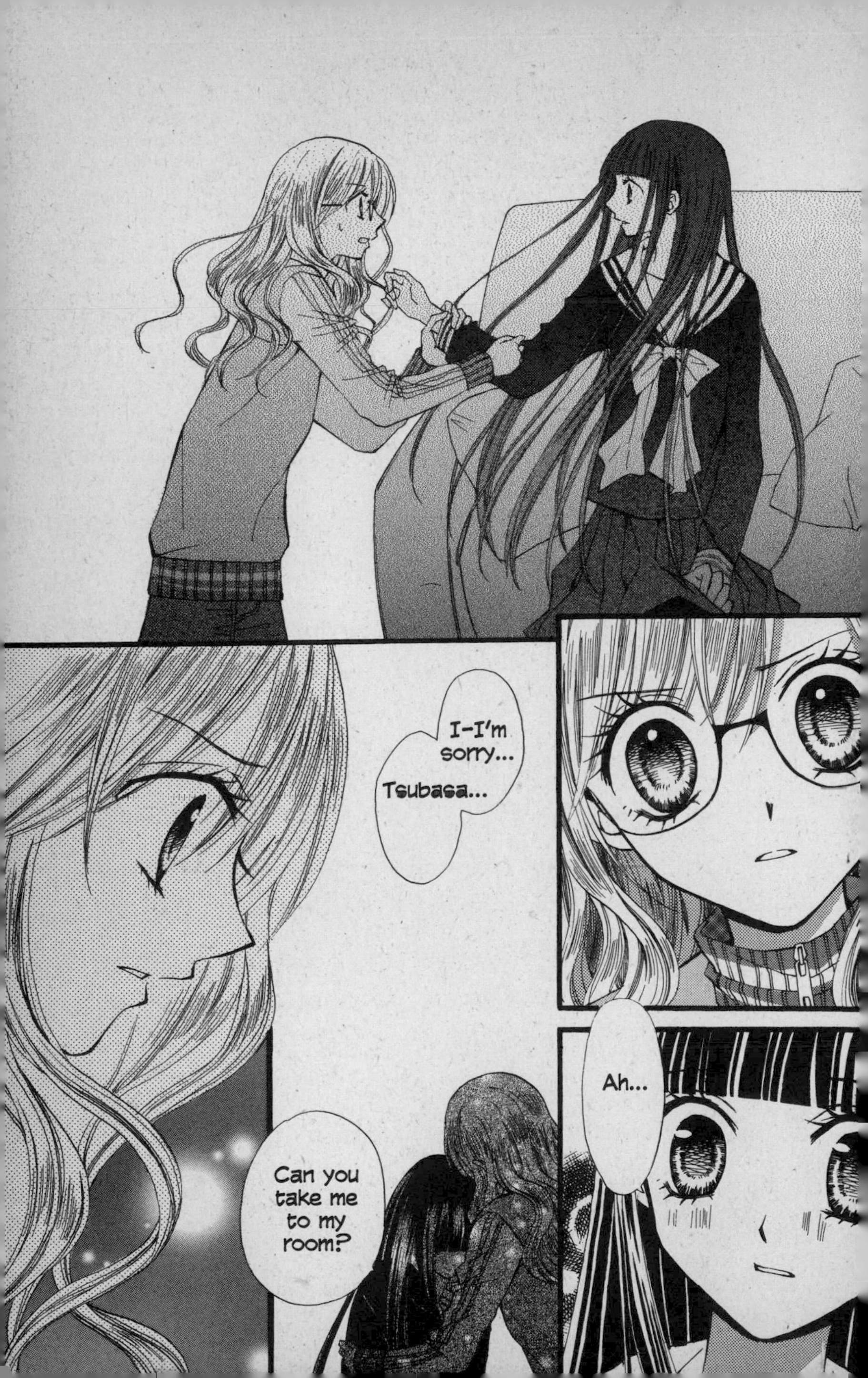
I-I'm sorry... Tsubasa...
Ah...
Can you take me to my room?

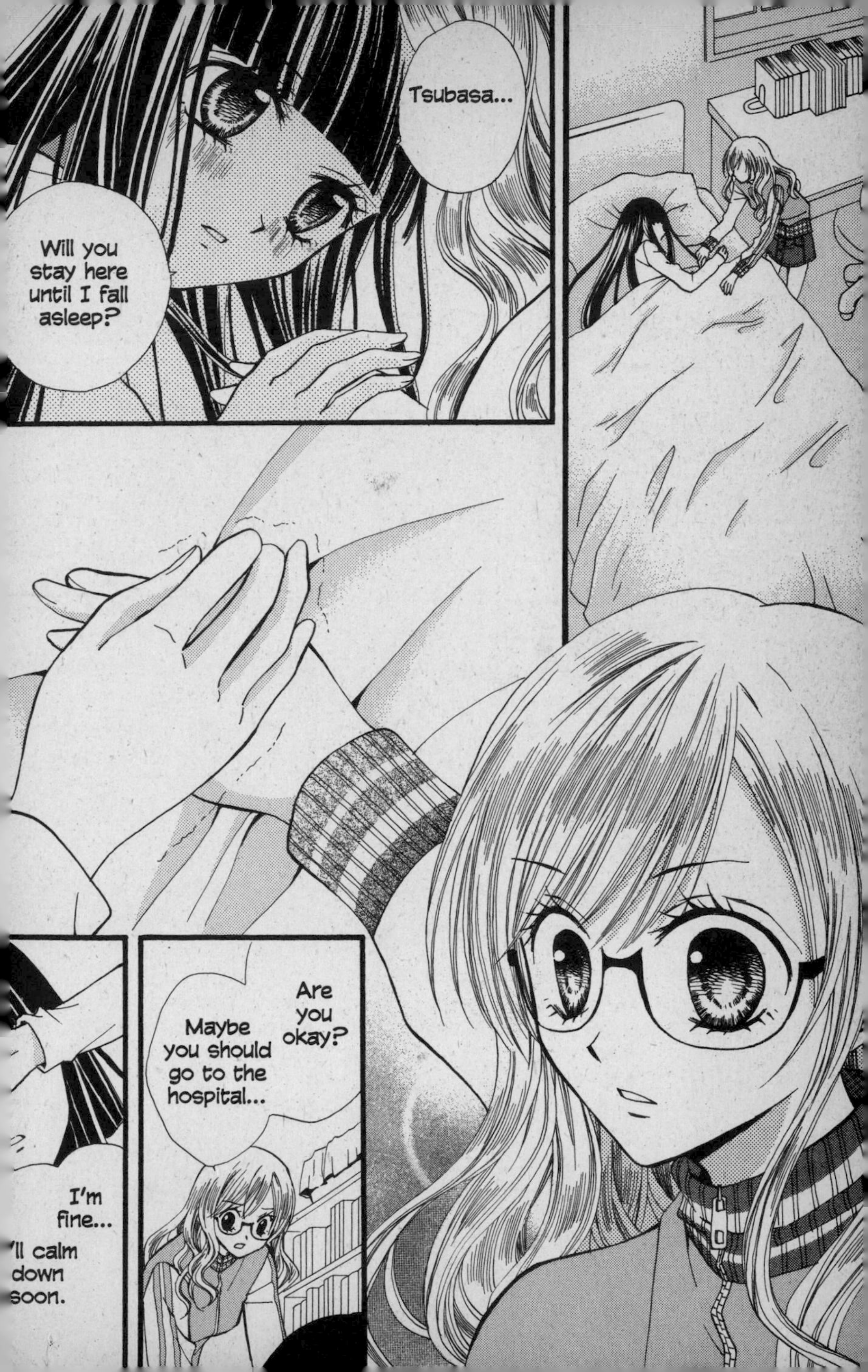
Tsubasa...
Will you stay here until I fall asleep?
Are you okay?
Maybe you should go to the hospital...
I'm fine...
'll calm down soon.

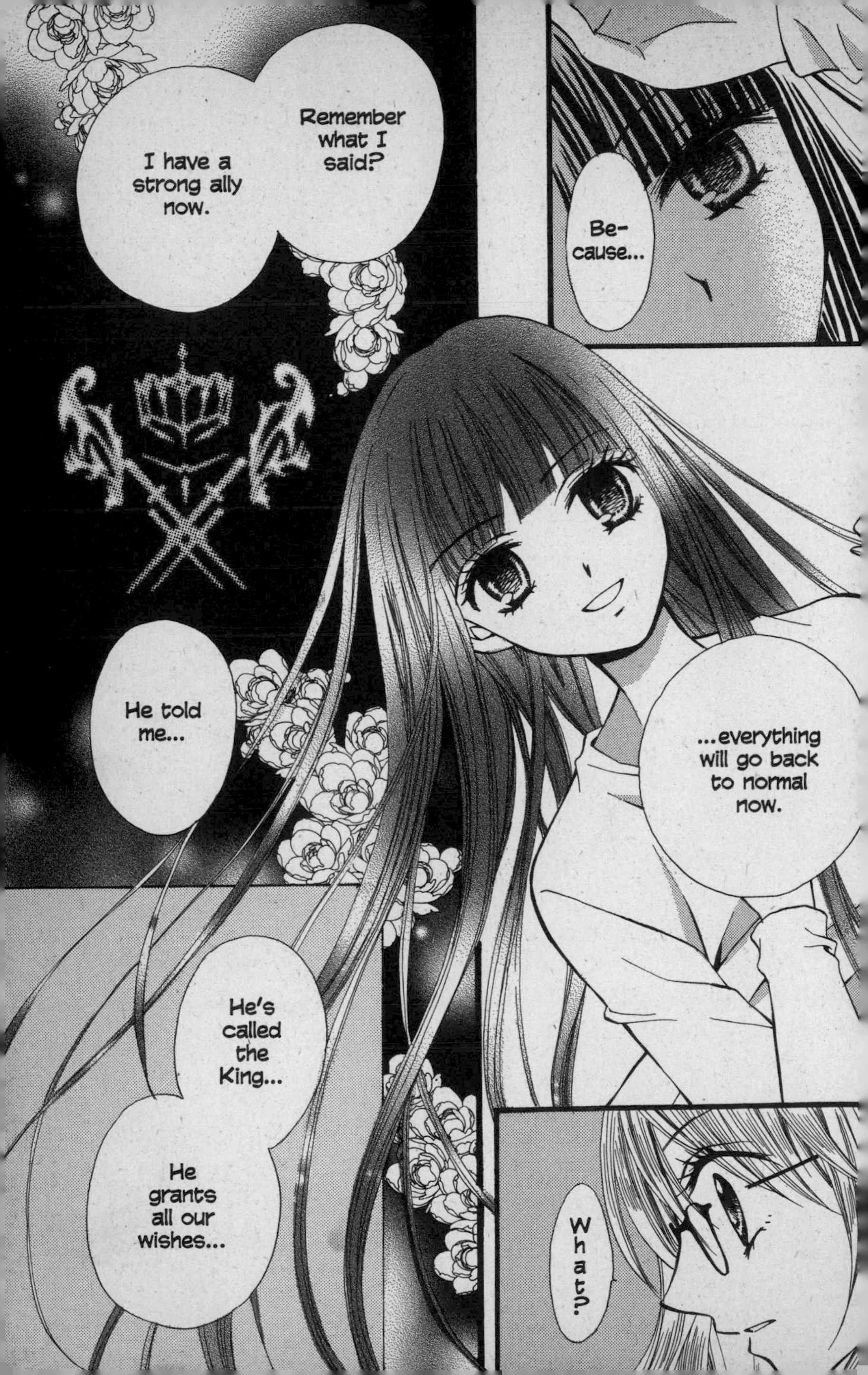
Be-cause...
...everything will go back to normal now.
Remember what I said?
I have a strong ally now.
He told me...
He's called the King...
He grants all our wishes...
What?

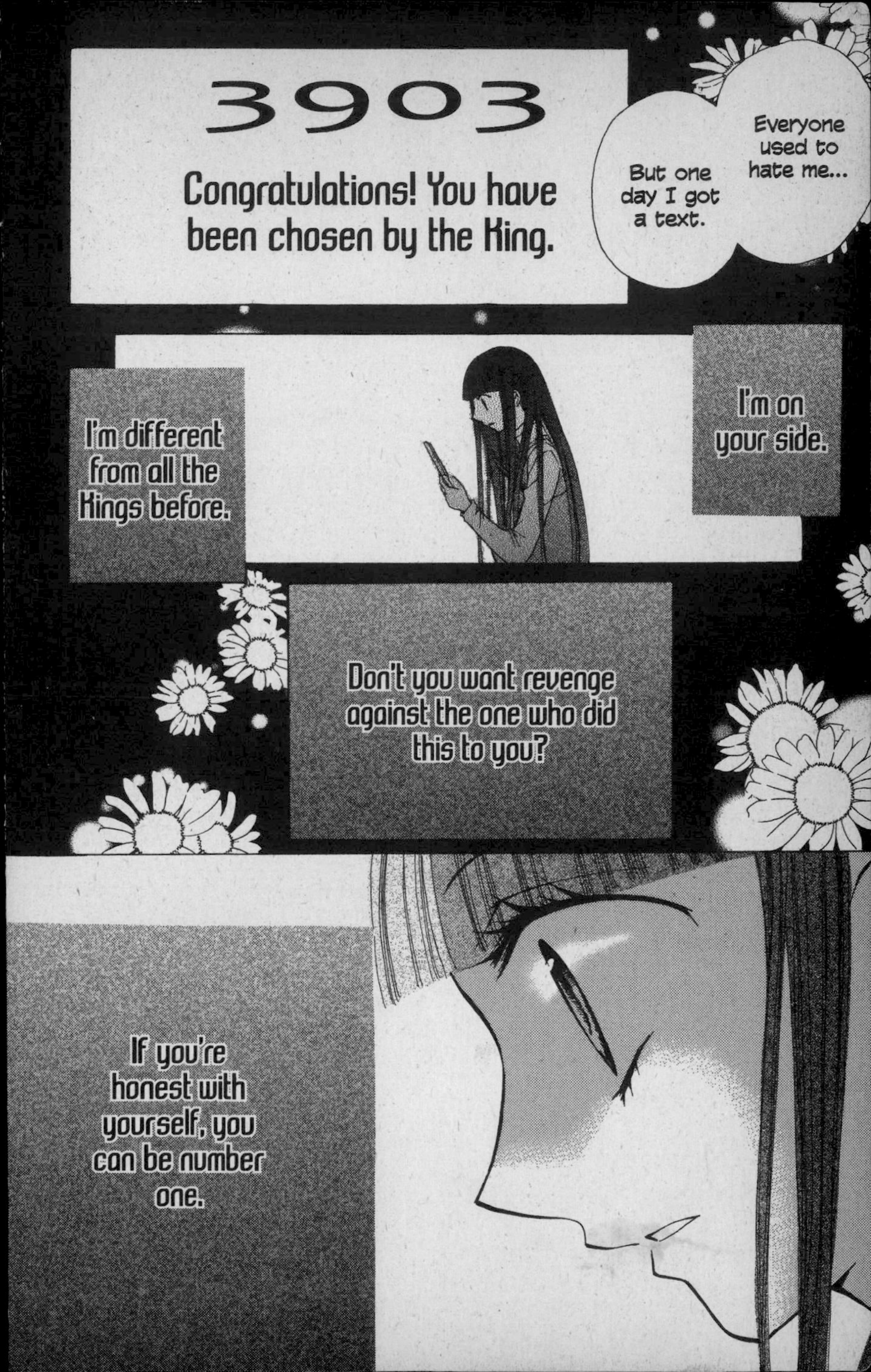
Everyone used to hate me...
But one day I got a text.
3903
Congratulations! You have been chosen by the King.
I'm on your side.
I'm different from all the Kings before.
Don't you want revenge against the one who did this to you?
If you're honest with yourself, you can be number one.

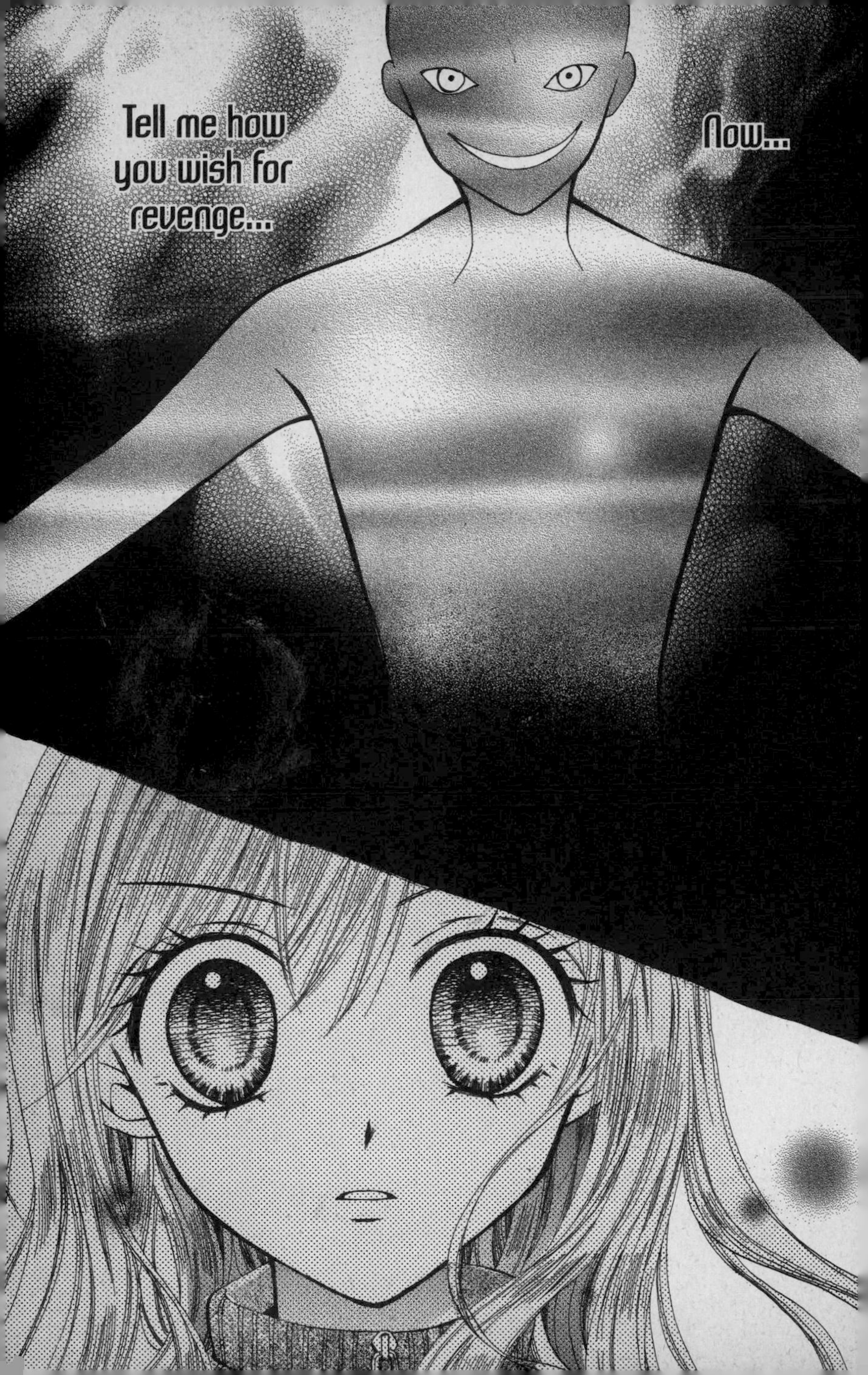
Now...
Tell me how you wish for revenge...

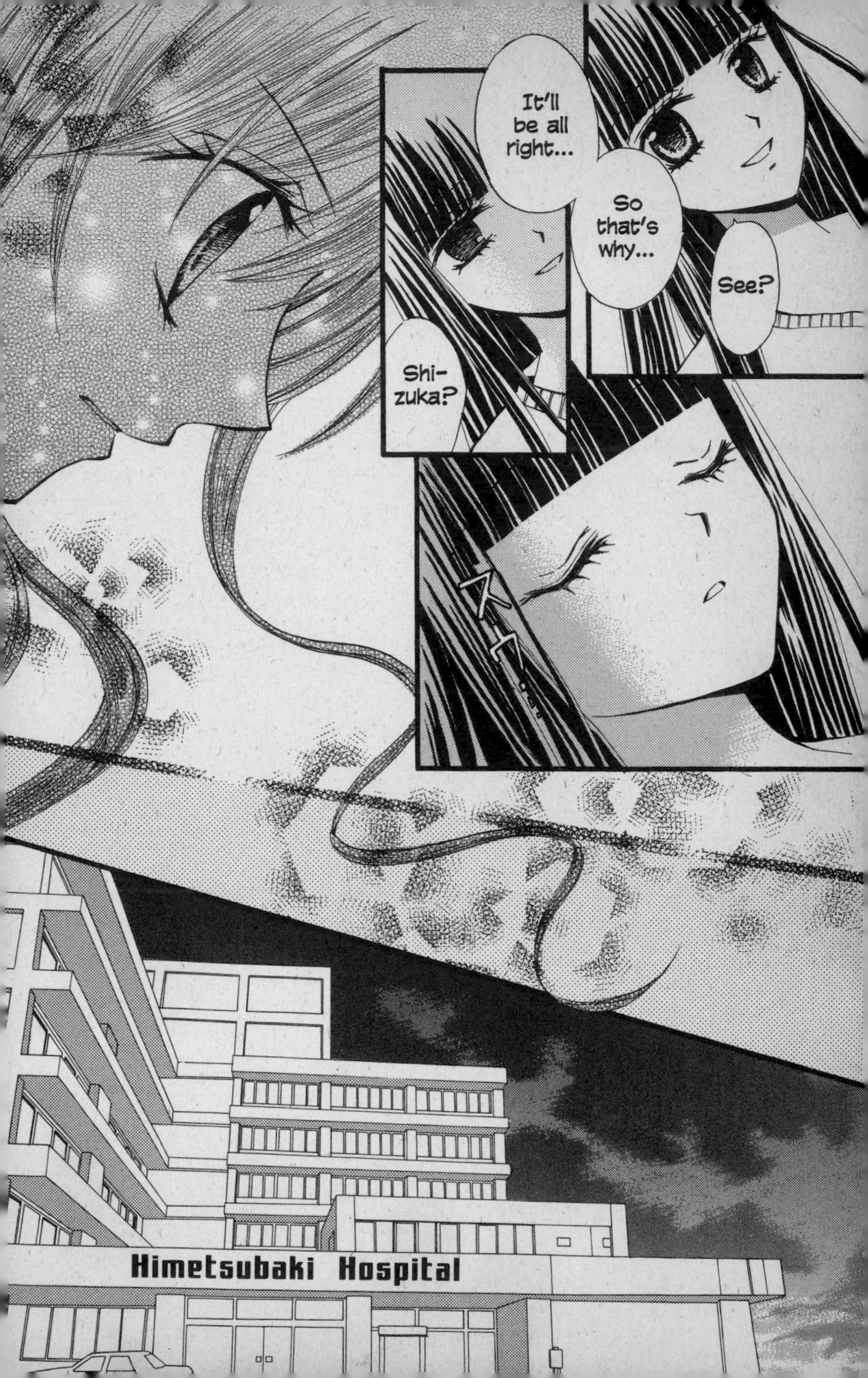
It'll be all right...
So that's why...
See?
Shi-zuka?
Himetsubaki Hospital

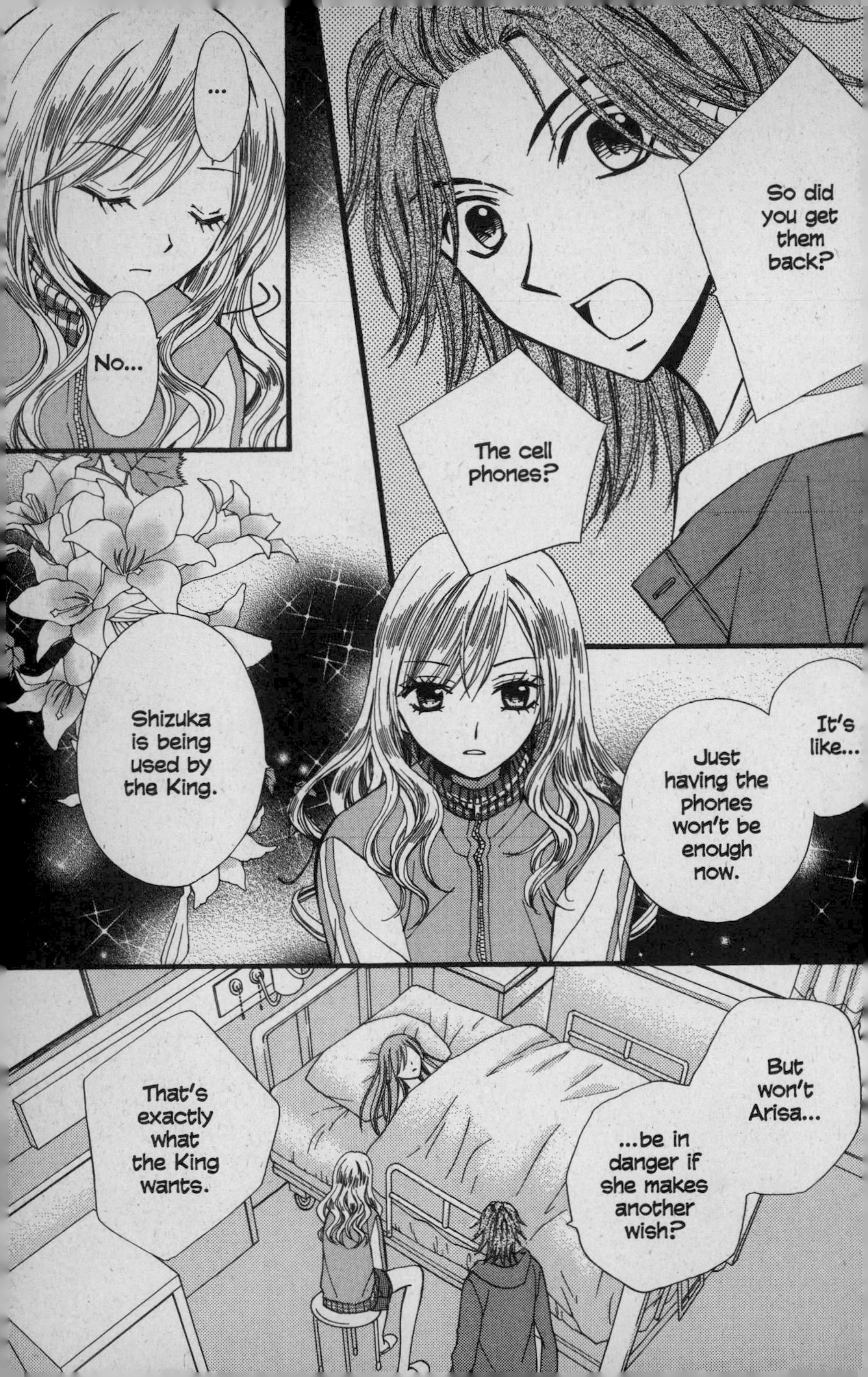
So did you get them back?
The cell phones?
...
No...
It's like...
Just having the phones won't be enough now.
Shizuka is being used by the King.
But won't Arisa...
...be in danger if she makes another wish?
That's exactly what the King wants.

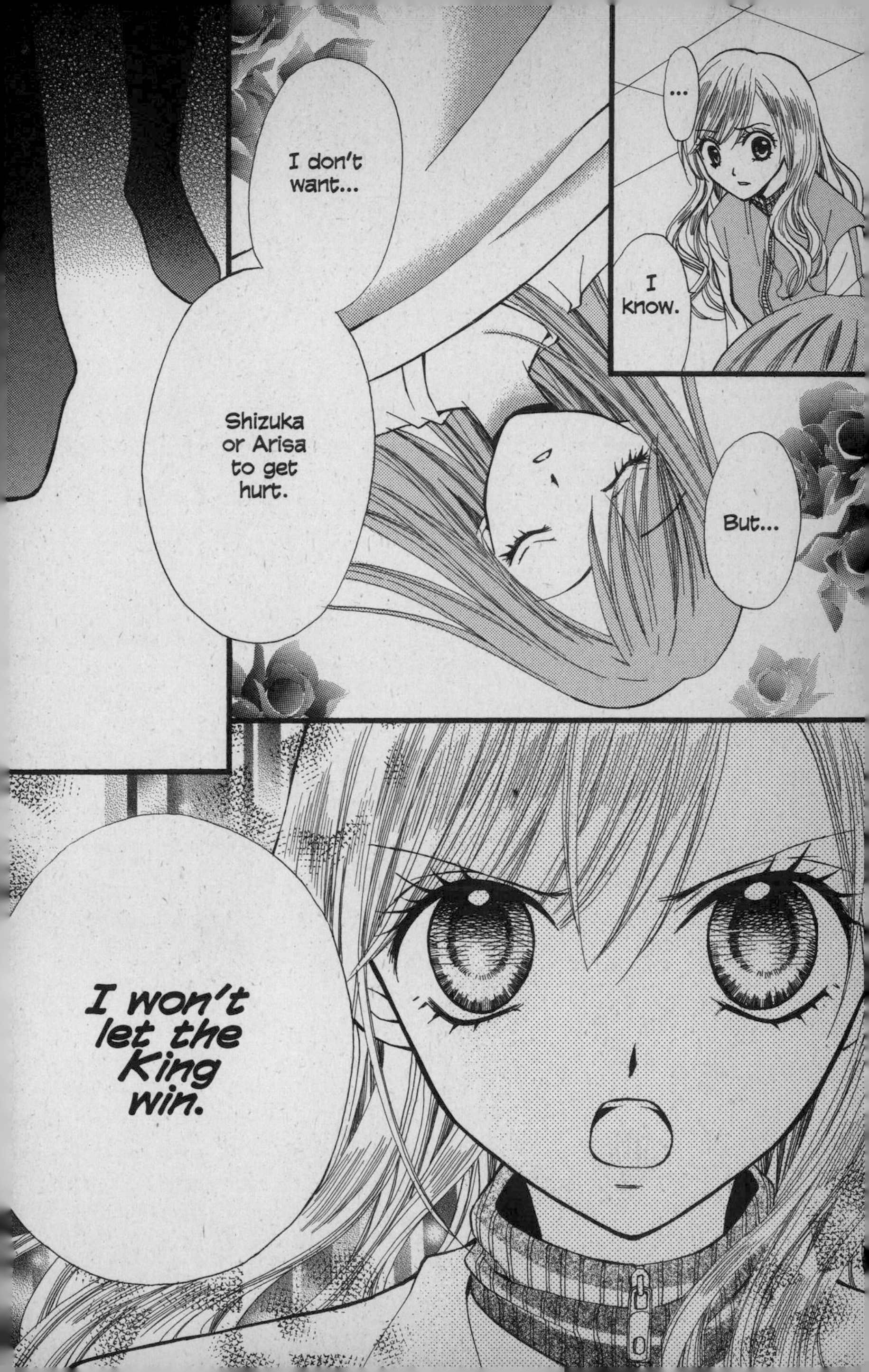
...
I know.
But...
I don't want...
Shizuka or Arisa to get hurt.
I won't let the King win.

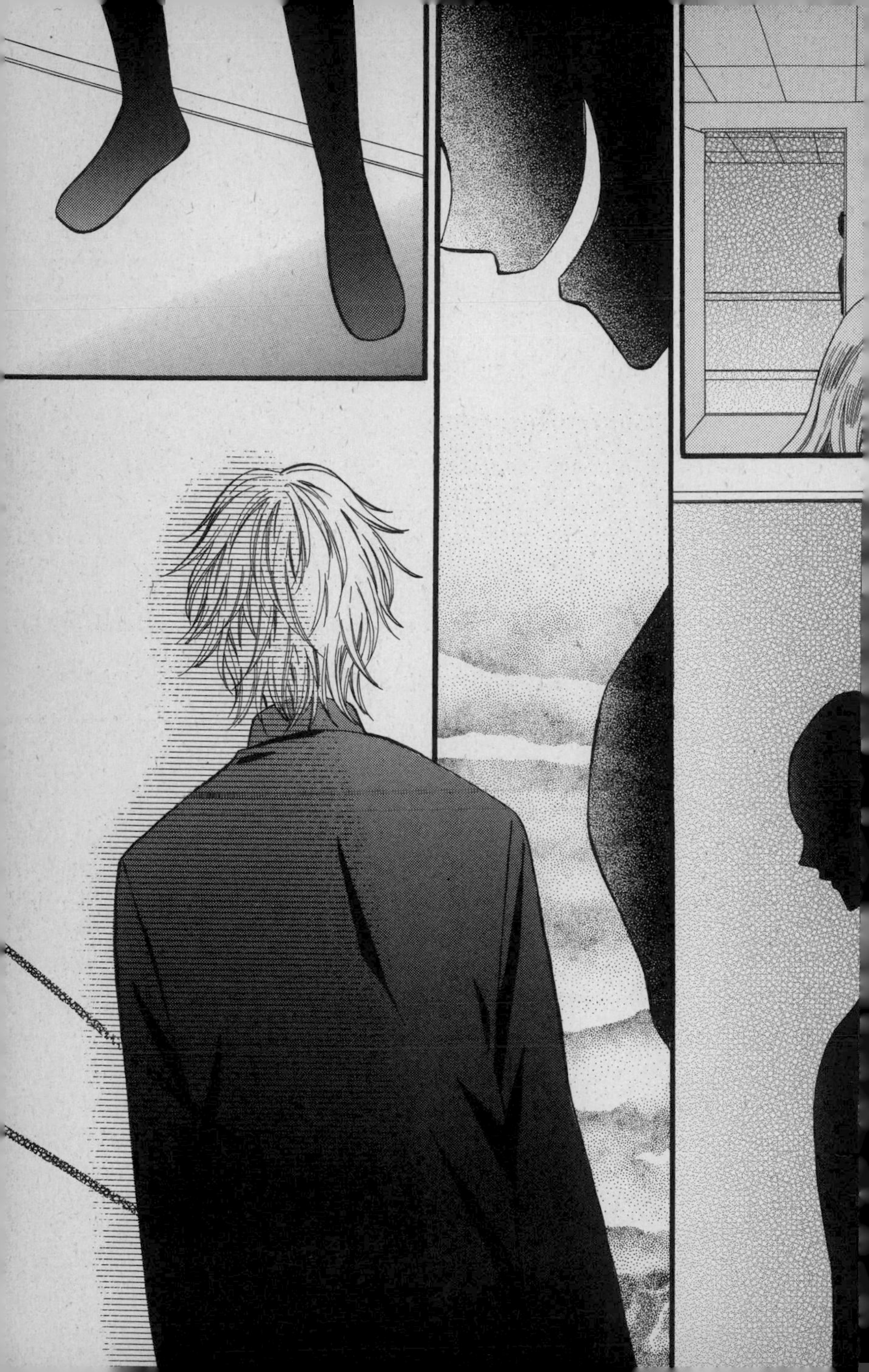

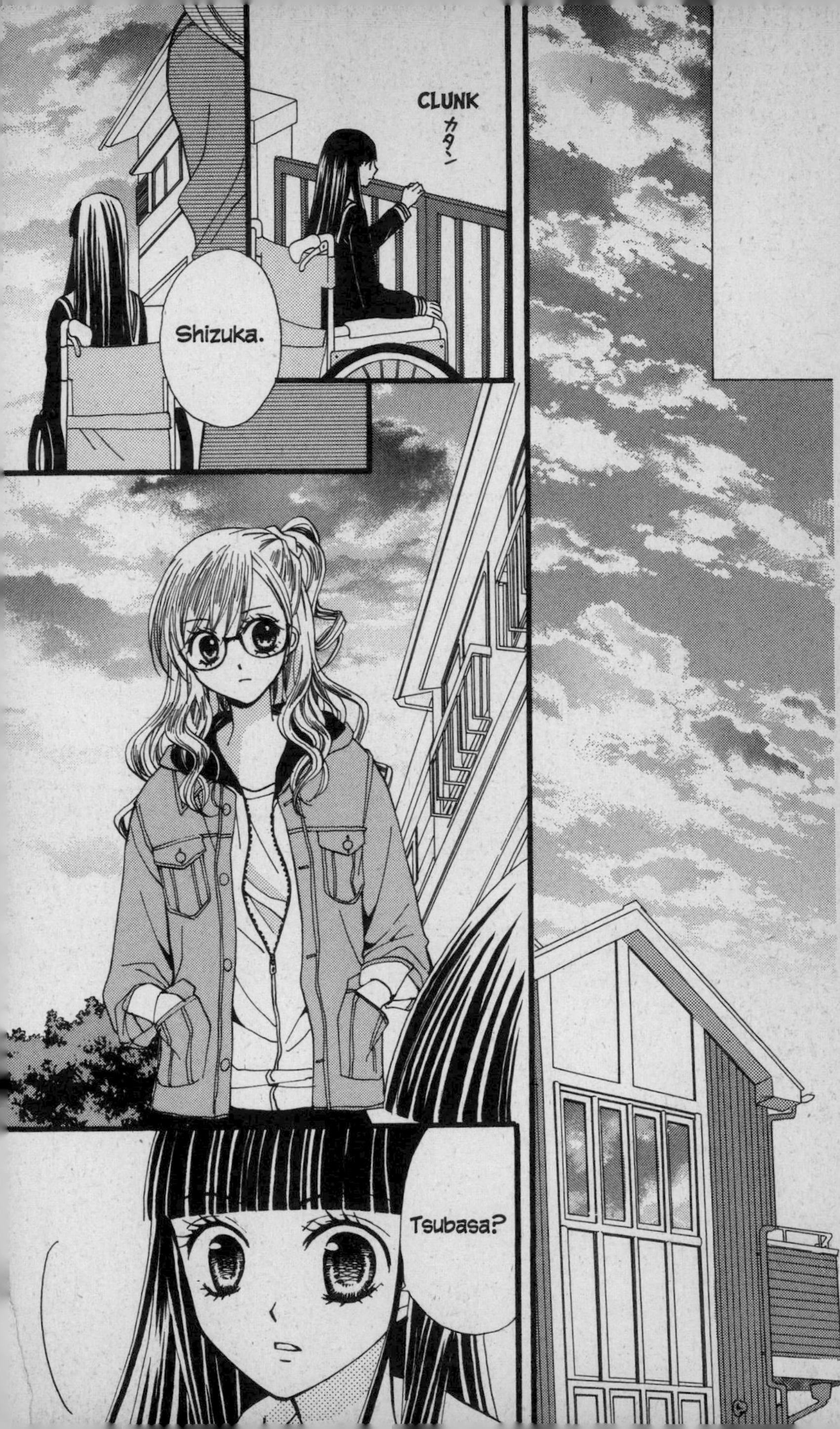
CLUNK
カタン
Shizuka.
Tsubasa?

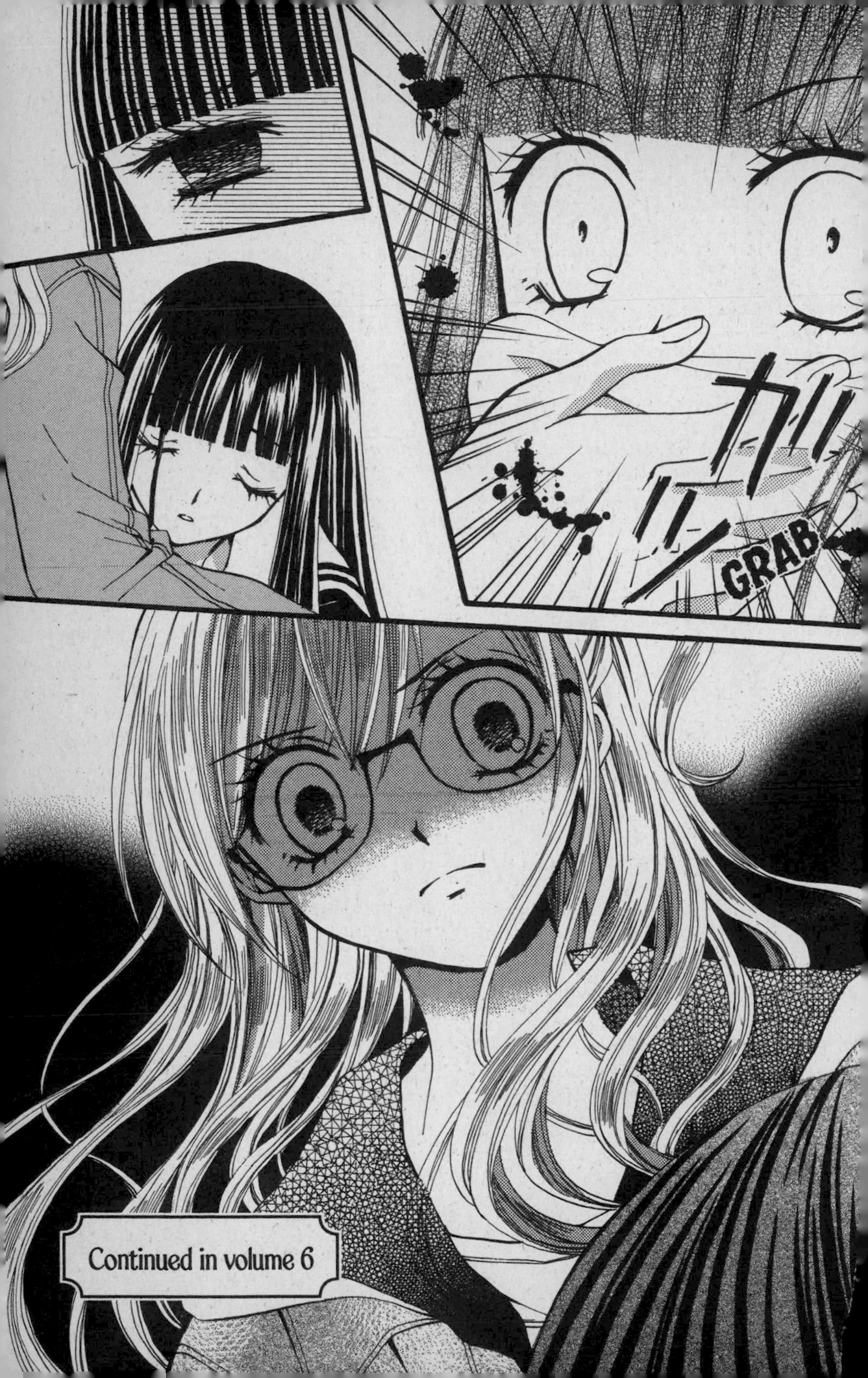
GRAB
Continued in volume 6

The Lost Manuscript Part 2 (For part one see volume 5)

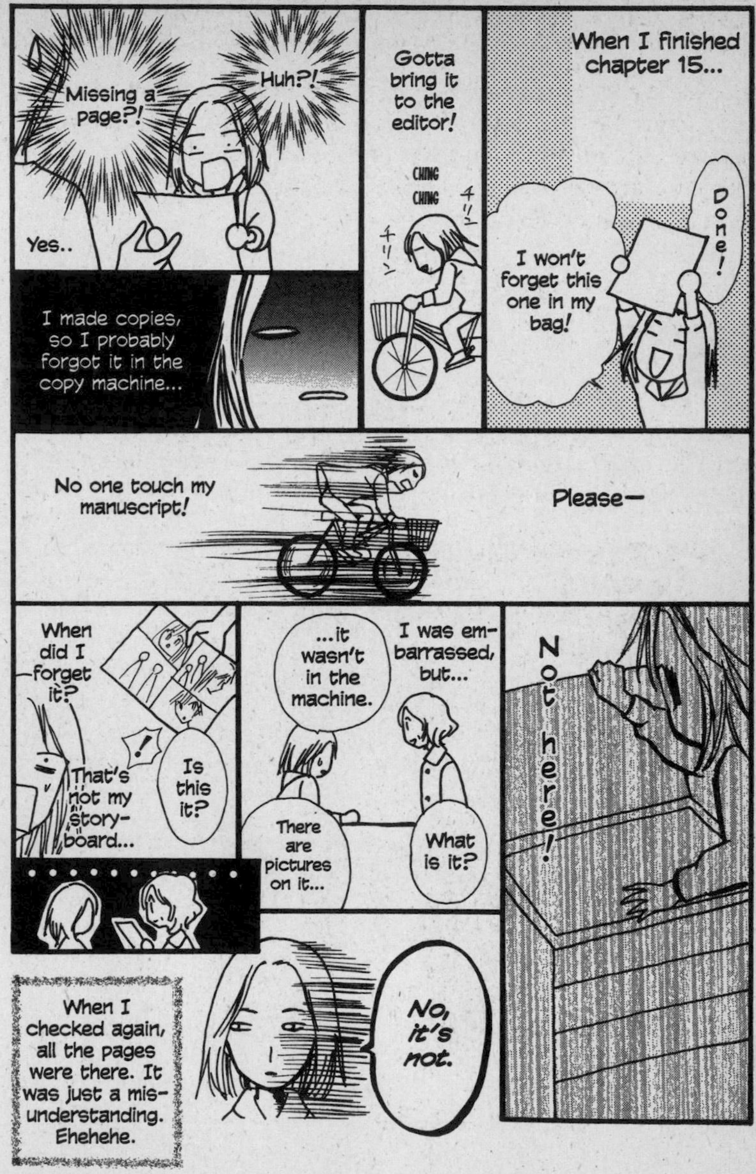
When I finished chapter 15...
Done!
I won't forget this one in my bag!
Gotta bring it to the editor!
CHING CHING
チリン チリン
Huh?!
Missing a page?!
Yes..
I made copies, so I probably forgot it in the copy machine...
Please—
No one touch my manuscript!
Not here!
I was embarrassed, but...
...it wasn't in the machine.
What is it?
There are pictures on it...
When did I forget it?
Is this it?
!
That's not my story-board...
• • • • • • • • • • • • •
No, it's not.
When I checked again, all the pages were there. It was just a mis-understanding. Ehehehe.

THE END

Translation Notes

Japanese is a tricky language for most Westerners, and translation is often more art than science. For your edification and reading pleasure, here are notes on some of the places where we could have gone in a different direction with our translation of the work, or where a Japanese cultural reference is used.

The King

In Japanese, there is no pronoun used to refer to the King. It is not clear in the Japanese whether the King is male or female. This is more difficult in English, so the King is referred to as "he" in this translation. Keep in mind this does not necessarily mean the identity of the King is a male (or isn't).

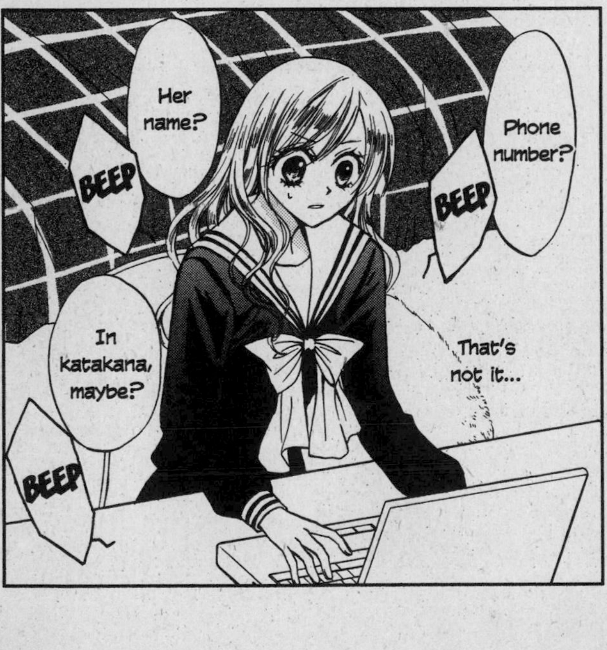

Phone number?
BEEP
Her name?
BEEP
That's not it...
In katakana, maybe?
BEEP

Preview of *Arisa*, Volume 6

We're pleased to present you a preview from volume 6. Please check our website, www.kodanshacomics.com, to see when this volume will be available in English. For now you'll have to make do with Japanese!

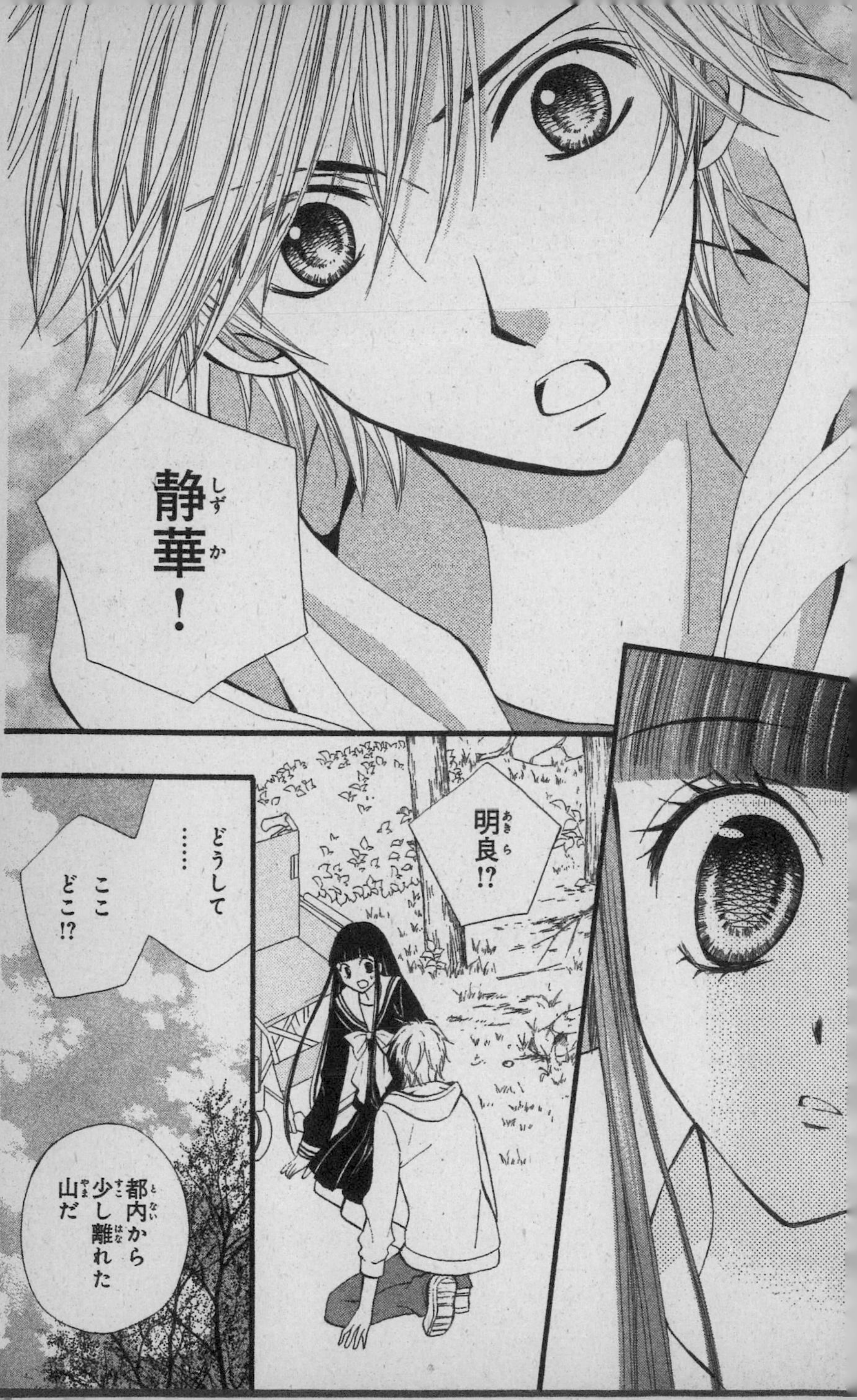
静華！
明良!?
どうして……
ここどこ!?
都内から少し離れた山だ

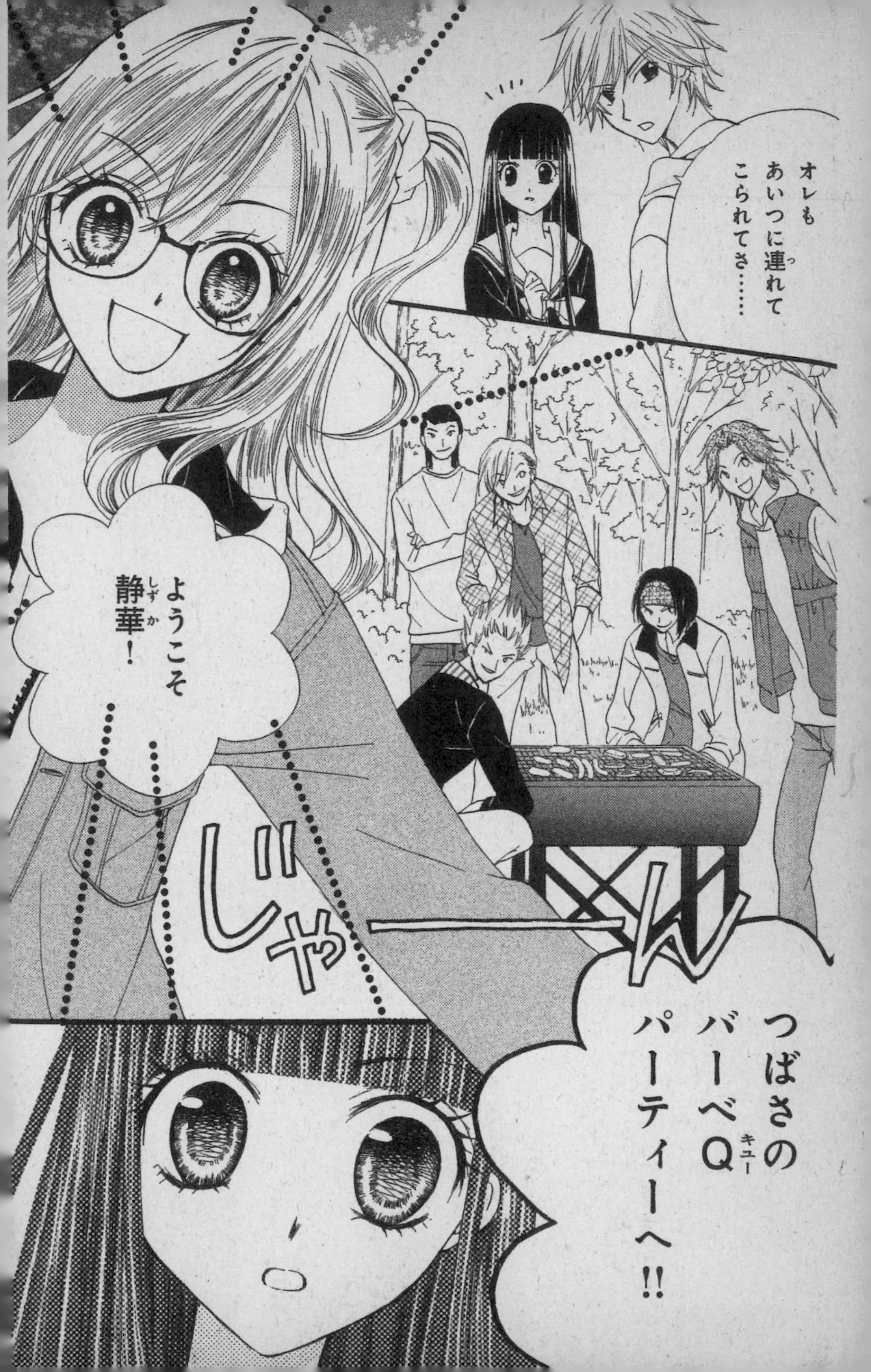
オレもあいつに連れてこられてさ……
ようこそ静華！
じゃーん
つばさのバーベQパーティーへ!!

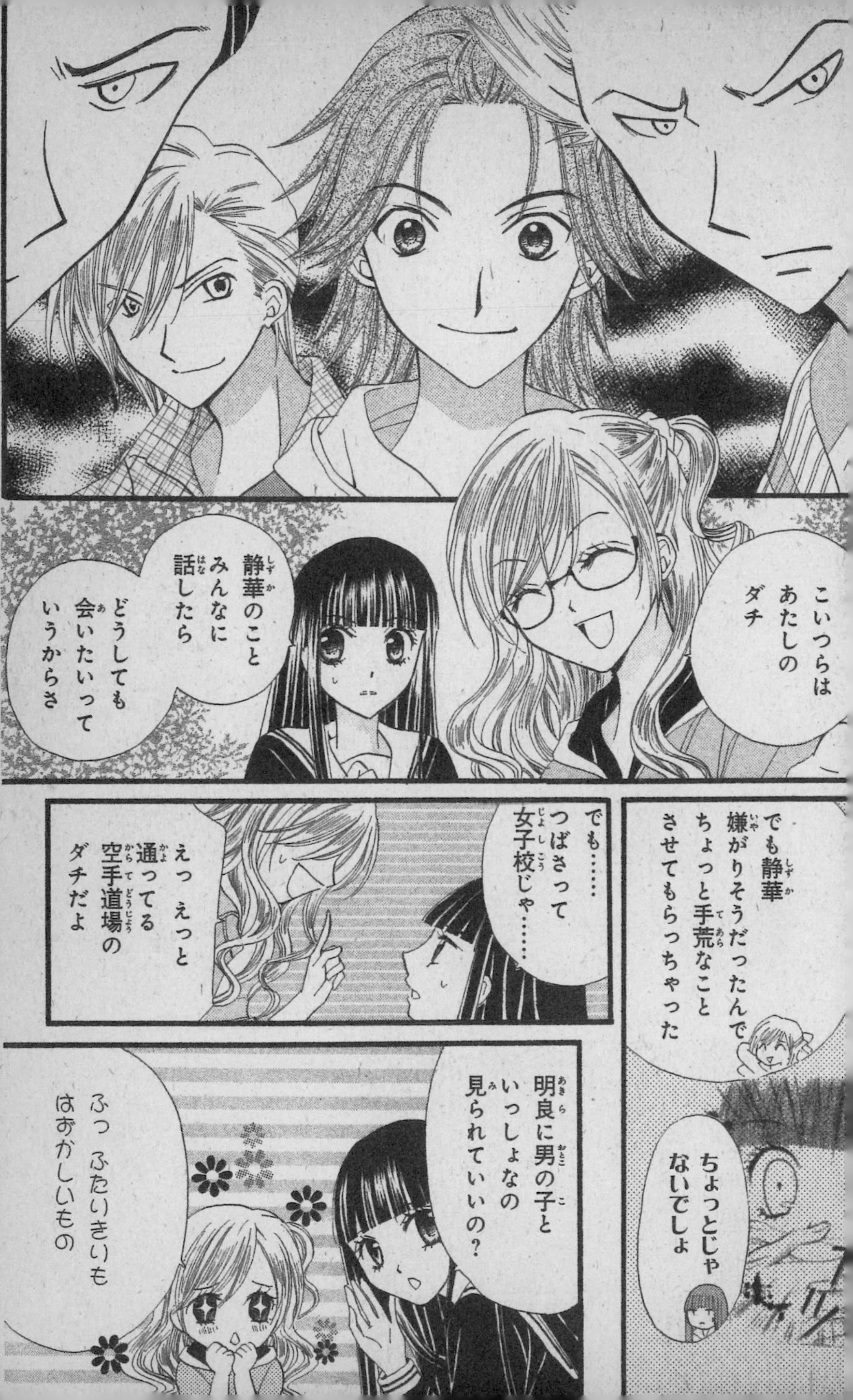
こいつらは あたしの ダチ
静華のこと みんなに 話したら どうしても 会いたいって いうからさ
でも静華 嫌がりそうだったんで ちょっと手荒なこと させてもらっちゃった
ちょっとじゃ ないでしょ
でも…… つばさって 女子校じゃ……
えっ えっと 通ってる 空手道場の ダチだよ
明良に男の子と いっしょなの 見られていいの？
ふっ ふたりきりも はずかしいもの

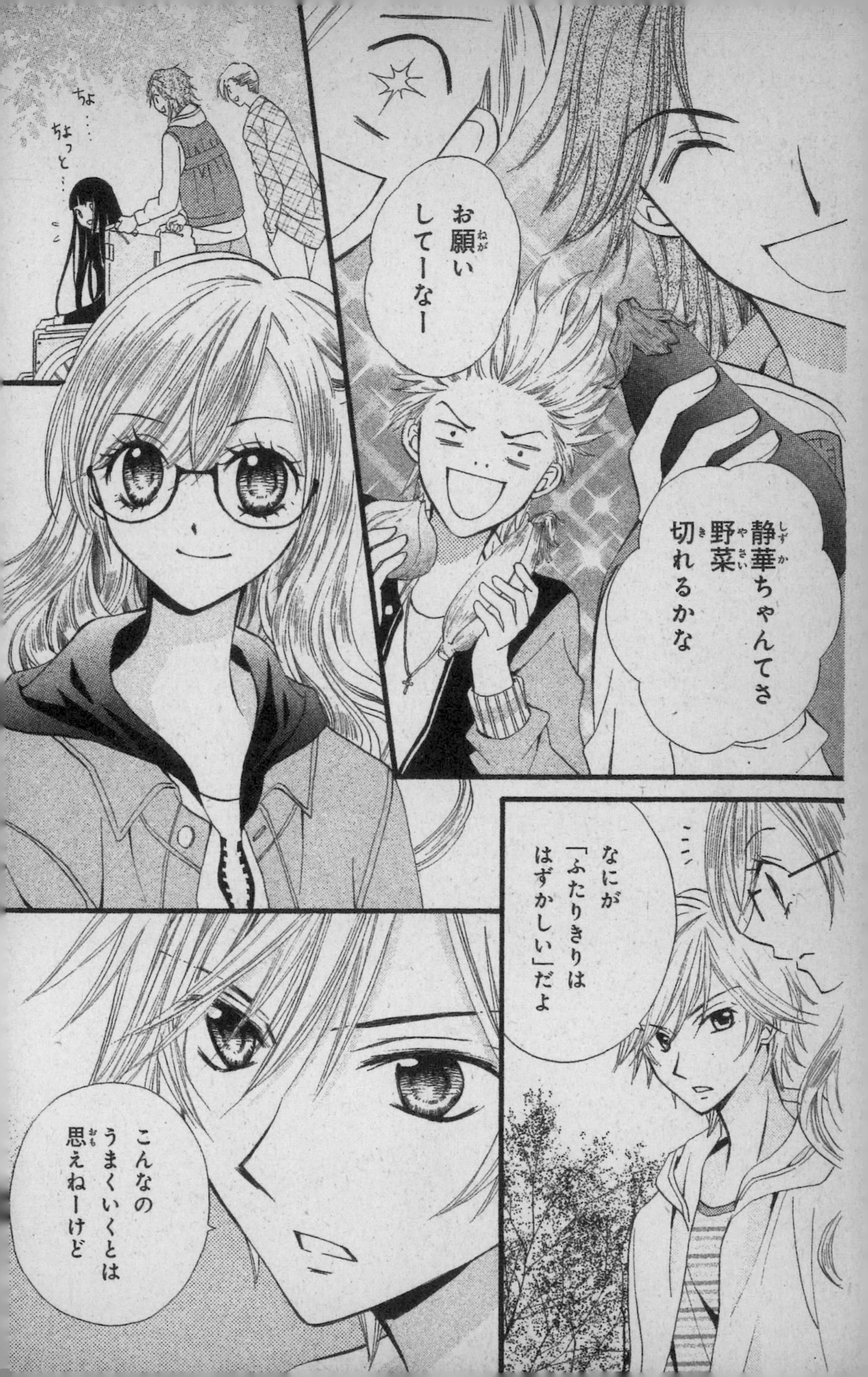
静華ちゃんてさ野菜切れるかな
お願いしてーなー
ちょ……ちょっと……
なにが「ふたりきりははずかしい」だよ
こんなのうまくいくとは思えねーけど

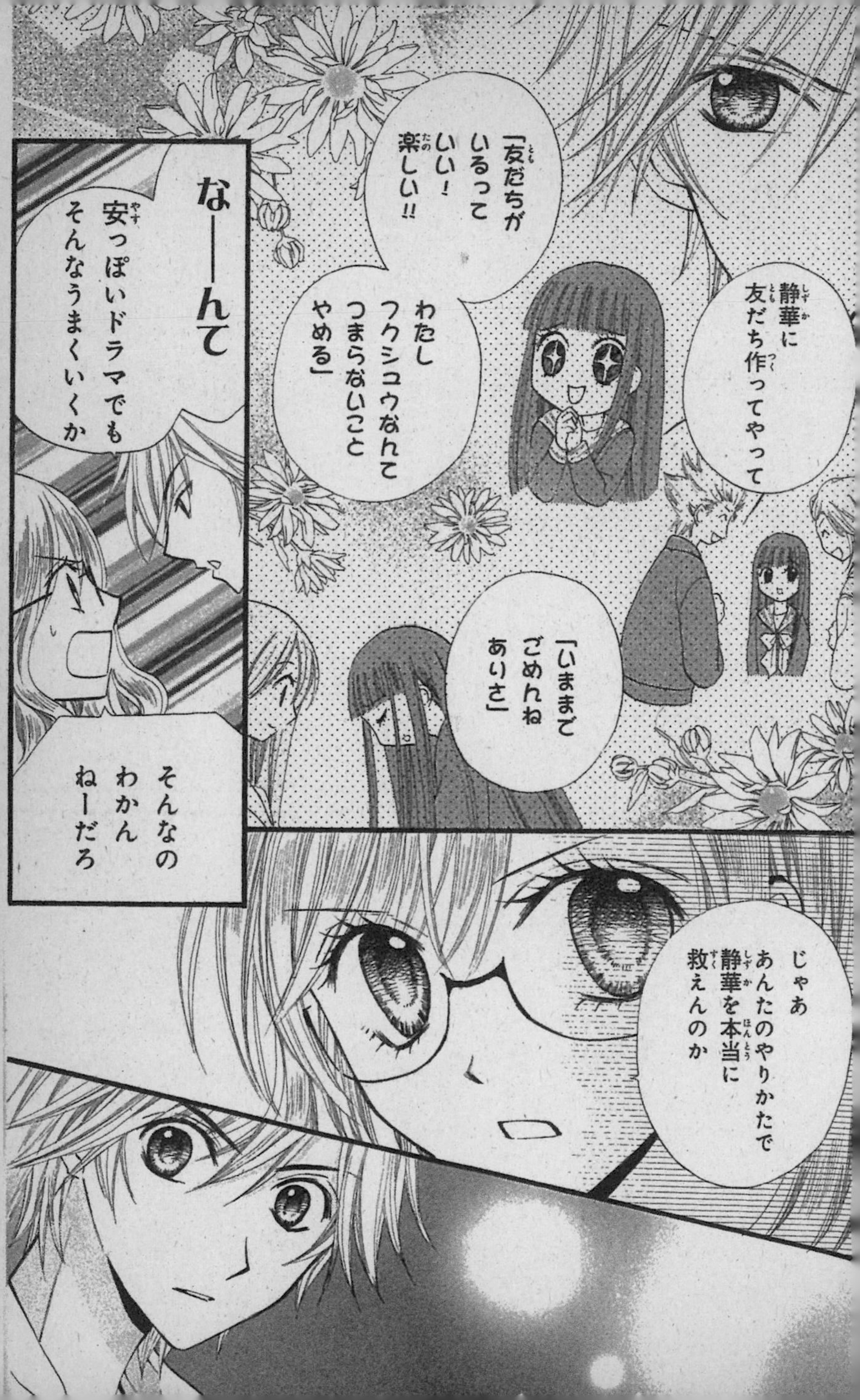
静華に友だち作ってやって
「友だちがいるっていい！楽しい!!
わたしフクシュウなんてつまらないことやめる」
「いままでごめんねありさ」
なーーんて
安っぽいドラマでもそんなうまくいくか
そんなのわかんねーだろ
じゃあ あんたのやりかたで静華を本当に救えんのか

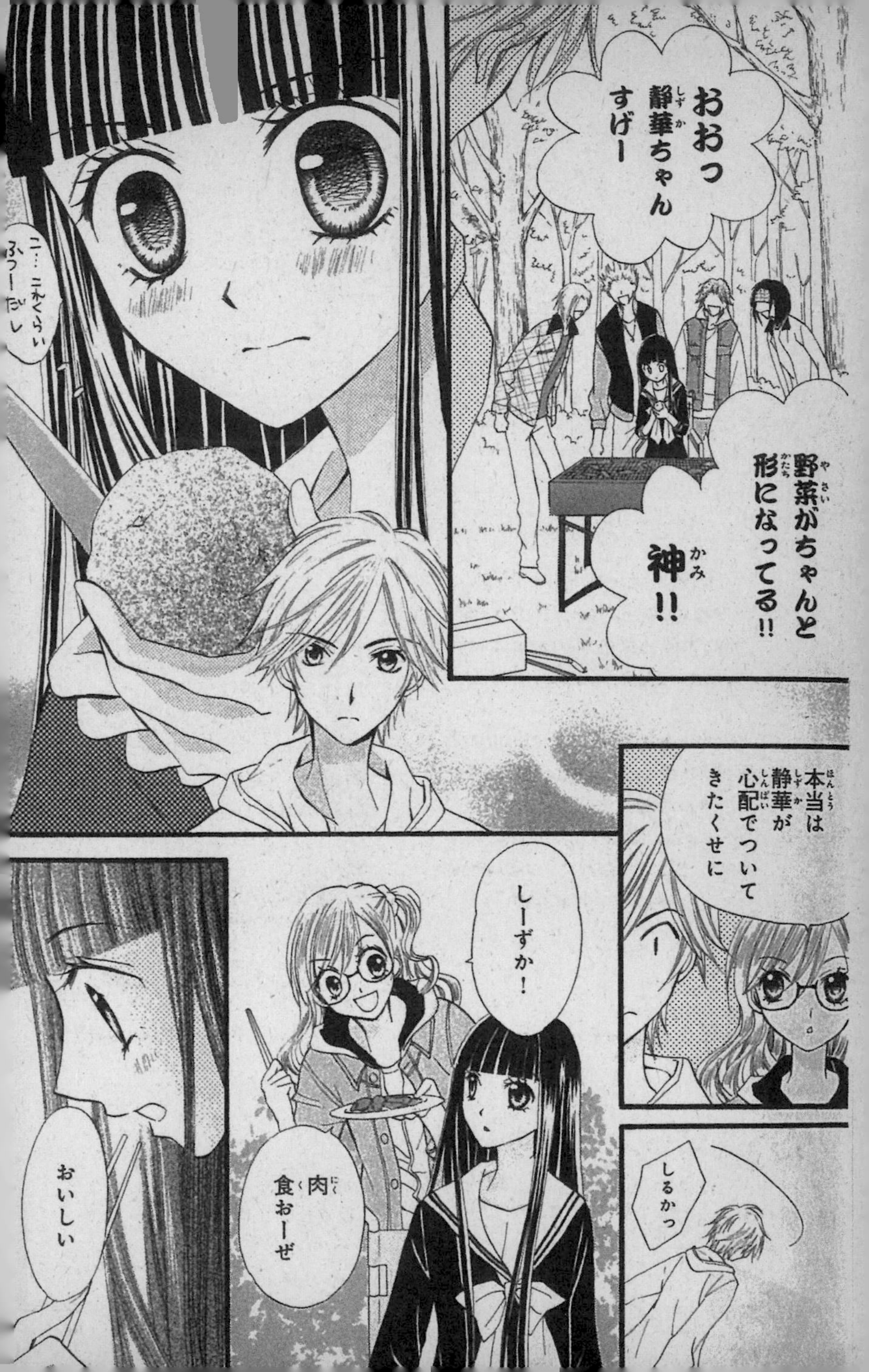
おおっ静華ちゃんすげー
野菜がちゃんと形になってる!! 神!!
こ…これくらいふつーだし
本当は静華が心配でついてきたくせに
しるかっ
しーずか！
肉食おーぜ
おいしい

BY TOMOKO HAYAKAWA

It's a beautiful, expansive mansion, and four handsome, fifteen-year-old friends are allowed to live in it for free! But there is one condition—within three years the young men must take the owner's niece and transform her into a proper lady befitting the palace in which they all live! How hard can it be?

Enter Sunako Nakahara, the horror-movie-loving, pock-faced, frizzy-haired, fashion-illiterate hermit who has a tendency to break into explosive nosebleeds whenever she sees anyone attractive. This project is going to take far more than our four heroes ever expected; it needs a miracle!

Ages: 16 +

Special extras in each volume! Read them all!

SHUGO CHARA!

PEACH-PIT
CREATORS OF *DEARS* AND *ROZEN MAIDEN*

Everybody at Seiyo Elementary thinks that stylish and supercool Amu has it all. But nobody knows the real Amu, a shy girl who wishes she had the courage to truly be herself. Changing Amu's life is going to take more than wishes and dreams—it's going to take a little magic! One morning, Amu finds a surprise in her bed: three strange little eggs. Each egg contains a Guardian Character, an angel-like being who can give her the power to be someone new. With the help of her Guardian Characters, Amu is about to discover that her true self is even more amazing than she ever dreamed.

Special extras in each volume! Read them all!

VISIT WWW.KODANSHACOMICS.COM TO:

- **View release date calendars for upcoming volumes**
- **Find out the latest about new Kodansha Comics series**

TOMARE!

[STOP!]

You're going the wrong way!

Manga is a completely different
type of reading experience.

To start at the *beginning*,
go to the *end*!

That's right! Authentic manga is read the traditional Japanese way—
from right to left. Exactly the *opposite* of how American books are read.
It's easy to follow: Just go to the other end of the book, and read each
page—and each panel—from the right side to the left side, starting at
the top right. Now you're experiencing manga as it was meant to be!